KRAYOLOGY

AN INDEPENDENT EXAMINATION
OF THE RISE AND DEMISE OF
THE BROTHERS KRAY: 1933-68

JOHN BENNETT

ISBN: 978-0-9931806-3-7 (hardback)
ISBN: 978-0-9931806-5-1 (ebook)

Published by Mango Books

www.mangobooks.co.uk
18 Soho Square
London W1D 3QL

KRAYOLOGY

CONTENTS

Introduction 1

1 "Why Did You Buy Two?" 9
2 Boys Will Be Boys 24
3 Seconds Out 41
4 The Rise of The Krays 60
5 Good Times, Bad Times 79
6 East Meets West 103
7 A Dangerous Business 130
8 The Untouchables 154
9 The Public Eye 180
10 Trouble Brewing 197
11 "Look Who's Here" 212
12 Errors of Judgement 236
13 "That Dog Won" 259
14 Release Me 282
15 Jack 'The Hat' 303
16 Culture of Violence 329
17 End of Empire 356

Afterword 367

Appendix One: Select Bibliography 373
Appendix Two: The Krays Family Tree 377
Appendix Three: Maps of the Krays' East End 381

Acknowledgements 387
Index 389

INTRODUCTION

Whether we wish to face up to it or not, crime fascinates. The simple (or in some cases not so simple) act of breaking the law, with its often serious ramifications for the perpetrator and the victims of the offence, can frighten us, appal us or excite us, often all at the same time. For those who have no criminal record, criminal behaviour and those individuals who execute it seemingly come from a world far removed from our own, yet it is one that we live uncomfortably close to and have done since man could first break those early unwritten rules. From the cunning acts of petty thieving and pick-pocketing ably demonstrated by any number of Charles Dickens's guttersnipes, to the barbaric horrors of the modern serial killer, the sheer weight and diversity of media concerning crime shows no sign of losing its appeal.

Much of the interest from the public in true crime can be seen as a safe way of experiencing taboos. Many are truly fascinated by the mindset of criminals, especially murderers, and seek to understand why anybody would bring themselves to commit such outrages. For some, it is the thrill of the chase, enjoying the often complex processes employed by crime-fighters to finally catch the perpetrator. The popularity of TV shows like the CSI franchise or the Sherlock Holmes stories are testament to that. However, for most of us, whether it is reading about Al Capone's gangland exploits in the USA, the daring escapades of the Great Train Robbers, or the sordid multiple homicides of somebody like John Christie of Rillington Place, this other world - the criminal world - is at a safe enough distance. Millions enjoy scary movies full of gore in the same way; it can be seen, gives that visceral thrill of watching something that wouldn't normally be enjoyed otherwise, and all from the safety and comfort of the cinema or the sofa.[1]

But crime has consequences, and not just for the criminal and his immediate victims; in certain forms of crime, the influence and cost can be far-reaching. Gang crime is a good example of this. The sheer number of people involved in gangs, whether they be Chicago mobsters of the 1920s or some Hackney street gang trading in drugs today, ensures that one violent or drastic action can have ramifications that bounce from one set of individuals to another, sometimes resulting in desperate acts of revenge, bloody shows of one-upmanship and, unfortunately, in too many cases violent injury or multiple deaths. When rival gangs play out their war games on the streets, the whole neighbourhood feels it.

'Gang culture' has always been with us; our earliest ancestors formed themselves into tribes, probably for self-preservation as much as anything, and that societal norm is still ingrained in communities across the globe, often where hardship is present. It gives a sense of safety in numbers, peer support and of course, when the going gets tough, dominance over the enemy, in whatever form that takes. In East London alone, an area of about five square miles, there are presently over fifty recorded gangs,[2] each with their own aggressively-guarded territory, sometimes defined by little more than a postcode, where being on the wrong side of the street can spell violence and tragedy.[3] These East End tribes are continuing a long tradition in this most fractious part of London, a tradition that arguably reached its zenith in the 1950s and 1960s when, with a public profile uncharacteristic of organised criminals, the Kray twins and their 'Firm' made their mark

1   Psychologist Glen D. Walters attributed three factors to this: *Tension* - through mystery, suspense, gore, terror, or shock; *Relevance* – the viewer needs to identify with either a protagonist or a situation; *Unrealism* - the understanding that what is on screen is obviously not really happening in the way it appears. 'Understanding the Popular Appeal of Horror Cinema: An Integrated-Interactive Model', *Journal of Media Psychology*, Volume 9, No. 2, Spring, 2004.

2   Revelling in such names as the True Tredegar Thugs, Devons Road Bloods, Brick Lane Massive, Manor Park Squad and the Loyal Soldiers.

3   A number of youths have been killed over little more than being in a rival gang's neighbourhood in what became known in the UK media as 'Postcode Wars.' In 2007, 16 year-old Nass Osawe was murdered on a bus in Islington (*Guardian*, 30 December 2007) and 15 year-old Steven Lewis died from stab wounds in East London in 2009 (*Daily Mail*, 30 January 2009), all because they were spotted in another gang's 'turf'. There are many more incidents.

on the British consciousness.

The story of Reginald and Ronald Kray, remarkable as it is, appears to warrant continual retelling. Identical twins, born in a poor and dirty part of London to a peculiar – some would say dysfunctional – family, they were bullies who hated bullies; heavy drinkers who hated drunks; identical twins who gradually became different in both appearance and temperament; bisexuals (openly so in Ronnie's case) in an age when homosexuality was illegal and 'the love that dare not speak its name';[4] they adored their mother with cloying devotion, yet were prone to awful acts of unprovoked violence; criminals who, rather than keeping their heads down, courted publicity and fame; they were at home in the exclusive clubs of the West End as much as they were in the dingy pubs of the East End. From humble beginnings as local tearaways, they moved into clubs and illegal gambling, protection rackets and fraud. They enjoyed tremendous luck when dealing with the law and the press, interpreting that luck as a *carte blanche* to do what they liked without fear of conviction, which ultimately led them to intercontinental high-end crime and, eventually, to murder. The story of the Kray twins is a contradiction-riddled one of survival, the desire for success and wealth, pride, and power games, all laced with shocking violence, paranoia, glamour and, strange as it may seem, some genuinely surreal comic moments. Add to that a whole cast of colourful, real-life characters from the realms of East End crime, sport, showbiz and the aristocracy and you have quite a saga. But is there anything left to be said?

Actually, there is quite a lot.

It was when reading the many books about the twins' rise and fall that I quickly began to realise that often the authors of these books, many of whom had worked alongside the twins and in some cases went down with them, had their own particular story to tell. That often meant that an account of a particular key event would change, dependent on the teller. Another frustrating characteristic of many of the books is that often, incidents are thrown into the mix without any reference to their position in the Kray story: "I remember one night when Reggie..." or "Around about that time..." are seen often. It is only by reading the different accounts that one can gradually

---

4   A phrase from the 1894 poem 'Two Loves' by Lord Alfred Douglas, and used at Oscar Wilde's gross indecency trial the following year, it has always been considered as a euphemism for homosexuality.

begin to work out what happened when. I believe this is important as it helps us chart the behaviour of the twins and their associates and the development of their criminal activities; there appears to be a definite progression and pattern. Also, accounts of the Krays' exploits are littered with names and places, many of them key to the unfolding story, and I was always left wanting to know a little bit more about them; "What was their background?", "Where exactly was that pub?" and similar questions regularly presented themselves. Thus, this book is a distillation of a wide variety of sources; written memoirs, filmed interviews, newspaper reports and archive documents from a number of institutions. I have attempted to produce a continuous and, hopefully, accurate narrative by bringing these together, using them appropriately, based on what I believe are their own merits.

The lynch-pin of this book are the archives in London relating to the Krays (notably held at the National Archives, London Metropolitan Archives and Tower Hamlets Library), which were an important resource for finding out a wealth of new information. The National Archives (the former Public Record Office) in Kew provided a rich seam of new material; in fact it is staggering. Much of their material relating to the Krays, mainly from the Metropolitan Police, is now open to the public and has provided incredible insight into all aspects of the case. Considering many of these files have been open for over a decade, it is surprising how little has been used before: admittedly, official documents had been examined and used by Martin Fido (1999), Craig Cabell (2002 and 2006) and James Morton (2008), but authors continue to produce books on the Krays and repeat inaccuracies which could have been eliminated through scrutiny of this important material.

Examining the official files does have its problems, however. Many people involved in the various cases had already been publicly named, thanks to press reporting at the time and later memoirs, and certainly the key figures in the Kray Firm were well known to many. We know, for example, who was present at the party when Reggie killed Jack McVitie. But there were many peripheral players in various incidents who, for divers reasons, were not named. Those names are there to be seen in the National Archives.

The problem arises regarding the issue of what should be said and what should be held back in regard to certain witnesses. The question was, "Do I now name them? Is there any legal or moral reason why they cannot be named, almost half a century after the event?" I sought advice from a number of sources and was given different opinions. Most said "I don't know – that's a difficult one." The answer came with a consultation with the National Archives itself; the bottom line was that if these names are in documents that are now open to public inspection, then there is no reason why they cannot be published. Due to the public nature of these files, it would only be a matter of time before the names were 'out there' in any case, and it was felt that if I didn't publish them in this book, somebody else would eventually anyway. And so, for the first time, the reader will know the identities of those who were witness to some of London's most notorious criminal deeds. For that reason I believe the chapter regarding the murder of George Cornell in 1966, for example, is a significant cornerstone of this book.

It is the same with some of the other cases and reports. Thus we get a unique insight into the 1950 assault charge levied against the twins; the 1956 GBH case against Ronnie Kray and others; Reggie's 1959 conviction for demanding money with menaces; the 1960 police investigation that ultimately led to the closure of the Double R Club and other 'businesses.' These early incidents are no mystery to the avid Kray readership, yet here we can hear the voices of the victims, the police and the twins themselves, culled from official statements. Much of this is bolstered by rare press reports from both local (East London) and national newspapers. We also have new material regarding the assault on the late Lenny Hamilton by Ronnie Kray, a number of previously unreported cases of protection, club takeovers and violence, Ronnie's complaint about police bribery in 1966, as well as details on the murder conspiracies managed by Alan Bruce Cooper.

Luckily, as I was putting the finishing touches to this manuscript, Secret Service files relating to the 1964 Boothby scandal were released, and so material from these interesting documents has made it into this book – in the nick of time. Further information from the archives sheds light on the escape of Frank Mitchell from Dartmoor, biographical detail on numerous key characters, most notably George Cornell and Jack McVitie, and the details surrounding the arrest of the Kray Firm in May 1968.

It is impossible to ignore the wealth of written material about the Krays: with this I have had to be selective in my approach. Some memoirs, usually those written by those who gave evidence against the twins and who therefore have nothing to lose in the telling, proved particularly enlightening. Others, where every reason to be embittered or to embroider the facts to suit a personal agenda was all too evident, were examined carefully. Needless to say, every memoir is a minefield and all were considered with respect to what they could positively bring to the story.

The memoirs of the Lee family proved exceptionally valuable and indeed confirmed several things about the Krays' early lives that I had already worked out through independent research. Maureen Flanagan also appears to be an astute, and surprisingly independent, observer of the Krays. As for the twins themselves, again, one must engage with the reasoning behind certain statements: Ronnie Kray appears to have had a very fragile grasp of the facts surrounding key events in his criminal career, whereas Reggie appeared more open. Charlie Kray's published memoirs were also useful, particularly over business dealings, although as with his brothers, discrepancies turn up in the retelling. Leonard 'Nipper' Read's writings, set down with the meticulous attention to detail one would expect of a long-standing and respected police officer, and usually based on official material, are also chock-full of vital information.

The opportunity to consult key Kray associates who are still alive, should that opportunity have arisen (Albert Donoghue and Chris Lambrianou were two that I could have been introduced to had I pushed for it), was considered, but I felt early on that they had already spoken out in their books and interviews for documentaries, and that I may only get a repeat of what was already available in the media. Having previously dealt with historical subjects beyond living memory, I decided to work from the premise that everybody in the story was dead, in order to make this study truly independent.

And so, by studying the numerous accounts given to us in the mass media, backed up with a wealth of official documentation, one can begin to pick away at the confusion and contradictions to identify the most likely version of events (or, if not, at least to give the reader the chance to make up their own mind). The possibility that this book, as a result of the use of unique sources, may be the most accurate account of the Kray years, is debatable. Some may take umbrage with some things mentioned, or disagree with conclusions offered, but that is the way when writing on any historical subject.

The narrative of this book ends in 1968, with the termination of the committal hearings at Bow Street Magistrates' Court. This was a decision made late in the writing process, as it was my original intention to thoroughly cover this and the ensuing 1969 trial at the Old Bailey. However, as writing progressed, it soon became apparent, from the sheer weight of documentation surrounding that lengthy trial - literally thousands of pages of statements and transcripts - that it would be impossible to do it justice in a single chapter, or even two. I do believe, however, that there is a dedicated and thorough retelling of that fascinating trial, waiting to be written, out there somewhere.

◆

The title of this book arose from the desire to examine many specific aspects of the Kray story in significant detail, essentially with the rigour of a historian. I feel that in a number of areas this has been achieved; whether it suddenly creates a field of historical research about the twins and their activities bearing that name, I doubt very much. But the title presented itself willingly from the Old Bailey trial transcripts of 1969; it came from an odd exchange between Detective Superintendent Leonard 'Nipper' Read and John Platts-Mills QC, who was representing Ronnie Kray, surrounding the investigative methods used by Read's team:

Platts-Mills: The whole science is called *Krayology* at Scotland Yard?
Read: I have never heard that term before.
Platts-Mills: Is it not?
Read: No, sir.
Judge Melford Stevenson: I hope we shall never hear it again.[5]

---

5   Quoted in Mrs X with James Morton; *Calling Time on the Krays: The Barmaid's Tale* (London: Little, Brown and Company 1996).

ONE

"WHY DID YOU BUY TWO?"

October 1933 had been pleasantly mild, with less rain than usual and more sunshine than anybody could hope to expect. The worst of the characteristic London fog had passed earlier that month and the temperature dropped drastically during the clear nights. One imagines that conditions were not conducive to playing outside. For many young children growing up in Hoxton, on the northern fringes of the East End of London, the street was the hopscotch playground, the racecourse, the battlefield and the football pitch, but on the evening of Tuesday 24 October, seven-year-old Charlie Kray and his cousin Joe Lee, constant companions owing to their similar ages, made do with playing indoors.

Charlie and his parents, Charles Snr and Violet, had moved to Stean Street, Hoxton, the previous year, and soon after their arrival Violet became pregnant – not that young Charlie had noticed. So it was with some puzzlement that, on that Tuesday evening, he and Joe, who had been playing quietly in the house so as not to disturb Violet (who appeared to them to be a little unwell) were asked to play outside in the cold. As an incentive they were given a penny each for some candy-floss and told to stay outside until they were called. They soon got used to the idea and spent the time running around the street and throwing stones at each other.[1] When they were summoned back inside, some time after 8.00pm, Joe's mother Cissy told Charlie to go

---

1   Joe Lee's personal account: Joe Lee, Rita Smith and Peter Gerrard; *Inside the Kray Family* (London: Carlton 2008).

upstairs, where a little surprise was waiting for him. He found his mother sitting up in bed, holding what looked like two little dolls.

"Say hello to your brothers," she said proudly.

Both had dark hair and dark eyes; already, one had been named Reginald and the other Ronald; and – aside from the different names – they appeared to be exactly the same. With the naïveté one may expect of a boy his age, Charlie asked, "Where did you get them from?"

Playing along, the motherly Violet replied, "I bought them."

Charlie's reply was straight out of some catalogue of 'funny things children say': "But why did you buy two?"[2]

Life would never be the same again.

◆

Now one of London's prime locations, on the cutting edge of modern urban living, Hoxton has come a long way since the 1930s, when Reggie and Ronnie Kray first came into the world. The transformation has been recent – only beginning about two decades ago, and unwinding gradually ever since – and, walking around its sprawling streets today, one is assaulted by a myriad of visual experiences: here, the down-at-heel grubbiness of yesteryear; there, its obvious reinvention with the street-cool ambience enjoyed by fashionable young 'hipsters.' Old warehouses are now home to trendy new-media companies and luxury apartments for those who have chosen Hoxton and neighbouring Shoreditch and Dalston as places to experience what has become known as 'urban chic'. Those properties which have not been taken over and have fallen into decay have become canvasses for the increasingly popular style of creative graffiti we now call 'street art'. Old pubs, once the preserve of rough and ready drinkers, have been taken over by young, ambitious tenants, catering for the new population with promises of obscure global beers, international cuisine and most importantly, free wi-fi. Hoxton, it can be said, has arguably become a brand name, and its increasing popularity has finally earned it its own London Overground Station[3] which sits perched on previously disused elevated railway lines, looking down on the discordant array of architecture below, old and new.

2   Charlie Kray's account. (Charlie Kray & Robin McGibbon; *Me and My Brothers* (London: Grafton 1988).

3   Opened on Geffreye Street in 2010 at the same time as Shoreditch High Street and Haggerston Stations, it is situated on the old Kingsland Viaduct.

It was the nineteenth century which essentially turned the former rural hamlets of Hoxton, Haggerston and Dalston into overcrowded industrial heartlands. Like many districts outside the boundaries of the City of London, it had once been a fresh and healthy environment sporting almshouses and hospitals, but as the industrial revolution began to make its mark, those trades unsuitable for the City settled there. A turning point came in 1820 with the construction of the Regent's Canal in the area. This was a vital transportation link across the northern suburbs of the time, allowing the transit of heavy goods from the new docks at Limehouse, through Stepney and Bow, across St Pancras to Hampstead and ultimately to the west and the confluence with the Grand Union Canal. This greatly influenced the trades of Hoxton and by the mid-nineteenth century, furniture-making was prevalent; the canal facilitated the transporting of heavy construction materials and the all-essential coal. Naturally, the arrival of an eager workforce swelled the population: these were mostly poor manual workers, and in time, the wealthy who had once dominated the exclusive pastures saw the future and moved on.

Access to the area was further enhanced by the arrival of the railways, but it came at a price: to build the extensive network, many residents were displaced when their homes were demolished, causing localised overcrowding and the truncation of numerous thoroughfares which, neglected and obscured from the main roads, would be allowed to decline, becoming unsanitary slums and the hiding places of the unlawful and dangerous.[4] A similar situation was developing in the heart of the East End – that is, in the districts of Whitechapel, Shoreditch and Bethnal Green to the south. When Charles Booth examined the areas of Hoxton and Shoreditch in the late 1880s, the growth of the area's characteristic industry was still ongoing, and his observations were hardly positive:

> *The character of the whole locality is working-class. Poverty is everywhere, with a considerable mixture of the very poor and vicious... Large numbers have been and are still being displaced by the encroachment of warehouses and factories.*[5]

---

4   Many of these shortened streets can still be seen running off the Kingsland Road and appear to exhibit the neglect and gloom of an earlier era.

5   Charles Booth; *Life and Labour of the People in London* (17 volumes published between 1883 and 1903).

By all accounts, Hoxton and its environs, though split vertically by the bustle of the Kingsland Road (a major route towards North London and the northern trade routes), formed a tough and tight neighbourhood. Hardship was a common experience, and there was little to be gained by not being staunch and resourceful. Often, need or frustration would beget aggression, often outside the public house after last orders, or sometimes, alas, in the home. It was into this uncompromising environment that James William Kray was born in April 1884.

Compared to some families, where, despite the high infant mortality rates, the number of offspring could run into double figures, James' own was comparatively small: he had a blood-sister, Betsy, and shared the family home with George, Albert and Jane, children from his mother Jane Wild's first marriage. His father, also called James, was a cork cutter, a semi-skilled trade that was much in demand, and he had married Jane only three months before young James's birth. The family had settled down at 40 St John's Terrace (called Gorsuch Street after 1909), a tiny little thoroughfare squashed between Kingsland Road and Hackney Road, and the street would be home to several generations of the Kray family in the decades to come. Young James began working as a cable-maker for the electrical companies, a secure and important job in the days when electricity was coming into its own as an energy source. At sixteen, he met Louisa Eliza Turner, and she quickly became pregnant; like James's parents before him they "did the right thing" and married in a hurry in 1901 at St Anne's Hoxton, only a month before the birth of their first child, James John Frederick.

After James Snr lost his job at the cable-maker's, things became less settled for the family. Despite the inconvenience of having to move home often, more children followed; John George in 1902, Albert Charles Giles in 1904, Charles David (the twins' father) in 1907, Alfred in 1909, William in 1911 and finally, three daughters, Elizabeth (born 1916 but died aged two), Dorothy (1919) and Charlotte (1921). With the advent of the First World War, James was quick to sign up with the King's Royal Rifle Company, a role that served his small but tough frame well. He was posted to France and went into battle at Ypres where he was wounded in the chest; he was subsequently returned to Britain. He had returned to a home full of children and, with no immediate prospects, struck out on his own as a 'wardrobe dealer', buying and selling on used clothes and other items at a profit. As with many East End men, James was no stranger to the odd fight or two; he took it up seriously as a way to earn extra money on the street and, of course, to build up a formidable reputation. When times were tough and tempers could easily fray, or when villains attempted to take liberties, a good pair of fists would always come in useful. He would often chance his arm at bare-knuckle boxing on the cobbles against all comers, becoming a feared opponent to any prospective adversary, and more so when he had had a few drinks. His method was aggressive, always pushing forward so that his opponent would be constantly on the defensive. Others, taking into account his sheer force and the fact that he didn't care who he fought or how hard he fought them, referred to him as 'Mad' Jimmy Kray.

His older sons, notably Charles, often accompanied him on his rounds of wheeling and dealing ('on the knocker', as it was known), and they set up a small stall on Brick Lane where they could sell on the clothing and other things they had bought. By all accounts it was acceptably lucrative. Young Charles would grow to keep the business going and would never work for a true employer, or 'guv'nor', in his life. He would become his father's son, working hard through the week, relishing his independence at work and at home, and at weekends enjoying the comfort of the public house.

◆

Jimmy Kray may have had his moments and his family may have garnered their own form of high profile in Hoxton, but the Lee family over in Bethnal Green were a different case altogether. It was they, with their remarkable family bond and extreme individual characters, who would have the most influence on the twins.

The major force of nature in the Lee family was James Charles, whose father, also called James (as was the tradition), was of Romany descent and commonly known as 'Crutcha' Lee, a title that nobody ever got round to finding the origins of. A butcher by trade, who had crossed the river from South London after James's birth, Crutcha's life had ended tragically and dramatically when he began to suffer from epileptic seizures. Indeed, so bad were these episodes, possibly exacerbated by drink, that sometimes Crutcha would not know what he was doing. On one occasion, he attacked his own family at night, a terrifying incident which led to his being institutionalised at Long

Grove Asylum in Epsom, where he remained for the rest of his life. Some have suggested that he may have suffered from the fits as the result of an accident in which he sustained a head injury after falling from a cart; or perhaps they were solely the consequence of heavy drinking. The latter reason may explain why his son James (usually referred to as Jimmy) remained a vociferous teetotaller all his life. Indeed, he would later say of his father that

> ...He weren't a bad man, except he took to alcohol and it ruined him as it's ruined many a good man. It made him epileptic. I can remember as a boy him having five and six attacks a day. And all the time he'd still be drinking.[6]

In 1898, Jimmy Lee married Mary Ann Houghton, who came from German and Irish parentage and whose family, from Whitechapel, the Lees deemed to be respectable. Mary Ann's family, however, never really took to Jimmy; he was quite a mercurial character, quick to settle even the mildest dispute with a punch, and his language was frequently unacceptable. Soon after the marriage, Jimmy and Mary Ann had a son (also called James); however, the usual curse of the age struck when the baby died in his father's arms after a convulsion. A second son, Joseph, was born in 1899. At this time, the Lees moved around often, rarely settling down. Times were hard, and when landlords complained about their non-payment of rent, the family would pack their things, sneak away during the night and find somewhere else at short notice; either that or Jimmy would tire of the landlord's protestations and solve the problem by 'upping him' or punching him on the jaw. The same fate often awaited anybody who slighted Jimmy. His skill and power as a pugilist were infamous, and his devastating left-hook, often delivered without warning, earned him the nickname 'The Southpaw Cannonball' or 'Cannonball Lee'. Whenever it came to rent disputes, the end result was always the same – a new home had to be found – and the family, beginning to grow, took lodgings in various locations around Mile End, Hackney and Bethnal Green. Daughter Rose was born in 1907, followed by Violet two years later, May in 1911 and finally John in 1914. By the time the last of the children was born, some semblance of a settled life was found in London Street, Bethnal Green, which ran alongside the elevated train line to Liverpool Street Station. With its noisome

6   John Pearson; *The Profession of Violence* (London: Weidenfeld & Nicolson 1972).

and dirty railway arches, London Street (later renamed Dunbridge Street)[7] would become a Lee stronghold for many decades to come.

Bethnal Green, close to the fringes of the City and with Whitechapel to the south, had, like Hoxton, once been a rural hamlet. For a long while it boasted fine houses and wide pastures ideal for market gardening. In the late eighteenth and early nineteenth centuries, the weaving trades began to show a marked increase, spreading as they did from neighbouring Spitalfields. From 1801 to 1821 the population of Bethnal Green more than doubled, and by 1831 it had trebled,[8] principally due to the arrival of French émigrés and Irish weavers, and to the rise of small-scale manufacturing such as the production of matchboxes, cigars and mattresses, much of which would be undertaken in the home, often in rooms which occupied whole families. By the 1860s, the character of Bethnal Green was beginning to be defined by the poor condition of many of its dwellings, with dirty streets lined with tumbledown worker's cottages. By the end of the nineteenth century, it had become home to some of the worst slums in London. The most notorious was the Old Nichol, a small enclave of filthy, leprous slums near the border with Shoreditch; with very few access points to main thoroughfares, its isolation caused it to become a breeding ground for social neglect and crime. Places like the Old Nichol were the last stop for many before entering the dreaded workhouse:

> *In some wretched cul de sac, partly inhabited by costers, the fetid yards are devoted to the donkeys, while fish are cured and dried in places which cannot be mentioned without loathing. Bandbox and lucifer-box makers, cane workers, clothespeg makers, shoemakers, and tailors, mostly earning only just enough to keep them from absolute starvation, swarm from roof to basement; and, as the owners of such houses have frequently bought the leases cheaply and spend nothing for repairs, the profits to the landlords are greater in proportion than those on a middle-class dwelling.*[9]

The poor, as always, could take some solace in the proximity of family. It was not unusual for children to live with their parents even after they had married and had families of their own, and often these

---

7   The name was changed in 1938.

8   Andrew August; *Poor Women's Lives: Gender, Work, and Poverty in Late-Victorian London* pp 35-36 (New Jersey: Fairleigh Dickinson University Press 1999).

9   "Dwellings of the Poor in Bethnal-Green"; *The Illustrated London News*, 24 October 1863.

extended families would dominate particular streets. A house-move could often mean taking a few belongings to a property merely doors away. As would become apparent, this was certainly true of the Lees in Bethnal Green.

The Lees were nothing if not extraordinary. Jimmy Lee, like Jimmy Kray, was happy to settle into the world of the bare-knuckle street fighter. Apparently Lee and Kray had met in several contests over the years, although Jimmy Lee always maintained that 'Mad' Jimmy Kray never got the better of him. But 'Cannonball' Lee was known as quite a character outside of the fighting culture of the East End. He was a real trooper, taking on any role to support his family; and, when he was not working, he marked himself out as quite an entertainer. He would often spend money on broken musical instruments which he would (often unsuccessfully) attempt to repair, and yet he always managed to squeeze some semblance of a tune out of them. He would sing, dance, recite poetry of his own devising and some tales of his escapades have become the stuff of legend. Some of them even appear to defy logic.

The most famous of these was the feat of placing a white-hot poker on his tongue without sustaining any personal harm, a trick he first attempted after seeing an African impressing crowds with it on the Mile End Waste. He claimed the secret was to ensure that the poker was heated to a certain temperature, for only then would it work: "You're safe enough, long as you see the poker's white-hot. If it's just red you lose your tongue" he once said.[10] Jimmy's other *pièce de résistance* was walking across beer bottles that had been placed on end. Not only could he do this with no trouble at all, but he could also apparently accomplish the feat with bottles that were placed on the rungs of ladders, from the top of which he would jump into an upturned barrel. He bet all comers £50 that they could not do the same and needless to say, he never had to pay up once. If it *is* true, it is a truly remarkable story. These acts he would take to the streets to entertain the neighbours or, often enough, around the music halls of the East End such as the People's Palace in Mile End or the Pavilion on Whitechapel Road; his last performance, when in his fifties, was at the Portsmouth Empire, after which he 'retired', concentrating on his less unconventional real job as a market porter.

---

10 John Pearson; *The Profession of Violence* (London: Weidenfeld & Nicolson 1972). .

Despite this image as an amusing *bon viveur*, albeit with a serious message for those who upset him, in the home Jimmy Lee was the boss. His word was law and nobody, including Mary Ann, was permitted to disagree. As a married couple they were entirely devoted, despite being like chalk and cheese, although later Mary Ann would take on some of Jimmy's more coarse verbal characteristics. Owing to Jimmy's strict teetotal manner, Mary Ann would often resort to smuggling alcohol into the house, or going out with friends from whom she could scrounge a few beers or whiskies. When her husband was out and about, either working or getting into any number of peculiar schemes, Mary Ann held the family together in the tradition of the East End mother and wife; but with three daughters to bring up, Jimmy made sure that they in particular adhered to his strict moral codes.

Bookended between the oldest and youngest of the Lee sons, Joe and John, the three girls, Rose, Violet and May appear to have had very distinctive characters. By far and away the most dominant character was the eldest daughter, Rose, a fiery, dark-haired girl who appears to have inherited her father's short fuse and tendency towards physical retribution for even the smallest slight. In the words of her brother Joe, "She should have been a boy, that one, because she was into everything. Always ready for a fight and never changed the rest of her life."[11] May, the youngest, was a less tempestuous character, always singing and 'larking about'. She was pretty and blonde and was later known as 'Dinah' by the local boys, after the words of the song of the same name – "Dinah, is there anyone finer...?"[12]

Violet Lee looked very much like May and according to the family was cheerful and often seemed to be in a world of her own, earning her the affectionate nickname of 'Doodle.' It was not unusual for her to be sent on a food errand, only to return having absent-mindedly eaten it on the way home. She enjoyed life, as did all the Lee sisters and, as she would later declare, had a happy childhood. The only problem, she felt, was her father's demands:

> He was terrible strict. Us girls all had to be in by nine o'clock, every night. I used to like life. Always have. And I was the one who couldn't get home on time. I used to go up Mare Street to the dance halls and I never could seem to get home on time, no matter how hard I tried.

---

11 Joe Lee, Rita Smith and Peter Gerrard; *Inside the Kray Family* (London: Carlton 2008).

12 Music by Harry Akst with lyrics by Sam Lewis and Joe Young; it was published in 1925.

*As my Dad worked in the market, he had to get up early, and I can
remember creeping up the stairs so's not to wake him.*[13]

Despite being very much unlike her sister Rose in terms of
temperament, it is clear that Violet (or 'Violi' as the family normally
called her), by her teenage years, had developed a quiet rebellious
streak, and it was probably in that youthful spirit that she would
quickly fall for attractive young Charles David Kray, two years her
senior.

Charlie Kray was by now well settled into the life of a travelling
wardrobe-dealer, working alongside his father. He had the gift of
the gab. Trade could be quite lucrative, so there was a bit of ready
money around, and these qualities, deemed desirable in the East End,
undoubtedly made a great impression on sixteen-year-old Violet Lee.
The problem was that he was a Kray, and they were already known
to the Lees: the family had all had dealings with the Krays at some
time, and Jimmy knew Charlie's father through his street-boxing days.
He had little time for them and to say that he was not happy about
his daughter's association with a Kray was putting it mildly. In fact,
the Lee family as a whole – bar Violet – were not enamoured with
them. Older brother Joe remembers them as a "flash mob really, like
travelling people,"[14] and when Rose first told him that Violet was
seeing Charlie, he could hear alarm bells ringing. An attempt by Joe
to have a 'quiet word' with Charlie about the situation was scuppered
before he could do so when Violet bravely brought her new paramour
round to the Lee home on London Street one Sunday. Everybody
was civil enough – even Jimmy, when he returned home from the
market – but the reception became somewhat frosty after that. Violet
sat giggling nervously as Charlie turned on the charm. After he left,
Jimmy flew into a rage and made his opinions known, telling her
that Charlie was no good for her and saying everything he could to
convince his daughter that she was making a mistake. She promised
not to see Charlie again, but continued to do so and for a while her
sisters would cover for her when she went out to see him. Her father
was not stupid and could see that something was going on, but still
nobody was prepared for what happened in March 1926. Violet left
home unannounced and married Charlie Kray.

13 John Pearson; *The Cult of Violence* (London: Orion Books 2001).
14 Joe Lee, Rita Smith and Peter Gerrard; *Inside the Kray Family* (London: Carlton 2008).

On 6 March 1926,[15] and with Violet lying about her age (as she was not yet eighteen), the couple had sneaked off to the registry office in Kingsland Road with Charlie's friend and close neighbour Harry Hopwood as best man.[16] Here they became man and wife, seemingly without anyone's blessing but their own. Jimmy Lee took it badly and, as far as he was concerned, Violet was no longer his daughter. Of course, living with her family after the wedding was not an option for Violet and her new husband; however, there was obviously a place for them back in Hoxton and they moved in with Charlie's aunt Betsy and her husband George Cook at Charlie's childhood home at 40 Gorsuch Street.[17]

It is clear that Violet was pregnant by this time, and this may explain the secrecy and swiftness of the marriage. On 9 July 1926, four months after the wedding, she gave birth to a son, Charles James.[18] The new arrival, probably to Violet's relief, produced a softening in her father's attitude; secretly he would ask the family how his grandson was getting on, although – stubborn as ever – Jimmy Lee still refused to talk to Charlie. In fact, he was determined that he would get his Violet back whether she was married or not, and one night he went with his eldest son, Joe, to 'rescue' her. On arriving at the house in Gorsuch Street, it sounded as though a party was going on inside. After knocking at the door, Jimmy shouted out that he wished to speak to his daughter, only to hear the voice of old Jimmy Kray say, "Tell the old bastard to fuck off." Jimmy began kicking violently at the front door and if Joe hadn't talked him out of it, he undoubtedly would have smashed the door in and wreaked havoc.

Despite the inter-family stress, young Charlie would later feel that his childhood had been a good one, largely down to the efforts of Violet:

15 In *The Cult of Violence* (2001), Violet tells John Pearson that her wedding took place on 6 March 1927, however records show the marriage in the first quarter of 1926. It is unlikely she would get her wedding anniversary date wrong, just the year.

16 There were a number of branches of the Hopwood family in Gorsuch Street at this time. Harry lived at No. 28.

17 By this time James and Louisa Kray, Charlie's parents, had moved a few doors down to 26 Gorsuch Street.

18 In *The Krays; The Image Shattered* (London: Robson 2002), Craig Cabell suggests that Violet was right about her wedding taking place in 1927 and that Charlie therefore would have been born out of wedlock. However, the dates shown in official documentation show that Violet and Charlie were already married, but that Violet was undoubtedly pregnant when the wedding took place.

As a mother she was unbeatable, simply the tops. And I have her to thank for giving me a wonderful, happy and secure childhood in an East End that suffered as much as anywhere from the Depression that bit into Britain in the late twenties and thirties. Hungry children roamed around Hackney in rags, stealing food from barrows and shops. But I was always well fed and dressed in smart clean clothes.[19]

Such words were often used to describe Violet Kray. Many people felt she was the salt of the earth, kind and generous to a tee, never used bad language and was always friendly and hospitable. In later years it would become a cliché as to how much she was adored by Ronnie and Reggie – and, indeed, how much that affection was reciprocated. But the Kray sons, for all their maternal veneration, talked of their father in less enthusiastic terms.

Although Violet may have been a conscientious and doting mother, she did not work. The money that allowed the Krays to exist more comfortably than some of their neighbours came from her husband's work 'on the knocker'. This meant that he would be away for much of the week, traversing London and in some cases the Home Counties and beyond, buying and selling. It made him a respectable living. But this relative affluence was tempered with the less salubrious side of East End life. Charlie usually made sure his wife had money for the housekeeping, even if it meant calling in a few favours, but what was left over invariably ended up in the pub, and Charlie's nature would often change for the worse once he'd had one too many drinks. The result was violence.

The abuse that Charlie Kray inflicted on his wife and eldest son is not often written about. Joe Lee and Rita Smith, the twins' cousins, published their memoirs in 2008,[20] and here they put forward a disquieting picture of a man who, when working or sober, was quiet and thoughtful, perhaps with a dark charm that helped him in his job, but who when in drink could be unpredictable and aggressive. Despite their own fieriness, the Lees took a dim view of Charlie's more public forms of violence – but that violence would manifest itself against his own family when alcohol was placed into the mix. Much of this would go unnoticed by Violet's parents and siblings for several years, until they were all living near each other. Whatever went on behind closed

19 Charlie Kray & Robin McGibbon; *Me and My Brothers* (London: Grafton 1988).
20 Joe Lee, Rita Smith and Peter Gerrard; *Inside the Kray Family* (London: Carlton 2008).

doors, though, young Charlie appeared unaffected. He was good-natured and quiet, and as he grew, was polite and eager to please. Uncle Joe later said that Charlie would often get a serious beating from his father and remembers one occasion when Charlie, off school with excruciating toothache, was ordered to get some fish for supper by his father (who had just returned from an after-work drinking session in the pub). Young Charlie, crying with pain, had to make his way to Kingsland Road and back to get the fish, only to be cruelly reprimanded by his father who described the fish he had brought back as rubbish, ripping it to pieces and making him go back and get something better.[21] But young Charlie never remonstrated with his father; nobody could when he was in that state. It was a blessing that Charlie Kray spent much of his time away from home working, but his return at weekends could often spell trouble. As Ronnie would later recall:

> *I don't have such happy memories as Reg about our father. During the periods he was at home he would often drink too much and come home and start shouting. This used to upset me and I used to think that one day, when I was bigger, I would give him a bloody good hiding – and later I did... He wasn't a bad man. But when he's had a drink, he got a bit silly.*[22]

In 1927, Rose Lee married William Wiltshire in Shoreditch and, as seemed to be the way of things, Rose must have been pregnant at the time, for a few months later she gave birth to their only son, also named William. The Wiltshires lived with Jimmy and Mary Ann Lee in their house on London Street, at the corner with Vallance Road. Then, in 1929, Violet found herself pregnant again. For somebody disposed towards motherhood as she was, it must have been a joyous piece of news and, already having a son, she felt – with a mother's intuition – that the next child would be a girl. As it turned out, she was correct; but little Violet, as the baby was named, died almost immediately. Again, accounts differ as to the circumstances of the baby's death: Reggie Kray would later go on to write that she was born prematurely,[23] but the Lees, perhaps less inclined to paint a rosy picture of the Kray side

---

21 Joe Lee, Rita Smith and Peter Gerrard; *Inside the Kray Family* (London: Carlton 2008).

22 Reggie & Ronnie Kray, with Fred Dinenage; *Our Story* (London: Sidgwick and Jackson 1988).

23 Reg Kray; *Reggie Kray's East End Stories* (London: Sphere 2010).

of the family, believed that there was a much more disturbing reason.

They claimed that the night before little Violet's birth, after a Sunday night in the pub, Charlie had given his wife one of his customary bashings. The following morning, with young Charlie at school and her husband preparing for a train journey out into the provinces to look for work, Violet was not well and was bleeding between her legs. She begged Charlie to stay with her, but he chose to ignore her pleas and was soon out the door; an hour later, little Violet Kray was born, and died in her mother's arms. She had dark eyes and masses of dark hair. The death of a child is traumatic to say the least and Violet sank into a depression and for a long while was bedridden with grief. A visiting doctor said to Charlie that she needed to get pregnant again, to have another child, or else she would begin to sink even lower. At this point, Violet may well have felt tremendous resentment for her husband; some members of the family even felt that this may have been the final straw in their already abusive marriage, but she stayed by him, tolerating him more than anything else. It has been said that – deep down – she hated Charlie, and many years later, when Charlie had softened his ways, she would make her bitterness about the marriage felt by putting him down, not accepting his offers of kindness and even exacerbating his chest complaint by shaking dusty cloths near him. Perhaps it was just as well he was away much of the time.

They say a change is as good as a rest and, by the early 1930s, Violet had begun to tire of living amidst the Kray family in Gorsuch Street. Her brother Joe had found vacant rooms at 68 Stean Street, Hoxton and moved in with his wife Cicely (Cissy) and young son Joe. Sharing the large house were Cissy's parents Edward and Caroline Whittington and a docker, William Budd,[24] leaving two rooms free on the upper floors. Charlie and Violet Kray moved in during 1932. Young Charlie found it all exciting, especially as there was a stable yard opposite their home, and, with cousin Joe always around for company, the two lads were allowed by the yard owner to play there or to watch the horses being groomed. All this must have contributed to Charlie's rose-tinted view of his childhood. Despite his father's frequent absence through work and his erratic, even troublesome behaviour when he was at home, the move must have been refreshing, like a new start. In early 1933, Violet fell pregnant again.

---

24 Electoral Register: Hackney – Shoreditch and Stoke Newington 1933.

On Tuesday 24 October 1933, as Charlie and Joe played outside in the cold with the promise of small change and sweets, Violet Kray gave birth to twins. The first, named Reginald, arrived at 8.00 p.m.; the second, Ronald, came ten minutes later.[25] They were named after Caroline Whittington's nephews – two names, already conveniently paired up within the extended family, for which Violet had long had a fondness.

25 Exact timings of birth are taken from the twins' birth certificates.

TWO

BOYS WILL BE BOYS

Perhaps it was with no little irony that on 23 October 1933, across the Atlantic in Greencastle, Indiana, a gang led by John Dillinger pulled off an audacious bank heist at the Central National Bank and Trust Co., netting them a cool \$74,802,[1] the largest take in any of their organised bank robberies. Dillinger would later be known as 'Public Enemy No. 1' by the US law enforcement authorities, a moniker which could easily have been attached to the two bouncing baby twins born in a poor part of London the day after that bank job. But that was thirty-five years away. When Reggie and Ronnie Kray were born there were no dark omens; no spontaneous storms over East London, no sinister premonitions from family or neighbours. Quite the opposite, for the arrival of twins was greeted with great joy, such as the arrival of any child into the world would provoke. It even softened the stubborn heart of Jimmy Lee, who was delighted by the birth as much as anybody else and allowed his rejecting of his errant Violet to subside. The arrival of the twins did much to reunite the Lee family. Of course, at this time, there was no knowing what the future would hold, yet an early photograph of the twins, taken on 8 February 1934, showed their potential characters already: Reggie looks out at the world with his customary furrowed, perhaps mistrustful brow; and Ronnie glares with the same look that, many years later, would inevitably be a precursor to trouble, serious trouble.

---

1   This would be approximately \$1.4 million at today's value.

The twins were a big distraction in the neighbourhood and, as Violet would walk them through the streets in their double pram, other mothers would coo over her two identical sons. As Violet would later recall:

> Everyone who saw 'em seemed to love 'em and everybody spoiled them. Somehow with the twins you couldn't help it. I always dressed the twins the same. They was such pretty babies. I made 'em both angora woolly hats and coats and they was real lovely, the two of them. Just like little bunny rabbits.[2]

To all intents and purposes, Reggie and Ronnie were their mother's pride and joy. With older brother Charlie having such an agreeable temperament, it would become easy to leave him to get on with his own childhood outside the somewhat cloying environment around the twins. But he was not averse to entering that world and, when Violet was busy, he would take them out, feeling some of the same pride that his mother did as neighbours leant over the pram to say how gorgeous his two little brothers were. Sharing the same bedroom, Charlie would look at them as they drifted off to sleep, feeling that their dark eyes lacked childhood innocence, as if they knew full well what was going on around them. He also noticed that they soon began to get used to being the centre of attention and demonstrated their unhappiness when they weren't. It was Reggie and Ronnie's first taste of the limelight.

For the first three years of their lives, the twins, as many are, were inseparable. However, that unique bond took its first test in late 1936 when Reggie came down with a raging fever. Ronnie soon followed suit and the pair were diagnosed as having contracted diphtheria. It could easily have been tragic, for in the 1930s diphtheria, a respiratory tract illness caused by the bacteria *Corynebacterium Diphtheriae*, was potentially fatal; prior to the development of widespread vaccination after 1940, it was a major cause of death in children. At the time Reggie and Ronnie contracted it, there had been a slight peak in cases, around 70,000 being recorded in England and Wales, of which approximately 500 resulted in death (more than was recorded for measles, scarlet fever or whooping cough).[3] Isolation was essential and, for the first

---

2   John Pearson; *The Profession of Violence* (London: Weidenfeld & Nicolson 1972).
3   Source: Record of mortality in England and Wales for 95 years as provided by the Office of National Statistics (published 1997).

time, the twins were separated; Reggie was sent to the North Eastern Fever Hospital in Tottenham[4] and Ronnie to Homerton Isolation Hospital in Hackney. It is unclear from the numerous accounts as to exactly how long they were hospitalised,[5] but what is generally accepted is that Reggie was quick to recover. Ronnie, however, was having difficulties and it wasn't looking too good for the younger twin. After a while, Reggie was well enough to go home, but Violet remained deeply concerned for Ronnie's well-being. After several months of having to look at him suffering from a distance through a glass partition, she decided that she knew what was best for him and, against the recommendations from the medical staff at Homerton, she took him back to Hoxton. "All he really needed was me and his Reggie," she would later declare.[6] Nursing him at home in Stean Street with all the attention that only a doting mother like Violet could muster, Ronnie gradually recovered. Although Charlie Snr was away much of the time working, leaving Violet to do the visiting and later, the nursing, he would always be aware of what she did for Ronnie: "It was his mother saved his life. If it 'adn't been for 'er and what she done for 'im, Ron'd have been a gonner", he would later admit.[7]

Diphtheria is not only an infectious disease of the throat and respiratory system; it also releases dangerous neurotoxins which can affect or even damage the central nervous system. After Ronnie's slow recovery, it was apparent that he had changed, and perhaps not for the better. He was slower, more prone to tantrums and, probably because of his prolonged separation from his family, noticeably more needy. In a way, this change in behaviour created a form of dominance in Ronnie: if he was not getting suitable attention, he would play up; once Violet had addressed his needs, he would smother her with affection. He became competitive in the strangest of ways, more so than the average twin, as several of the family attest. Billy Wiltshire, an older cousin, later recalled one occasion when Ronnie flew into a tantrum because he counted more peas on Reggie's dinner plate than were on his own. Outside the home it would be Ronnie whose spontaneity and newly aggressive nature would cause him to get

4   Now St Ann's Hospital.

5   Patient registers are usually confidential for 100 years (certainly in the case of St Ann's) so it is impossible at this time to gain access to the specific admission and discharge dates in this instance.

6   John Pearson; *The Cult of Violence* (London: Orion Books 2001).

7   Ibid.

involved in little scraps with local kids or assorted mischief which Reggie felt compelled to join in with, either to assist his twin brother or to get him out of the trouble he had created for himself.

It may be a simplistic overview, but what was happening was that the twins were now developing distinctive personality traits. Reggie was the brighter, more socially articulate brother who, out of filial loyalty, was being roped into behaviour that compensated for Ronnie's unpredictability and difficult nature. As effectively two parts of the same person and, through their close bond as identical twins, there was a sense of *Yin and Yang* to their relationship. They did everything together, but there was definitely a difference in the way they perceived situations. Together they were one rounded personality; perhaps good and bad is too strong a description, but it seemed that Reggie would often struggle to keep Ronnie's more wayward character traits in check, a factor that would bedevil Reggie for the rest of their lives together as free men.

With the Kray family reunited in Stean Street, things continued as normal. Violet ensured her sons were well-fed and well-dressed and Charlie Snr continued to bring in the housekeeping, pounding the streets of London and beyond 'on the knocker'. Young Charlie was now attending school in Laburnum Street and had shown sporting promise, earning him a place in the football team. He was soon getting involved in athletics and of course it would not be long before the Kray and Lee family traditions of pugilism would make its mark on the young Charlie, who became interested in boxing. He was serious about his sport and was encouraged by his father, who would take him to boxing events at local venues and ensure that Charlie had the best kit that a child of the East End could possibly want. Grandfather Jimmy Kray, known to the brothers as 'Farvie', was a constant source of riveting boxing stories from his younger days, and young Charlie was enthralled by tales of great fighters like Ted 'Kid' Lewis, himself a native of Hoxton, and others. Despite this, Violet was never enamoured of her son's interest in boxing, thinking that it was too dangerous. She was even less happy about any fighting in the street; Charlie was a generally easy-going boy, but he was fit and physically strong and could hold his own in any scrap. For young boys in Hoxton, fighting came with the territory, a way of settling disputes or garnering respect. It wasn't long before Charlie got involved in his first street fight. It shows the mindset of 1930s Hoxton that this fight was observed by a circle of adults who, as Charlie later recalled, "watched us slug it out for nearly an hour. Afterwards they made us shake hands as though we had been fighting purely for their entertainment."[8] Whatever he got up to on the streets or at school, he was always careful to clean himself up afterwards, so as not to upset his mother.

However, change was soon in the air. Charlie Snr's often difficult behaviour was causing friction in the Stean Street home and Violet, despite the relaxation of tensions within the Lee family following the birth of Reggie and Ronnie, was still somewhat distanced from the nucleus of her own flesh and blood. In time, Charlie and Violet were encouraged to look for somewhere else to live.

The oft-repeated story about the move to Bethnal Green has usually been that one of the twins' aunts, either May or Rose, was living in a house in Vallance Road and that the property next door, No. 178, had become available. The story continued that a chance for the Lees to live more closely together was swiftly grasped, and the Kray family moved into one of the small row of terraced houses occupied by various Lees, that part of Vallance Road being known locally as 'Lee Corner' or 'Lee Street'. But this was not so. Aunt Rose was living with her husband and son next door to her parents in a flat at 45 Dunbridge Street (as London Street had been recently renamed); May and Albert Filler had married in 1936 and were living in Union Crescent, Bethnal Green, with their little daughter Rita. John Lee, who married Maude Frith in 1938, was at Wilmot Street with his in-laws.[9] Also, the Krays had moved out of Stean Street in late 1937 and had at first settled in dingy rooms at 1 Dunloe Place, off the Hackney Road. Violet's brother Joe described it as "A right dump... Up an alley it was and gas-lit, even then."[10] Soon they were on the move again and briefly lived above a shop with Bertha and Thomas Mayer at 218 Hackney Road.[11]

No doubt Rose or her parents, living close by, must have been aware that 178 Vallance Road was up for grabs,[12] and told Violet about it. Charlie and Violet were the first of that extended family to arrive at Vallance Road, in the late summer of 1939. No. 178 was one of a line of workers' cottages with two rooms on the ground floor, a kitchen

8 Charlie Kray & Robin McGibbon; *Me and My Brothers* (London: Grafton 1988).
9 All addresses taken from electoral registers, 1937-39.
10 Joe Lee, Rita Smith and Peter Gerrard; *Inside the Kray Family* (London: Carlton 2008).
11 Electoral Register for Tower Hamlets – Bethnal Green 1939.
12 The house had been occupied for several years by a widow, Matilda Wood, and her children. This information is courtesy of Adam Wood.

and a scullery out the back and the standard outside lavatory in the little back yard. Upstairs there were three rooms, but it was certainly no palace; Reggie would later say, "I won't mince words, it was a dump."[13] Like the neighbouring properties, it was infested with mice and shook every time a Liverpool Street train flew by on the nearby railway arches, but to the five-strong Kray family, it was their first chance to truly have a real home of their own. Charlie Snr must have been impressed as he went so far as to have legitimate business cards printed, complete with contact address. There seemed to be a sense of permanence and, indeed, for the next thirty years it would become their one true home; only the coming of the demolition contractors at the end of the 1960s would see them move on.

At this time Reggie and Ronnie began their formal education, attending Wood Close School in nearby Cheshire Street. It was an imposing but not unattractive building, built in the regular London County Council Board School style in 1900,[14] and the twins enjoyed their short and disrupted time there. One thing they noticed, just as brother Charlie had several years before at Laburnum Street, was how much better dressed they seemed compared to their classmates. Many of them had cut-down cast-offs, frayed shirts and broken plimsolls. This was quite an education in itself for the twins, who became aware for the first time of how well they were looked after by their family and how hard others must have had it. Reggie would later paint a rosy picture of his time there:

> I took to schooling like a duck to water. I may not have been top of the class but I was a long way from the bottom. My main highlight of the day was when all the pupils were gathered together in the main hall first thing in the morning to sing such hymns as 'Down in Virginia', 'The Maple Leaf' and 'The Four Leaf Clover.' You'll see the headmaster's choice had a rather international flavour that would have been lost on us kids as we sang our hearts out, accompanied on an echoing piano.[15]

13 Reggie & Ronnie Kray, with Fred Dinenage; *Our Story* (London: Sidgwick and Jackson 1988).

14 The school closed in 1953, reopening in 1959 as St Gregory the Great Secondary School until that institution moved to other buildings. After becoming a temporary site for Swanlea School until the opening of its new buildings in Brady Street in 1993, it was taken over by William Davis Primary School, who occupy the site today. Information from William Davis School website: www.williamdavisprimaryschool.wordpress.com/school-history.

15 Reg Kray; *Reggie Kray's East End Stories* (London: Sphere 2010).

There were also daily rest periods when the pupils were made to sleep in the afternoon on small camp beds; supervised by a member of staff, there were strict rules about talking and giggling. Break time meant playtime, allowing the children ample opportunity to run off their pent-up energies. Sometimes an innocent bump or knock could escalate into a confrontation and, as in all schools, playground fights were a big draw until the teachers arrived to break them up. It was at Wood Close that Reggie claimed to have had his first fight, with an older boy named George Tappin whom Reggie described as 'a bully'. When he arrived home that day, brother Charlie apparently took one look at the results on Reggie's face and suggested that learning some boxing skills would not go amiss.

The proximity of her parents and older sister, as well as all three Kray brothers being in regular education, would have made life easier for Violet, who, often left alone with her children in her husband's absences, could breeze through such lop-sided parenting with familial support. It was undoubtedly this arrangement which would have the most significant influence on the upbringing of Reggie and Ronnie Kray. But the promise of any hard-won stability was about to be dashed by the onset of war.

The full impact of that most devastating of global conflicts, the Second World War, was slow to make its mark on the people of Britain. Known as the 'Phoney War' from its declaration in September 1939 until May 1940, the first eight months of the war in Europe were primarily naval. There were no land offensives and any enemy action was specifically targeting fleets at sea or naval bases.[16] Despite the immediate sense of there being no danger to London from the skies, extensive evacuation procedures were now being instigated across the country, predominantly aimed at children and women. The Kray family stuck it out in Bethnal Green as Operation Pied Piper, as it was known, saw the evacuation of 3.5 million people to rural locations far and wide.

By early 1940, however, the impending threat of air-raids over London, part of what became known as the Battle of Britain, saw to it that the Kray family needed to move on. After all, they were based in the East End, a prime target for bombing with its docks and factories and the nearby railway line to Liverpool Street, a major London

16 The first Luftwaffe air raid was directed at British warships based at Rosyth on the Firth of Forth in Scotland in October 1939.

terminus, added to the risk of living in Vallance Road. Perhaps with great reluctance, Violet took the twins, accompanied by her sister May and her young daughter Rita, to Hadleigh in Suffolk. Brother Charlie, by now almost a young man, would join them occasionally in that most picturesque part of the countryside. The family were billeted at East House,[17] a large 17th century property in George Street, Hadleigh, owned by Dr. Arthur Hurrell Style and his wife Clare.[18] The twins may well have been taught to show good manners to those who treated them well and who garnered their respect, but they were fundamentally two little East End boys, for the first time in their lives released from the tough and dirty surroundings of Bethnal Green into an exciting new environment. How they would be perceived by their new host would be relative, for Clare Style's world was markedly different, refined and most certainly middle class. Nearly thirty years later, she would have this to say about her wartime guests:

> My first thought was: what horrible little boys. And so they were. They were full of rough and tumble and quite unlike my own children. I recall vividly how shocked I was that they could not read. I spent long periods teaching them to read. When they showed some mastery, I insisted they learn the Lord's Prayer.[19]

Despite Mrs. Style's reservations, the twins loved Suffolk, starting a love affair with the county that lasted for the rest of their lives. Ronnie was particularly enamoured by it, relishing the sense of space and freedom so removed from the hustle and bustle of East London. Even as an older man he would recall his time in Hadleigh with a child-like wonder:

> ...the quietness, the peacefulness of it, the fresh air, nice scenery, nice countryside - different from London. We used to go to a big 'ill called Constitution Hill and used to go sledging there in the winter-time. We had a good time there, you know. We used to go apple-scrumping and all that, you know. Very nice there. We used to play cowboys and Indians...[20]

17 The house was Grade II listed in 1950 and sold by the Style family in 1963 (*Hadleigh Community News*; September 2014).

18 All accounts written about the Krays' time away from London state that the family name was 'Styles', however it was actually Dr. Arthur *Style* as his name can be found as such in medical registers. Some accounts also make out that Mrs. Style was a widow, when in fact her husband did not die until 1953. She passed away in 1974.

19 *Daily Mirror*, 5 March 1969.

20 1989 interview with Robin McGibbon in Broadmoor from *The Kray Tapes* (Glasgow: Harper Perennial Talking Book 2008).

One little incident that Ronnie confessed to was having accidentally shot another boy in the eye with a slug-gun, a typically boyish *faux pas*, but a strange portent of what was to come decades later. At one point Charlie joined them and, now in his teens, found work in a local fish and chip shop and later as a tea boy in a local factory. Like his younger brothers, he found the countryside to his liking.

It may have been a quiet and wholly safe idyll, but Violet was soon missing Bethnal Green and her family. Her husband would occasionally visit when he wasn't working and his interest in the local pubs during his brief stays may not have endeared him to the Style household or the locals of Hadleigh; accordingly, the decision was made, after little more than a year away, to decamp back to London. By this time aerial bombing had started in earnest. The Krays may have missed the most devastating raids of the Blitz, but air raids were still a regular enough occurrence to make the return to Vallance Road a highly risky proposition.

But, to most eight-year-old boys, war was exciting, like watching a movie acted out in real time, and the overwhelming dangers were always obscured by a keen sense of adventure. The nearest shelters were under the railway arches by Bethnal Green Junction Station, just round the corner from Vallance Road,[21] and the wail of the sirens would produce a great exodus from the streets into these cavernous spaces, which in all fairness would probably have offered very little protection from a direct hit. People made the most of it and, with their immediate family in tow, Reggie and Ronnie could always be guaranteed a good time, whether it was to peek out of the arches to watch fighter planes battle it out overhead in dogfights, look on at the tracer fire and searchlights sweeping the sky at night or, inside the shelter, become a part of Grandad Lee's 'cabaret'. Jimmy Lee would often take advantage of the captive audience to pull out his repertoire of tricks and music and the twins would look proudly on as their Grandfather did his bit for wartime morale. Once the all-clear siren sounded, it was out into the shattered streets, climbing over ruins, collecting shrapnel and getting into all manner of little scrapes with other groups of children from the neighbourhood. Joining them on these escapades would be their school friend Laurie O'Leary, whose family lived down the road in Cheshire Street.

21 On Three Colts Lane, it is now Bethnal Green Overground Station.

Significantly, it was during these war years that the Lee family consolidated their presence in Vallance Road. Gradually, perhaps as a result of the evacuations, the houses adjoining No. 178 became vacant. Violet's younger brother John moved into 172 with his wife Maude and some of her family, and Rose Wiltshire and her son Billy moved into 176, next to the Krays. No. 174 was empty and as good as derelict, but May and Albert approached the landlord and offered to do the house up. The landlord must have thought they were mad as the property was in a bad way, but Jimmy Lee knew a builder who did the work cheaply, and so the house was made fit and the Fillers moved in. With three sisters and a brother all now in adjoining houses and with their parents a few doors down at the corner, 'Lee Street' was complete.

The close proximity of such a close (and fractious) family would have a lasting effect on the young Kray twins. Their cousin Billy Wiltshire, despite being older than them, was now a frequent companion on the bomb sites of Bethnal Green. As he, Reggie, Ronnie, Laurie O'Leary and others would play on the ruins, he would assert his authority over these little boys with physical aggression. Billy's potentially dangerous behaviour was no surprise, considering the temperament of his mother, Rose. Her marriage had floundered and she and Billy Snr had since parted company, supposedly on amicable terms; however, despite the proximity of family, young Billy would perhaps draw more from his mother's attitude than anybody else. Aggression, settling disputes or slights with a punch or a beating, was well-engrained in Lee culture, but the twins' Aunt Rose was something else altogether. She would take no nonsense from anybody, and any perceived wrong would be met with immediate retaliation, both verbal and physical. With all due respect, if all the stories of Rose's confrontations and the reasons that sparked them off were true, a modern court would see fit to place an Anti-Social Behaviour Order on her. But she adored the twins and they in turn thought she was wonderful. Rose was the one that would stick up for them, cheerfully let them off the hook when she was party to any of their misdemeanours; to the twins, she was the kindly aunt who would turn a blind eye and let them get away with all sorts and give them little treats into the bargain. Ronnie was particularly fond of her and it is interesting to note how his own developing spontaneous temper and its repercussions would mirror Rose's. In the street, the pub, the market, man or woman – if anybody upset Rose Wiltshire, they would receive a mouthful of abuse and a few punches for their trouble, even if it was actually Rose who was in the wrong all along.

Billy's behaviour with the twins and their friends reflected this. Games on the rubble would result in Billy intentionally hitting somebody in the head with a brick, or, if he did not get his way, inflicting hard punches that would leave vivid bruises. Even at the local baths in Cheshire Street one was not safe, and one of his favourite schemes was to climb over the partitions into somebody else's bath cubicle and hold his victim's head underwater longer than was entirely advisable. Like his mother he was quick-tempered, and on one occasion whilst camping in Chingford with the twins and a friend named Ronnie Gill, he waited until they had put up their own tent and gone inside before pulling out the support strut. As the tent collapsed around the three boys, Billy exclaimed, "Fuck the camping, let's get back to Vallance Road."[22] In the words of Joe Lee:

> I've got to say he was a right little bastard... If you was looking for odds on which of the boys would turn out a gangster and end their days behind the door you wouldn't have got even money on him.[23]

Ironically, after serving in Malta he emerged from the army a different man and went on to live a straight and hardworking life as a market porter at Covent Garden. However, for the twins, Billy's behaviour as older cousin was all grist to the mill: "Because he was older than us, we just accepted the treatment he handed out,"[24] Reggie would later recall. As far as they were concerned, what with their father's occasional lapses into heavy-handedness, Grandad Lee's quick temper and ready fist and Aunt Rose's own excursions into blind aggression, all this was frankly normal. Granted, there is nothing normal (or desirable) about a family that regularly inflicts violence on its own or others, but the twins grew up in that maelstrom and it probably shaped their attitudes to getting what they wanted from life as much as anything else. They didn't shy away from violence because it was a part of their life, part of their inner programming: with the family (and especially Violet) spoiling them and increasing their egos by treating them differently, and pending the addition of a few extra

22 Reggie Kray; *Born Fighter* (London: Arrow Books 1991).

23 Joe Lee, Rita Smith and Peter Gerrard; *Inside the Kray Family* (London: Carlton 2008).

24 Reg Kray; *Reggie Kray's East End Stories* (London: Sphere 2010).

ingredients, a potent mix was being prepared.

One ingredient was a mistrust of the law. Since time immemorial, one of the codes of the East End had been 'thou shall not grass', for any problem that should be sorted should be done so within the community on its own terms, not via the police. Importantly, the Second World War saw a massive increase in criminal activity, and specifically in black market trading. Goods purloined in less than legal ways would be sold on in similar circumstances and, with its glut of street markets like Brick Lane, Watney Street and Petticoat Lane, to name but a few, the East End became a ready conduit for 'fenced' goods. Criminal it may have been, but ordinary communities were willing to turn a blind eye, for, in most cases, the buying and selling of stolen goods became a way of survival, a way of acquiring essentials and little luxuries that wartime rationing had made hard to come by. Any perceived interference by the police would have been most unwelcome.

The East End was awash with colourful characters. The Kray twins would come to hear of these underworld types through their grandfathers, who had mixed with many of them during their street-fighting years. Some of them would be regular visitors to Grandad Lee's home and, although he accommodated them as far as a fireside chat and a cup of tea, he made sure he never got involved in any of their scams. As Ronnie would go on to remember:

> ...we really admired the famous local villains like Johnny Spinks, Timmy Hayes and the greatest of them all, Dodger Mullins and Wassle Newman. All great fighters, but in a different way to Ted [Lewis]. They were East End villains of the old style. Fearsome, tough fighting men who didn't give a toss for anyone. Even the coppers were scared stiff of them. They ruled the streets of the East End when we were kids but they always played by rules which we admired.[25]

Grandma Lee, Mary Ann, would contribute her own stories of growing up off Brick Lane in the late 1880s and of being told that 'Leather Apron' (the first nickname given to the proto-serial killer we now call Jack the Ripper) had committed another gruesome murder near her home. A whole collection of unusual characters, many

---

25 Reggie & Ronnie Kray, with Fred Dinenage; *Our Story* (London: Sidgwick and Jackson 1988).

working on the other side of the law, were brought to life by the Lees and the Krays, undoubtedly instilling the notion of *criminal celebrity* in the twins. These were fanciful, legendary stories about real people, some of whom would actually pass within the Kray orbit, and it was yet another constituent in the way the twins would come to see life in the future, and their part in it.

By the time the Krays returned to Bethnal Green, men of fighting age[26] were receiving their military call-up papers, and that, of course, would eventually include Charles Kray Snr. But Charlie had other ideas.

As far as his sons were concerned, Charlie refused to join up on account of his being the sole breadwinner in the family. In retrospect, they looked up to his decision to opt out of army life with great admiration, as he had risked so much to ensure and maintain the livelihood of his wife and children. That's what they said, anyhow. Whether this was entirely the case is difficult to ascertain, as it is always easy to throw an accusation of cowardice at any man who refuses to fight for his country without giving the authorities a solid reason why. Sure, there were many conscientious objectors who were put to work in essential civilian jobs or in non-combative roles within the military, but Charlie Kray, for whatever reason, just let it go and went on the run. He valued his independence, never worked under anybody else and wasn't going to let the advance of Nazism change that.

As the war rolled on, the twins' father remained at large, evading the military police with no small amount of luck. He would put in the occasional appearance, taking a risk as he did so. When situations got tight, Violet or her sons would have to cover for him. Charlie Snr would hide in various locations at the house if the police called whilst he was there: under the sink alcove, in the cupboard under the stairs or in the coal hole in the back yard. Sometimes he would jump over the fence in the back yard and hide in Rose's house next door. One morning, the twins awoke to find two policemen standing at the end of their bed asking where their father was, but Violet had primed them with the stock response that they hadn't seen him in ages and that their parents were getting a divorce. Aunt Rose only helped to reinforce the barrier between them and the police – "She'd have a right go at the

26 Aged 18-41 years.

officers, four-letter words and all."[27] The twins duly became complicit in their father's desertion, learning how to outwit the law and, at the same time, building on their resentment against the authority that, at that point, seemed to be hell-bent on taking the family bread-winner away from them.

On one occasion, Charlie, realising that hanging around Bethnal Green would make him more vulnerable to capture, went south of the river to stay with a friend in Camberwell Green, and it may be here that he fell in with a young villain named Francis Fraser, who had also deserted from the forces. Charlie and Frankie, as he was known, used to drink together, and occasionally the pair would return to Vallance Road where Violet, hospitable as ever, would cook them a meal. In time, the twins called him 'Uncle Frank',[28] and later he would consolidate his ties with the underworld in South London, become known to all as 'Mad' Frankie Fraser, and quickly grow into one of London's most notorious gangland figures (after the twins themselves).

Older brother Charlie was now settling into his own life. He had got himself a job as a messenger boy at Lloyd's in the City, earning him eighteen shillings a week; his spare time was devoted to his passion for boxing. Grandad Lee set up a punchbag in an upstairs room at No. 178 and the twins would watch enthralled as Charlie would go through his moves; then they would ask if they could have a go themselves. Charlie went from the Coronet Junior Club to the Crown and Manor youth club, both in Hoxton, training three nights a week. After recovering from a serious bout of rheumatic fever in 1943, he joined the naval cadets at Hackney Wick. The cadets had excellent boxing facilities which Charlie took advantage of and, as a welterweight, he began entering competitions. There was money in it too, and before long Charlie was proving himself to be a very capable boxer, winning trophies and thinking seriously about turning professional. Once the twins saw these accolades being brought home, they were keen to grab some of the action themselves. Charlie turned the upstairs room into a more functional gymnasium and Reggie and Ronnie began to join their brother in his early morning road running, or 'road work.' They would invite their friends round to use the gym equipment and spar, and Violet would make them all tea and sandwiches; the boys

---

27 Charlie Kray & Robin McGibbon; *Me and My Brothers* (London: Grafton 1988).
28 According to Fraser in a number of television interviews, including *The Krays and Fred Dinenage*; Talent TV South Production (broadcast 15 March 2010).

were having fun and, as long as nobody got hurt, Violet was happy to let them all get on with it.

When they were ten, Charlie took the twins to the Robert Browning Institute in Elephant and Castle, South London, where they gave a demonstration of their acquired boxing talent. The observing trainer was duly impressed and signed them up immediately. Also around this time, they participated in their first public display of boxing at Alfie Stewart's boxing booth, which had set itself up on a bombsite in Turin Street, Hackney. Five boxers took to the ring in all and the twins looked on in awe and excitement, swept up in the cheering and adrenaline of the crowd. During a break, Alfie Stewart invited members of the audience to come up and have a go in the ring themselves. Perhaps unsurprisingly it was Ronnie who leapt at the chance but, owing to his size and age, found himself without an opponent. It was only natural for his twin to make the offer and Reggie climbed into the ring. Stripped to the waist and wearing shabby boxing gloves, the twins fought three rounds, resulting in a battered nose for Ronnie and a bruised face for Reggie, with Stewart declaring the match a draw to an appreciative crowd. They were paid seven shillings and six pence between them and walked back to Vallance Road with their handy earnings, their bruises and their confidence boosted.

By 1944, the war at home was beginning to lose its impetus. The frequent air-raids of four years earlier had subsided, but there was still the risk from the new terror weapon which the Germans had begun to unleash upon their enemies: the flying bomb. The V1 rocket, or 'Doodlebug', was a terrifying missile, arbitrary in its target and falling to earth only after a moment's silence once its fuel had been spent. The first had fallen not too far away in Grove Road, Bow, in June 1944. Its follow-up, the V2 (first used in September 1944), was the first true ballistic missile, more powerful and devastating than its predecessor, and Vallance Road became one of several locations which felt its effect. On the morning of 25 March 1945, a V2 rocket struck Hughes Mansions, three blocks of 1920s dwellings situated on the southern stretch of Vallance Road, beyond the railway bridge and less than a quarter of a mile from the Kray home. The small houses at 'Lee Corner' were subjected to the shock wave, blowing out windows and dislodging objects indoors. It was an event that made a lasting impression on the twins, as some of the 134 people killed at Hughes Mansions were well known to them and their family. In fact, the Krays and the Lees were lucky to keep their own homes, as incendiary and high explosive bombs had seriously damaged or totally destroyed a number of the buildings in the immediate vicinity. The whole row from 170 to 180 Vallance Road was subject to blast damage,[29] the bakery at the end had to be demolished, and John and Maude's house at 172 was particularly affected. Before long they would open a café opposite, on the corner with Cheshire Street and it would soon become their home.[30]

However, by this time, Reggie and Ronnie had seen their first significant brush with the law.

Some time between 1944 and 1946,[31] the twins, accompanied by their friend Alfie Miller, spent one of their customary days out in the suburbs around Chingford. Reggie had brought his slug gun with him, a .177 Diana air rifle, for use as a prop in their games of 'Cowboys and Indians'. On the return train journey, the boys were in playful mood and Reggie fired the gun out of the carriage window. As far as they were concerned, nobody got hurt, and they weren't even aware of where the pellet had ended up. The guard, however, noticed what they had done and shut them in his carriage; when the train pulled up at Liverpool Street, two railway detectives were waiting for them. After the officers interrogated them in a small room, the twins were driven back to Vallance Road where Violet was told that this would not be the end of the matter.

The railway police had made veiled threats about the boys ending up in a youth detention centre – Borstal, as such places were commonly known – and this terrifying possibility hung over the Kray family for a whole month before Reggie was put before a magistrate at Toynbee Hall Juvenile Court in Whitechapel and charged with discharging a firearm. With a sense of overwhelming relief, Reggie was bound over to keep the peace, given a stern talking-to and allowed to go. Violet and Aunt Rose, who had attended the hearing, were relieved but emotional. For the twins, however, this was to be a formative experience. Not only were the police after their father, coming to their

29 London County Council Bomb Damage Maps 1939-45, as held at the London Metropolitan Archives.

30 According to electoral registers and Kelly's Post Office Directories, 119 Cheshire Street was formerly a hairdresser's and became Lee's Café in 1947. It was closed in 1957.

31 This date is an estimate only. It is impossible to say exactly when the events described actually happened. Some accounts (including Reggie's) say the twins were ten-years-old; others, including Colin Fry in *The Krays - The Final Countdown* (Edinburgh: Starlyte 2001), say they were twelve. The records of the Inner London Juvenile Court at Toynbee Hall are held in the London Metropolitan Archives (PS/IJ/0-2) but are not available for public inspection at the time of writing.

home and making life difficult, but now even they, as young boys, could not get away with what they felt were childish hijinks without feeling bullied by the law. As far as Reggie was concerned:

> I felt nothing but hatred for the police, railway or not, and the establishment that had put my family through a month of emotional hell. In my mind they had become and would remain THE ENEMY. My young mind couldn't comprehend such a thing as the establishment, but later on I would realise that this experience was my first conflict with those faceless powers-that-be, a conflict that would become greater.[32]

32 Reg Kray; *Reggie Kray's East End Stories* (London: Sphere 2010).

THREE

SECONDS OUT

As young boys, the twins were always active. Whether they were sparring with brother Charlie, playing in the streets with improvised box-carts, or travelling to suburban adventures by train, they had energy to spare. They relished making a little money on the side, a perk of helping their Uncle Joe at his job in Billingsgate Market, or accompanying their father's friend Harry Hopwood 'on the knocker'. Sometimes they would work with their grandfather Jimmy Kray on his stall in Brick Lane, using their break times to dodge through the swarming market crowds and develop their footwork reflexes. Charlie was by now back in Civvy-street after being discharged from the Navy on medical grounds (he had been suffering from migraines), and was working with his father 'on the knocker'. As much as he admired his father's hard graft and ability to charm his customers into handing over profitable merchandise, he wasn't keen on his drinking after work. Charlie Snr's watering hole of choice was the '99 Public House' on Moorgate, close to Broad Street Station and an ideal stopping-off point after a long day in the provinces.[1] It was a place he spent many hours, much to the chagrin of his family.

At twelve years old, once the schools had reopened after the war, Reggie and Ronnie started at Scawfell Street LCC School,[2] behind

---

1 The '99 Public House' was a nickname given to the Crown & Anchor at 99 Finsbury Pavement, Moorgate. It has since been demolished but would have stood at the junction with Ropemaker Street.

2 Often described as Daneford Street School, this comes from a report made by Detective Superintendent Leonard Read in 1968; CRIM 1/4900 (National Archives).

the Hackney Road. As with Wood Close, they enjoyed their time at Scawfell and by all accounts were popular with fellow pupils and staff alike. Reggie was particularly fond of English and Ronnie enjoyed general knowledge. Years later, their principal teacher, William Evans, described his former students with great affection:

> *Salt of the earth, the twins; never the slightest trouble to anyone who knew how to handle them. Course they were tough and they were fighters, but they weren't the sort that rolled around or spat in each other's faces or used knives as some of them do today. If they had to be punished they'd take it like gents. And if there was anything to be done in school they'd be utterly cooperative.*[3]

Evans' account reveals a strange dichotomy that stayed with the twins throughout their lives: despite being known as tough kids early on and violent underworld characters with little respect for others later, they maintained a high regard for the middle and upper classes whom they deemed 'their betters'. This was a character trait instilled in them by their parents, and one individual who was on the receiving end of such respect would go on to be a highly important figure in the twins' life.

Father Richard Neville Hetherington came to the parish of Bethnal Green in 1945 after previously serving at St Barnabas in Ealing, West London. A strong and verbally forthright character who enjoyed his cigarettes and scotch, he came to know the twins when they joined the youth club attached to St James the Great Church on Bethnal Green Road. He too remembered the twins with some affection:

> *They were extremely kind boys and would do anything for me except actually come to church. But they were both exceptionally polite, to old folk in particular, and they took trouble over people.*[4]

Just as compliant as they were in school, they loved to help out with church events such as jumble sales, and often approached Father Hetherington for things to do. On one occasion, they gave him a packet of cigarettes as a gift by secretly putting it into his pocket whilst keeping him talking, as they knew he would not accept if they offered it outright: Hetherington later claimed that he would refuse gifts from the twins as he could never be sure how those gifts had been acquired.

3 Evans interviewed by John Pearson for *The Profession of Violence*.
4 From his obituary in the *Daily Telegraph*, 14 January 1990.

To their elders, at least, Reggie and Ronnie therefore maintained a veneer of deference that was perhaps not replicated in their general conduct out on the streets of Bethnal Green. As identical twins they were still often the focus of attention, but sometimes this was unwanted attention from local youths who would pick on them, and then find themselves on the receiving end of a dual assault. The twins fought as one; they were strong and fit and if one of them found himself in an altercation with any local 'hard-nuts', the other would always be there to back him up. Singly, they were formidable: together, they were a force of nature. This combined strength would see to it that they had the confidence to hold their own and ultimately ensure that things always went their way.

Undoubtedly, they were earning their 'chops' on the streets of Bethnal Green, and it was an accomplishment echoed in their boxing. With Charlie Simms training them at the Robert Browning Club and older brother Charlie introducing his own skills to the mix, boxing became the twins' obsession, their potential path to fame and success, and they gave it their all. They joined the Webbe Boys' Club, the Oxford Boys' Club and ultimately the Repton Club in Cheshire Street, a few hundred yards from their home. As schoolboys, they clocked up an impressive track record: Reggie became schoolboy champion of Hackney, a Great Britain schoolboy finalist and the 1948 London schoolboy champion. In 1949, he became the South East Divisional Youth Club Champion, and the London ATC (Air Training Corps) Champion. Ronnie enjoyed similar successes as Hackney Schoolboy champion, also winning the London Junior Championship in 1946 and 1947, as well as ATC titles. Ronnie also beat Reggie in the 1946 Hackney Schools Championships and the match was reported in the press – apparently they were so alike that judges found it difficult to award the right points to the right twin.[5]

All the while, they were attending other clubs and gymnasiums across London, such as Klein's Gym in Great Portland Street and Solomon's in Windmill Street, meeting some of their boxing heroes and often sparring with them. All of this combined to give them a truly rounded boxing education, and they delighted in meeting the big names of the boxing world, for they were utterly star-struck. They developed distinctive styles. Reggie, as has often been said, had all the

---

5   *The Star*, 5 November 1946.

makings of a champion, strong in technique and self-discipline, able to hold back when necessary and willing to listen to advice. Ronnie, whose temperament was more spontaneous and unpredictable than that of his twin, was a real 'slugger', winning by sheer brute force and relentless onslaught. If boxing was in their genes, then Reggie was like Jimmy 'Cannonball' Lee in his approach; Ronnie, it seems, had inherited the drive and aggression of 'Mad' Jimmy Kray. It was these differing approaches which would ensure that Reggie would soon become the more talented fighter and gain greater success in the years to come.

On leaving school in December 1948,[6] they initially had ideas about getting into the building trade, and worked for a roofer as odd-job boys. After only a few weeks they had had enough of the filth and burns from the hot asphalt, and they left. On 8 January 1949, they began working for Farren and Barrow at Billingsgate Market, earning £2 a week, a job acquired though their Uncle Joe. Reggie was hired as a trainee in sales and Ronnie, less glamorously, was an 'empty boy', charged with the job of collecting empty boxes from around the market. They left on 30 April, and at the end of May, Reggie got work at Fielder's Tinsmiths on Redchurch Street, Bethnal Green, taking home £3 a week until he left on 17 June to go fruit picking in Wisbech, Cambridgeshire, for a working holiday. The twins, accompanied by their friends and family all enjoyed the rigorous outdoor work and the clean country air, but it was purely seasonal work and by October 1949, the brothers were again on the lookout for employment. On 6 October, Reggie got work with Davis Feather Mills on Whitechapel High Street before being dismissed six days later as 'unsuitable' and from then on bounced around various labouring jobs.[7]

Despite their skill and enthusiasm for boxing, and their apparent keenness to get a 'proper job', on the dirty streets of the East End they were soon carving out a niche as adolescent tearaways to be reckoned with. Brother Charlie marked the age of fourteen as the turning point:

> *Suddenly they started staying out late and neglecting their morning roadwork. They became very secretive about where they were going, what they were doing, who they were seeing. Mum was very concerned but she bit her tongue. She put it down to their age:*

6   CRIM 1/4900 (National Archives).
7   Ibid.

*they were probably going through that 'growing up' stage and she
didn't want to appear a moaner.*[8]

What was happening was that the twins were quickly beginning to
be dragged into a youth street-culture that had begun to germinate
now that the war was over and curfews and controls had been
abolished. Youths would hang around the streets, forming themselves
into small gangs and marking out their territories, settling disputes
with fights. Reggie and Ronnie now had a name for themselves; apart
from the fact that they came from a prominent, even notorious, local
family and stood out as identical twins, they were now also gaining
column inches in the local press for their boxing and their pictures
were beginning to grace the pages of the *East London Advertiser*.
They were now becoming mini-legends of Bethnal Green and Father
Hetherington would later blame this ego-boosting publicity for the
twins' evolution from 'polite young lads making good' to aggressive
street thugs.

They were beginning to gain a negative reputation in the cinemas
and dancehalls of the East End, and therefore began to frequent places
further afield, such as Hackney and Tottenham. On Sunday mornings,
they would congregate with some of their friends like Laurie O'Leary
and Pat Butler outside a record stall in Cobb Street, one of the many
thoroughfares that make up the renowned Petticoat Lane Market,
where they would catch up on the latest gossip. One particular
morning, when the twins were sixteen, they were hanging around
Cobb Street as usual when a group of three men moved through the
crowd and went into Ziggy's Cafe,[9] another popular haunt for the
twins and their friends. The men were smartly dressed, almost in the
style of flash Chicago gangsters, and, as they approached, the crowds
parted for them, and the street cries and shouting became hushed
muttering. It was Little Hymie Rosen,[10] Moishe Blueboy[11] and, leading
the way, the legendary Jack Spot.

Born Jacob Colmore in Mile End in 1912, Spot grew up as Jack Comer

8   Charlie Kray & Robin McGibbon; *Me and My Brothers* (London: Grafton 1988).
9   Situated at No. 4 Cobb Street. It has remained an eating place and is now Moo Cantina, an
    Argentinian restaurant.
10 Also known as 'Little Hymie' or 'Hymie the Yid', he was a boxer from Aldgate who was
    active inside and outside the ring during the 1930s.
11 His real name was Morris Goldstein and like Rosen was a former boxer, hailing from
    Stepney. It was said that he had a discoloured testicle and was sometimes called 'Blueball'
    by those who knew him well enough to get away with it. 'Blueboy' was the polite version.

in Whitechapel in the slums of Fieldgate Mansions, Whitechapel, becoming part of a gang at the age of seven. This gang of Jewish youths would regularly do battle with the Catholic boys from the school along their street, and, as was the way with many youngsters in the East End, a life of crime was soon to follow. Throughout the 1930s and '40s, Spot, so named because of a large mole on his face, worked alongside Billy Hill, another prominent London crime lord, and together they jostled for the title of 'King of the Underworld'. Their criminal enterprise revolved around protection rackets, illegal gambling, controlling bookmakers' pitches at race meetings, and high-stakes robbery. Spot was well-known, feared and respected throughout the East End, backed as he was by his tough, loyal gang which included Blueboy, Rosen, Bernard Schack (known as 'Sonny the Yank') and Solly Kankus, usually referred to as 'Solly the Turk' owing to his dark complexion.[12]

By the time Ronnie and Reggie saw Jack Spot and his henchmen in Cobb Street that morning, Spot and Hill had begun to drift apart, and within a decade they would both sensibly retire on the spoils of their criminal careers with their respective 'Kings of the Underworld' titles relatively intact. But the image of the strong, dapper men eliciting hushed respect from the masses was intoxicating, and Ronnie Kray was paying particular attention. He asked Laurie O'Leary what would happen if he shot Jack Spot, to which O'Leary made it plain that this would not be a good idea for all of them.[13] Ronnie, it seems, was already thinking big, thinking ahead, perhaps picturing himself as Spot's natural successor. Indeed, that year the twins had acquired their first gun from a local criminal. Weapons had become *de rigueur* for the youth-gangs of London; the twins, practically unbeatable as a dual fighting-force, were perfectly capable of settling disputes with their fists, but if rivals were 'tooled up' with coshes, knives or razors, the ante would have to be upped. Daggers, swords and other bladed weapons were easy to come by in the markets or 'on the knocker', but a firearm, a somewhat rarer currency, would be seen as the ultimate leveller. The gun was quickly added to the growing arsenal of weapons which the twins secreted under their bed at Vallance Road.

Just how far Reggie and Ronnie had ventured into the violent world

12 James Morton, Jerry Parker; *Gangland Bosses: The Lives of Jack Spot and Billy Hill* (London: Sphere 2005).
13 Laurie O'Leary; *Ronnie Kray – A Man Amongst Men* (London: Headline 2001).

of street-culture was amply demonstrated in early 1950, when they first felt the serious attentions of the law and ended up appearing at the Old Bailey on a charge of Grievous Bodily Harm (GBH).

On the evening of 12 March 1950, Roy Harvey, a clerk from Dalston, had gone to Barrie's Dance Hall in The Narrow Way, off Mare Street in Hackney, with some friends, in a group which included Denis Seigenberg and Walter Burch. It was a busy Sunday night at the hall and the multifarious gangs and collectives from the East End were well represented, including the Krays and their friends. There appeared to have been no trouble that night. Seigenberg, Harvey and Burch left at 11.00 p.m. and, as they walked along the road, they became aware of a large group of about thirty youths following behind. Among them were eighteen-year-old Thomas Organ, seventeen-year-old Patrick Aucott and the Kray twins; Harvey knew them all by sight and was aware that they had been in the dance hall. Suddenly, without warning, Harvey was viciously attacked – he was punched by Aucott and, falling to the ground, was repeatedly kicked, beaten and struck with heavy objects by multiple assailants. Seigenberg and Burch managed to get away,[14] but Sheila Coates, who had witnessed the incident, tried to help Harvey once the mob had moved on. Lying in the blood beside Harvey was a length of bicycle chain and two lavatory chains with handles, which had been used in the assault.

Harvey's injuries were severe; examined the following day by Dr. Stanley Turtle, a medical practitioner based in Clapton, he was found to have "two contusions of both eyes. There was a weal across the bridge of the nose which was consistent with a blow from a fist or something blunt. On the right side of the neck he had four weals and on the side of his chin two weals, consistent with the use of a chain..."[15] Burch remembered seeing one of the Kray twins and the incident was also witnessed by a passing insurance broker, Stephen Norris, who confirmed that the twins were there, as did Sheila Coates. Aucott, Organ, Reggie and Ronnie were arrested and charged on remand with causing GBH. There were five appearances at North London

14 Seigenberg, as Dennis Stafford, was given a life sentence (along with Michael Luvaglio) for the murder of Angus Sibbett in Newcastle in 1967. Known as the 'One Armed Bandit' murder, or the 'Body in the Boot' case, it was apparently the inspiration for the 1971 Michael Caine movie *Get Carter*. Stafford and Luvaglio were released on license in 1979, but Stafford was imprisoned in 1989 for breach of his license and again in 1994 for forging travellers' cheques.

15 *East London Advertiser*, 31 March 1950.

Magistrates' Court,[16] during which evidence came to light that Harvey had received a threatening letter and that Coates had been warned that "a razor would be put across her face" if she gave evidence. In early May, the case went to the Old Bailey.

Undoubtedly the twins were present during the incident and had some part in the ensuing fight. In his statement, Reggie admitted that they were there (with twenty or thirty others) and that both he and Ronnie acted violently:

> I saw my brother Ron striking a fellow in the face. I joined in and also struck this fellow and another in the face. I did not use any weapons in the fight. I saw one man lying on the pavement but I am not sure if it was one of the men I hit.[17]

Ronnie's statement is particularly interesting as it connects him to a cosh that had been confiscated from Organ by the first officer at the scene, PC Kenneth Wilkinson:

> About 10.30 p.m. I went to the lavatory and found a cosh lying beside the urinal. I picked it up and put it in my pocket. I went into the dance hall and Tommy Organ was standing by the lavatory entrance. I handed him the cosh & said "You had better take this there is going to be trouble."[18]

When Organ was searched by PC Wilkinson, he did indeed have a cosh on him, but said that he hadn't used it and that he "had it bunged on me at Barry's [sic]."[19] This backs up Ronnie's claim, but it does suggest a disingenuous act on Ronnie's part: seemingly unarmed, he was quite happy to dump an offensive weapon on somebody else. Ronnie may have been aware that some trouble was going to occur and that he would probably be in the thick of it – maybe he even thought that he might be the instigator. Either way, he was more than happy for somebody else to take the rap for possessing a weapon which would have come in handy during any potential fracas. The twins would often get others involved in their plans, sometimes to detract from their own responsibility, or for some form of backup.

It is not clear if the twins used any weapons in the fight, or indeed

---

16 Reported in the *East London Advertiser* 17, 24, 31 March and 21, 28 April 1950.

17 Statement by Reggie Kray taken 13 March 1950; CRIM 1/2064 (National Archives).

18 Statement by Ronnie Kray taken 13 March 1950; CRIM 1/2064 (National Archives).

19 From PC Wilkinson's statement taken 4 April 1950. Ibid.

whether they were responsible for getting a third party to make the threats against Harvey and the key witnesses, yet this tactic seemed to work. Identifications became shaky, statements were withdrawn and the twins' role in this locally significant incident could not be fully accounted for at the Old Bailey trial; as a result, they were acquitted. One element in their salvation was character witness testimony from Laurie O'Leary, Pat Butler[20] and most significantly, Father Hetherington. Uncle Joe Lee generally felt that Hetherington spoke from the heart when he supported the twins in their moments of need, "and honestly believed, when they got into trouble, it was a bit out of the ordinary and they would soon straighten out. I'm afraid to say he made a bit of a misjudgement."[21]

In fact, Reggie and Ronnie were rather good at hiding their dubious activities from their family and those whom they respected. Because he was away so often, it was comparatively easy to keep their father in the dark, and brother Charlie was now finding it difficult to get his younger siblings to listen to his fraternal advice. But the twins had the undying loyalty of their mother and her sisters. Violet turned a deaf ear if she heard anything negative about her two boys, or simply convinced herself that they were good sons and that any bad stories that came her way were the product of spite and malice. Aunt Rose welcomed any such stories with a wink and a nod, practically condoning their behaviour. Nanny Lee and her daughters would also set upon anybody who talked badly about the twins within their earshot. The bottom line appears to be that Reggie and Ronnie were very used to being the centre of attention, and, whatever they did, they were backed up to the last by the most dominant members of their family. In a word, they were spoilt rotten and were blessed with the luck of the devil.

Ronnie's first official crime, and the one that kick-started his criminal record, was a conviction on 31 October 1950 at the Friend's House Juvenile Court for attempting to drive away a car without consent, the punishment being one day's police detention. The following day, the twins appeared at Old Street Magistrates' Court on a charge of assaulting a police officer. One evening that October, Bethnal Green PC Donald Baynton was making street enquiries regarding a fight that had recently taken place at the Mansford Youth Club, in Mansford

20 O'Leary and Butler appeared in court on 8 May 1950, according to the subpoena.
21 Joe Lee, Rita Smith and Peter Gerrard; *Inside the Kray Family* (London: Carlton 2008).

Street. Outside a cafe on Bethnal Green Road,[22] he approached a group of youths and asked one of them if they had been in a fight recently. The boy replied that he had not, at which PC Baynton prodded him hard in the back; the boy responded instinctively by hitting Baynton in the face and quickly ran off. It was Ronnie Kray.

Ronnie was soon traced and taken to Bethnal Green Police Station. There he was beaten black and blue by a coterie of officers. Reggie, in the meantime, having heard about the incident, called in at the station, only to be met by PC Baynton, who let him know that some of the officers had given Ronnie a taste of his own medicine. Reggie ran off, knowing full well that Baynton would follow; when Baynton turned a blind corner, Reggie was waiting. A few punches to Baynton's face and he was away.

Brother Charlie went to the station to see Ronnie for himself and was appalled at the state he was in. His face was battered and his shirt was torn and bloodstained. Charlie kicked up a fuss, almost getting arrested himself. Back home at Vallance Road later that day, Ronnie sat nursing his wounds whilst Violet sobbed and Charlie debated with his father as to whether some form of legal action might be warranted. A knock on the door signalled the arrival of an Inspector, accompanied by PC Baynton: they were looking for Reggie, who was now also to be charged with assaulting a police officer.

After some terse words, Reggie arrived and it was agreed that he should turn himself in. Charlie said that if any harm came to Reggie, then the family would go to the papers, but the officers suggested otherwise. Both twins would have to appear before a magistrate on the assault charges, and the Krays were advised to keep quiet about what had happened to Ronnie, otherwise things would become difficult. The police had a trump card: Charlie Snr was still officially on the run from the army,[23] but they were willing to turn a blind eye in this instance if the matter of Ron's beating went no further. After the appearance at Old Street Magistrates' Court, the twins were given two years' probation and let go, and Reggie's own criminal record began in earnest.[24] But just as Reggie's air gun incident had affected his feelings about the forces of authority, so this new trouble

22 Some accounts say it was Pellicci's at No. 332 Bethnal Green Road, but Laurie O'Leary states confidently that it was outside Hooker's Cafe on the corner of Mape Street.

23 In 1953, the House of Lords voted to give an amnesty to all army deserters from the Second World War, to mark the coronation of Queen Elizabeth.

24 Ronnie's Criminal Record Office (CRO) number was 38912/50; Reggie's was 39340/50.

only served to reinforce Ronnie's hatred of the police. And again the family's indulgent attitude did nothing to restrict the growth of the twins' hostility.

◆

These trials and tribulations with the law did not interfere with the twins' progress as boxers, and in the summer of 1951 they turned professional. Charlie had already started his pro boxing career in 1948, just prior to his marriage to Doris 'Dolly' Moore,[25] and was proving to be a very successful welterweight. By the time his brothers followed in his footsteps, Charlie had fought sixteen professional bouts, winning eleven, losing four and drawing once.[26] The twins fought at lightweight level and Reggie, in particular, was showing tremendous promise in the ring. From July 1951 to the end of that year, Reggie won all seven of his professional fights, including two knock-outs. Ronnie, in the same period, had six fights, winning four and losing two. Significantly, all of Ronnie's wins were knock-outs. Their manager, the American Jackie Jordan, refused to pay the twins their fee unless both were present, because, after their first professional fight on 31 July 1951 at the Mile End Arena, he had accidentally paid one of them twice, because he could not tell them apart.[27]

Famously, on 11 December 1951, all three Kray brothers fought on the same bill at the Albert Hall in what would be their last recorded professional bouts. Charlie's opponent was Lew Lazar from Aldgate; Lazar apparently exhibited the best performance of the night, described in the press as "a fine exhibition of hard and accurate punching" to which "the very game Charlie Kray" succumbed in the third round.[28] Characteristically, Reggie won, beating Clapham-based opponent Bobby Manito (whom he had also beaten in his first professional fight) on points, and Ronnie was outpointed by Bill Sliney. It is often stated that Ronnie was actually disqualified for being too violent, but there appears to be no mention of this in the boxing records[29] or in the press of the time, and this may be a sensationalistic exaggeration by authors keen to identify early signs of the violence

25 They were married on Christmas Day 1948 and set up home at the Krays' house in Vallance Road. Son Gary Charles was born in 1951.
26 Records found at Boxrec.com; boxrec.com/list_bouts.php?human_id=38955&cat=boxer.
27 Ibid.
28 *Daily Mirror*, 12 December 1951.
29 All three Kray brothers' professional boxing details can be found at boxrec.com.

for which Ronnie would later become notorious.

Throughout 1951, the twins were not only asserting themselves as professional boxers. They were also busy reinforcing their profile in the streets. They had begun to frequent the Tottenham Royal Ballroom, a popular meeting place for a wide variety of East and North London gangs, and were making themselves known to any potential competition. They would show up mob-handed with about twenty associates, ferried there in an old army van driven by their friend Googie Lane, and they soon came to the attention of William and Ronald Webb, local Tottenham villains who had begun to dominate the Royal with their own loyal following. As Billy Webb later recalled:

> At first I never paid them a lot of attention and thought of them as a couple of actors out to impress people – all night long they sat poker faced and glaring at everyone. They had their own little gang always close at hand, which proved they didn't then, and never would, have the courage to have a fight on their own.[30]

On one occasion, one of the Webbs' friends had insulted the twins' cousin Rita at the Royal, and the détente between East and North looked about to break into an almighty battle. Ultimately, on the night that all hell could have broken loose, Reggie approached the Webbs and cordially asked that the friend give Rita an apology and all would be forgotten. According to Rita, that apology was given in front of the whole crowd in the Royal. Bloodshed had been avoided, and the Krays and the Webbs entered into a relationship of unspoken acknowledgement, for a while at least.

In February 1952, two envelopes arrived at Vallance Road containing the twins' National Service call-up papers. Since 1939, conscription to the armed forces had been compulsory for all men between the ages of seventeen to twenty-one, for a period of eighteen months; in 1950, following the outbreak of the Korean War, the period was extended to two years, and thus it was expected that Reggie and Ronnie would serve their time in the military from March 1952 to 1954. What ensued was the twins' first major battle against the establishment – with the British Army itself.

On 20 March 1952, the Kray twins arrived willingly at the Tower of London to begin their two years as conscripts to the Royal Fusiliers, an infantry regiment that had been formed in 1685 from two companies

---

30 Billy Webb; *Running With The Krays* (Edinburgh: Mainstream Publishing 1993).

of guards based at the Tower. What happened on that first day has gone down in legend. Along with a number of their fellow conscripts, the two identical Kray brothers went through their initiation into National Service life. The squadron corporal began giving instructions about conduct, describing the rules about the maintenance of kit, and detailing other such regulations, and the twins suddenly began to walk off. When challenged, one of them apparently said, "We don't care for it here, we're off home to see our mum."[31] Naturally unhappy about being made a fool of, the corporal took hold of one of the twins and was promptly knocked to the floor. Reggie and Ronnie then strolled out, took a bus to Whitechapel and were home in time for tea. The experience had left them in a foul temper and, rather than tell their mother what had happened, they went out and spent the night at the Tottenham Royal. The following morning, military police arrived at Vallance Road and took the bleary-eyed twins back to the Tower.

Their punishment was lenient considering they had struck an officer, but the question of who had actually committed the assault remained unresolved, for the twins reactivated their old ploy of confusing the authorities with their identical appearance, and thus the issue of who actually hit the officer was never properly resolved. They were given one week's detention in the guardroom. As they whiled away their time, eating the drab food and sleeping on the cold hard floor, they were joined by another youth who had obviously incurred the army's displeasure, Richard 'Dickie' Morgan.

Dickie Morgan was a thief from Mile End with a strong criminal pedigree. He lived with his parents and brothers at 32 Clinton Road, close to Mile End Underground Station, and had recently been released from Portland Borstal in order to do his National Service. In fact, Morgan had been sentenced to borstal training or approved school no less than eight times since the age of ten, for robbery, larceny and stealing.[32] His father John had just been imprisoned for his part in a warehouse raid, and his overweight older brother John 'Chunky' Morgan was in Parkhurst. Another brother was also serving time in borstal. In Morgan, the twins saw a kindred spirit, somebody who constantly presented two fingers to the law and authority, offset with a sense of humour that must have given everybody light relief. When the week in the guardroom was over, the twins took advantage

31 John Pearson; *The Profession of Violence* (London: Weidenfeld & Nicolson 1972).
32 Morgan's CRO No. was 177255/48; CRIM 1/4927 (National Archives).

of the relaxed security and absconded again, this time taking Dickie with them.

A useful bolt-hole was the Morgan house in Clinton Road. Dickie's mother Janet was a truly accommodating host, used to putting up with all manner of criminal types. This was remarkable to the twins, for although their own family was full of real characters, they were essentially 'straight'; at Clinton Road, however, lawlessness was a way of life and there was no judgement, just acceptance. Dickie Morgan would introduce them to some of the local petty criminals and regale them with stories of the illegal activities of his own family and friends. In turn, Reggie and Ronnie would introduce Morgan to their world in Bethnal Green and the safer environs of the Tottenham Royal. The occasional trips to Vallance Road for fresh clothes were risky, so their appearances there were sporadic to say the least. Violet could not hide her concern on these infrequent visits, but the twins assured her they were doing fine.

They reignited their acquaintance with Billy Webb, who was now on the run from the army himself. Via Webb, they managed to set themselves up in a squalid flat in Finsbury Park in North London, but before long, the presence of a couple of National Service-eligible East End teenagers in a predominantly Irish neighbourhood began to attract suspicion, and so they took lodgings in Peckham, south of the river. Other useful bolt-holes were the Lyons Corner Houses in London's West End and the Vienna Rooms on Edgware Road, or a seedy hotel in Piccadilly; all of these establishments maintained a regular clientèle of deserters, petty criminals and others on the edge of society (including homosexuals) who were dodging the attentions of the law. As an education for their future, it would be invaluable.

One evening, the twins found themselves in a contretemps with a police officer who attempted to arrest them in Maidman Street, Mile End. Passing by was local thief Lenny Hamilton, who was at that time on his way home from work at Billingsgate Fish Market. Seeing two young men being accosted by a burly older man, Hamilton leapt in and the twins escaped; Hamilton was arrested for his troubles, and was taken to Arbour Square Police Station. "Do you know what you've done?" said the officer. "Them two young fellows was the Kray twins and now they've got away. They're on the run from the army." Hamilton, who was none the wiser, apologised and was grateful to be let off.[33] This was his first encounter, albeit brief, with Reggie and Ronnie Kray; it would not be his last, for years later Lenny Hamilton would begin a criminal relationship with the twins that would end dramatically.

But the twins' luck ran out in October 1952 when, on one of their brief visits home, they were picked up by PC Roy Fisher who knew them by sight. This time they were separated: Ronnie remained at Wellington barracks in the Tower, whilst Reggie was sent to the Fusiliers' own punishment institution at Purfleet. Independently, they began making life difficult for the authorities. Reggie got into innumerable scraps with any over-zealous prison officer who dared attempt to inflict discipline upon him, receiving two court-martials. Ronnie tried to convince his captors that he was going mad. Reggie had already attempted such tactics at the Tower when he had pretended to hang himself, a ploy that had cut no ice with the guards. Ronnie's attempts were less sinister – he would throw a tantrum and refuse to don his uniform or, comically, only shave half of his face.

The twins were reunited for a month at Colchester Military Detention Barracks, but after their return to the Tower absconded again. In late 1952, they set themselves up for a fall after being approached by the ubiquitous PC Fisher who had found them outside the Orange Cafe in Burdett Road, Mile End. The twins appealed for leniency – after all, Christmas was only round the corner; however, despite the cordiality of their plea, PC Fisher told them that he could not neglect his duty. With that, one of the twins pushed Fisher over a wall and the two made good their escape. It was not long before they were found again, but now they would also be charged with assaulting a police officer. On 26 February 1953, Reggie and Ronnie were sentenced to one month's imprisonment at Wormwood Scrubs, something that earned them a few column inches in the national press.[34] This would be their first true taste of life on the inside.

After their month in prison, which apparently had passed uneventfully, they were taken to Howe Barracks guardroom in Canterbury, awaiting court martial for repeated desertion and other misdemeanours. It appears that the army had now come to the conclusion that these two unwilling conscripts were in no way going

33 Interview from the Spitalfields Life website, posted 1 September 2010. spitalfieldslife. com/2010/09/01/lenny-hamilton-jewel-thief-2.
34 *Daily Mirror*, 27 February 1953.

to fulfil their military obligations. And they were right. At Canterbury, Reggie and Ronnie, now reunited with Dickie Morgan, made the authorities' life hell, taking any opportunity to create chaos, lash out at their captors and prove that the army would be well shot of them. Cells were smashed up, bedding and clothing was burnt, guards had chamber pots tipped over them. The company flag was cut into smithereens. On one occasion, Reggie managed to get hold of a pair of handcuffs and cuffed a guard to the bars of his cell door. Another time, at the behest of the twins, the keys to the officers' mess went down a drain, resulting in a time-wasting search by guards who now could not get any food or drink. With Dickie Morgan and fellow partner in crime Ted Bryant, they managed to climb onto the prison roof and sat there ignoring the pleas and the threats whilst Reggie squeezed a tune out of an old mouth organ.

Only one man could make the difference and that was Corporal Ted Haines. In that strange twist of respect that the twins had for those they considered their betters, Haines had Reggie and Ronnie in the palm of his hand. He was extremely experienced and had seen it all before, so when it was his turn to calm the twins down, he dealt with them in a calm, almost laid back manner. The twins felt they were being treated with respect by somebody who did not shout them down, and the feeling was duly reciprocated. It was Haines's efforts that calmly got the Krays, Morgan and Bryant off the prison roof.

In the early spring of 1953 there was one more attempt at escape. This time the twins, Morgan and Bryant overpowered a number of guards and made it out of the prison compound, intending to rendezvous with a van round the corner, in which sat their father, along with Harry Hopwood and his brother George. The fugitives took a wrong turning and could not find the van, but time was of the essence and they had to keep running, especially since a gaggle of prison guards were in hot pursuit. They jumped walls and waded waist-deep through a river before finding an old, decrepit van to steal. Heading back to London, the van broke down after ten miles, forcing the escapees to take the journey on foot. Another vehicle was taken but the four only got as far as Eltham before a group of motorcycle police caught up with them.

On 3 April 1953, they were all sent to Shepton Mallett military prison, convicted of numerous counts of assault and desertion; Bryant, being a full-time soldier as opposed to a conscript, received twelve months. Even though this would see out the end of their time in the army, the twins were still up to their old tricks. They received a few visits from their family and, on her only visit, cousin Rita went to see Ronnie, who was still shaving only half his face. He noticed her looking with some distaste at a brown spatter up one of the walls and, immediately knowing what she was thinking, said, "Don't look so disgusted, Rita, it's only cocoa. I slung it up there to piss them off."[35] Despite his predicament, Ronnie Kray still had his characteristic sense of humour.

On 13 November 1953,[36] without fulfilling their full two years, Reggie and Ronnie were released from the army, which surely would have been relieved to see the back of them. They were back in Bethnal Green as free men, twenty-years-old and with a dishonourable discharge from the Royal Fusiliers and a one-month prison sentence for assaulting a police officer behind them. Their criminal records were growing, and so their boxing careers, as a result, were effectively over: with such a reputation, the Boxing Board of Control would have no choice but to refuse the twins a licence. Ronnie didn't really appear interested any more in any case, although Reggie, who had tried to sort himself out a little after release, began his roadwork again and by some stroke of luck was granted a licence after PC Fisher, the constable they had knocked over at Christmas 1952, gave him a good reference. It wasn't long before the enthusiasm died off, however. To older brother Charlie, it was terribly frustrating. He felt that with their skills and fitness they could have made good army physical fitness instructors, but the twins, it seems, knew better:

> To me it had all been a terrible waste... I went to see them in hiding in various parts of London and tried to persuade them to give themselves up. I told them the Forces favoured sportsmen; they could do well with their boxing talent. But it was a waste of breath.[37]

Interestingly, had the Kray brothers taken their time in the army seriously, they may well have gone into battle with a more hostile enemy: in August 1952, the Royal Fusiliers entered the Korean War, a conflict in which many National Service conscripts found themselves

35 Joe Lee, Rita Smith and Peter Gerrard; *Inside the Kray Family* (London: Carlton 2008).
36 CRIM 1/4900 (National Archives).
37 Charlie Kray & Robin McGibbon; *Me and My Brothers* (London:Grafton 1988).

involved.[38] Destiny, it seems, had a different calling.

Those disjointed months on the run in 1952 and 1953, and their time at Shepton Mallett, had been an education in many ways. It taught the twins resilience and self-sufficiency, and how to keep their wits about them. But it also brought them face to face with the machinations of the London underworld and the colourful characters who practised the various disciplines of crime. The West End twilight world and the modest East End cafe hang-outs had introduced them to influential villains. Wally's Cafe near the Hackney bus station was a particular favourite. Islington's Nash brothers – Johnny, Jimmy, Roy and Ronnie – would go there, as well as kleptomaniac Billy Bellamy and Ronnie Diamond, head of the Diamond Gang. Many of these individuals were older than the Krays and already had convictions for robbery and violence under their belts. One of the regular customers was Hackney's own Tommy Smithson, regarded by the twins as a true hero. He was a loner, unallied to any gang, and a compulsive gambler who financed his life through protection rackets and the running of illegal gambling 'spielers' and snooker halls. He held no store in material possessions and spent anything he earned on enjoying himself. He was incorrigible and feared nobody in a fight, the result being innumerable wounds from old altercations which earned him the name 'Scarface' and 'Mr. Loser', as he did not always come out of these fights with the upper hand. As far as the twins were concerned, though, he was certainly worthy of their respect and admiration.[39]

The Lyons Corner House in the West End,[40] introduced to them by Billy Webb, was another of Smithson's hang-outs, as he had opened a spieler in nearby Archer Street, round the back of Shaftsbury Avenue. Such places were the haunts of the underworld, where villains could spend the hours and plans could be made. The twins and Webb often stayed in Archer Street when the club was closed, with Reggie and Ronnie choosing to sleep on the snooker tables. Homosexuals also frequented the Corner House; at that time homosexuality was

---

38 One man who was also posted to the Fusiliers in 1952 and who ended up serving in the Korean War was a young Maurice Micklewhite, later of course to become the actor Michael Caine.

39 Smithson would eventually die in 1958 after he was shot in a disagreement with a Maltese gang. The twins often claimed that they attended his funeral at St Patrick's Roman Catholic Cemetery in Leytonstone that year, although Ronnie would have been in prison at that time.

40 There were a number of these establishments very close together at this time and it is unclear which particular one was favoured by the twins in the early 1950s.

illegal,[41] and gay men would meet there, and runaway boys who had been ostracised by their families hid away there. It was at this time that Billy Webb became aware of Ronnie Kray's sexuality, noticing how Ronnie would look at the young men in the cafe. One night, Ronnie had struck up a brief conversation with a flamboyant regular known to all as 'The Duchess', who instinctively felt that Ronnie was gay. When Billy Webb asked him how he was so sure, he apparently replied, "It takes one to know one, and that's definitely a queen."[42] As Ronnie became more open about his sexuality in this somewhat liberated environment, he would happily tell Webb that he liked a certain boy, or that somebody had "a nice compact bum." Any boy he fancied would be called "a prospect",[43] but, despite this apparent openness, the issue of Ron's homosexuality (or bisexuality) was not something he readily mentioned to just anybody. It was still effectively a closed subject.

With their new criminal contacts and their swift introduction to the school of villainy whilst on the run, the twins had earned a little income from selling stolen goods, or 'fencing' as it is known in the underworld. But they had learnt of a wealth of possibilities which gave them a template for the future ahead, and the thought of mere thieving for a living did not have an enormous amount of appeal. Sure, they were well known, respected and even feared in their native East End, but there needed to be a catalyst to bring that strong-arm attitude together with a way of earning a crust. Whether it was legal or not didn't matter.

41 In the UK homosexuality was decriminalised for men over the age of twenty-one in July 1967. The age was reduced to eighteen in 1994 and then sixteen, bringing it into line with the heterosexual age of consent, in 2000.
42 Billy Webb; *Running With The Krays* (Edinburgh: Mainstream Publishing 1993).
43 Ibid.

FOUR

THE RISE OF THE KRAYS

Around 1952, Samuel Martin opened a billiard hall in Eric Street, a nondescript little turning tucked behind Mile End Underground Station. The premises had once been the 702-seater Forrest's Electrodrome Cinema, which had first opened in 1910 and closed, never to re-open, in June 1940, during the height of the Blitz. The building had been used thereafter as a factory and a warehouse, but, by all accounts, as a billiard hall it was considered a bit of a 'dive', a hangout for all manner of shady characters, petty thieves and National Service dodgers. By 1954, it was somewhat let go: its paintwork needed refreshing and the green baize on its few tables was looking distinctively grey from the cigarette ash that had been carelessly flicked over it by players.

After their release from the army in late 1953, the Regal Billiard Hall was a popular haunt for Reggie, Ronnie and their new partner in crime, Dickie Morgan; it was one of a number of places they frequented in those strange, open-ended days after being demobbed. There were also the cafes around the Mile End Road and, frequently, Ziggy's Cafe off Petticoat Lane. The twins continued to use the Vienna Rooms as their base for a while, revelling in the company of experienced villains, with some of whom they had rubbed shoulders in the more fractious days of desertion. It was here that they finally acquainted themselves with Jack Spot and his loyal gang. They would also become friendly with an associate of Spot whom they had met as young boxers many years before, Robert Edward Denis Ramsey: he was also an ex-boxer, and had previously been one of Billy Hill's right-hand men.[1] Bobby Ramsey, thirteen years older than the twins, was a smart dresser and drove a big American car, and had dated the twins' cousin Rita for a short while until she found out about the company he kept.

Reggie and Ronnie would spend many an hour listening to the stories these seasoned criminals had to tell, and soaked up the 'education' they had to offer. Billy Hill, Spot's old partner, was also a regular user of the Vienna Rooms; Reggie in particular looked up to Hill as a potential role model:

> *He was very physical and could be violent when necessary – he wasn't powerfully built, but he could be vicious with a knife. At the same time he had a good brain and this appealed to me. I learnt a lot by observing the way he put his thoughts into action.*[2]

They began their life of crime in earnest. At first, they got involved in little fraud scams and thieving, taking a cut in the proceeds of fencing off the stolen goods. Loads were purloined from delivery lorries, warehouses were robbed and valuables would make their way from the London docks by various means, away from the prying eyes of customs officials. Another scam revolved around supplying (for a fee) young National Service conscripts with bogus medical certificates aimed at to keeping them out of the forces, and involved a doctor they had known from their days as young boxers at the Repton Club, Dr. Morris Blasker.

Dr. Blasker was certainly a character. Born in Stepney in 1904, he was a compulsive gambler and a lover of opera, having also been a competent pianist and violinist as a boy; his tenure as Repton's medico probably came about owing to his former abilities as a boxer. He operated from his little surgery at 2 Manchester Grove on the Isle of Dogs, and in years to come would be a vital link in keeping those injured in gangland altercations out of mainstream hospitals and thus away from the prying eyes of the law,[3] removing bullets and stitching

---

1   Ramsey fought 69 professional fights between 1939 and 1947, winning 26, losing 33 and drawing nine. Although this is not the greatest boxing record, Ramsey was held in very high esteem amongst the boxing fraternity. He died in 2004.

2   Reggie Kray; *Born Fighter* (London: Arrow Books 1991).

3   Blasker came up before the General Medical Council on at least one occasion for supplying false documents and certificates for the illegal procurement of passports. In 1961 he was nearly struck off the Medical Register, but was acquitted. He died in 1974 and Blasker Walk on the Isle of Dogs was named after him after a campaign by local residents. An affectionate overview of his career can be found at islandhistory.wordpress.com/tag/dr-blasker.

up faces with no questions asked.

The twins soon had their fingers in a lot of pies and the money began to trickle in, hardly any of it legal. But whilst use of the Vienna Rooms and other West End establishments may have been fruitful in cementing useful relations with top-class villains like Jack Spot and Billy Hill, a more permanent base in the East End would soon present itself in the form of Samuel Martin's Regal Billiard Hall. The twins had been taking note of the problems Martin had been having with fights and violence, an unsurprising characteristic of the place considering its clientele. Martin had even tried to use a large Alsatian dog as a deterrent but it went mad after continually having firecrackers thrown at it, and before long, with the violence seeming to escalate, he was ready to throw in the towel.[4] This is when Reggie and Ronnie stepped forward with an offer that signalled their first 'takeover', using a methodology that they would employ for the rest of their careers to establish their influence in clubs, gambling houses and pubs.

They offered to 'look after' the Regal for £5 a week, borrowing money off Charlie to smarten the place up and promising to deal with trouble efficiently and quickly. They would keep the money from the snooker tables and the refreshment bar and give Martin a cut of the earnings. By the end of 1954, the Kray twins, aged only twenty-one, were on the first rung of their business ladder.

It wasn't long before the fortunes of the Regal and thus the twins looked more promising. It became popular, any aggravation from customers was swiftly quashed, and, although the dubious nature of the clientele had not really changed, those now frequenting the hall were known to the Krays and their friends and thus the rules of conduct were known to all. A small coterie of trusted 'sidekicks' was now developing: Dickie Morgan and his brother 'Chunky' (now out of prison); Colin 'Duke' Osbourne, the product of a respectable Westminster family and nicknamed with reference to his gentlemanly manners,[5] who had become a lover of Ronnie's; Henry 'Checker' Berry; Eddie Alford; and Pat Butler. On the sidelines was Thomas Walter Welch, who was sometimes known as Tommy Brown and, more often, just as 'The Bear' on account of his sheer size; he was a boxer and a friend of old Charlie Kray who was fond of the twins and always looked

---

4   Colin Fry & Charlie Kray; *Doing the Business* (London: John Blake 1993).
5   Leonard Read & James Morton; *Nipper Read: The Man Who Nicked the Krays* (London: MacDonald & Co 1991).

out for them. Another regular at the Regal who endeared himself to the Kray brothers was young Harry Abrahams. This gathering was a loose prototype of what would later become known as 'The Firm', that ever-shifting crew of sidekicks, henchmen and hangers-on which would later contain some of London's most famous villains.

The Regal was not only a place for the Krays' expanding troupe of associates to meet and plan new schemes. A small forecourt doubled up as a used-car lot, adding extra income to the now-profitable enterprise. Stolen goods could be stored in the hall before they were sold on, and weapons could be hidden in strategic places, ready to be used at short notice. Ronnie was now particularly taken by weapons: he had amassed a terrifying collection of knives, razors, swords and cutlasses, as well as a number of guns. Another service the twins offered was support for those who had recently been released from prison, for, now having money to spare, they were happy to give financial assistance to the displaced ex-con, sometimes finding them a place to stay whilst they settled back into society. It was also a way of garnering favour and building a growing criminal network.

At this time, there were lots of little gangs or 'teams' scattered around the East End, each firmly defending their own interests and territory: the Bethnal Green Mob (of which the Krays had once been a part), the Poplar Mob, the Limehouse Mob and so on. The success of the Regal would soon attract unwelcome attention from those who felt that the Krays were taking a step too far out of Bethnal Green and were beginning to encroach on their borders. One of the more notorious of these gangs was the Watney Street Gang, which mainly consisted of dockers and was based around the Poplar and Shadwell areas south of Whitechapel; in the same area were well-established Maltese gangs who controlled much of the prostitution. With their reputation building, the Krays would be forced to step up to challenges, the result being confrontations that would become the stuff of legend.

It was the Maltese who notoriously came up against a progressively more violent Ronnie Kray one night as the Regal was shutting up shop. They arrived cocksure in the belief that they could scare the twins into paying them for protection, an arrangement which the Krays certainly did not need. "Protection from what?" Ronnie is said to have remarked before pulling a cutlass from behind the bar and chasing the unwanted guests, now with their tails firmly between their legs, out into the street. As they jumped into their car, Ronnie lashed out at the vehicle with the weapon, smashing the windows and generally causing havoc with the paintwork.[6] The Maltese threat was over before it had begun.

Billy Webb's suggestion that the twins could only challenge their rivals mob-handed was, therefore, not entirely correct – at least, not at this point in their career. While Reggie and Ronnie were still finding their feet in the lion's den of gangland, they were frequently more than capable of holding their own unassisted. In fact, Charlie Kray always maintained that there was one particular incident that sealed their reputation as forces to be reckoned with on their home turf.

One evening at about 10.00 p.m., Charlie was at home in Vallance Road when Reggie returned from some engagement to find that Ronnie was out. He was at the Coach and Horses pub in Mile End Road[7] and had left a message for Reggie to meet him there, but as far as Charlie was concerned, it was pointless for Reggie to go there as it was so close to closing time. Reggie, sensing he may be needed, was insistent on going, however, and swiftly joined his brother, who was with Pat Butler, in the pub. Also in the bar were a group of about nine young men who apparently had been looking over at them and mentioning the Kray name. Ronnie felt there may be some trouble looming and it was said by Charlie that Reggie had, with the supposed telepathy of twins, sensed it too, hence his willingness to join his brother so late in the evening. Tension began to mount. Pat Butler, who was not a fighter by any means, was told to keep out of the way, at which point Reggie and Ronnie simultaneously stormed out of the pub, as if they had lost their nerve. Once outside, they doubled back and re-entered the pub through a different door. Four of the gang had followed them outside and whilst they stood about looking for their quarry, the twins took on the five men still in the bar. Punches were thrown, beer glasses and chairs were used as weapons and the youths were soon sprawled about the floor of the bar. When the other four re-entered the pub, it was a simple matter for the twins to finish them off. It was two against nine and Reggie and Ronnie had left them all in a bloody heap on the floor. One of the men, Billy Donovan, was

6   In 1990's movie *The Krays*, the incident is depicted with Ronnie impaling the hand of one gang member on a snooker table and twisting it sadistically. It is not clear whether this actually happened.
7   This was at 380 Mile End Road, opposite Queen Mary College. It was demolished c.1958.

hospitalised with a badly damaged eye, but he never told on the twins and once he had recovered developed a friendship with his attackers. Loyalties like this, born out of a violent initial confrontation where the code of 'thou shalt not grass' was adhered to, were how some garnered the twins' respect, and a number of their associates would fall into the Kray's orbit in this way.[8]

On another occasion a few weeks later, the twins were visiting a cafe on the Commercial Road and, upon leaving, were confronted by about ten members of the Watney Street Gang who wanted to show the famous Bethnal Green boys that they were getting a little too close to their 'manor'. Without any preliminary words or threats, the twins instinctively knew what had to be done and swiftly floored six of the Watney Streeters. The remaining members of the gang ran off quickly. It would be incidents like these (and particularly the fight in the Coach and Horses) which soon became the talk of the East End and served to cement the Krays' reputation as young men not to be messed with. Any attempts by potential rivals or local tough guys to put the twins in their place were invariably doomed to failure when put up against the dual fighting force that was Reggie and Ronnie Kray.

One associate of the Watney Street Gang was George Myers, a man who would go on to play a highly significant role in the story of the brothers Kray. Information about Myers is, however, often fragmented or inconsistent, so it is worth looking at his background in more detail. Born in St-George-in-the-East, Stepney, on 13 November 1927, he was one of seven children born to Mary Ann Garrett and a father who, for the moment, remains elusive. Older brother James would later say that their parents were not married[9] and that he and his siblings - with the exception of George, who never managed to get round to it - had changed their name by deed poll from Myers to Cornell. Certainly there is no record of any marriage between Mary Ann Garrett and a Myers or even a Cornell. Mary Ann was recorded as living with a Joseph Cornell in Everard Street, St George-in-the-East, around the time of George's birth, but even though this gives tantalising leads, it still fails to definitively clear up the mystery. What is probably the

---

8 Charlie Kray speaks of this incident in *Me and My Brothers* and in *The Kray Tapes* interviews with Robin McGibbon, suggesting that the twins were only about seventeen at the time. Laurie O'Leary puts the incident after the Regal takeover when they were twenty-one, a more likely place in the chronology since they were drinking in a pub.

9 From his statement on identifying the body of his brother on 18 March 1966; MEPO 2/11406, f. 19 (National Archives).

case is that George and his siblings were born to a man called Myers who may well have disappeared from the scene, to be replaced by Joseph Cornell in the mother's and thus the family's affections.

When he wasn't getting into trouble, Cornell worked at Billingsgate fish market where he would occasionally get help from Lenny Hamilton, who described Cornell as "a very tough man who could handle himself against anyone," but "not a liberty taker."[10] Billy Webb described him as "a fighting man" and "a bit of a loner."[11] Billy Frost, a later Kray associate and driver, knew him well and, like many, spoke kindly of the man:

> I liked George Cornell; George had done me a couple of favours, 'cause more or less we all lived very close to each other, me, George Cornell and that; we were all in the Watney Street region, Commercial Road. We had a lot of respect for George, he was a very tough man.[12]

He certainly was 'a tough man'. George would switch between the names Myers and Cornell, as can be seen on his lengthy criminal record, which would ultimately show his willingness to use violence.[13] His first conviction (as Myers) came on 30 October 1944, for stealing chickens; in May the following year he was bound over for three years for garage-breaking and larceny after stealing goods worth £327 8s 10d. In 1950 (as Cornell), he received his first prison sentence, of fifteen months, after being convicted at the Central Criminal Court for unlawful wounding and malicious damage. In 1952, he received substantial fines for assault and wilful damage and then, the following year, another spell in prison for shopbreaking (stealing cigarettes and razor blades). No sooner was Cornell free than, again as Myers, he assaulted two police officers and used insulting words and behaviour, getting off with a 40 shilling fine.

George Cornell, as he is always known, would go on to face several more spells in prison, one for malicious wounding when he is believed to have slashed a woman's face with a blade. His last spell in prison was in 1963, but it must have been after one of these prior convictions

10 Lenny Hamilton & Craig Cabell; *Getting Away With Murder* (London: John Blake 2006).
11 Billy Webb; *Running With The Krays* (Edinburgh: Mainstream Publishing 1993).
12 Billy Frost interview with Steve Wraith and Liam Galvin. www.youtube.com/watch?v= u1SU tilKmcY.
13 Cornell's CRO number was 35545/44; MEPO 2/10923 (National Archives).

in the 1950s that he went to the twins for assistance.[14] Cornell was extended this courtesy as an ex-con and Eastender, and, although he was friendly with the Krays, they would never become what one could describe as close friends. In 1955, Cornell married Olive Hudd from Camberwell and he soon decamped south of the river where he would ultimately thrive in the South London underworld. Consequently, his good relationship with the Krays would sour, triggering a significant course of events which would result in catastrophe over a decade later.

◆

One notable incident around this time involving the twins was remarkable in that not only did it demonstrate the levels of violence of which they were now capable and to which they were willing to resort, but it would probably be the closest they got to being hanged.

One night, Reggie and Ronnie were having a drink with Harry Abrahams, one of the regulars from the Regal, in a club in Tottenham Court Road and Abrahams was given some money to get a round of drinks. A thick-set African man started manhandling Abrahams after he had accidentally bumped into him at the bar and so the twins came to Abrahams' defence. Both were 'tooled up' – Ronnie had a long knife tucked into the waistband of his trousers and Reggie had a wooden police truncheon – and set about the African with frightening ferocity. Reggie was first, smashing the man across the head with the truncheon so hard that it broke and then Ronnie contributed to the mayhem, stabbing the African in the side twice as he lay on the ground bleeding profusely from the serious head wound. As the twins and Abrahams dashed out of the club to a car, they were followed by a few friends of the injured man, but a few punches settled the score and before long Reggie, Ronnie and Abrahams were away, heading for Vallance Road.

The next morning, Bobby Ramsey came to the Krays' house with a friend, Lorraine, and told the twins that they had heard about the assault and that word had it that the African had died from his injuries. The possibility that they had committed murder was, at this stage at least, a frightening thought, punishable at the time by execution, but Ramsey was able to furnish the twins with the names of some of the witnesses in the club, who were later approached and told to say nothing. Nonetheless, the police were soon on the twins'

14 Reggie Kray; *Born Fighter* (London: Arrow Books 1991).

trail, so they hired a barrister on the recommendation of their father and contacted West End Central Police Station. To their relief, the African was not dead, but Reggie and Ronnie were now wanted on a charge of attempted murder. They were put into an identity parade and the African faced his attackers, but he was only able to pick out Ronnie and another unrelated man. The barrister interjected that the African was unable to identify both his clients and immediately called a halt to proceedings. The twins had got away with it and were soon celebrating in the 99 Public House with their father; the barrister was also given £50 for his good work.[15]

The Kray twins were by now showing that they were becoming a major force in East End underworld circles. Such achievement did not go unnoticed by Jack Spot and Billy Hill and the twins were reasonably happy to endear themselves to both, but for different reasons. In the case of Jack Spot, it was really to further their own ends. In 1955, at the suggestion of Spot, they were hired as controllers for various betting pitches at point-to-point races and flat races at Epsom. Many villains of the time would attend these race meetings, protecting the various bookmakers from any unwelcome interest and ensuring they obtained their usual, if not the best, pitches: the threat of gang-related trouble was therefore always a possibility. Billy Hill often had the best pitches, minded by Billie Blythe and the twins' father's old acquaintance Frankie Fraser; but the presence of such hard-nosed and potentially dangerous villains held no store with Reggie and Ronnie. They showed nothing but contempt for the whole set-up, over-indulging in the hospitality tents and making everybody with eyes to see aware that they were afraid of nobody. It was their way of showing that Jack Spot was not the overlord he once was and that the Krays were going to fill his position:

> It wasn't that we liked him. We despised him really. We just turned out with Spotty to show everyone that we was the up-and-coming firm and didn't give a fuck for anyone. Old Spotty understood. Whatever else he may have been he wasn't stupid. He knew quite well that though we were there in theory as his friends, we meant to end up taking over from him.[16]

15 Reggie Kray; *Born Fighter* (London: Arrow Books 1991).
16 John Pearson; *The Profession of Violence* (London: Weidenfeld & Nicolson 1972).

As far as Reggie and Ronnie were concerned, Billy Hill was the man. He once tested their loyalty by calling them up at some ungodly hour, asking that they come to his Bayswater flat immediately, which the twins, driven by Charlie and fully armed, duly did. On arrival, Hill confessed to calling on them just to see if he could rely on them to be there for him without question; obviously satisfied that he could, he threw them a huge bundle of notes for their trouble. On one occasion, Reggie and two friends were refused entry to the 21 Rooms, a West End nightclub, and dealt with the rebuttal by flooring the doormen. On hearing that Hill ran the protection at the club, they went to see him to smooth things over, only to be told that they had done him a massive favour, as the owners of the club would now realise that Hill's protection was needed; accordingly, he would continue to reap the financial benefits. Again, the twins were rewarded handsomely by the retiring gang lord for this little incident.[17]

Reggie and Ronnie's brief association with Jack Spot helped them to forge friendships with members of his circle. Sammy Lederman was a small, older man and a one-time Whitechapel thief who was now a long-time resident of Soho, where he worked as a self-styled theatrical agent. Moishe Blueboy became a good friend: as well as being a boxer and wrestler, he was also an exceptional crooked card player. It was through Blueboy that the twins were introduced to Geoff Allen, a wealthy property dealer from Smith's Green in Essex, and by all appearances a tweedy country gentleman who seemed, on the outside at least, to be everything the Krays and their ilk were not. One night, whilst drinking with Spot's gang, a man named Jack Pokla told Blueboy that he had met "a mug from the country who has plenty of money", namely Allen.[18] The idea was to play cards with Allen and fleece him out of a considerable portion of his obvious wealth. Allen was keen to play and eventually, at his home in Smith's Green, a marathon game of cards took place, with Blueboy doing what he did best and winning several thousand pounds off his unwitting victim. Despite this, Allen seemed convivial enough and, when the game was over, told Ron, Reg and Blueboy to go to a nearby pub and that he would be over with the winnings in an hour.

They waited. And waited. Fortunately, somebody remembered Allen's telephone number and Moishe called him to find out what

17 Ibid.
18 Reggie Kray; *Born Fighter* (London: Arrow Books 1991).

was happening. He wasn't expecting the reply. "I knew all along I was being conned, and if you come near this cottage, you'll find me waiting with a shotgun."[19] The twins obviously saw something interesting in Geoff Allen and called on him a few days later, extending the offer of doing a little business together in the future. They got on well and Allen would come to be a useful man to have around when the Krays became successful themselves.

◆

As well as running the Regal Billiard Hall, the twins had moved into protection and had begun to target local car dealers. It was a simple premise: they had their own little concern on the Regal forecourt and if others wanted to be 'the competition', then they would have to pay for the privilege. A couple of heavies armed with a hammer or some paint-stripper would soon see to it that any rival car dealers understood the arrangement. One dealer, Johnny Hutton, under the protection of the twins, soon discovered the kind of service he was paying for when he sold a car to a docker who brought it back after a day, complaining that it had all manner of problems. The docker, getting no satisfaction, threatened to return mob-handed and settle the score. Hutton, of course, merely called the Krays. What happened next would be comical if it were not so much of an omen of things to come.

The next day, the docker returned, alone, apologising that although there were problems with the car, he realised that he had not been intentionally misled, and the two men came to an amicable arrangement. Then Ronnie, who had been staking out the car dealership, burst in holding a gun, shot the docker in the leg and walked. Hutton's face must have been a picture as the strident figure of Ronnie Kray stormed out of the shop, with the docker lying on the ground, crying in pain from a bullet wound he most certainly did not merit. Reggie, exasperated at his brother's first foray into justice by firearms, undertook a damage-limitation procedure. Ronnie's gunpowder-marked clothes were disposed of and he went into hiding for a little while in Walthamstow until the issue had been effectively buried. Reggie attended an identity parade at Mile End Hospital in Bancroft Road before the injured man and was identified as the gunman (unsurprisingly, considering the twins' similarity in

19 Reggie Kray; *Born Fighter* (London: Arrow Books 1991).

appearance). It was an easy task for Reggie to produce identification and an alibi, so he was let go and Tommy 'Red Face' Plumley, a local fixer from Brick Lane, got to work convincing Johnny Hutton and the docker that the matter needn't go any further. Apparently, the whole clean-up operation had cost Hutton a cool £3,000, enough for the now permanently-scarred and partially-disabled docker to open his own sweetshop.[20] Importantly, Ronnie had escaped yet another charge of attempted murder.

It was around this time, therefore – around 1956 – that Ronnie Kray's distinct personality traits began to come to the fore. For one, the clientele at the Regal had begun to include young men who hung around Ronnie in particular. They were not necessarily villains, but Ronnie appeared to enjoy their company. By this time, brother Charlie had started up his own travel business and frequented the Regal less and less, partly due to his own work and family commitments and partly because he regarded the increasing use of the billiard hall by the local criminal fraternity with some distaste. One day, on one of his visits, he noticed that as he passed Ronnie and some of the regulars they stopped talking, as if there was something they didn't want Charlie to hear. This had been going on for a while, so Charlie asked what was going on. It transpires that they had been talking about the one thing that the elder Kray brother was still not party to: Ronnie's sexuality.

Characteristically, Ronnie just came out with it: he was bisexual. Charlie couldn't believe what he was hearing. His younger brother was certainly not effeminate or camp – he was a 'man's man' – but, unlike other members of the family who appeared to just accept Ronnie for what he was, Charlie just couldn't understand it, and certainly didn't like it. "Can't believe it. He's told me he's the other way and I think it's fucking disgusting," he said to cousin Joe later that day. "He's admitted it and I'm so wild I want to knock it out of him."[21] Ultimately, of course, there was nothing Charlie could knock out of Ronnie and blood is, after all, thicker than water. Only their father would see it the same way.[22] Like everything else Ronnie did, it was always a case of "there's

20 Ibid.

21 Joe Lee, Rita Smith and Peter Gerrard; *Inside the Kray Family* (London: Carlton 2008).

22 In Mickey Fawcett's book *Krayzy Days* (Brighton: Pen Press 2013), Fawcett recounts a fierce confrontation between Charlie Snr and Ronnie in the kitchen at Vallance Road after Charlie had heard from regulars at the 99 Public House that Ronnie was homosexual. "Oh you make me sick, it's disgusting," Charlie apparently said.

no point crying over spilt milk", and the issue of his sexuality would be something that everybody around him, including his father and older brother, would just have to get used to.

The other issue, of course was his tendency towards – and his apparent enjoyment of – violence. Throughout the ascent of the Krays as young underworld players, it had been noted that Ronnie in particular took great pleasure in organising the various crimes and attacks on rivals. He was meticulous, treating such planning as one would a serious military operation and, as a result, he had earned the nickname of 'The Colonel',[23] a soubriquet given to him by flamboyant Teddy Boy and occasional early Kray associate Lionel 'Curly' King.[24] It was a title Ronnie embraced. His love of weapons, something Reggie was less bothered about, meant that he quickly acquired an extensive arsenal of guns, knives, razors, swords and cutlasses and he would spend hours in the back yard at Vallance Road honing blades to lethal perfection.

But it was his ability to lose all reason at the drop of a hat and unleash a torrent of violence that made him different to Reggie. Reggie was brutal when necessary, but could reign in his aggressive instincts when the moment required it. It was easier to placate Reggie, although often he would not forget the original reason for his anger and wait patiently for an opportunity to make his point, usually with devastating consequences. Sometimes he could wait days or even months. Ronnie (like his Aunt Rose, who was such an influence on him) would deal with perceived slights, insults and threats without a moment's hesitation. On one occasion during the early days of the Regal, he and Reggie had been invited for a drink in a pub by a rival gang, only to be insulted by them. The twins did what they do best, felling the gang with a devastating dual onslaught, but, when it was all over, Ronnie continued to beat one of the gang senseless and had to be dragged away before he sent the man to the morgue. Such behaviour from Ronnie was becoming par for the course, and whether anybody could see the way things were going at this stage is

23 During the Old Bailey trial in 1969, Ronnie told Kenneth Jones QC that he had been known as 'The Colonel' since he was seventeen-years-old (*Daily Mirror*, 1 February 1969).
24 King's real name is given by his son Paul who contributed to the East London Forum in 2013 (www.eastlondonforum.com/viewtopic.php?f=8&t=11411&start=45). Curly King later moved out to Israel to escape unwanted police attention, becoming quite a well-known figure there. He eventually moved back to England in the mid-1980s. He has since died.

not clear; nevertheless, he was increasingly using extreme violence as a way of making a point or settling a score.

The twins, such strong characters as they were, would also fight each other. Sibling rivalry is not an uncommon thing and the unique bonds of twinship would no doubt make such relationships more extreme. With the Kray background of aggression and the brothers' own strength and ability as boxers, their fights would be incendiary:

Sometimes they would scream and fight and slag each other off. They would get into proper fist fights. But sometimes Reggie would blaze back at Ronnie, and Ronnie would sit there and take it. Sometimes it was the other way round...

When these guys narked each other up we wouldn't interfere. You didn't interfere with them two. That would be like trying to separate two Dobermanns: they'd both turn on you...[25]

◆

Bobby Ramsey, being older than the twins, had a lot more experience behind him. Apart from being able to straddle both the Hill and Spot camps in their heyday (as the twins also appeared to do later), he had a stake in a number of clubs in the West End, one being the Stragglers in Cambridge Circus. It was not a select or plush establishment by any stretch of the imagination. Much of its clientele consisted of tough dockers from the East End who had been encouraged to drink there by Ramsey's business partner Billy Jones, who worked on the London Docks in Wapping and who had quite an influence in the allocation of labour there. The club had a licence to stay open later than the pubs but, of course, the hospitality would still continue after hours, making it an attractive proposition for hardened drinkers. Dockers associated with the Watney Street gang became regular visitors; however, these tough characters, George Cornell among them, were not always good to have around once the drink had taken hold.

Ramsey was concerned that this boisterous, sometimes foul-mouthed presence at the Stragglers was not necessarily conducive to regular business, and suggested that his young friends, Reggie and Ronnie Kray, do a little door-work there and use their particular 'talents' to make sure there was no inappropriate behaviour in the club. The twins were keen and this move constituted their first

25 Albert Donoghue & Martin Short; *The Enforcer* (London: John Blake 2002).

tentative steps into West End clubland. However, their growing involvement with Bobby Ramsey was to prove significant. A feud had developed between Billy Jones and a man called Charlie Martin over the distribution and allocation of dock labour down in Wapping. The feud soon spilled over into violence and Jones was beaten up by Martin. What ensued was a dangerous spiral of revenge.

The day after Jones was attacked Bobby Ramsey went to avenge his friend and beat up Martin. Two days later, Martin and his friends took the fight back to Ramsey by severely assaulting him outside a pub, the Artichoke, on The Highway in Wapping. Things were getting out of hand, and Ronnie Kray was keen to help his friend and finish the matter once and for all; he was all for using a gun, an indicator of his growing interest in serious and dangerous retribution.

At 8.00 p.m. on the night of 28 August 1956, Charlie Martin's brother Terry went into the Britannia pub[26] on Chapman Street, a narrow thoroughfare running off Watney Street by Shadwell Station. There were a number of people there he knew and so he settled down to a few pints and a game of cards with three others – Bill Patmore, Dick Agate and another man, whose name Terry Martin didn't know. At about 9.45 p.m. the door of the Britannia opened and one of the Kray twins (nobody could tell which one) came in and told Martin to go outside. Bobby Ramsey then pushed his way in and was aggressive from the outset; he said, "I want you," in a rough tone and proceeded to pull out a bayonet that had been secreted down his trousers.[27] As Martin reluctantly complied and began to walk out the door, he was struck on the back of the head and bundled outside by the unidentified Kray.

In the street was a group of men including the other Kray and Billy Jones, who struck Martin round the head as soon as he was outside:

> I couldn't say what he hit me with. I saw him raise his hand. I felt something hit me in the back and I went on the floor where I got a number of kicks and felt something come across my legs together. It was not a blow because I was hit with something on both legs at the same time.

---

26 The Britannia was run by Alfred Weeks whose family had run the pub since 1876 and would do so until 1983. It closed in 2005 and was converted into a fried chicken fast food outlet. The pub sign at the top of the building on the corner still remains.

27 Witness statement of Richard Hackett, 5 September 1956; CRIM 1/2747 (National Archives).

*When I felt the blow on my back as I came through the door I felt
a sharp pain in my back. I couldn't move my shoulder. At the time I
received the blow in my back Ramsey was behind me. I don't know
where the bayonet was.*[28]

After the assault on Martin, the group scattered and Ramsey, Jones
and the twins sped off in two cars. Martin was led back into the pub by
two customers and was taken to the London Hospital where he was
examined by the house surgeon, Dr. David Williams. Williams' report
shows the extent of Terry Martin's injuries:

*He was suffering from many lacerations. There were two gaping
lacerations at the back of the head – one an inch in length, the other
one and a half inches long. I put in three stitches and five stitches
respectively. One tooth was very loose and was extracted, another
tooth was considerably loosened. On the upper surface of the right
shoulder was a laceration of about half to three quarters of an inch
long at the entrance. Examined under anaesthetic it was found to
be one and a half inches in depth, penetrating the right shoulder
joint. Several layers of stitches were inserted. On the upper part of
the back at the right was a laceration four and a half inches deep
and about an inch long, skirting the ribs. I found a notch in one of
the ribs. This also required several layers of stitches.*[29]

Martin was kept in hospital for eight days, after which he still did
not have full movement of his shoulder.

Soon after the incident, the Buick containing Ramsey and Ronnie
Kray was stopped by the police in Morgan Street, Mile End.[30] When
the two men were found to have bloodstains on their clothing, the
police took possession of a bayonet, a machete and a crowbar. Ronnie
was also found to have a loaded 'Young American' revolver in his
jacket pocket. When Ronnie was questioned about the gun at Leman
Street Police Station, he remarked that he kept the gun in case of
trouble at the Billiard Hall. Interestingly, the bullets had been filed
down, but interviewing officer Sgt Walter Cooper could not be certain
whether this was to make them fit the chamber of the revolver or
for some other reason; he did note, however, that the nature of the
filing had effectively turned the bullets into potentially devastating

28 Statement of Terence Martin, 18 September 1956; Ibid.
29 Statement of Dr. David Owen Williams, 18 September 1956; Ibid.
30 *East London Advertiser*; 31 August 1956.

'dum-dums'.[31] Reggie and Billy Jones went voluntarily to Leman Street Police Station and Ramsey, Jones and the Krays were quickly charged with causing grievous bodily harm on Terence Martin. Ronnie was also charged with possessing an offensive weapon and with having no certification to authorise such possession.

Bloodstains in Ramsey's car, on the bayonet, machete and crowbar, and on clothing worn by all four defendants was found to be Group A, such a common blood type that Dr. Lewis Nicholls of the Metropolitan Police Laboratory stated that they "were of such a general nature that it could not be determined whether or not they were human."[32] Despite the uncertainty of the forensic evidence, the case went to trial at the Old Bailey in October 1956; Charlie Kray Snr had written a very humble letter at the last minute, pleading with the authorities to show leniency towards his two sons:

> *If you will at least believe me Sir – they are the most respectful & good natured lads anybody could wish to meet, so kind to my wife & I & everybody in their thoughts & actions & only do good to everybody & with my guidance & my wife & son Charles (the eldest brother) they will make good...*

> *They are at present in a good business with every chance of making good. Can I appeal to you again for a chance to enable this lad of mine to lead a moral & good life. Hoping my appeal may receive your kind consideration & mercy.*[33]

The day Charlie wrote that letter – Friday 4 November – Reggie, who had pleaded not guilty to the GBH charge, was acquitted and formally discharged. The verdict for the others, given the following day, was not so good: Ramsey, who had pleaded guilty, received seven years' imprisonment, and Jones and Ronnie received three years each. Prosecutor Victor Durand said how lucky Martin was to have survived the attack and, after passing sentence, recorder Sir Gerald Dodson stressed the pre-meditated nature of the assault and paused to pass comment on what he saw as a worrying trend:

> *It would seem there has existed a state of gang warfare for some time, dangerous to all concerned and flouting and scorning the law*

---

31 Statement of Detective Sergeant Walter Cooper, 18 September 1956; CRIM 1/2747 (National Archives).
32 *East London Advertiser*, 21 September 1956.
33 Letter from Charles Kray, CRIM 1/2747 (National Archives).

*regardless of life. You plunged what otherwise is a respectable part
of the East End into an abyss of brutality.*[34]

The twins were now separated again as Ronnie began his three-
year sentence at Wandsworth Prison, a Category B institution.[35]
By all accounts he appeared to settle in very well. On his arrival he
was greeted by a friendly face, Dickie Morgan, who at that time was
serving a sentence for robbery; and, with the Krays' reputation well-
known via the prison grapevine, Ronnie enjoyed a certain amount of
respect. He could command a degree of influence, participating in the
distribution and mild luxury of the all-important tobacco 'currency',
and his incarceration was shared with like-minded villains to whom
he could relate.

It seemed that his three years was going to pass quickly and
relatively peacefully in the tough environment of Wandsworth (even
more quickly if he earned remission for good behaviour), and that he
would be reunited with his brother before he knew it. To those who
knew him well, however, Ronnie was beginning to show mild paranoid
traits, something certainly noticed by old friend Laurie O'Leary;
for the moment, however, this peculiarity was not too marked. The
prison authorities were obviously impressed with how he was coping
and soon they began to think he would be suitable for a less punishing
regime.

It was recommended that he be transferred to a prison with a more
lenient system and, on 19 June 1957, he was taken to Camp Hill Prison
on the Isle of Wight. Camp Hill, just outside Newport, was a Category
C institution[36] opened in 1912 by Winston Churchill (who was then
Home Secretary). It had a more relaxed system and its inmates were
generally less serious offenders, certainly not high risk; many were
deemed suitable for training in new skills to prepare them for the
outside world. For a career criminal, one would imagine that the offer
of softer conditions would be thought of as a trip down easy street.
Not so Ronald Kray. Ronnie liked the frisson of being a criminal, the
planning, the necessary violence, the adrenaline; he was 'the Colonel',
working his way up the ladder to notoriety and ultimately, power and

---

34 *East London Advertiser*, 9 November 1956.

35 Category B prisons are described as being for inmates "who do not require maximum
security, but for whom escape still needs to be very difficult."

36 For prisoners "who cannot be trusted in open conditions but who are unlikely to try to
escape."

success. In Wandsworth he had been 'somebody', and the different regimen of Camp Hill did not suit his temperament at all. The other inmates were too 'straight', nothing like him, and there was no covert system of perks to be milked like there was in Wandsworth. In addition, the isolation from his friends and family back on the mainland resulted in less frequent visits, and the prolonged loneliness began to affect him.

It wasn't long before he began to make his mark. On 7 August 1957, the Governor of Camp Hill wrote a memorandum to Head Office outlining his concerns regarding Ronnie's attitude:

He is a surly, lazy prisoner, whose whole attitude borders on non-co-operation. He has made it quite obvious that he has no intention of making any attempt to benefit from the training facilities at this prison.

His violent tendencies were also manifesting themselves again:

Although he still has a comparatively short record, it includes two convictions for assault on the police. He is a young man of violent and uncontrollable temper, who has already been on report here for assault on another prisoner, and for using improper language to an officer and damaging prison property. In the latter case, because his Assistant Governor had refused him permission to attend the Gymnastic Class, he swore at his Hall Officer and smashed a table tennis table which was standing in the hall. He was in such a fit of temper that he was quite unable to control his actions.[37]

It can be said that Ronnie's noticeable downward slide into mental illness began at Camp Hill. From here on in, his behaviour would become increasingly disturbed and the authorities had to act.

---

37 Ronald Kray's prison file; HO 336/865 (National Archives).

FIVE

GOOD TIMES, BAD TIMES

If the summer of 1957 could be seen as the beginning of Ronnie Kray's annus horribilis, it would provide his twin brother with different fortunes. It is possibly a mark of how much influence Ronnie had over Reggie that when the former was taken out of the equation, the latter's more astute, keen nose for business and relative affability would come to the fore.

The Regal was still doing well and, with the other sidelines also proving lucrative, Reggie, constantly on the lookout for new opportunities, had acquired no small taste for further expansion. One day in the spring of 1957, a local tearaway named David Cohen approached Reggie, telling him that there was an empty property on the Bow Road which he felt would make a good club. Cohen had had some disagreements with a man named Joe Abrahams (who owned a drinking club near the Regal) and hinted, somewhat disingenuously, that if Reggie opened a similar establishment, it would probably be a lot better than Abrahams's one. Reggie's interest was piqued and inquiries were made with the property owner, a likeable Jewish man who had plush offices in Park Lane. The owner had no objection to the property's potential use as a club and a deal was struck; Reggie borrowed the first quarterly rent from car-dealer Johnny Hutton, and he was in business.[1]

The big house at 145 Bow Road was not in good shape aesthetically and needed extensive redecoration inside to bring it up to scratch.

---

1   Reggie Kray; *Born Fighter* (London: Arrow Books 1991).

Reggie had all the legal paperwork, including licences, but it took the promise of a partnership with brother Charlie, who could see the potential of the place, to secure money to stock the bar. Together, they got to work on making it the place to be seen in the East End. The premise was simple: a club for drinking and live music where people could come – men, women, wives and girlfriends – for a relaxing and enjoyable night out without any trouble; a little flavour of West End club life in East London. It would be called the Double R in honour of the twins, for although Ronnie was presently indisposed, there was no question that he was part of it too. Registered on 6 May 1957,[2] its opening night, a Wednesday, was by all accounts a success.

Reggie was in his element as an accomplished host, making the guests feel welcome and becoming a friendly presence around the club whilst Charlie stayed in the background, sometimes manning the bar or dealing with the day-to-day business. Often, Reggie would man the doors himself, a task he enjoyed and which allowed him a level of control, but the main doormen were Tommy 'The Bear' Welch and a formidable Scotsman, Patrick 'Big' Pat Connolly. Connolly, who up to that time had no criminal record,[3] was only one of several men who would become part of the Krays' 'Firm' during the Double R years; some would stay with the twins until the bitter end.

There were Alfred 'Limehouse' Willey, whose knowledge of the intricacies of gambling odds more than made up for the twins' own lack of numeracy; long-time friend Georgie Osbourne (not to be confused with 'Dukey' Osbourne); Billy Donovan, whose silence after being assaulted by the twins in the Coach and Horses several years before had earned him their respect and a place in their inner circle, as well as a job on the door of the Double R; and Sammy Lederman, the theatre promoter and former Jack Spot sidekick, who was never too far away. Edward 'Mad Teddy' Smith was a thief and shopbreaker with a string of convictions[4] who thought of himself as a bit of a writer and had forged a homosexual relationship with Ronnie and was known as an unpredictable character when drunk, hence his nickname. On the sidelines were Mickey Fawcett, a trusted outsider from the Silvertown area by the Thames who had become a Double R regular; Alfie Teale,

2   CRIM 1/4900 (National Archives).
3   He would later be convicted for five offences between November 1957 and February 1968, ranging from receiving stolen goods to possession of a firearm, CRO No. 22062/50; CRIM 1/4900 (National Archives).
4   Smith's CRO No. 31336/49; MEPO 2/10763 (National Archives).

whose acquaintance with Teddy Smith had brought him into the club; and old face Lenny Hamilton. Hamilton, a jewel thief who was later allied to Harry Abrahams's offshoot gang,[5] had been approached by the twins in the Regal after they recognised him as the man who had prevented their arrest years before, when they were on the run. Doing odd jobs for the twins was William Exley, a former boxer who lived in Woodseer Street, off Brick Lane in Spitalfields; unlike most of the others, he had no criminal record at that time[6] and suffered from a heart problem, but he would come to be used more by the Krays over the next few years.

Other associates were Dave Forland, Dickie Moughton, Dave Simmonds and Johnny Davis, names that are often forgotten today. None of these individuals were straight, of course, but the Double R itself, perhaps with Charlie's influence, was set out from the off to be a legitimate business. It had a jukebox to entertain the guests when live music, performed on the dedicated stage, was unavailable. It had a car park which sometimes doubled up as a used-car lot, further adding to the Kray income. And it had a gymnasium and boxing ring upstairs: this latter addition was opened with much fanfare by British boxing great Henry Cooper who apparently, after realising the thread of villainy that permeated the attendees of the opening, left quickly once the proceedings were winding down.

Outside of the club, however, Reggie could still be relied upon to exercise a little muscle when he felt it necessary. This was usually directed at businesses that he felt were in direct competition with his own interests. Soon after opening the Double R, Reggie set up a gambling club, a 'spieler', at 8 Wellington Way, off Mile End Road, which turned out to be another lucrative venture. Not long afterwards, on 5 August 1957, Stephen Martin, the father of Charlie and Terry Martin, opened his own club at 1a Campbell Road, a street opposite the Double R and only a few blocks along from Wellington Way; the building was owned by Anwar Haque and thus the club was known as the Anglo-Pakistani Club. This was too close to be acceptable, and Reggie felt that this was a liberty taken by the family responsible for Ronnie's three-year prison sentence, so he soon went to work to drive

---

5   According to Hamilton, Abrahams began to distance himself from the Krays around 1960 and set up his own firm specialising in security van robbery. Lenny Hamilton & Craig Cabell; *Getting Away With Murder* (London: John Blake 2006).

6   He would later receive a conviction for illegally receiving wines and spirits to the value of £306 in 1959. Exley's CRO No. was 43107/59; MEPO 2/10763 (National Archives).

them out. In his own later account,[7] he claimed that he had arranged for their club to be firebombed, but archive documents[8] show that this was not the case.

On 14 August, at about 8.50 p.m., Stephen Martin left the club in the hands of a barman (known as 'Ginger') so he could go for a drink with a friend at the Bow Bells pub nearby. Whilst relaxing in the saloon bar, Martin was told by an associate who worked at Bloom's kosher restaurant that something had happened to his club soon after he had left, and he swiftly went back to investigate. According to 'Ginger', who had apparently been struck in the face during the incident, a group of eight to ten men had turned up and wilfully caused damage to the furniture and fittings. In one room the chairs were broken, a wardrobe had been damaged and the glass in it smashed. In another room, the chandelier had been ripped out of the ceiling and the telephone had been smashed, and in the kitchen area a cabinet and glassware had been broken. The men were all quite large and 'Ginger' believed he would recognise one of them again. The cost of the damage was estimated at £35.[9]

In his statement, Stephen Martin strongly hinted that this incident was linked to the current ill-feeling between his family and the Krays, and thus Reggie and Charlie were brought in for questioning over the issue. Of course, they strenuously denied any involvement in the matter, and there was nothing to connect them with it in terms of evidence – even fingerprint analysis at the scene drew a blank.[10] It was obvious that this case was going nowhere, and the whole affair was swiftly drawn to a close on 16 August when Martin announced his decision to drop the issue entirely:

> *I have given the matter some further thought and I have decided that I do not wish Police to take any further enquiries in the matter as I feel that if I take it further it may cause more trouble from the people responsible.*[11]

There is obviously a distinct whiff of trepidation here, and this can be seen as the first officially documented indication that the Krays

7   Reggie Kray; *Born Fighter* (London: Arrow Books 1991).
8   MEPO 2/9753 (National Archives).
9   About £600 in today's money.
10 Report by Detective Sergeant N. Barrett, 16 September 1957; MEPO 2/9753 (National Archives).
11 Statement by Stephen Martin, 16 August 1957; Ibid.

would purposefully foster intimidation, and thus a reluctance to speak on the part of those threatened, creating what later became known as the 'Wall of Fear' or 'Wall of Silence'. The police made a note that the club was probably used for unlicensed gaming and speculated that Martin had backed off to avoid any further unwelcomed interest from the law. This was typical: many businesses and individuals targeted by the Krays were operating illegally in their own right, and so recourse to the authorities was often not an option, allowing the Krays to manipulate the situation as they wished. The Martin family were obviously bold enough to speak out, but ultimately, like many others, there was little they could do. Even though the investigation into the Anglo-Pakistani Club affair fizzled out, Reggie later shamefully boasted that, after discussions with Anwar Haque, he became a partner in the club (along with Charlie and Ronnie *in absentia*), and gave friends James Woods and Ernest John 'Jackie' Reynolds the responsibility of looking after the day-to-day interests. They would all take a slice of the profits.[12]

The Krays now had a successful club and the control of two profitable spielers to further line their pockets. Things were going very well.

◆

On the day Stephen Martin backed off, Ronnie Kray was transferred from Camp Hill to Winchester Prison. He had been regarded as unsuitable for training – in fact, totally unsuitable for Camp Hill at all – and, significantly, Winchester had a psychiatric unit where he was placed under observation. Back in London, it was business as usual. Fortunes with the Billiard Hall had taken a new turn and in September 1957, Reggie's solicitors wrote to the governor of Winchester Prison requesting that Ronnie be transferred to a prison nearer to London owing to their joint business interests, particularly relating to the sale of the Regal. It appears that Reggie was planning to buy the billiard hall outright, as, up until then, their involvement had merely been an 'arrangement' between them and Samuel Martin. Despite a petition written by Ronnie to the same effect,[13] the request was refused; nonetheless, the Regal soon passed into the hands of the Kray twins,

---

12 Report by Detective Inspector B. Devonald, 17 June 1960; MEPO 2/9974 (National Archives).

13 Reggie and Ronnie's requests are contained in Ronnie's prison file; HO 336/865 (National Archives).

who became the official proprietors in 1958.[14]

Ronnie may have been of little use in business meetings, even if he had obtained his transfer. His time at Winchester was punctuated with periods of disturbing behaviour. Eventually, the medical officer diagnosed a case of 'prison psychosis'[15] and, from here on, Ronnie's mental health would go into steep decline, with one incident particularly having a disastrous effect.

It had been known by the family for two years that Aunt Rose was ill with leukaemia. The knowledge that she had a condition which, in those days, was untreatable, was a terrible blow to all, but Rose treated the threat of death with the same pugnacity with which she treated life. Three weeks before the illness took her life, she was still up to her old tricks, despite frequent trips to hospital and the onset of debilitating weakness. She had a fight with a woman outside a grocer's in Bethnal Green Road – the fallout from a previous altercation – and, after knocking the woman over a stall covered in eggs, proceeded to leap on her and continue the onslaught. Right up to her death, Rose declared that the matter was not over; however, she never got round to finishing it off. The family had decided that she would not die in hospital and as time went by they took it in turns to look after her at the Kray house in Vallance Road. As Violet later recalled:

> The doctors warned us that the end would come with a haemorrhage and that it wouldn't be nice to see. Her feet swelled up and the rest of her went thin as a rake. Then on Christmas Eve the bleeding started.[16]

The twins' favourite aunt died on Christmas Day 1957. All this time, the family had been insistent that her condition be kept from Ronnie; not only was he especially fond of Rose, but it was perhaps wisely felt that such news should not be passed to him whilst he was having problems of his own. In the care of Winchester's psychiatric unit, Ronnie had been seen to be doing well and responding gradually to treatment, but on 27 December he received a letter from Reggie telling him the bad news about Rose. The effect was devastating. By that evening, Ronnie had become incoherent and aggressive and was

14 The 1959 Kelly's Post Office Directory (which documents the year 1958) records R and R Kray as owners for the first time.

15 John Pearson; *The Profession of Violence* (London: Weidenfeld & Nicolson 1972).

16 Ibid.

put into a straitjacket. At times he was uncontrollably violent and was often kept isolated as much for the safety of the other patients and hospital staff as for his own. In a partially redacted report on Ronnie's mental condition, the authorities described him as "potentially dangerous in that he has persecutory ideas, and on one occasion ran across the prison landings in an attempt to attack another prisoner."[17] A further devastating blow to the Kray family came when, on 12 February 1958, Ronnie was certified; a telegram was swiftly sent by the governor of Winchester to Vallance Road with the bad news: "Your son Ronald Kray certified insane."

On 20 February 1958, Ronnie was transferred to Long Grove Hospital near Epsom in Surrey, the same institution in which his great-grandfather 'Crutcha' Lee had ended his days many decades before. Originally Long Grove Lunatic Asylum, it had been built in 1906 and held up to 2,000 patients, most of whom came from London.[18] There were 1,800 patients at Long Grove at the time of Ronnie's confinement, only six of whom had come from prisons, and it was the policy of the hospital that everybody, convicts or otherwise, would be treated the same. Under closer expert supervision, Ronnie's behaviour could be monitored more effectively, and he displayed some very unusual symptoms. As Ronnie himself said years later:

> I wouldn't move but sat all day huddled round the radiator. I wasn't quite sure who I was. The radiator seemed the only friend I had because it was warm. I was completely on my own and funny things used to come into my mind...
>
> I didn't recognize anyone, even though Reggie and my mother visited me. Sometimes I thought I'd kill myself to stop someone else doing it first.[19]

He was quickly put on powerful tranquilisers, including Stemetil, a brand name for Prochlorperazine Mesilate, which inhibits the production of dopamine, a neurochemical believed to be the cause of certain psychotic illnesses, including schizophrenia. The medication helped to curb his more violent tendencies, but it made him slow and

---

17 Ronnie's mental health file, HO 336/883, has a number of closed documents which are exempt from any Freedom of Information ruling as the material was medical information given in confidence.

18 It closed in 1992 and was mostly demolished, although surviving parts of the hospital were converted into apartments and are now part of the Clarendon Park development.

19 John Pearson; *The Profession of Violence* (London: Weidenfeld & Nicolson 1972).

affected his memory, and the family were saddened by what they saw when they visited him. Often, he wouldn't recognize them. Cousin Joe Lee drove Violet and Charlie Snr to the hospital on a number of occasions, but Joe always felt that it was a waste of time as Ronnie just looked at them blankly and said nothing. The twins' father for one was not convinced that Ronnie's behaviour was genuine, feeling like he was pulling a fast one on the authorities just as he'd tried to do with the army. They could not really decide for themselves if he was truly insane, and in all probability they just refused to believe it – Violet, in particular, again thought she knew her son better than anybody – but they were certainly concerned about the effect the medication seemed to have on him. The question of Ronnie's eventual freedom also arose: according to his record at Winchester,[20] the earliest release date with remission would have been 29 October 1958, but he was now held at Long Grove, and the authorities there had recommended that he stay for a further seventeen months, making a release date before the beginning of 1960 unlikely. It wasn't long before Reggie made the decision to get Ronnie out of Long Grove, no matter what it took. But Reggie couldn't do it alone; Joe Lee was approached first but refused to have anything to do with such a plan, and brother Charlie was initially against it too. He eventually agreed to it on the promise that he would not have to be there when it happened.

By May 1958, Ronnie's condition must have stabilised to some extent, otherwise he probably would not have been able to willingly participate in the plot to free him, which was planned very carefully over several weeks of visits. The big day was going to be Monday 26 May, and, during a visit the week before, Violet, who was obviously doing what was expected of her by Reggie, had told Ronnie to wear his blue suit, grey check shirt, red tie and black shoes. The plan revolved around the twins' similarity to each other, which at that time was still very pronounced; they had often got out of scrapes by using their identical appearance, putting doubt into the minds of their accusers as to which twin was responsible for the particular misdemeanour. On this occasion there was more at stake. It was truly audacious, but could the twins pull it off?

When the day came, Reggie, Georgie Osbourne, 'Curly' King and a few other friends drove to Long Grove in two cars. At 2.00 p.m., Reggie

---

20 Ronnie's prison file; HO 336/865 (National Archives).

and Osbourne went into the building armed with an old photo album and permits authorising them to visit Ward M, the ward for serious cases where Ronnie was being confined.[21] Reggie was wearing clothes that he knew matched those that Ronnie had been instructed to wear, and completed the effect with an overcoat; he had also had his hair cut in a similar way. Once the visit commenced, the pair sat with Ronnie, perusing the photo album and making a point of laughing uproariously at its contents. It was usually down to visitors to collect refreshments from the little canteen in the reception hall and normally Reggie would go off at some point and bring the tea. With the guards roaming the hall, teatime came and Reggie got up and walked out to the canteen and never came back. It was actually Ronnie, now wearing Reggie's overcoat whilst his twin kept his head down, who had left the visiting hall and within minutes he had left the building, crossed the grounds, left the main gate and was speeding away in one of the two getaway cars. After a while, the guards noticed something amiss and one of them looked closely at Reggie; realising what had happened, he said, "You've pulled a flanker." When he was accused of letting Ronnie go, Reggie said coolly, "It's your job to look after him, not mine."[22] Alarms sounded and Reggie and his companions were detained, but by then Ronnie was long gone.

It took two hours for Reggie to confirm who he was and at 4.00 p.m. he and Osbourne were allowed to go. Brother Charlie, who had spent several nail-biting hours by the phone at the Double R Club, was relieved to hear that it had all gone according to plan. It had been a unique deception, clever and certainly daring in its execution, and it had gone faultlessly; the hospital staff who had allowed Ronnie to pass through security gates had been totally convinced that he was his brother. For the authorities, however, it was a grave cause for concern and the story, which appeared in the national press over the next two days, reflected their worries. Ronnie, as far as they were concerned was "a violent criminal"[23] whose freedom was a danger to the public; one newspaper announced that he suffered from "a persecution mania" and that "he may use violence if he thinks he is near recapture."[24] Reggie was questioned by the police the day after

21 *Daily Herald*, 28 May 1958.
22 Reggie Kray; *Born Fighter* (London: Arrow Books 1991).
23 *The News Chronicle*; 28 May 1958.
24 *Daily Telegraph*; 28 May 1958.

and, when talking to the press, he characteristically pulled a veil over his involvement:

> *I was with him a few minutes before he disappeared from the hospital on Whit Monday afternoon. But I don't know how he escaped. I am in the clear. The police have been to see me but I have told them I know nothing about my brother's escape.*[25]

The fact that the twins were dressed identically was, to Reggie, "a coincidence. We are identical twins. We think alike."[26]

The escape was the easy part, it seems. Now came the difficult job of keeping Ronnie out of the way of the authorities for six months. The reason for this particular time limit stemmed from a loophole in the law at that time which stated that if somebody certified insane could remain at large for six months without incident, they would automatically have their certification rescinded and would have to be reassessed. The plan was to have Ronnie pass through this period without issue, so that he could return to regular prison and finish the remainder of his sentence. Reggie called on the services of Geoff Allen, who at that time had a property near Hadleigh, Suffolk (where the twins were evacuated during the war), which had extensive wooded grounds and an isolated caravan: it was a perfect location to hide Ronnie. And so it was that the fugitive Kray was installed in Allen's rural retreat, with a small roster of minders to keep him company, supply him with drink, cigarettes and food and, if Ronnie so desired, young male company.

It wasn't long after the escape that the Superintendent of Long Grove contacted Charlie and asked to see him and Reggie at the hospital. Although he complimented the brothers on the clever plan, he also told them that Ronnie was seriously ill and needed appropriate medical attention.[27] Freeing him had been an enormous mistake and before long, the Superintendent said, he would be proved right.

With all the media attention, it was unwise for Reggie to see Ronnie for a while, and he stayed away for a week. But Ronnie's isolation was not good for him. For one, he was now separated from the expert attention Long Grove could give him and he did not have access to the vital medication that helped curb his psychotic tendencies. He became

---

25 *Daily Mirror*, 28 May 1958.

26 Ibid.

27 Charlie Kray & Robin McGibbon; *Me and My Brothers* (London: Grafton 1988).

increasingly restless, sometimes paranoid, and he was becoming a handful for his minders. His requests to go to London became more frequent, but it was totally out of the question, not that this mattered to Ronnie. To solve the problem of Ronnie's restlessness and his fears that he was going to be in and out of mental institutions for the rest of his life, he was taken to a Harley Street psychiatrist under an assumed name, giving a false story about suffering from nerves prior to an impending wedding. The psychiatrist ultimately gave Ronnie a clean bill of mental health and the paperwork to go with it. Geed up by this, he continued his requests to go to London; eventually his brothers relented and Ronnie was pleased that he could spend some time near family and friends.

Ronnie did manage to stay in the East End in a safe house in Adelina Grove, behind the Whitechapel Road, and he was able, often posing as Reggie, to go for little walks and stop by the occasional nearby pub, such as the Grave Maurice[28] – and, of course, the Double R. When things got a little hot in East London, he would stay at flats in Finchley or Fulham, but the longer he was in London, the more risky his situation was likely to become. Despite the Harley Street psychiatrist's diagnosis, Ronnie was still not well and his illness would manifest itself more noticeably as the months went by. Heavy drinking had caused him to put on weight and he became frequently morose and anti-social. Cousin Joe remembers one occasion when both twins were at their house in Vallance Road and he was left to look after Ronnie whilst Reggie went out briefly.

> *Well I looked at him and he looked at me as though he'd never seen me before. He was so strange I couldn't think of anything to say, then after five minutes of this he said, "Who are you then?" I thought he was having a laugh except he was dead serious. I said, "I'm Joey – your Cousin Joey." He screwed up his eyes and gave me one of his looks and said, "You in here as well?" but I could tell he didn't have a clue who I was. I tried all kinds to liven him up, but he wouldn't even look at me, let alone answer.*[29]

On occasion, his paranoia would take over and he would often believe that his family were spies, out to get him. They were now

---

28 The Grave Maurice at 269 Whitechapel Road was a favourite of Ronnie's and the twins would often conduct business meetings in the booths in the main bar. It became part of the 'Q Bar' franchise in 2004 and closed in 2010. It is now a 'Paddy Power' betting shop.

29 Joe Lee, Rita Smith and Peter Gerrard; *Inside the Kray Family* (London: Carlton 2008).

deeply worried for Ronnie's welfare and, after a while, even Reggie was beginning to think that his brother should not be out and about like he was. Eventually it was decided to turn Ronnie in to the authorities, for his own good. It was with no small amount of regret that Ronnie was taken away at 2 a.m. one morning; Reggie was concerned that he would be thought of as a 'grass' for telling the authorities where his brother was, but he was quickly convinced that it was all for Ronnie's own good.

Once he was safely at Long Grove Ronnie responded well to treatment, and the medication he received put him back on an even keel. The six months at liberty had successfully scratched his certification of insanity and he was released from Long Grove on 18 November 1958[30] to see out the end of his original sentence at Wandsworth. It was during this final brief spell of imprisonment, just prior to his release, that Ronnie met Frank Mitchell.

By the time Ronnie Kray met him, Frank Samuel Mitchell had become a British criminal legend and the scourge of the prison system. Born into a family of seven children in Canning Town on 19 May 1929, Mitchell's first brush with the law came at the age of nine when he stole a bicycle. Rather than castigate his son, Mitchell's father thought that taking him to the police would teach him a lesson, but the police did not send the young boy away with a telling off: instead, they pressed charges and Mitchell appeared at juvenile court on 25 April 1939 and was bound over for twelve months.[31] Alas, Mitchell senior's good intentions unwittingly awakened a mistrust of authority in his son, a predilection for making acquaintances with villainous characters, involving himself in crime and ultimately immersing him in a downward spiral of punishment and rebellion.

From 1946 Frank Mitchell was bounced from youth detention centre to Borstal and back, usually for shop-breaking and larceny, with notable regularity. His first prison sentence, for twelve months, was given on 9 February 1948. On another occasion, in August 1952, he received three months for receiving a stolen revolver[32] and with a growing number of misdemeanours under his belt, he rapidly became trapped by the criminal punishment system. When detained, he was a

---

30 Date taken from Ronnie's pre-trial medical report, 2 December 1968; CRIM 1/4927 (National Archives).

31 Mitchell's CRO No. was 24467/46; DPP 2/3006 (National Archives).

32 Ibid.

thorn in the side of the authorities, violent towards guards and other convicts alike if they incurred his displeasure. He played a major part in riots at Rochester Borstal while quickly building a reputation within the prison system. In maturity, he was an imposing, extremely powerful young man, 6 feet 1 inch in height and with a chest that apparently measured 54 inches. He was incredibly strong, obsessed with keeping fit and maintaining that strength, and yet he could be a gentle giant, reminding one of the character of George in Steinbeck's *Of Mice and Men*. He was often prone to displaying his physical strength by demonstrating his ability to do seemingly endless press-ups, or lifting up fellow inmates or prison wardens alike with one hand. His crushing bear-hug was particularly disarming. As former prison officer Derek Brisco once admitted:

> *I think there was a hidden agenda for him, it was like a demon-stration that, you know, "I really am a powerful man and although I'm a nice pleasant guy, theoretically there could be another side to me if things went wrong."* [33]

Yet despite his size and formidable presence, many believed that Frank Mitchell had the mental age of a thirteen-year-old boy at most. It was a dangerous combination.

In 1955, he was declared 'mentally defective' and was sent to Rampton Secure Hospital in Nottinghamshire, a maximum-security psychiatric hospital. On 18 January 1957, he escaped with fellow inmate Richard Maskell after getting duplicate prison keys made. They terrorised the villages around Rampton for several days and attacked a man, Leonard Collingburn, with an iron bar before stealing clothing and money. They were recaptured by police at a roadblock on the Great North Road in Newark, where the efforts of PC Bernard Briddon earned him a British Empire Medal for gallantry.[34]

Mitchell was sent to Broadmoor, the famous high-security psychiatric hospital in Crowthorne, Berkshire, but escaped on the morning of 8 July 1958 after again employing duplicate keys, sawing through bars and leaving a dummy in his bed to dupe officers into thinking he was still there. Mentally, Frank Mitchell may have been backward, but he was nothing if not ingenious when it came to escaping from prison.

---

33 Interview with Derek Brisco from *The Krays – Unfinished Business* (Carlton Television 1999); Channel 4, UK broadcast 10 January 2000.

34 'Farewell to PC who captured fugitives', *Worksop Guardian*, 17 August 2001.

Immediately after his escape, at about 5.30 a.m., he broke into the Wokingham house of Edward and Eva Peggs. It was a most bizarre encounter, for not only was Mitchell frighteningly aggressive (at one time he tried to throttle both Mr. and Mrs. Peggs and threatened them with a hatchet and a billy-hook) but he was gradually calmed by his resourceful victims, who made him a cup of tea and bathed his cut feet. He eventually escaped with some clothing after an hour and thirty minutes at the house. Through the resulting press coverage, this incident sealed Mitchell's legend, his choice of weapons giving him the name 'The Mad Axeman', a title that would stay with him for the rest of his life and beyond his eventual death. The media was full of warnings about Mitchell's character, describing him as "a particularly dangerous man who will be especially dangerous to anyone who may try to apprehend him."[35] Mr. and Mrs. Peggs must have been only too aware of what this meant and yet Eva Peggs, when interviewed on television, was very quick to state that Mitchell was harmless as long as he got what he wanted.[36]

Foolishly, this dangerous fugitive gave away his identity to two down-and-outs who went to the police, and Mitchell was apprehended on a bus after only thirty-six hours of freedom.[37] As a consequence, on 2 October 1958, 'The Mad Axeman' was sentenced at Berkshire Assizes to life imprisonment for robbery with violence and sent to Wandsworth Prison, where he began what would be his fateful relationship with the Krays. With his young mind prone to hero-worship, it was not long before Mitchell began to idolise Ronnie, a form of fandom which would ultimately lead the unstable giant to disaster.

◆

Late 1958 was a busy time for Reggie. As a successful, handsome businessman with no small amount of money and influence around the East End, he had quickly become a prominent local figure and (perhaps unsurprisingly) was attractive to women. But up until this point, there was little to suggest that either of the twins was that enamoured with the opposite sex; in Ronnie's case, his confession of bisexuality with a preference for young men was the obvious

35 *Evening Times*, 8 July 1958.
36 Footage of this interview can be seen in the documentary 'The Krays – Unfinished Business'
37 *Evening Times*, 8 July 1958.

reason why. In fact, Ronnie was known to regard women, with the exception of his mother and other female members of his close family, with disdain. The world in which Ronnie Kray had chosen to live was a violent, man's world, where there was no room for feminine distractions. He had seen numerous associates drift away from the twins' criminal enterprise because of girlfriends or marriage, and that was certainly not going to happen to him: "Fuckin' women. Make you end up like a fuckin' girl yourself."[38] But despite Ronnie's open preference for young male company and his dislike of most women, the question of the twins' sexuality has often provoked differing opinions.

In all likelihood they were both bisexual. Homosexual acts were still a criminal offence in the late 1950s, yet Ronnie knew what he was and how he felt and stuck to his instinct in the same way that he approached much of his life: that was how it was and if anybody didn't like it, it was their problem, not his. Reggie, despite being the 'other half' of the same person and practically identical genetically and in upbringing, had a more cautious outlook. He was easier to placate and more willing to see another side of the situation; often mistrustful or cautious in certain ways, he could sometimes be relied upon to weigh up a situation or even ask advice before responding, something which Ronnie, powered by his illness, rarely did. Thus he may have been all too aware of his sexuality and, perhaps, chose to suppress the homosexual element of it, seeing it as shameful or a mark of not being a true man. He later admitted to his future wife, Roberta Jones, that he had experimented with homosexuality as a young man, but that "he had never perceived himself as even bisexual until he was almost fifty."[39] But Reggie was certainly open to relationships with women; he adored his cousin Rita, suggesting on one occasion that had they not been related, she would have made his ideal woman.

Certainly, during those successful early days of the Double R Club, he was attractive to the opposite sex and the time he spent outside the sweep of Ronnie's withering judgement was punctuated with brief affairs. The women would be wined and dined, taken to Vallance Road to sleep overnight and then just cast aside like a playboy's plaything. This is something that Ronnie would not have tolerated; he would have badgered Reggie about wasting his time with women,

38 John Pearson; *Notorious* (London: Century 2010).
39 Roberta Kray; *Reg Kray: A Man Apart* (London: Sidgwick & Jackson 2002).

and so Reggie would keep his heterosexual desires under wraps out of loyalty to his brother and to maintain calm waters. But with Ronnie away and success and money at his fingertips, Reggie spent those last years of the 1950s putting himself about. It was even suggested many decades later that he had fathered a child with a dancer he had met at the Double R.[40] But man-about-town Reggie was about to embark on the most important relationship of his life, outside of his brother and mother, for it was around this time that he met fifteen-year-old Frances Shea.

Despite his love of impressive cars, Reggie was a hopeless driver; stories are legion about his often dangerous forays behind the wheel, sometimes ending up with a wrecked vehicle or, at the very least, a terrified passenger vowing never to ride with him again. Therefore, it was always handy to have a driver on call, and in those heady days of the Double R, young Frank 'Frankie' Shea fitted the bill perfectly. It has been said that Frankie Shea had got to know the twins as a visitor to the Regal when he was seventeen, and by the age of eighteen he had set himself up in business at a car lot in North London. Frankie was no angel and involved himself in a number of villainous enterprises, one of which was 'rolling' prostitutes' clients; this would be done by hiding in a room as a prostitute serviced her customer and, whilst in the throes of what had been paid for, the unwitting man would be unaware that his wallet was being stolen from his discarded clothing.[41] His partner in crime in much of this was Chris Lambrianou, the older brother of Frankie's old school friend Tony.

The eldest of five brothers from a Cypriot/Irish family, Christopher Lambrianou was born on Christmas Day 1938 and had a criminal record going back to the age of nine, when he had been bound over for one year for 'shopbreaking and larceny of food.'[42] Throughout his teenage years he went through the Borstal system and later a few spells in prison, convicted for offences such as housebreaking, being in possession of an offensive weapon, common assault and malicious

40 In 2001, 42-year-old Sandra Ireson claimed publicly that she was the daughter of Reggie, born out of an eight-month affair he had with dancer Greta Harper in 1958. Ireson visited Reggie in prison in 1998 and he did not challenge her over the claims. He was keen to know if it was true, but left the 'ball in her court'; he was soon involved in Charlie's case for drug trafficking and never got the chance to get meet or get in touch with Ireson again before his death. (*Sunday Mirror*, 11 March 2001.)

41 Chris Lambrianou and Robin McGibbon; *Escape From the Kray Madness* (London: Sidgwick and Jackson 1995).

42 CRO No. 26068/55; DPP 2/4583 (National Archives).

damage. In 1960, he would be given a two-month prison sentence for living off immoral earnings, probably a result of his work with Frankie. Chris Lambrianou was a bit of loner, used to doing his own thing, but he had carved out a reputation around Hackney and the East End as a man to be reckoned with. His brother Tony said of him:

> *He was a man of very changeable moods, and if someone upset him he didn't think, he acted. He wasn't a man you could turn your back on, and he would hold a grudge badly...*
>
> *He had to have the best things in life, and he had to have them right away. If he wanted something, he just went and got it. I always looked up to him because he was the livewire of the family.*[43]

Thomas Anthony 'Tony' Lambrianou,[44] three years younger than Chris, was also making an impact around their home turf of Dalston and Haggerston. Whereas his older brother tended to plough his own furrow, Tony had a small gang which included younger brother Jimmy, and together they would go on to work the local dancehalls and clubs, earning money from protection, as well as other choice acts of villainy. It would be lucrative: Tony would be earning up to £130-£140 per week by the early 1960s.[45] He, like many in the East End of London, was fully aware of the Krays' reputation by the late 1950s, but it would be a little while yet before the Lambrianou brothers found themselves being drawn into the Krays' world; they would come to have a more significant role to play in the story many years later.

Reggie had gone to Frankie Shea's car sales forecourt looking for a replacement for the Vanguard he was driving at the time and although Shea didn't have anything to Reggie's liking, they struck up a good relationship immediately; before long Frankie became Reggie's driver. Reggie described him as

> *...a good-looking kid with brown eyes, dark hair and an olive complexion. As a driver he was the best I had come across, while his personality made him exceptional company.*[46]

Frank Shea was born in October 1939 to Frank Snr and Florence Elsie Shea (commonly called Elsie),[47] and they lived at 57 Ormsby

43 Tony Lambrianou with Carol Clerk; *Inside the Firm* (London: Smith Gryphon 1991).
44 This name is given in the BMD register.
45 Tony Lambrianou with Carol Clerk; *Inside the Firm* (London: Smith Gryphon 1991).
46 Reg Kray; *Reggie Kray's East End Stories* (London: Sphere 2010).
47 Details from the BMD register of marriages, 1938.

Street in Hoxton, a long street of humble terraced cottages sandwiched between the Hackney and Kingsland Roads. In September 1943, he was joined by younger sister Frances Elsie, who would later become the centre of Reggie's attention. By the time he first met her, Frances was beginning to blossom into a very attractive young woman (although she was still at school) and Reggie was taken by her immediately. One side of his nature was his unfailing commitment to whatever he did; Reggie Kray rarely did things by halves and whether it was boxing, organising clubs (or taking over other people's clubs), exacting vengeance or starting up new money-making opportunities, he went into everything 100%. And so it was with Frances Shea. But he did have his doubts. Frances was still very young and cousin Rita remembers that he went to her seeking advice or even justification for his new obsession:

> He used to go round to the Shea house to see Frank. That's when she would come in from school. And one day Reggie came to see me and said, "I wanna ask you something. Frankie Shea's got a sister. Oh, he's got a lovely sister. She's so nice. I do like her. But... I think she's too young for me. She's still at school." I said, when she leaves school, ask her out with you. And he kept on about her.
>
> Reggie said, "She's got lovely eyes. Don't you think I'm a bit too old?" I'd say, "Not really. If she wants to go out with you, what's the difference?" [48]

Both the Shea siblings were good looking, but Frances had a beautiful, open face, set off with thick dark hair and large, doe-like brown eyes. Reggie thought she was 'saucy'. Whatever his sexual preference up to that point, regardless of his brother's influence, the first time Reggie saw Frances at the doorstep in Ormsby Street would be a defining moment in both their lives.

◆

Ronnie's mental health continued to be a problem, with his occasional periods of paranoia causing distress for his family. In his darkest moments he would rail against his brothers, accusing them of being imposters; or otherwise he would fail to acknowledge them at all. He would become sporadically reclusive, refusing to attend family gatherings or parties at the Double R. Medication was sought via the friendly face of Dr. Morris Blasker, but Ronnie was not under

48 Jacky Hyams; *Frances: The Tragic Bride* (London: John Blake 2014).

supervision for his drugs, and this led to erratic dosages which, when combined with the increasing quantities of alcohol that he was imbibing, resulted in alarming fluctuations in behaviour. Significantly, the combination of his illness, alcohol and drugs began to change Ronnie's appearance. Up until this time, he and Reggie had looked almost identical (and certainly seemed completely alike to those who did not know them intimately), but now Ronnie's features began to bloat. His eyes bulged, his face was puffy and he was putting on weight.

A terrifying incident occurred one night just before Christmas 1958 when Ronnie, who had been taken to a pub by Charlie and friends, began to behave strangely. Slamming his glass on the table, Ronnie stormed out, only to turn on his brother in the street when he tried to help him. Fortunately, 'Curly' King was passing and Ronnie, strangely, recognised him immediately and accepted his invitation to relax at the Regal. Before long, however, Ronnie had started prowling around the billiard hall in an obvious state of distress. He ended the episode by standing in the middle of the hall, staring into space, before collapsing on his knees. He had had a seizure which could have affected him one way or the other – either as a passing condition with a swift recovery period, or as an ultimate mental breakdown from which he would never emerge. On 19 December, he was taken to St Clement's Hospital on the Mile End Road in Bow, where until 4 January he received the care he once again so desperately needed. Before long, he was (relatively speaking, at least) as right as rain and was really able for the first time to talk about what he had been going through: some of the time he realised what was happening to him but couldn't stop himself, and most of the time he knew that those he rejected were truly his own loved ones, but still he could not help denying it. Brother Charlie recalled:

> *The price he had to pay was immense. Drugs would be a part of his life forever: four different tablets a day, an injection once a month. Ronnie accepted it without complaint; he realized how unwell he was and he knew the drugs kept away the paranoia and the eventual distrust that would lead to extreme violence.*[49]

With Ronnie seemingly stable, it was business as usual, although one bit of 'business' turned out to be less than fortuitous for Reggie.

---

49 Charlie Kray & Robin McGibbon; *Me and My Brothers* (London: Grafton 1988).

Daniel Dennis Shay (also known as Dennis Schay or Schai),[50] was another regular at the Regal billiard hall. He was thirteen years older than the twins and had a long criminal record dating back to 1936 (mostly for stealing motor vehicles), and had served a total of nearly eight years in prison for various convictions. According to Reggie's memoirs,[51] in February 1959 Shay had asked Reggie to accompany him to a shop, Swiss Travel Goods Limited, at 267 Finchley Road, north-west London,[52] to help him recover a gambling debt from the shop owner, a man named Murray Podro. Georgie Osbourne, Reggie's friend who had been complicit in Ronnie's breakout from Long Grove, came along for the ride, although it is claimed that, originally, the pair were not too keen on going. On arrival, Shay asked Reggie and Osbourne to come in and look around the shop (which sold leather goods) whilst he spoke to Podro. An argument broke out and Reggie moved in, head-butting Podro and giving him a black eye. As far as Reggie's side of the story goes, the fact that he had given Podro a card for the Double R Club before the trouble started led the police to his doorstep soon after, and Reggie, Shay and Osbourne were arrested for demanding money with menaces. As would be expected, Reggie's latter-day account[53] is not quite the truth. It appears that Daniel Shay had got him involved as a little muscle in a scam to extort money from Podro, if the official statements given to the police at the time are anything to go by.

According to Murray Podro, Shay had come to his shop at about 11.30 a.m. on 3 February 1959, looking to buy a briefcase. Choosing one with a disappearing handle, he told Podro that he would pay for it the next day, before changing the subject quickly and asking whether Podro had a car. When he said he did, Shay gave him his business card, for Maryland Motors in Stratford,[54] and suggested that Podro buy a Jaguar or a Chevrolet from him on hire purchase. But Podro was happy with his own car and, besides, Shay's offer was to buy on hire purchase: fail to pay the repayment instalments and then let the HP company repossess the vehicle after three months. It was a common

---

50 A name registered on his CRO record (6794/37) held at the National Archives.

51 Reggie Kray; *Born Fighter* (London: Arrow Books 1991).

52 Report by Detective Sergeant Albert Evans, 26 February 1959; MEPO 2/10075 (National Archives).

53 Reggie Kray; *Born Fighter* (London: Arrow Books 1991).

54 The original is kept at MEPO 2/10075 (National Archives).

enough scam. Podro was still not impressed, saying, "That's a funny way to run a business."[55] Shay left the shop promising he would be back in the morning to pay for the briefcase.

At 1.15 p.m. the following day, Shay returned – but this time he was not alone. Reggie and Georgie Osbourne were with him, but, strangely, according to Podro, Shay introduced them as the Kray twins.[56] He then accused Podro of overcharging him for a suitcase he hadn't actually paid for, and when Podro pointed this out to him and told him not to be "idiotic", Shay pulled out an umbrella from a display stand and waved it in Podro's face, saying "Don't you call me an idiot." Then came the crunch: Shay demanded £100 from Podro and threatened to have him kidnapped and cut to pieces if he did not comply. When Podro protested that he didn't have that sort of money to throw about, Shay took hold of him and hit him in the face, followed by Reggie who did the same. Shay then kneed or punched Podro hard in the chest before the two men, accompanied by Osbourne (who had merely been guarding the shop door) left. Shay's parting words were ominous: "You can go to the law if you like, but we'll be back and we want the money."[57]

Reggie Kray and anybody else can say what they like about this incident, but one thing is certain – it was extortion, pure and simple. Osbourne and Reggie may not quite have been aware what they were getting themselves into (Reggie had given Podro the Double R business card when first introduced), but by hitting Podro hard enough to bloody his face, nose and cause bruising, Reggie was in it up to his eyebrows.

Fortunately for Murray Podro, Shay never got his money. Podro informed the police at West Hampstead Station later that day and Detective Sergeant Perry Newell and PC Jeremiah Fallon hid at the back of the shop until Shay returned the following day, 5 February, at about 12.50 p.m., accompanied by a driver, Joseph Rood.[58] Shay denied everything with an audacious set of lies, even though Newell and Fallon had overheard a telephone conversation between Shay and

55 Statement by Murray Podro, 5 February 1959; CRIM 1/3142 (National Archives).
56 In his statement dated 12 February 1959, George Osbourne said that Shay introduced them as Mr. Kray and George; ibid.
57 Statement by Murray Podro, 2 March 1959; ibid.
58 Report by Detective Sergeant Albert Evans, 26 February 1959; MEPO 2/10075 (National Archives).

Podro earlier which made it quite clear what was going on.[59] Between 10 and 12 February, Shay, Reggie and Osbourne were rounded up and charged with demanding money with menaces.[60] Ronnie's name came up owing to Shay's initial introduction of his two companions as 'the Kray twins', but all involved were adamant that Ronnie was not in the least bit involved. Ronnie was eventually arrested on 12 February and was cooperative enough to give the police a statement,[61] claiming that he was at the Regal the entire morning of the incident, and then spent much of the day in pubs, particularly "The Ball" in Stratford.[62] He had a number of witnesses who could corroborate his story.

On 10 April 1959, Reggie was sentenced to eighteen months' imprisonment for 'demanding money with menaces and with intent to steal same.'[63] The case had received a fair amount of press coverage and the verdict elicited some fairly strong headlines, one comparing the three convicted men of "using Chicago–type protection methods."[64] On 22 September 1959, however, Reggie was granted bail[65] pending an appeal against his conviction and for a while at least, he was back in the East End and back in the saddle; which was just as well, for although Ronnie may have outwardly appeared more rational, his essential character traits were now proving to be a headache for his brothers as far as business was concerned. The Double R Club, which for nearly two years had been a veritable money pit and was by now attracting the patronage of celebrities such as Jackie Collins, George Sewell and Barbara Windsor,[66] had begun to suffer as a result of Ronnie's presence. Undoubtedly he was part of the set-up, but he failed to see the club as a profit-making business like Reggie and Charlie did. They had worked hard to make it into the success it was,

---

59 Detective Sergeants Evans and Newell, along with PC Fallon, were recommended for a commendation for their part in the case on 29 April 1959; MEPO 2/10075 (National Archives).

60 Statement of Detective Sergeant Albert Evans, 2 March 1959; ibid.

61 Statement by Ronald Kray, 12 February 1959; MEPO 2/10075 (National Archives).

62 Ronnie said "Ball", however there is no record of a pub of that name; there is, however a Bull, and it is likely the word was mistranscribed.

63 George Osbourne received the same sentence and Daniel Shay received three years.

64 *East London Advertiser*, 17 October 1959.

65 Report by Detective Sergeant Albert Evans, 5 October 1960; MEPO 2/10075 (National Archives).

66 It was around this time that Charlie Kray began an affair with Windsor, despite being married with one child at that time. It was agreed to end the relationship, according to Charlie, because he felt he could not break up his own family when son Gary was so young. Charlie and Windsor remained firm friends, however.

but when Ronnie became a regular presence, profits began to dwindle. For all his problems, Ronnie Kray was certainly a man of mercurial personality; prone to violence and fits of rage at the merest pretence, he could also be uncharacteristically goofy, with a sense of humour that could sometimes be seen as immensely child-like. As part of the Double R entertainment, he would occasionally bring dwarves to the club, or a giant, just to liven things up a bit. It was not to everybody's taste. But he was also incredibly generous, giving large amounts of money to anybody he trusted or liked who had fallen on hard times, or who had imminent debts they could not pay. Word soon got round that the twins could be relied on to help out ex-convicts or wives of those who had been put away, just as they had done during the early years of the Regal. The problem was, the money for friends, favours and free drinks was coming straight out of the Double R's cash register.

Reggie and Charlie often remonstrated with Ronnie, but there was often no reasoning with him:

> "What do you want to do – show ourselves up?" He said, "People come home expecting to be given something. Do you want us to get a bad name? Do you want people to think we're tight?"
>
> Reggie said, "We'd better slow down, that's all. We're overdoing it."
>
> Ronnie wouldn't have it. "You think we are, but I don't. It's not going to change. That's how it's going to be." [67]

The character of the club was also changing. Mickey Fawcett, who had become a regular at both the Double R and the Wellington Way spieler, had certainly noticed a difference once Ronnie had begun to make his mark:

> ...it was different at the Double R once the Colonel had come home. The Krays' place wasn't somewhere you'd go out with a girlfriend or with the wife. You had to be on your guard and know who Ronnie Kray was speaking to and who was out of bounds. There was one bloke who we were told to ignore one night – a reporter for the Sunday People called Tom Bryant. His crime was to file a nasty piece about a friend of Ronnie's called Frank Mitchell. He called him 'the Mad Axeman'. [68]

Elsewhere, the twins were looking forward to the future. In June 1959, they had applied for planning permission to turn the Regal

---

67 Charlie Kray & Robin McGibbon; *Me and My Brothers* (London: Grafton 1988).
68 Mickey Fawcett; *Krayzy Days* (Pen Press 2013).

into a private members' club and in August of that year had applied for a music and dancing licence. Although the use as a billiard hall had been approved until 30 June 1960, they were obviously hoping to improve the profile of their first business venture. After a survey of the building was conducted in September 1959, however, they withdrew the entertainments licence application for reasons best known to themselves.[69]

But it wasn't just Ronnie's unpredictably carefree nature and domineering behaviour that would instigate the decline of the Double R Club. Reggie had recently become the subject of police interest when he helped 25-year-old Ronald Marwood go into hiding in early 1959, knowing that he was wanted for stabbing PC Raymond Summers to death outside a club on Seven Sisters Road in North London on 14 December 1958. The police had heard that Reggie was somehow involved with Marwood's concealment and visited him at the Double R, making suggestions that they knew where he was hiding the fugitive.[70] Later, Reggie was interrogated at Bow Police Station and was told in no uncertain terms that, although they could not prove anything, the police knew what he was up to. "I was told by the governor of the station that they knew I had looked after Marwood, so in future the spotlight would be on me wherever I went and in whatever premises I opened as clubs."[71]

It was an ominous threat and, indeed, Scotland Yard would soon be taking a closer look at the activities of the twins and prominent London villains in general.

---

69 Applications in file GLC/AR/BR/17/036264 (London Metropolitan Archives).

70 Marwood gave himself up at Caledonian Road Police Station on 27 January 1959 and confessed to killing PC Summers. He was charged with capital murder and hanged at Pentonville Prison on 8 May 1959.

71 Reggie Kray; *Born Fighter* (London: Arrow Books 1991).

SIX

EAST MEETS WEST

The end of the 1950s saw a blossoming of organised criminal gangs in London. Undoubtedly Billy Hill still cast a shadow that loomed over much of West London's villainy, pulling strings from his luxury flat in Bayswater or his Moroccan bolt-hole in Tangier, but the capital itself was noticeably carved up between East, North and South. Indisputably, East London belonged to the Krays; any other smaller firms, be they localised street gangs like the Watney Streeters or more serious concerns such as the Maltese organisations who controlled prostitution, were resigned either to toe the Kray line or to keep their heads down. The Nash brothers, whom the twins had got to know when on the run from the army, were lords of North London, working out of Islington, but the Krays were on good terms with the Nashes and there was always a tacit understanding about remaining on their own ground and not treading on each other's toes.

The most prominent figures in South London were the Richardson brothers, Eddie and Charlie, a veritable money-making machine if ever there was one. Together they had amassed a small fortune in the predominantly legitimate scrap-metal business; Charlie Richardson also owned a pharmacy, yet they too were not averse to dealing in protection and fraud to boost their coffers. Undeniably, the Richardsons had far more going for them intellectually (the Krays tended to enforce their will by brawn rather than brains), and of course they were a lot more low-key than the twins, operating quietly and carefully without attracting media attention. They too had their own gang of sidekicks and henchmen, one of whom was George Cornell, now firmly rooted in Camberwell after his marriage in 1955. He would be joined later by Frankie Fraser after he had seen the benefits of working with the Richardsons, to the point where he became so involved with their immediate operations that he would turn down an offer to work with the twins.

Fraser's nickname – 'Mad' Frank – was well-earned. Born into an impoverished family in Lambeth, South London, in 1923, his first criminal experience came at the age of ten, and his first conviction at sixteen.[1] During the Second World War he sought to take advantage of the criminal opportunities made available by the black market, blackouts and the dearth of regular police officers, and found himself in and out of Borstal throughout 1940 and Wandsworth Prison the following year.[2] Conscripted into the army, he chose the villain's path and went on the run, during which time he became acquainted with the twins' father Charlie. In 1947, he was again imprisoned for a smash-and-grab raid on a jeweller's shop, and after his release in March 1949 began working with Billy Hill and Albert Dimes before being imprisoned again in 1951 for various offences including malicious damage and actual bodily harm. Whilst at Durham Prison, his violence led him to be certified insane and on 9 February 1955, he began a five month stay in Broadmoor. On 2 May 1956, he was involved in a vicious knife attack on Jack Spot outside his home in West London, which, far from earning him money, significantly improved his notoriety within the London underworld, but for which he received a seven year prison sentence. A career criminal of the highest order, Fraser was notorious – he was later to say, "I'm not frightened of nothing and no-one. Never have been, never will be."[3]

But perhaps the most respected of the South London criminal fraternity was Frederick Gerald Foreman, whose own independent firm of bank robbers and safe-blowers, formed in 1956 and which included future Great Train Robbers Buster Edwards and Tommy Wisbey, had achieved considerable success. Born in 1932, Freddie Foreman had known the twins' brother Charlie for some time and had occasionally worked with him and his partner 'Stan the Fence'

1 Fraser's CRO No. was 22868/39; MEPO 10933 (National Archives).
2 Fraser is famously quoted on numerous occasions as saying that the war years were the best of his life and that he never forgave the Nazis for surrendering.
3 Interview with Fred Dinenage from *The Krays By Fred Dinenage*, (Talent TV South), UK Broadcast 15 March 2010.

in the selling of stolen goods. Despite Charlie's more law-abiding reputation, the nature of his upbringing and the East End culture had seen to it that even he was not entirely squeaky clean, having received a fine at Stratford Magistrates' Court on 22 August 1951 for stealing twenty pieces of zinc guttering.[4] Foreman was truly independent and was comfortably able to spend time in the East End, visiting Charlie and other acquaintances, as well as enjoying the anonymity that being across the river, away from the attentions of the South London police, afforded him. This relationship came in very handy around 1959 when Foreman found himself on the run from his native Lambeth after a van he had used in a robbery in Southampton was traced back to him. The Krays came to the rescue.

> Charlie and the twins found me a nice little flat in Adeline [sic] Grove, right opposite the Blind Beggar pub run by Jimmy and Patsy Quill in the Sixties – lovely people who were later to go onto bigger and better things...
>
> Ronnie, Reg and Charlie used to pop around and I would go to the Double R Club, the pool hall, the Blind Beggar and many other pubs in the area. It was mostly Jewish food over there and you got all these characters like Sammy the Yid, Nobby Clarke, Bill Ackerman, Limehouse Willey and Leslie Berman. They were all part of the organisation, working at the local spielers. I used to pop in there to pass the time, though I never played cards.[5]

The twins' relationships with the Nash brothers and Foreman demonstrated that if everybody knew where they stood, if territory was respected, and if a helping hand was there for the right people, then trouble could be avoided and profitable work could be shared. As far as the south Londoners were concerned, Eddie and Charlie Richardson always maintained that the twins were no threat to them and vice versa. The Krays may have seen it differently, but it was their relationship with the Nash brothers that garnered them undue attention in early 1960 and helped the police put a temporary squeeze on their activities.

One evening in February 1960, Reggie had been drinking in the Green Dragon Club, a small spieler down a narrow passage called

---

4   This would remain Charlie's only conviction until 1969. His CRO No. was 3380/1951; CRIM 1/4900 (National Archives).

5   Freddie Foreman; *Freddie Foreman: The Godfather of British Crime* (London: John Blake 2007).

Green Dragon Yard, off Whitechapel High Street, with Sonny the Yank (Bernard Schack), the former Jack Spot henchman. The club was owned by George Mizel, Bill Ackerman and Matty Constantino, and had first been targeted for protection by the Krays the previous year. The co-owners were paying the twins £40 per week following an 'intervention' by about eight men who did some significant damage a few weeks after the club opened;[6] as a result of their 'services', the Krays were regular visitors, although as neither were card-players, they mainly used it as a social haunt.

That particular night, after a pleasant enough drink, Reggie was preparing to leave when Sonny called him 'son' in what Reggie felt was a somewhat patronising, even insulting, manner. Without another word, Reggie punched and head-butted him, breaking his jaw. The result of Reggie Kray's violent impatience was hospitalisation for Sonny the Yank, but the two would see each other again a day or two later at the London Hospital when Reggie went to visit an old boxing friend, Billy Ambrose, who was in the same ward recovering from a gunshot wound. The incident in which Ambrose received that wound would be seen as one of the most notorious acts of gangland violence in the East End up to that point, and it became the catalyst for police interest in the Kray's affairs.

The Pen Club stood on Duval Street in Spitalfields, in a row of shabby buildings facing the Spitalfields Fruit and Wool Exchange.[7] It was apparently named in honour of a robbery at the Parker Pen factory, the proceeds of which had been used to set the club up,[8] and, like many such establishments across London, it was the haunt of many a villain. At about midnight on 6 February 1960, Selwyn Keith Cooney, also known as 'Leeds Jimmy Neill', a West End nightclub owner, visited the Pen Club with barmaid Joan Bending. Not long after, Jimmy Nash and his girlfriend Doreen Masters arrived, accompanied by former boxers Joey Pyle and John Read. It was believed that Nash's brother Ronnie had been beaten up by Cooney in a Notting Hill nightclub some time before and revenge was in the air,[9] so when Masters pointed out

6   Statement by George Mizel taken at Central Office, New Scotland Yard, 16 May 1968; MEPO 2/11387, ff. 834-6 (National Archives).

7   Before 1904, Duval Street had been known as Dorset Street, an infamous thoroughfare known for its criminal element and a number of murders, including that of Mary Jane Kelly in November 1888, widely considered to be the last atrocity committed by Jack the Ripper.

8   James Morton; *East End Gangland* (London: Little, Brown and Company 2000).

9   *East London Advertiser*, 11 March 1960.

Cooney to Nash, things took a turn for the worse: accompanied by Pyle and Read, Nash violently attacked Cooney, first punching him in the face so hard that his nose was broken.[10]

A free-for-all ensued, with other club members, including Billy Ambrose, setting about Nash, Pyle and Read in Cooney's defence, before shots rang out. According to witnesses, Nash pulled a gun and began shooting, first hitting Billy Ambrose in the stomach and then Cooney – almost at point blank range – in the head, before fleeing with his companions. Ambrose, though seriously injured, managed with others to drag Cooney out into Duval Street; leaving him on the pavement, he drove himself to the London Hospital, where he gave a false account of what had happened to him. Ambrose was lucky, but Cooney had died instantly from the gunshot wound to the head.[11]

The resulting trial began at the Old Bailey on 21 April 1960: ultimately, Nash was acquitted of murder on 4 May (as one witness could not be found and two others had withdrawn their evidence), but was found guilty of the beating he had given Cooney beforehand and sentenced to three years' imprisonment.[12] The trial had been of great interest not just to the public, but also to many key players in London's underworld, who were present in the public gallery throughout much of the proceedings. Of course, the Kray twins, in solidarity with Jimmy Nash, were conspicuously in attendance throughout much of the trial and the police could not help but notice. In fact, at this time, the Krays and their business premises were being closely watched by the police. And the Krays knew it.

On 26 April, they had instructed their solicitors to write to Scotland Yard announcing that they knew they were under scrutiny and to emphatically deny that they had any criminal interests:[13] this was a common enough tactic by figures in the criminal underworld, an attempt to pre-empt any action by the police, but Scotland Yard's Flying Squad had certainly done their homework. In a lengthy report, filed soon after the Pen Club verdict, Detective Superintendent Tommy Butler outlined the information gathered about the twins and

---

10 Ibid.

11 The Metropolitan Police files and the DPP records for the Pen Club case are held at the National Archives; however, they are closed to the public until 2033 and 2038 respectively.

12 At this time, Jimmy Nash's brother Roy was serving a prison sentence (for manslaughter), as was another brother, John (for carrying an offensive weapon with intent).

13 Report by Detective Superintendent Tommy Butler, 6 May 1960; MEPO 2/9974, f. 3A (National Archives).

their associates.

> *They are well known in London criminal circles as "THE TWINS".*
>
> *They are the joint owners of the "Double R" Club, Bow Road, E. This is a low-drinking club, which can only be described as a sink of iniquity. They are careful to adhere closely to all club regulations, but every visitor to it is either (a) a convicted criminal or (b) one of the many degraded lower class newspaper reporters seeking "colour", "drama" or so-called atmosphere for rubbishy news items. They also own the Regal Billiards Hall, Eric Street, Bow, E.3.*
>
> *During the last three years the Kray twins and their older brother Charles James KRAY, C.R.O. No. 33830/1951, assisted by the notorious NASH family, have welded themselves into a formidable criminal association.*
>
> *They have organised the "Protection" technique, and the keystones of their confederacy are VIOLENCE and INTIMIDATION. At present this is mainly directed towards club owners, cafe proprietors, billiard hall owners, publicans, and motor car dealers, operating in the East End of London. That they will spread their operations to other districts in due course may be taken for granted.*
>
> *Their reputation is already such that persons threatened almost frantically deny visitations by anyone connected with the Kray twins. Not one victim can be persuaded to give evidence against anyone connected with their organisation.*
>
> *The fact that Ronald Kray is certainly mentally unstable (to put it at the very least) is of immense importance to the others, and adds considerably to the victim's undeniable urge to comply with demands made upon him, and to his atrocious memory when questioned by Police at a later stage.*[14]

But it was not just the police who had strong things to say about the increasingly formidable Kray 'empire'. They had also received an anonymous letter, presumably from an East End resident who was certainly not backward in coming forward about what he saw as a reign of terror in his part of London. This letter is reproduced here in full and the spelling mistakes and grammar (or lack of it) are as in the original:

---

14 Ibid.

Dear Sir,

In the best interests of the community I should like you to know that on Tuesday there did appear a photograph of Five men, it was printed in the daily sketch and headed that these men were Cooneys killers friends, all these men have got very violent records having served terms of imprisonment from seven years, there was the two Kray brothers one was sentenced to 18 months some time last year but only done 3 months of he's sentence and was supposed to be let out on appeal, since he has been home on appeal he has been successfully running organiszed crime they have been operating all sorts of gambling clubs in the east end of London in the Bow district, it is pretty evident that these men are not doing these things without some assistance from the police why is this being allowed to continue they are getting money from all sorts of operations they have been known to have machine guns and shot guns in hordes what exactly is going on when it is common knowledge and the police are powerless to do anything about it it will not stop at this one murder and I think that you should make some effort to stop it, probe into the way that this man Kray has been able to come out on appeal as his case is only one of many things that require looking into I am not able to disclose my identitie as when you hand this letter to the police they will use there resorces to find out where this letter came from and condem me for writing it but I can assure you that it is in everybody's interest that I am informing you of these matters I trust that you make every effort at your resorces to try and fetch these people to book and allow law abiding citizens to go peacefully about these gangsters are paying no taxed and have been amassing a small fortune at the expense of the community just look into their records yourself and you will see what is going on. There are two familys here in the east end namely the Nashes and Kray's brothers that have been having a glorious time on the proceeds of violence and crime so I think that they are the real organizers of this business but they are getting more money than you get in the way of renumation trusting you give this matter you early attention I

Annomous

Shut up these gambling clubs and conviscate the equipment that they are using frut machine and prostutes that they are living off of [15]

---

15 MEPO 2/9974, f. 1C (National Archives).

The result of such interest was a police raid on both the Wellington Way Social Club and the Double R, executed on the same day, 3 June 1960.

At the Wellington Way spieler, raided at 3.10 p.m., twenty seven people were present; sixteen of them had criminal records, including Jackie Reynolds, the part-owner, and one Frank Shea, the father of Reggie's girlfriend Frances, who had unwittingly taken a job there. All were fined for attending an illegal betting house; however, the Krays themselves were absent. At the Double R, raided that evening at 10.50 p.m., forty-seven people were present, including Ronnie Kray, Harry Abrahams, Johnny Davis, friends Pat Butler and Richard Moughton and boxing brothers Edward and Henry 'Checker' Berry.[16] It was discovered that the club had no drinking licence and thus Reggie, 'Big' Pat Connolly (who was described as the club secretary) and Johnny Davis were charged with selling intoxicating liquor without a justice's licence.[17] Ronnie was bound over at a cost of £10 to keep away from gaming houses for twelve months.[18] A number of people had their car registration numbers logged as part of the police crackdown, including Charlie and Reggie Kray, Teddy Smith, and 'Checker' Berry. Significantly for the Krays, the police recommended that the club should be abolished: "every endeavour is being made to get the premises disqualified", read a report.[19] By the end of 1960, the Double R Club,[20] the Wellington Way spieler and even the Regal had closed down for good. The Krays still had their ways of raking in money, and weren't far away from sealing a deal that would restore their temporarily battered pride, but it was a significant blow nonetheless and a first strike for the Metropolitan Police who, for the remainder of the decade would embark on an on-off attempt to bring them down for good.

◆

16 Report by Detective Inspector B. Devonald, 17 June 1960; MEPO 2/9974, f. 1A (National Archives).

17 Reggie was forced to pay a total of £25 in fines against five charges of selling alcohol without a licence (and £25 costs), plus £5 for not having a dancing and music licence, at Thames Magistrates' Court on 9 September 1960.

18 He had also been fined on 7 March for attempting to bribe a police officer and driving without a licence.

19 Report by Detective Inspector B. Devonald, 17 June 1960; MEPO 2/9974, f. 1A (National Archives).

20 Struck off on 11 September 1960; CRIM 1/4900 (National Archives).

By now, Reggie was well and truly courting Frances Shea, who had left school and was working in the Strand in a clerical job. Despite the impending misfortunes of 1960, whether it was through the police clampdown or Ronnie's recklessness, Reggie was more than keen to offer the young Frances a life like no other. And who could resist the charms of a handsome local man who wore elegant bespoke suits, drove expensive cars and who appeared so successful in 'business' that he could afford to take the subject of his affections to smart West End clubs and shower her with gifts? For many East End women in those days, the choices were few: a low level job which would be given up for marriage, children and the promise of a basic existence as a housewife with limited options to travel or see the high-life... these expectations were taken as read, but Reginald Kray was not part of that world. He was a real catch and Frances, with her striking good looks, was a real catch for him. Whatever his sexuality up to that point, Reggie certainly felt that a settled life with a lovely girl and the possibility of having a family was on the agenda, and with his strong, driven personality, like everything he did, he did not court Frances by halves. In February 1960, he had taken her to the Astor Club in Mayfair's Berkeley Square[21] and in May they flew to Jersey, experiences that, for a sixteen-year-old girl from Hackney, were only the stuff of dreams. Reggie already knew her brother Frankie and he had even offered Frank Shea Snr work in the Wellington Way club (where he was unfortunately found later that year). Mother Elsie, for the moment, kept her own counsel on this dapper, polite man whose business enterprises and the way he managed them were no real secret.

Ronnie, however, was less impressed by Reggie's love life. Certainly, Ronnie could be sentimental: he could display a strong sense of humour and he could fall in love or into deep infatuation with the boys he was attracted to, but he never allowed this to cause him to lose focus on what he felt was important. As far as he was concerned, women watered down the criminal drive. They had too much influence where it was not wanted and what Ronnie Kray wanted was to live that organised life of crime unfettered, to storm along on a wave of control and violence as 'The Colonel' working from 'Fort Vallance', and relishing the power it provided. With Reggie keen to show a more

21 The Nash brothers were paid protection money by the club, so Reggie and his associates would have been more than welcome there.

respectable side to the public (and particularly to Frances's parents), Ronnie felt that his twin had gone soft. But perhaps what he feared more than anything was losing his brother. Keeping the Kray empire going, of course, was still a major concern and it was fortuitous that, as the police were making their plans to squeeze the twins, the Krays had already met an important man who would take their criminal enterprise to the next level: Leslie James Payne.

The so-called 'Firm', the Krays' entourage of drivers, minders and henchmen was never static. People would come and go over the years and the twins were always on the lookout for potential members who could bring something to their business dealings. Men like 'Duke' Osbourne and Charles 'Nobby' Clarke (an old friend of brother Charlie) were loosely-appointed armourers at various times; little redheaded Thomas Patrick Cowley, who had a number of convictions for burglary and keeping illegal gaming houses,[22] had a certain amount of nous when it came to the workings of business; Sammy Lederman was a link to the West End and celebrities who could raise the Kray profile. Leslie Payne would prove to be, for a while at least, a most valuable addition to the ranks.

Born in Paddington, London, in 1927, Payne came from a diverse background: his mother was from an impoverished family, his father from a well-to-do one, and the latter had originally trained as a solicitor before deafness curtailed his legal career and he was forced into more menial work by his disability. Payne had served as an Infantry Sergeant during the war and had seen incredible hardship and violence at the battle of Monte Cassino in 1944, and thus he would never be too intimidated by the more aggressive elements within the underworld. During his army days, he became adept at making money through illicit means, and, after being demobbed in 1947, he took this skill into the outside world. With his broad-shouldered good looks and his confident and well-spoken manner, he had the deportment of an Old Etonian and was able to speak in a language that professional people understood. He was essentially a businessman, and often a good one at that; but he had chosen to exercise his talents in the criminal subculture, abetted by his partner, a cunning accountant named Frederick Gore, whom Payne described as "a comedian, an innocent."[23]

22 Cowley's CRO No. was 34163/57; CRIM 1/4927 (National Archives).
23 Leslie Payne; *The Brotherhood* (London: Michael Joseph 1973).

Payne first met the Krays indirectly through his car-dealership business in Stratford: on one particular occasion in 1959, a business arrangement with another dealership had gone wrong, with the owners claiming that Payne owed them money. When Payne refused to pay them, they mentioned that they had 'influential friends' by way of a veiled threat, which initially cut no ice with Payne. Those 'influential friends' turned out to be the twins. When Payne faced the music and met them, he was able to bend them to his way of thinking and they even took his side against the other dealership, who they felt had been using their reputation in vain. Perhaps because of his keen intelligence and appearance of breeding, the Krays took a liking to Payne and would visit him often, probably aware that he could be a useful ally. They were also very willing to defend him: one day, he had a minor altercation with Bobby Ramsey, the old Kray associate who worked for him part-time at the dealership. The relationship between the Krays and Ramsey had soured since the 1956 Terry Martin assault case, and, having heard through the grapevine about the small spat, the twins came over with members of the Firm to sort things out. When Ramsey challenged either of them to a 'straightener' (a straightforward, stand-up fight that would be forgotten about once honour had been satisfied), Ronnie replied, "Straight up fight? We haven't come here for that. We've come here to hurt you."[24] They then beat Ramsey up.

What Leslie Payne and Freddie Gore had made much of their money from, and what they would bring to the Krays' arsenal of money-making schemes, was the long-firm fraud. John Pearson described it in very basic terms thus:

> *The theory of the long-firm fraud was simple and probably started with the Ancient Greeks. It involved buying up large quantities of goods on credit, selling them off for cash as cheaply and as fast as possible, and then disappearing with the money. End of story.*[25]

Long-firm frauds involve setting up a legitimate company or companies and then buying stock from various suppliers. Bills are initially paid promptly so that in time, a good line of credit is built up, from which point stock is bought on credit: in other words, nothing is paid for straight away. Once a huge amount of stock is acquired and

24 Ibid.
25 John Pearson; *Notorious* (London: Century 2010).

warehouses are full, with bills outstanding, the stock is sold off quickly at desirable prices, all company offices and paperwork disappear and a large amount of money is made for the partners in the fraud. There would always be a front-man who, if things went wrong, would be willing to take the rap and spend a few months in prison if he got caught, but Leslie Payne could certainly see the advantage of having heavyweight associates like the Krays behind him should anybody direct unwanted attention their way or attempt to take over the operation.

"When it came to organised, effective violence," said Payne, "they were quite simply the best in the business."[26]

Payne and Gore made the acquisition of huge amounts of money through long-firm frauds extremely easy. They set up a company, Carsten Securities Limited, as a front (the first of several companies that were created to operate the frauds) and all the twins really needed to do was sit back, let the experts get on with it, and reap the benefits. It was also through Payne and his ability to say the right things to the right people (unlike the twins who were not known for their subtlety or even their intelligence) that the Krays were able get their feet under the boardroom table of Esmeralda's Barn, a club in Wilton Place, Knightsbridge. It was a prime location from which to extend their influence into the wealthy West End of London, frequented as it was by the rich, titled and privileged. Some accounts suggest that the twins had become aware of the club through Ronnie's vague dealings with Peter Rachman, the notorious Notting Hill slum landlord and pimp,[27] who employed their old friend Dickie Morgan as 'muscle', but there appears to be no consensus on what Rachman's actual involvement was.[28] Colin Fry and Charlie Kray suggested that the deal was done by Charlie, Payne and Gore after a tip off from one 'Commander Diamond' and that Ronnie and Reggie weren't even there when the deal was brokered.[29] John Pearson described a meeting between the twins, Payne, Gore and one of the four investors in Esmeralda's Barn, Stefan De Faye.[30] Whole control of

26 John Pearson; *Notorious* (London: Century 2010).
27 James Morton; *The Krays: Crime Archive* (London: National Archives 2008).
28 One suggestion was that the Krays, via Morgan, were trying to muscle in on Rachman's business. Rachman was said to have some involvement in the running of Esmeralda's Barn and that he had offered the Krays a stake in it to get them off his back.
29 Colin Fry & Charlie Kray; *Doing the Business* (London: John Blake 1993).
30 John Pearson; *Notorious* (London: Century 2010).

the Barn was vested in a holding company called Hotel Organisations Ltd, which turned out to be De Faye alone. The idea was to buy Hotel Organisations Ltd for £1,000, thus removing any responsibilities and 'worries' from De Faye. When De Faye claimed he didn't have any worries, Payne assured him that he needn't be so sure, as the twins glared on. Payne had worked his magic and thus Reggie and Ronnie became sleeping partners in Esmeralda's Barn.[31] He also suggested the involvement of Mowbray Henry Gordon Howard, the Sixth Earl of Effingham, as a front man on the premise that the Earl, an inveterate gambler, womaniser and drunkard, would enjoy having his name on the Barn's headed notepaper and the little extra money that came with it, and that the involvement of the aristocracy would look good for the twins.

The hijacking of Esmeralda's Barn and the partnership with Leslie Payne and Freddie Gore began a new period in the activities of the Krays. The timing could not have been better, for the Gaming Act of 1960 was about to be passed, making gambling legal beyond the racecourse, and the government had begun to soften to the idea as many establishments began installing casinos. Esmeralda's Barn followed suit, with a discotheque in the basement and a restaurant to add to the income. It also staged entertainment, boasting the Walker Brothers, the Everly Brothers and a young Eric Clapton as performers on their first rungs up the ladder of stardom: Clapton would later recall one occasion where he sat in with the house band and played to an audience of two, the twins themselves, who sat at the back of the room and glared blankly at the players.[32] In those early days, Payne's long-firm activities were bringing in sizeable amounts of money, making the cut from the gambling at the Barn, estimated at £800 a week,[33] seem meagre by comparison, but the Wilton Place establishment was nothing if not a status booster for the twins. Reggie was back in his element, enchanting the rich clientele with his cockney charm and presumably wowing Frances with his improved standing in London's nightlife. For Ronnie, it was another open wallet and the discotheque in the basement, run by a lady called Ginette,

31 The twins would officially become directors on 8 January 1962; Report by Detective Superintendent Leonard Read, undated (1968); CRIM 1/4900 (National Archives).
32 Eric Clapton; *The Autobiography* (London: Arrow 2008). Clapton had a few encounters with the Kray circle and corresponded with Reggie many years later when the latter was in prison.
33 Just over £12,000 equivalent today.

became the regular haunt of West London's gay community, lesbians in particular. Here Ronnie met other homosexuals who, rather than hiding their sexuality, openly flaunted and enjoyed it, and this often led to a more relaxed Ronald Kray. It also introduced a less starchy clientele to the club, in the form of the 'gambling playboy'.

On 26 July 1960, Reggie's appeal against his 1959 conviction for demanding money with menaces was rejected and he turned himself in to the authorities before returning to Wandsworth Prison to see out his sentence.[34] His relationship with Frances was reduced to letters and visits when it was practical, but Reggie suffered from the distance between them. If he received letters less than twice a week, he would fret terribly and on one occasion was in such a bad mood that, in a letter to Frances, he confessed that "I nearly choked a fella in my cell for having too much to say."[35]

Whilst Reggie was in Wandsworth, he met Frank Mitchell for the first time. Mitchell must have thought all his Christmases had come at once now that he was able to meet the twin brother of his legendary friend Ronnie. But Reggie also met another fellow convict who had just been transferred from Exeter Prison: Jack Dennis McVitie, known to all as 'Jack the Hat' on account of the fact that he always wore a hat to hide his thinning hair.

McVitie was born on 19 April 1932 in Battersea, South London and was one of five children along with brothers Henry, Leonard and Fred, and a sister Jean.[36] During the Second World War, the McVitie family broke up and he lived with an aunt in Gilbey Road, Tooting, and later, with a family known as the Hutchinsons. His first in a long line of criminal convictions came in October 1946 when he was bound over at Buntingford Juvenile Court for stealing a watch and cigarettes.[37] At the age of fourteen he met Marie Esther Marney, a pupil at Western Road Secondary Modern School for Girls in Mitcham, who was a year his junior. McVitie (whom everyone at the time called 'Dennis') and Marie became engaged whilst still in their teens and, immediately

---

34 Report by Detective Sergeant Albert Evans, 10 August 1960; MEPO 2/10075 (National Archives).

35 Jacky Hyams; *Frances: The Tragic Bride* (London: John Blake 2014).

36 Jean was murdered in the 1950s in London, and Fred and Leonard were living in Wales by the 1960s - Henry lived in Leicester. Statement given by Henry McVitie on 16 October 1968; MEPO 2/11404, ff. 1545-6 (National Archives).

37 McVitie's CRO No. was 36413/46; DPP 2/4583, ff. 86-8 (National Archives).

38 Marriage certificate held at National Archives; CRIM 1/4927.

after, Marie fell pregnant. A daughter, Mary Elizabeth was born at St James' Hospital, Balham, on 6 September 1950, whilst McVitie was undertaking his National Service, and three weeks later, he and Marie tied the knot at Wandsworth Registry Office.[38]

The marriage was doomed, as the only time Marie ever got to see her husband was when he was on army detention in Reading, and pretty soon she left him. When McVitie went to see his wife and child at her parents' house, his father-in-law told him to go away and never return; it was the last time Marie would ever see McVitie. She had no communication with him, never received any maintenance payments for the child and, despite entering a long-term relationship with another man, Henry Cooper, which resulted in more children, she never married Cooper and never divorced McVitie either.[39]

McVitie's criminal life gathered pace from March 1952; Borstal training followed another conviction for stealing and, four months later, one month imprisonment and further time in Borstal for assaulting a police officer. Four separate prison terms followed over the next four years, for offences ranging from stealing to assault. In 1954, McVitie had met Sylvia Ann Mitchell, who was to briefly become his common-law wife and the mother of his second child, Tony Jackson McVitie, in 1958.[40] They drifted apart after McVitie was sentenced to seven years' imprisonment on 3 April 1959 after being found guilty, with three other men, of being in possession of explosives for an unlawful purpose and possessing a flick-knife in public.[41]

By all accounts, Jack McVitie feared very few people and could certainly handle himself. He was 5 feet 9 inches tall and heavily built, with blue eyes and, on his hands, arms and chest numerous tattoos, with one particular adornment, on his left wrist, reading 'ANN'.[42] Despite his later reputation as an unpredictable liability who drank to excess and mixed alcohol with drugs, some in the criminal fraternity spoke well of him.

---

39 Information about McVitie's past taken from a statement given by Marie Cooper at Guildford Police Station, 29 January 1969; MEPO 2/11388, ff.2273-4 (National Archives).

40 Statement by Sylvia McVitie/Mitchell taken at New Scotland Yard, 22 January 1969; MEPO 2/11388, f.2275 (National Archives).

41 Information from McVitie's application for Habeas Corpus, 1959-60; J 167/74 (National Archives).

42 Information from missing persons application dated 13 November 1967; MEPO 2/11388, f.1432 (National Archives).

Lenny Hamilton looked up to him:

> *...he was more of a man than anyone on the Firm because he was not a yes man. Jack was his own man and I admired him because he said what he thought and nobody can blame him for the way he was. You speak as you find and I always liked Jack McVitie.*[43]

Tony Lambrianou, on one hand, could be rather complimentary about him: "He was a generous man and he had a very good sense of humour. He was flamboyant, loved to be the centre of attention and enjoyed having women around him."[44] And yet he was certainly aware of McVitie's other traits: "Let's not whitewash it. Jack McVitie was a man of violence... He didn't have a care in the world. He didn't give a monkey's for anything."[45] Freddie Foreman regarded him as "a loudmouth," and thought that, "all told, he was a bit of a nut";[46] his own wife described him as "a thief, spiteful and very quick tempered."[47]

It appears that Jack the Hat's unpredictability meant he could be all things to all men, depending on the situation. Reggie Kray claimed he was originally impressed by McVitie at their first meeting, as fellow convict Ray Rosa, who had made the introduction, had told him that McVitie had previously assaulted the governor of Exeter Prison, the much maligned Mr. Steinhausen, which was why he had been moved to Wandsworth.[48] Frankie Fraser, also at Exeter at that time, said that McVitie had got involved in a fight with a prison officer and as a result he was severely beaten in his cell.[49]

With Reggie away in prison, Ronnie was now beginning to dominate Esmeralda's Barn with his own brand of hospitality and was flexing his muscles in other areas of the Kray business empire. As with his effect on the Double R Club previously, this was not necessarily a good thing. Apart from his own tendency to raid the coffers when a little 'small change' was needed, he could also be very inconsistent when it came to ensuring customers paid their gaming debts. One such character

43 Lenny Hamilton & Craig Cabell; *Getting Away With Murder* (London: John Blake 2006).
44 Tony Lambrianou with Carol Clerk; *Inside the Firm* (London: Smith Gryphon 1991).
45 Ibid.
46 Freddie Foreman; *Freddie Foreman: The Godfather of British Crime* (London: John Blake 2007).
47 Statement given by Marie Cooper at Guildford Police Station, 29 January 1969; MEPO 2/11388, ff.2273-4 (National Archives).
48 Reggie Kray; *Born Fighter* (London: Arrow Books 1991).
49 Frankie Fraser with James Morton; *Mad Frank – Memoirs of a Life of Crime* (Sphere Books 1994).

was the painter Lucian Freud, a compulsive gambler who owed the Barn £1,400 which he had no way of paying. He offered Ronnie a painting, which was refused, but Ronnie just wiped the debt away, for no other reason than he liked Freud. Thankfully, perhaps owing to the more content Ronnie, a result of his finally 'coming out' in the welcoming environment of Ginette's gay disco, and his sense of having closed the class divide between East and West, violence was rarely necessary. But even after Reggie came out of prison on 25 February 1961, he was powerless to stop Ronnie from once again messing with something that they had all believed would be the making of them. Despite this, Esmeralda's Barn continued to attract the wealthy and privileged who were willing to part with their money and the Krays and their business partners were happy to take it off them. For a while at least, the Krays were becoming extremely wealthy and could now afford numerous holidays abroad for themselves and their parents. If the more familiar environs of Britain were preferable, then there was their caravan down at Steeple Bay in Essex,[50] which they would go to most weekends during the warmer months. Life was good.

But there was always something around the corner with the Krays. Reggie had not been out of prison long when he was arrested on a charge of burglary. Apparently a woman, Lily Hertzberg, had seen him leaving her husband's flat in Stoke Newington with jewellery that was subsequently valued at £502. Ronnie was also arrested for apparently trying the door handles of parked cars in Dalston, presumably with the intent to steal. Unsure whether the Hertzbergs had been put up to framing Reggie by the police, the Krays made them a deal; they knew full well it hadn't been Reggie that Lily had seen – after all, what would he want with thieving when money was rolling in from all his other concerns? – so, according to Charlie,[51] they offered the Hertzbergs £500 to tell the truth in court, which they could collect once Reggie had been freed. Reggie was acquitted; the Hertzbergs never got their money in the end, but by then it was too late, and Reggie was out. Ronnie was acquitted of his charge when he was able to provide eight witnesses, including a private detective, who gave him cast-iron alibis. In May 1961, as they celebrated their joint acquittals in a local pub, Reggie told the press:

---

50 Situated in Southminster, close to the River Blackwater, it is now called Steeple Bay Holiday Park.

51 Charlie Kray & Robin McGibbon; *Me and My Brothers* (London: Grafton 1988).

Some villains in London are trying to put the finger on us. We are the victims of a vendetta. But we've both had very fair trials and are glad we have proved we are going straight.

We admit we've been in trouble, but that was years ago and we served our punishment. Now when anything goes wrong there are people who always try to blame the Kray brothers.[52]

If these were attempts by the police to frame the twins, the Kray brothers had shown that they were more than capable of proving that these were minor irritants that were pretty easy to brush off. Secretly, however, Reggie was shaken when the police first called at Vallance Road to arrest him – not because he feared the police or was worried that he would not be able to cope with the consequences, but because he was worried about what Frances would think. His feelings for the young Miss Shea were running very deep indeed. In fact, in his letters from Wandsworth, sent in late 1960, he had already suggested that he would like to get married as soon as possible. Frances, although not averse to the idea, felt that she was too young, but made the encouraging suggestions that "I want to get married not next year, but the July after"[53] which she felt would give them plenty of time to organise the wedding properly and even get a home built specially for them.

◆

Long-firms, Esmeralda's Barn, protection money from any number of sources – it all made for a very lucrative start to the Swinging Sixties for the brothers Kray. They also managed to find themselves a partnership in another significant club, The Cambridge Rooms on Kingston Bypass. But it wasn't all glamour and rubbing shoulders with the rich, famous and influential. The twins, despite their success, were still very fond of their East End roots and they were still regular patrons, along with the Firm, of various local pubs. They were particularly fond of the Grave Maurice on Whitechapel Road with its little booths that were ideal for small meetings; the Crown and Anchor on Cheshire Street[54] (just behind their house on Vallance Road) was conveniently close to home, as was The Lion on Tapp Street, by

---

52 *Daily Express*, 17 May 1961.
53 Jacky Hyams; *Frances: The Tragic Bride* (London: John Blake 2014).
54 This pub stood on what is now the corner of Chester and Kelsey Streets after the redevelopment of the Cheshire Street area, and was closed down and demolished c.1972.

Bethnal Green station. This pub, which saw much activity, was known as 'Madge's' and later as 'The Widow's' after the landlady Margaret Joseph, whose husband John had died.[55] Another favourite was the Old Horns, a little further afield in Warner Place, off the Hackney Road, which was run by the twins' old boxing friend Teddy Berry.[56]

With their feet firmly in both the West and East End, there remained the allure of starting up a successor to the Double R Club on home territory, and, with money to invest, the Krays opened the Kentucky Club at 106a Mile End Road in late 1961.[57] With all their contacts, famous or otherwise, the Kentucky was an immediate success and would see some of their most memorable nights in the East End. Partly, this was due to their growing interest in charity work, seen by the twins as not just a way of giving to their community, but also as a way of lifting their standing and respect with the straight folk of London. They had already made a point of making public collections for what they called 'the aways', families of those whose husbands or fathers were in prison, or for the newly released convicts who needed to quickly find their feet financially after spells in prison. This, however, relied on donations, usually dropped into a bucket that was passed around, from the assembled members of the Firm, and probably others, on any given night out. Often it was spontaneous, but importantly, it relied on the generosity of others; still, the twins considered that it proved their devotion to good causes. With high profile clubs on their books like the Cambridge Rooms, Esmeralda's Barn and the Kentucky, and with good relations with the Mayor of Bethnal Green, Robert Hare, the Krays could now exercise their charitable instincts with highly publicised displays of generosity that would instil the legend that they gave freely to those in need, a premise still spoken of by some today. In November 1962, they bought £200 worth of tickets for a charity show at the Repton Boxing Club on Cheshire Street for the British Empire Cancer Campaign Appeal, and Ronnie donated four trophies. Some of these affairs attracted more

55 The Lion closed down in 2002 and has since been converted into private flats. The old Truman brewery sign still sits on the side wall and can be seen from trains arriving at Bethnal Green Station.

56 It went through a number of different names in later years, including 'Warners' and 'Jeremiah Bullfrog' before closing in 1997. It is now in use as the Bethnal Green Montessori School.

57 Registered on 11 September 1961; Report by Detective Inspector Leonard Read, undated (1968); CRIM 1/4900 (National Archives).

publicity than others, but their most well-known charity event, which involved the Kentucky, was the result of a brief foray into the movie industry.

In 1962, Joan Littlewood was making a film of the stage play *Sparrers Can't Sing*, originally written by actor Stephen Lewis,[58] and which had previously been performed at the Theatre Royal in Stratford (of which Littlewood was the director) in 1960. The movie version used many of Littlewood's original cast from her Theatre Workshop production, including Barbara Windsor in her first film role, and it was shot on location in Limehouse, Stepney and Stratford. When Littlewood suggested using a real East End club for one scene, Windsor called on Charlie and Reggie Kray, whom she knew from the Double R days (quite intimately in Charlie's case), who allowed the Kentucky to become a film location. The Krays became even more involved when photographer, TV personality and general bon viveur Dan Farson[59] managed to get some locals as extras. As Windsor later remembered:

> And he'd gone down the docks and he'd got all these extras who were effing and blinding and saying they'd like to screw this one and that one on the set. So Reggie got to hear of it and they took them aside - there was quite a fight - because they didn't like all that swearing.[60]

The Kentucky appeared in one of the final scenes of the movie when the lead, James Booth, calls on the club. When he is allowed in, the door opens to reveal two bouncers; it was Firm members 'Big' Pat Connolly and 'Limehouse' Willey making cameo appearances, and it has been said that if you blink, you may miss Reggie Kray sitting at a drumkit in one scene.

It was the premiere of the film on 27 February 1963 which brought the Krays' hospitality into its own. The mayor of Bethnal Green, Robert Hare, had asked them if they could help by selling tickets for the event which was to be held at the ABC Empire Cinema on Mile End Road,[61] almost opposite the Kentucky. Obligingly, they took £500

---

58 Lewis would later become most famous in Britain for his portrayal of 'Blakey' in popular TV sitcom *On the Buses* which ran from 1969 to 1973 and spawned three feature films. He died in August 2015.

59 At that time, Farson (1927-1997) was living in Narrow Street, Limehouse and ran the Waterman's Arms pub on Glenaffric Avenue, Isle of Dogs.

60 Interview with Barbara Windsor; *The Guardian*, 7 December 2001.

61 This is now the popular Genesis Cinema. It was reopened in 1999 with a screening of *Sparrows Can't Sing* with Barbara Windsor as guest of honour.

worth and apparently sold them all. The proceeds were in aid of the Docklands Settlement charity whose patron was Princess Margaret, and this meant that this occasion would therefore be the East End's first Royal Premiere. As it turned out, Princess Margaret could not attend as she was suffering from influenza, but her husband, Anthony Armstrong-Jones, was there, along with stars from the film and other celebrities of the day, including Ronald Frazer, Charlie Drake, Roger Moore and East End singer Queenie Watts. After the event, a large crowd went for further drinks at the Kentucky and later, some even went on to Esmeralda's Barn. All in all it was a tremendous success and helped to seal the Kentucky's reputation as the place to be in the East End. As Reggie fondly recalled two decades later:

> It was on that night, with me and Ron done up like dogs' dinners in our bow ties and dinner jackets, and surrounded by the rich and famous, that I realised that we were well on the way to making it to the top. I felt so powerful that night. I felt like nothing was going to stop us. The good times were back for the Kray twins and, by Christ, we did have some good times and some good laughs at the Kentucky.[62]

One particularly amusing incident involved Ronnie and his unique sense of humour. One of the acts at the Kentucky was 'Tex the Dwarf', a midget in a huge cowboy hat, whom Ronnie brought in to 'liven things up' every once in a while. One night, Ronnie also brought in a donkey and got Tex to sit on it for everybody's amusement. At that point, a bookmaker who owed the twins a considerable amount of money walked in, prompting Ronnie to angrily berate him in front of the assembled guests. The bookmaker beat a hasty retreat, but the vision of London's most feared villain holding a donkey with a dwarf sitting on it whilst he furiously read the riot act was, in Reggie's words, "bloody hilarious."[63]

Real violence was never too far away, however, and it was usually of Ronnie's doing. One evening at the Kentucky, one of the Krays' drinking companions made a throwaway joke at Ronnie's expense, suggesting that he needed to 'go to the country' as he was putting on a bit of weight. When the man went to the toilet, Ronnie followed him in and promptly cut him down the face with a knife, resulting

---

62 Reggie & Ronnie Kray, with Fred Dinenage; *Our Story* (London: Sidgwick and Jackson 1988).

63 Ibid.

in the man acquiring over seventy stitches and the nickname 'tram lines'.[64] One awful incident which took place in March 1962, involving an unnamed and obviously traumatised witness, came to light during enquiries many years after the event. It has never previously been recounted.[65]

The witness was the co-owner (with a man named Reg Power) of Adams Casino Enterprises, based in Fetter Lane in the City of London. In 1961, the Krays had been introduced to the men and had a number of cordial meetings with them, whereupon the subject of protection had been raised. This was just a passing thing until, later that year, the twins, along with 'Big' Pat Connolly, had come right out and demanded £1,000 per week protection money, backed by threats to the unnamed man's family if he did not wish to comply. Eventually, a deal was struck whereby Reg Power would pay the Firm £500, in cash, every week. This arrangement went on week after week throughout the early part of 1962, and the punitive payments began to have a detrimental effect on the fortunes of Adams Casino Enterprises. Reg Power passed away, and, in March, the unnamed man made a payment by banker's draft, rather than cash, an act which apparently stirred the ire of the Firm.

He was abducted and taken to an undisclosed location by two men, Charles Mitchell and Danny Allpress, and subjected to a beating. First, he was deliberately pushed down a flight of stairs. Once recovered and sitting down, the man asked his captors what the matter was, and was told, "You'll find out in a minute." When a third man arrived, all three began knocking the hapless victim around the room before ordering him to strip. Once completely naked, his hands and ankles were bound and he was seated on a hard kitchen chair: it was at this point that Mitchell said, "Banker's drafts, eh? I'll give you banker's drafts – I'm going to teach you a lesson," at which the man perhaps gained a vague insight into the reason for his predicament. Mitchell struck the man around the head, hard enough for him to fall off the chair onto the floor, after which all three men began raining blows on their victim with long pieces of rubber hose. A knife was pushed into his leg near the ankle and twisted so that it ground against bone, and was left hanging out of the wound until it fell out of its own accord.

64 Interview with Albert Donoghue from *The Krays: Lords of the Underworld*; Channel 4 UK, broadcast 23 June 1997.
65 Statement made by anonymous witness at Central Office, New Scotland Yard, 29 May 1968; MEPO 2/11388, ff.1843-1865 (National Archives).

And then, obviously in a traumatised state, the man noticed that the Kray twins were also in the room, watching proceedings.

One of the twins (the man was not sure which) walked over to an electric fire and pulled the flex out of the back of it, exposing the live wires. The man was thrown onto the ground and the unidentified Kray proceeded to electrocute the man's genitalia and anus until he passed out. When he came to, complaining that he'd had enough, the twins told the man what they were after: "You know you've had enough. Do you fully understand what we want? We're taking over your business."

Ultimately, in July 1962, the man signed Adams Casino Enterprises over to John Bryant, a representative of the Krays, after receiving further threats and (on a night when the Firm knew he was out) having his flat in Tottenham Court Road burgled. To say this was demanding money with menaces is an understatement. It has often been claimed by those who knew the twins that they never approached people for protection money, or forced their services on people, and that that those who felt they needed protection, minders, doormen, or any other Kray specialities, could come to them voluntarily. Undoubtedly, many probably did approach the twins of their own volition, but incidents like this, set down in a signed statement by somebody too intimidated to reveal his name, proves that the Krays were more than willing to bully their way into a business venture. The twins would have recourse to similar tactics in the future.

The most infamous incident of this period (because it has been spoken about so often) was when Lenny Hamilton came up against the wrong end of Ronnie's madness. Hamilton had become part of Harry Abrahams' gang of robbers after Abrahams had begun to distance himself from the Krays' activities at the end of the 1950s. One evening in the Regency Club in Stoke Newington,[66] Hamilton was with Abrahams and a number of his gang when an altercation broke out between Hamilton and a man named Bonner Ward: this resulted in Ward attempting to cut Hamilton across the back with a razor in the toilets, failing, and having his nose broken in return. 'Big' Pat Connolly was present and word must have reached the twins soon after. This was problematic: Bonner Ward was the son of veteran London villain Henry 'Buller' Ward, who had been well-respected and feared in the

---

66 This was at 240a Amhurst Road and had opened in 1959. It was run by brothers John and Anthony Barry from 1960 until its closure in 1970.

criminal fraternity from the early 1950s onward. He knew the Krays pretty well and had helped them at various times through the years, but had always stopped short of becoming a true member of the Firm. It was this friendship, which would later turn sour, which led Ronnie Kray to exact revenge on Hamilton, on Ward's behalf.

Hamilton, who at that time was still on good terms with the Krays, was told by Andy Paul, a doorman at Esmeralda's Barn who had been lodging with him, that he was wanted by Ronnie at the club. It was 1.00 a.m., but it was never a good idea to ignore a request from Ronnie, or even to keep him waiting, so Hamilton donned a suit and took a cab to Knightsbridge. On arriving at Esmeralda's Barn, he was directed to the club's small kitchen and found Ronnie there with about eight other men, including 'Limehouse' Willey, David Forland, Billy Exley and Leslie Payne. After telling Hamilton to sit in an armchair by the cooker, Ronnie began mumbling something about the fight at the Regency before calmly telling him that he could leave. Hamilton was perplexed to say the least, but then things took a turn for the worse. What happened next has been recounted many times, mainly by Hamilton in his books and interviews, however, what follows is his original account taken from the official statement he gave the police years later:

> Ronnie Kray was standing in front of the cooker and pointing to the armchair said, "Sit down there Len", which I did.
>
> I looked away to see who else was in the room and as I moved my head back into the original position I saw him holding a cold steel knife sharpener. Instinctively I thought it was a poker because it was glowing red hot for he had just taken it off the gas ring.
>
> Holding it in his hand he slashed it right across my left cheek. I felt a searing pain flash through my head. There was a horrible smell of burning flesh and I thought he was going to kill me.
>
> I jumped up – turned round and faced him. The steel was still glowing red and Ronnie appeared mad. He shouted, "Fucking well hold him you cunt." He kept shouting to Payne, "Hold him! Hold him!" He appeared very frightened but he got behind me and held my arms because Ronnie kept shouting at him.
>
> Ronnie then stared at me – nearly nose to nose, with a mad glare in his eyes. He said, "We don't like anybody using our names."
>
> I could not talk or move because I was too frightened. I would have passed out had it not been through fear. It was fear alone that kept me on my feet.

He then placed the red hot poker again across the bottom of the same cheek touching the bottom lip. There was a smell of burning flesh – a blinding light in my eyes – a terrible stinging pain as though all my face was on fire.

Ronnie Kray then placed the red hot steel right across my head and my hair shrivelled as though I had a centre parting. I had a big scar on my skull for several months afterwards.

Ronnie was enjoying himself – he looked like a nut case. He then kept burning my suit. He placed the red hot steel on both shoulders and burnt holes in it.

The steel began to cool because it was not so hot as when he placed it on my right arm because the material only scorched.

He held the poker in front of my eyes and said, "If you say anything about this out of here you will get both your eyes burnt out next time." He then continued by saying, "He's had enough – fuck off."

I nearly fell down the stairs and I heard somebody laugh. As I got to the taxi I had my hands covering my face.[67]

Hamilton had been so scared, he had wet himself.[68]

I must have looked bad because the driver did not want to take me. He did take me to friends in the East End. I had blisters on my left cheek and on my right shoulder. My coat was burned in several places, and there were singed lines in my hair. My friends gave me yellow ointment to put on my burns. The blisters broke and scabs formed. I did not go out for nearly two weeks. My left eye started to blur so I went to the casualty department of Moorfields Eye Hospital. I was treated there with eye drops. I did not go back. I told the doctor there that I had walked into some hot steel rods in a friend's tubular steel furniture factory. He did not believe me. The scabs did not go for four weeks.[69]

It was a sadistic and utterly premeditated assault, which Hamilton later claimed Ronnie had seemed to enjoy: "He was making all sorts of funny noises. He grunted and groaned as if he was having sex and reaching his final climax."[70]

---

67 Statement by Lenny Hamilton taken at Central Office, New Scotland Yard, 28 February 1968; MEPO 2/11387, ff.684-694 (National Archives).

68 Lenny Hamilton & Craig Cabell; *Getting Away With Murder* (London: John Blake 2006).

69 Hamilton quoted in a Report of a medical examination at 146 Harley Street, London, by Dr. David Paul, 3 July 1968; MEPO 2/11387, ff.1046-9.

70 Lenny Hamilton & Craig Cabell; *Getting Away With Murder* (London: John Blake 2006).

But Lenny Hamilton was of the old school, and with Ronnie's threat lingering in his mind, did not take the matter any further. In fact, he was absolutely terrified. Soon after, George Cornell, who had been friendly with Hamilton from the days when they had worked together at Billingsgate Market, gave Hamilton's wife some money and told her to make sure her husband was looked after; he was followed soon after by Charlie Kray with yet another financial incentive, this time to keep quiet. But for Hamilton, the relationship was well and truly over and he would go on to become one of the Krays' most outspoken critics. Obviously, this horrid incident did not go unnoticed by members of the Abrahams gang either: one of them, Albert Donoghue, infamously spoke out about the assault, with perhaps unexpected consequences.

Albert Donoghue was born in 1935 in Dublin, Ireland, and had moved to the East End with his parents and three sisters when he was one-year-old. Soon after the move, Donoghue's father died; his mother later married a man named Barry with whom she had eight more children and Albert would occasionally use the Barry name, especially later when he had turned to crime and a handy alias was needed to confuse the authorities. He used violence from a young age, grew to be a strong, tall man and, like many others in his circle, went through the Borstal system. In the late 1950s, he worked with a gang robbing banks and payroll vans, as well as working the racecourse betting pitches for Albert Dimes, Billy Hill's lieutenant, just as the twins had done for Jack Spot only a few years earlier. He received his first major prison sentence on 25 February 1958, fifteen months for 'factorybreaking with intent'.[71]

Donoghue's brother-in-law was Billy Donovan, a member of the Kray Firm and one-time doorman at the Double R Club, and over the course of a couple of years the twins would drift in and out of Donoghue's criminal life as a consequence. It was through working alongside the likes of Harry Abrahams and Lenny Hamilton that he got to know about the incident with the latter at Esmeralda's Barn.

Hamilton, however, had not told anybody in the Abrahams gang who had actually burnt him, so when Donoghue spoke out about the incident, he was blissfully unaware that it had been committed by the most dangerous member of what, at that time, was probably the most dangerous criminal organisation in London.

71 CRIM 1/4900 (National Archives).

"If they'd done that to me," he said, "I'd have blown their heads off."[72]

Soon after, on 17 September 1962, Donoghue was given a three-year prison sentence after being found guilty of attempted larceny of £3,000 during a payroll robbery, and was sent to Pentonville. It was whilst he was at 'The 'Ville', that somebody told the Krays what Donoghue had said about Hamilton's torturer; thinking that he was making a threat about them (they did not realise that he was unaware of who was responsible), they kept a mental note of it. Reggie, in particular, was very good at storing up grudges in order to exact retribution a long while after (in contrast to Ronnie, who usually responded immediately). Donoghue's own come-uppance would be a while in coming.

72 Albert Donoghue & Martin Short; *The Enforcer* (London: John Blake 2002).

SEVEN

A DANGEROUS BUSINESS

By 1963, the Kray 'empire' was well on its way to achieving the sort of success that the twins had always dreamed of. They had a loyal Firm to back them in their criminal endeavours, were running clubs in the lucrative West End and, on their own turf, mixing with their heroes and other celebrities, raking in large amounts of money with Leslie Payne's long-firm frauds and, of course, still benefitting from their protection rackets. These rackets usually came in two forms: 'pensions' and 'nipping'. The latter was reserved for small businesses, minor clubs, gambling houses and pubs, where the price of protection may be a few bottles of booze once in a while, or the free use of any number of vehicles from a car dealership. 'Pensions' were a more substantial payment, usually extracted from larger businesses, particularly clubs in the West End. By the early Sixties, the Krays had used their presence in West London to get their foot in the door of local nightclubs that were willing (and able) to fork out large sums of money for their 'services'.

One place that managed to slip away from the Krays' attentions was comedian Peter Cook's satirical Establishment Club in Soho.[1] By the early 1960s, Cook had carved out a niche in British entertainment as one quarter of the 'Beyond the Fringe' team (with Dudley Moore, Alan Bennett and Jonathan Miller), had become a much sought after writer and performer, and had used some of his acquired wealth to help out

1   Opened in October 1961 at 18 Greek Street, London. After setting up a second club in New York in 1963, Cook closed the London premises in 1964.

130

satirical magazine *Private Eye*. This made him a doyen of satirical comedy, something his keen wit and considerable intelligence were perfectly suited for, and the Establishment took the form of a pioneering political cabaret. Cook, in a later interview, remembered when he met Reggie and Ronnie Kray:

> I remember the Kray twins came round just before we were about to open, and they said, "This is a very nice place you've got here, a lot of lighting and a lot of projection equipment and so on, and it would be dreadful, wouldn't it, if the wrong element came in and started smashing the place up? And we're willing to put people on the door to keep those types of element out, because we know these elements and we can keep them out."
>
> I knew perfectly well they were indeed the element that I didn't want to have in, and so I said, "Well thank you very much, that's very kind of you, but the police are just around the corner, so if there's any trouble, I'm sure we'll call them and they'll do their best." Never saw them again.[2]

Not all club owners possessed Cook's unflappable manner, and thus numerous popular venues became part of the Kray setup: as well as West End casinos, they had protection money coming in from places like Le Monde, the Pigalle Restaurant in Piccadilly[3] and the Starlite in Mayfair,[4] all of which paid protection on a sliding scale, the amount payable depending on the clubs' individual turnover. On their own manor, they controlled various small clubs such as the Little Dragon in Whitechapel (an offshoot of the Green Dragon), the nearby Greatorex Club on Greatorex Street, the 20th Century Club on Brick Lane, several spielers and cab firms, as well as car dealerships. They weren't raking in untold wealth from these protection rackets, but it was sufficient to keep the Firm ticking over; meanwhile, Leslie Payne and Freddie Gore's careful business frauds were adding quite significantly to the coffers.

Esmeralda's Barn, however, was already beginning to falter, despite the enthusiasm with which the Krays forced their way into the enterprise, and the healthy income it had once provided. Ronnie's unique sense of how a business should be run was proving problematic,

2   Cook interviewed in *Clive James – Postcard from London*, first broadcast BBC Television (UK), 31 July 1991.
3   196 Piccadilly, W1.
4   Often erroneously spelt 'Starlight', it was at 5 Stratford Place, W1.

and the twins' insistence on maintaining a regular presence in the club (and, of course, bringing their friends and dubious associates with them) was another factor. Admittedly, some of the Barn's well-heeled clientele were somewhat enchanted by the East End villains who now appeared to be sharing the gambling tables with them, as if their incongruous presence brought a sense of danger and excitement which rarely existed in their own privileged world. Freddie Foreman, for one, could see the problems ahead:

> *It was a big mistake because, instead of leaving it alone, keeping away from there and popping their head in every now and then, they took the East End to Knightsbridge... I suppose the Knightsbridge set, they found it amusing to start with, seeing all these scar-faces and pug-uglies roaming around. And they're sitting down with an East End cab driver, and a Lord or Lady somebody or other on the other side, and of course when a few cheques were made out and they were a bit late being honoured, the twins – two or three weeks would go by – they'd be round there putting pickaxes through Rolls Royces and things like that.*[5]

One regular at the Barn's gambling tables who was not looked upon as favourably as some when it came to honouring his debts was David Litvinoff, one of the more bizarre 'characters' in the Kray story.

Born to a poor Jewish family in the East End, like his more well-known half-brother, the writer and poet Emanuel Litvinoff,[6] he showed a keen intelligence and a gift for words. David, however, was also an incorrigible rake and a promiscuous homosexual, with a penchant for impressing anybody who would listen with extravagant stories, and horrifying others with cruel, sometimes scatological humour. On one occasion, when asked to look after a friend's baby, he defecated into the child's potty, just to see the look of horror on the mother's face when, on returning, she believed, just for a moment, that her little child had produced such a colossal stool. As a larger than life figure, he had managed to endear himself as an unofficial court jester to the fashionable Knightsbridge and Chelsea set. His gambling habit was considerable and he had racked up a debt with Esmeralda's

---

5   Interview featured in the TV documentary *The Notorious Kray Twins* (Aubrey Powell Partnership Production 2001).

6   Emanuel Litvinoff (1915-2011) was a poet and writer who was described as one of the great unsung writers of the 20th century. He was also a tireless campaigner for the liberation of the Soviet Jewry from persecution from the 1950s onwards.

Barn totalling more than £3,000, which, naturally, he could not pay. Ronnie Kray was less sympathetic to Litvinoff than he had been with Lucian Freud and demanded the money back, but Litvinoff could not oblige, and therefore offered Ronnie the remaining lease on his plush apartment at 4 Ashburn Place, near Gloucester Road, which he shared with his lover, Robert Buckley, in lieu of payment.[7] Ronnie moved in with the pair, with Litvinoff working as a 'procurer', supplying his new tenant with young men. One legendary incident, involving Litvinoff and an alleged debt, has also been associated with the Krays: around this time, somebody (it has never truly been ascertained who) took a sword to Litvinoff's mouth, cutting gaping wounds into his cheeks which gave him a peculiar smile once they had healed. Some, like journalist Lynn Lewis, have intimated that Ronnie did it as punishment for non-payment of debts,[8] and it is interesting to note that the Krays never denied being responsible for the attack.[9]

The Krays' foothold in the West End had also increased their reputation enough for them to come to the attention of the American Mafia, of whom the twins, particularly Ronnie, had aspired to become the British equivalent. Following the overthrow of Cuban president Fulgencio Batista in 1959, Fidel Castro assumed military and political power and sought to overturn Batista's long-standing Mafia sympathies by pushing the syndicates out of Cuba: in October 1960, Castro nationalised the hotel-casinos and effectively outlawed gambling. Thus the Mafia bosses were looking to expand their interests overseas and had begun to make inroads into the West End of London, investing in the now legal casinos. And so it was that the Krays met Angelo Bruno, the Philadelphia Don (who had known Billy Hill's associate Albert Dimes), Dino Cellini and most importantly, Meyer Lansky.

Lansky had built up a gambling empire second to none in Florida, New Orleans, Cuba, the Bahamas, and most significantly, Las Vegas. Cellini, apart from running his own casinos in Havana, also ran establishments for Lansky in New York, but the two soon realised

7   The address is usually given (erroneously) as Ashburn Gardens, however David Litvinoff's name can be seen in the electoral registers of Ashburn Place at that time.
8   Lewis confidently stated this in the TV documentary *The Notorious Kray Twins* (Aubrey Powell Partnership Production 2001).
9   The incident was portrayed in the 1990 film *The Krays* (Dir. Peter Medak), with Ronnie (Gary Kemp) wielding the sword in what was one of the more excruciatingly unpleasant scenes in the movie.

that Cuba was a no-go area and fled before Castro could begin rounding up the Mob. With the London gambling scene in its infancy, Lansky and his associates could see an endless stream of lucrative possibilities in organised crime over the Atlantic, and having heard of the Krays as major figures in the London underworld (probably via Dimes), tentatively approached them with the proposition that they supply protection for the Mafia-run clubs. For the twins, this was an opportunity not to be missed, with the potential for bringing in large financial rewards as well as cementing relationships with the Mob (with all its prestige and power) as an important bonus. But for the moment, initial introductions aside and tacit agreements in place, this liaison was put on the backburner whilst the Krays forged other international links.

In late 1962, Leslie Payne had been approached by Ernest Shinwell, the son of former defence minister Manny Shinwell,[10] regarding a perfectly legitimate development project to build 3,000 new homes and a shopping centre on a 654-acre site in Enugu, the new capital of Eastern Nigeria. Development had begun apace in Nigeria following its independence from the Commonwealth in 1960 and Payne could immediately see this as a tremendous opportunity, not simply because it promised a tidy profit for doing very little, but because it could also raise the twins' prestige as players on the international stage. The Richardson brothers already had a stake in a diamond mine in South Africa and it was perhaps felt that by involving themselves in the Enugu project, the Krays could redress the balance in an ambitious game of one-upmanship.

Payne and Freddie Gore used the profits of various long-firm companies to inject initial money into the project, named the Great African Safari (or GAS for short), and also sought potential investors from the numerous well-heeled members of West End society with whom they had been rubbing shoulders. One was Robert James Graham Boothby, Baron Boothby of Buchan and Rattray Head, who, as well as being a major and often controversial figure in British politics, would go on to give the Krays, himself, the press and, ultimately, the government a major headache.

Bob Boothby, without a doubt, balanced a tremendous political

---

10 Emanuel Shinwell was Chairman of the Parliamentary Labour Party from 1964-67 and was made Baron Shinwell of Easington in 1970. On his death in 1986, at the age of 101, he was the second longest-lived MP after Theodore Cooke Taylor.

career with a lifestyle that was scandalous by any politician's standards. At the young age of twenty-four he was elected Conservative MP for Aberdeen and Kincardine East, a post he held for twenty-six years until that particular constituency was dissolved in 1950. Subsequently, he was MP for its successor, East Aberdeenshire, until he gave up the seat on his acceptance of a peerage in 1958. In the meantime, he had become Private Secretary to the Chancellor of the Exchequer, Winston Churchill, in 1926 and had once met Hitler, an experience that led him to be a firm opponent of appeasement. During the Second World War, he held the post of Parliamentary Secretary to the Ministry of Food, and it was whilst serving in this post that he experienced his first minor political scandal when, after advocating the distribution of seized Czechoslovakian assets to Czech citizens living in Britain, he failed to declare that he had a financial interest in the policy, a contravention of House of Commons rules. He was forced to resign in 1941 and joined the Royal Air Force. With the advent of television in the 1950s, Boothby carved out a niche as probably the country's first media-savvy politician, appearing on numerous talk shows and earning himself a reputation as a veritable raconteur, although it has to be said that his stories, though entertaining, were not always strictly true. Nonetheless, he was an extremely popular figure in British politics.

But if Boothby's political and public life was eventful, then his private life was positively brimming with the sort of behaviour that tabloid scandals are made of. He once said of himself that, "If I really told the full story of my private life, I think I'd make half a million pounds, but I'd have to spend the rest of my life in Tahiti, and I don't particularly want to do that."[11] He was an inveterate gambler, something he admitted freely to; but what he was less inclined to admit, outside of trusted friends and tolerant members of his own family, was his bisexuality. His cousin, the journalist and broadcaster Ludovic Kennedy, claimed that Boothby once told him, "I don't know if I like the girls better than the boys, or the boys better than the girls!"[12] This, however, did not stop him having a thirty-year affair with Dorothy Macmillan, wife of Harold Macmillan, the one-time Prime Minister.[13] Macmillan was fully

11 Interviewed on *Tonight*, 14 March 1962.
12 Kennedy interviewed in *The Krays: Lords of the Underworld*; Channel 4 UK, broadcast 23 June 1997.
13 Macmillan (1894-1986) was Conservative Prime Minister from 1957 to 1963.

aware of the relationship and refused to divorce his wife, so, in 1935, Boothby married Diana Cavendish, Dorothy's cousin; but it was not to last, and the marriage was dissolved after two years.[14] Officially, he had no children, but Kennedy maintained that Boothby had actually had three children born out of relationships with other men's wives, two with one woman, and one with another.[15] Robert Boothby's serious affections, however, lay in the direction of young men, and it is no surprise that he had been a campaigner for homosexual law reform since 1954.[16]

By 1963, Boothby was in a relationship with Leslie Holt, a young man who would become a catalyst for the elder statesman's introduction to the Krays. Boothby claimed that Holt was introduced to him by the twins after they had rescued a stolen cheque written in Boothby's name at Esmeralda's Barn. Boothby was visited by the "two smooth looking characters" and was extremely grateful, after which he was offered the services "of a nice young chauffeur whom they described as pleasant and fair haired."[17] Holt, however, always maintained that he introduced Ronnie Kray to Boothby at one of the homosexual parties they attended together.

This was apparently no brief 'fling'; observers within British Intelligence noted that "Boothby has been using him [Holt] for a long time. He has given him expensive cars and they have been to the opera together a couple of times, which is rather bold. They are genuinely attached; this is no fly-by-night affair."[18]

Leslie Stanley Holt was born in 1937 to a poor family in Shoreditch. Like many young men from this tough quarter of London, he had fallen into criminality at a young age and had spent plenty of time in Borstal, as well as in the ring as an amateur boxer under the name Johnny Kidd. By the 1960s, the elfin, good-looking young man, who was flamboyantly bisexual, had carved out a career as a cat-burglar and rent-boy and as a 'man about town', Leslie Holt was, on the face of it, the epitome of the Swinging Sixties scene. His targets were the rich and entitled, and it was the wealthy patrons of London club

14 Boothby would later marry Wanda Sanna, a Sardinian woman thirty-three years his junior, in 1967.
15 Matthew Parris & Kevin Maguire; *Great Parliamentary Scandals: Five Centuries of Calumny, Smear and Innuendo* (London: Robson Books 2004).
16 Robert Rhodes James; *Bob Boothby: A Portrait* (London: Hodder & Stoughton 1991).
17 Security Service Report, 24 July 1964; KV 2/4097 (National Archives).
18 Security Service Report 285/27, 15 July 1964; KV 2/4097 (National Archives).

life whose stolen property and sexual favours lined Holt's pockets. Importantly, Holt had once had a flat in Cedra Court, Cazenove Road, in Stoke Newington[19] and by 1963, the handsome Art-Deco apartment building had acquired two new residents: Ronnie and Reggie Kray.

Ronnie was the first of the twins to move in, as early as summer 1962, taking over Flat 8 on the first floor, which was actually leased in Leslie Payne's name. In fact, for many months, the resident porter, Frederick Cox, called Ronnie 'Mr. Payne', even after somebody had told him who his newest resident actually was:[20] one assumes Ronnie must have seen the funny side of it. This was Ronnie's first real taste of independence from the apron strings of Vallance Road (the brief time with David Litvinoff at Ashburn Place notwithstanding), and he decorated the roomy apartment opulently with drapes and other souvenirs brought back from his trips abroad, and a formidable fish tank, and installed a large, four-poster bed in which to entertain his numerous lovers. In the summer of 1963, Reggie began renting the apartment immediately below Ronnie's, Flat 1 on the ground floor, suggesting that the twins could never be too far apart from each other.

Inevitably, Leslie Holt entered into a relationship with Ronnie Kray, and so the lover's triangle that constituted Kray, Holt and Boothby brought the two disparate, seedy worlds together. But there was one other ingredient that added to the dangerous concoction – a relationship between Kray associate 'Mad' Teddy Smith and Labour politician Tom Driberg, a friend of Boothby.

Born in Islington in January 1932, Smith had once been one of Ronnie's lovers and although he fancied himself as a bit of a writer,[21] he was a villain through and through. Since the age of seventeen he had accumulated a total of nine convictions for armed robbery, assaulting a police officer, and most commonly, theft: he had only recently been released from prison after serving a fifteen-month

---

19 Bobby Teale with Clare Campbell: *Bringing Down the Krays* (London: Ebury Publishing 2012).

20 Statement of Frederick Cox, taken at Central Office, New Scotland Yard, 4 June 1968; MEPO 2/11388, ff.1978-1981 (National Archives).

21 Under the name of Ted Smith he later penned a play called 'The Top Bunk' which was accepted by the BBC. The synopsis of the play, which was broadcast on *Thirty-Minute Theatre* in colour on 30 October 1967, said: "Two old lags who share the same cell have got prison life down to a fine art. They are upset when an outsider, a public school type and a first timer, is made to live with them, and bowled over when he reveals a sinister side to his nature, which makes him their natural leader, entitled to the position of prestige – the top bunk."

sentence for stealing a car.[22] Emotionally, he enjoyed the dangerous side of homosexual relationships, with a penchant for rough sex. He could be amusing and friendly, but when drunk, he could change in a heartbeat, showing an aptitude for violence which earned him his nickname.

Tom Driberg appeared to be cut from nearly the same cloth as Bob Boothby. The former *Daily Express* journalist, who had found popularity by penning the weekly 'William Hickey' column for the paper, had become an MP in 1942 and, despite being a staunch Labour politician, became an unlikely wartime supporter of Boothby's former boss, Winston Churchill. In 1957, Driberg became chairman of the Labour party and later, as MP for Barking, was a strong voice in the campaign against nuclear weapons. Like Boothby, he had entered into a marriage (in 1951) which was effectively a sham, and his wife, former Suffolk County councillor Ena Binfield, despite being aware of her husband's sexual preferences, tried to alter his lifestyle, with little success. Although they were ultimately to live apart, they never formally separated and were still legally married on Driberg's death in 1976.

Driberg made no secret of his homosexuality: he was often arrested for sexual acts with men in public places (or 'cottaging') but was always able to pull strings with the authorities to have these misdemeanours covered up. He was also a serious gambler, and it is through this latter activity that he came to discover Esmeralda's Barn, a perfect haunt with its gay club downstairs and casino above, all complemented by the seedy frisson of exposure to a little East End villainy. During his relationship with Teddy Smith, it has been said that Driberg would inform his new lover of any unattended homes that were ripe for burglary, usually the abodes of wealthy and titled members of London society whose jewel boxes, antiques and art collections would prove to be profitable for Smith's own particular line of work.

Like David Litvinoff's flat in Ashburn Place, Ronnie Kray's apartment in Cedra Court would become a communal centre for illicit, homosexual abandon. Ronnie liked company and he liked parties, especially those where he could rub shoulders with celebrity figures. In Flat 8, he could do just that, with the added bonus that he and his noted guests could indulge their sexual proclivities or watch pornographic films (or both) in a semi-chaotic fug of serious drinking.

22 Smith's CRO number was 31336/49; MEPO 2/10680 (National Archives).

Boothby and Driberg availed themselves of Ronnie's hospitality on a number of occasions, and Frederick Cox, the caretaker of Cedra Court, would later note that "on Thursdays and Fridays there would be a lot of male visitors to flat No. 8."[23]

Whilst Ronnie Kray, Leslie Holt and Teddy Smith may well have found these shenanigans ego-boosting, stimulating and profitable, Boothby, Driberg and any number of their unidentified high-profile friends were playing a phenomenally dangerous game.

◆

Early in 1964, Payne made an exploratory trip to Enugu, the first of many, and on his return he spoke to the Krays, telling them that if they were involved they could easily enjoy a considerable slice of all potential profit from the deal. Payne and the ever-present Freddie Gore were made co-directors of the Elukukwu Co. Ltd. along with the Enugu minister for health, Mr. Okwo Uko, a man named Eluwa, who was a nominee of the President, Dr. Michael Okpara, and a civil servant. Each of the Nigerian building contractors hired to do the work were to pay £5,000 each, up front, for the privilege of receiving their first contracts.[24]

Payne's second visit to Enugu was the only time Ronnie and Reggie came along together to get their bearings. The group were treated like kings, were chauffeured around in top-of-the-range cars, and met local dignitaries, including President Okpara. A second visit for Ronnie, this time without Reggie (who felt that one of them had to be back home minding the business), allowed him to fully let his child-like curiosity run amok. He was unfazed by being in a wildly foreign environment, and took advantage of all the perks offered to him. He indulged in local delicacies, was fascinated by the athletic young African boys and furthermore, was curious about the criminal side of Enugu. One thing he asked for was a guided tour of Enugu's prison, which made the British penal system look like a holiday camp. He took numerous tours through the jungle and was fascinated to hear tales about Nigerian organised crime and the violent lengths that local criminals would go to in order to maintain a reign of terror in the state. The jungle was a dangerous place, the prisons were almost barbaric, but at the end of

---

23 Statement of Frederick Cox, taken at Central Office, New Scotland Yard, 4 June 1968; MEPO 2/11388, ff.1978-1981 (National Archives).

24 Leslie Payne; *The Brotherhood* (London: Michael Joseph 1973).

a long day's sightseeing, Ronnie could always retire to the bar of the newly built, luxurious Hotel Presidential.

Soon after Ronnie's grand tour of Enugu, Charlie Kray accompanied Payne to Nigeria. The first payment of £5,000 was due from one of the contractors and it would be Charlie, present in the role of 'tourist', who would be pocketing the money on behalf of the Firm. He promptly took it back to Bethnal Green and divided it up. And so, as money changed hands, plans were drawn up and business was conducted without problems, the Nigerian project seemed to be going according to plan. But what the Krays were not aware of was the increasing interest from Scotland Yard, looking into their domestic activities. Nobody had complained of any specific wrongdoing, but the police were again scrutinising the increasing evidence of the existence of the Kray criminal empire, particularly the protection rackets and long-firm frauds. The twins were spreading themselves pretty thinly across London, and their prominence both east and west of the city made their activities that bit more conspicuous.

Inertia within the Metropolitan Police and an apparent reluctance to tackle the big names in the London underworld had allowed the twins to prosper without too much interference. Yes, they had felt some pressure before, particularly during 1960, but the urge to bring the Krays to book had soon fizzled out. Now, Scotland Yard were beginning to take the matter seriously and the Krays and their associates were under heavy surveillance from the police intelligence service, C11:[25] it was this scrutiny that revealed the comings and goings of the great and the good at Cedra Court. Unwittingly, in addition to collecting intelligence about the Krays' business dealings, the police were also becoming party to a veritable hornets' nest.

In early 1964, the Krays decided to put their continuing acquaintance with Boothby to good use, and Ronnie went to his home at 1 Eaton Square, Mayfair, in an official capacity, in order to discuss the peer's potential investment in the Nigeria project. Boothby would ultimately pass on the opportunity owing to his other commitments, but there were certainly at least two, probably three, meetings between him and Ronnie at Eaton Square, where business was on the agenda. At the second meeting, with Leslie Holt and Teddy Smith

25 C11 branch was part of the Metropolitan Police CID. Its officers were drawn from all branches of the police service, and contributed to inquiries being conducted by other parts of the Metropolitan Police, and by other police forces, through surveillance of those suspected of involvement in major crime.

in attendance, Ronnie had invited photographer Bernard Black along to take photographs: after all, the opportunity of having one's photograph taken with such an eminent and titled man like Boothby was something that Ronnie Kray, with his love of basking in the glow of celebrity, could not pass up. Black took a number of shots, including one of Boothby and Ronnie posing for the camera with drinks and a couple of them sitting on the sofa; in one, they were accompanied by Leslie Holt.[26] It all looked rather business-like and civilised.

It was July when the otherwise secret world of Boothby, Kray and others embroiled in their activities became public. Norman Lucas, a former police officer who had become one of the most well-informed and respected crime journalists of the day, had discovered from one of his regular contacts at Scotland Yard that the investigation into the Krays was building up to such an extent that police action was imminent. Lucas was also informed of the goings-on involving Robert Boothby and Tom Driberg, which had been observed by the C11 surveillance teams. The issue of perceived homosexual activities is said to have emerged after a tip-off from the Krays' North London on/off rivals the Nash brothers. During the early 1960s, when newspapers like the *Daily Mirror* were running their anti-gangland campaigns, the Nashes quickly became fed up with being pestered by the press. One of the brothers apparently told a journalist, "I'll give you a real story if you leave me alone", and promptly went on to speak about an alleged affair between Boothby and Ronnie Kray, having probably got Ronnie and Leslie Holt mixed up.[27] But this was not all. It had also come to light, via Conservative MPs Brigadier Terence Clarke and George Burnaby Drayson, that Boothby and Driberg had been seen importuning young men at White City dog track and keeping company there with known criminals who frequented such places in order to dispose of their ill-gotten monetary gains.[28]

Lucas penned an incendiary article, based on his insider knowledge, for the *Sunday Mirror*, a popular newspaper with a circulation of around five million, which recently, under the auspices of Mirror Group's editorial director Hugh Cudlipp, had been cultivating allegiances with the Labour Party in the run-up to the 1964 general

26 On 20 October 2010, John Pearson's personal copies of these photographs, along with other personal effects relating to the Krays, sold at auction. One photo alone sold for £550 and the whole collection fetched a staggering £21,000.

27 Security Service Report 285/27, 15 July 1964; KV 2/4097 (National Archives).

28 'Secret - Note for the Record', memo; PREM 11/4689, f.50 (National Archives).

election. Cudlipp, however, was on holiday when Lucas submitted the article and it was thus down to Cecil Harmsworth King, Chairman of the International Publishing Corporation (IPC), to decide whether the piece should go out. King gave it the green light, something that Hugh Cudlipp in all likelihood would not have done: less than a year after the devastating Profumo affair,[29] which saw the resignation of Prime Minister, Harold MacMillan, to be replaced by the unprepared Alec Douglas-Home, another major political scandal was the last thing anybody in politics wanted so close to an election. But with Mirror Group's ties to the Labour party, a devastating blow to the flailing Conservative government, ensuring a Labour landslide in the autumn, was a tempting proposition. Cecil King was obviously in the mood to ruffle a few feathers, as well as to cement his place as one of the movers and shakers of British journalism. And so it was that Lucas's article appeared on the front page of the *Sunday Mirror* on 12 July 1964. 'PEER AND A GANGSTER: YARD PROBE', ran the headline:

A top level Scotland Yard investigation into the alleged homosexual relationship between a prominent peer and a leading thug in the London underworld has been ordered by Metropolitan Police Commissioner Sir Joseph Simpson. The peer concerned is a household name and Yard detectives are inquiring into allegations that he has a "relationship" with a man who has criminal convictions and is alleged to be involved in a West End protection racket.[30]

The article made numerous claims, including the involvement of clergymen, the peer and the thug's mutual attendance of supposed Mayfair parties, the private activities of said peer during visits to Brighton with other 'prominent public men', and blackmail. To say that Norman Lucas, with the blessing of Cecil King and the *Sunday Mirror*'s editor, Reginald Payne, had detonated a bomb within the political establishment is putting it mildly.

Boothby was in Vittel, France, with his friend Colin Coote (the editor of the *Daily Telegraph*) when the article hit the newsstands, but he had

29 This was a British political scandal originating from a brief sexual relationship in 1961 between John Profumo, the Secretary of State for War in the Macmillan government, and Christine Keeler, a young would-be model. In March 1963, Profumo denied any involvement to the House of Commons, but after being forced to admit the truth a few weeks later, he resigned. Keeler was also alleged to have been having a relationship with a Soviet naval attaché, creating a potential security risk. Macmillan, who had publicly backed Profumo, resigned soon after.
30 *Sunday Mirror*: 12 July 1964.

picked up a copy at the airport on his return. In a letter he later wrote to qualify his side of the story to the Home Secretary, Henry Brooke, Boothby claimed that "when we saw the headline 'The Peer and the Gangster' we had a lot of fun guessing who the Peer could possibly be. Imagine my surprise when a friend of mine in Fleet Street rang me up after I got back and said that it was me!"[31] This, of course, was utter nonsense: Boothby may have been indiscreet and even foolish, but he wasn't entirely stupid, and he realised immediately who the article was referring to. The claim that a Fleet Street journalist telephoned him is also not true. In fact, Boothby phoned Tom Driberg and begged him to do what he could to get him out of trouble.[32] Driberg had always managed to wriggle out of his own scandals, so it was felt that he might be able to help Boothby with his own predicament, and with Driberg closely linked to the whole situation, he himself would do well to make sure that such help would be forthcoming.

The next day, Bernard Black visited the offices of the Mirror Group and, no doubt in receipt of some undisclosed sum, deposited his photographs of the meeting at Eaton Square. This was yet another potentially disastrous development for Boothby: here, then, was proof that the peer had indeed met the gangster, which was now sitting in the hands of a press organisation that seemed hell-bent on justifying its claims. Fortunately for all concerned, the *Mirror* had not named the men involved in the brewing scandal, but Black's images, if published, would seal Boothby's (and probably the Conservative government's) fate. Black soon had a change of heart and returned to the *Mirror* offices asking for his photographs back, claiming that they weren't really his to sell.[33] The *Mirror* refused to hand them over and consequently, Black served a writ restraining the newspaper from publishing the pictures.[34] Those involved in publishing the initial story were interviewed by the police on 14 July and were told in no uncertain terms that they were obliged to bring any information implicating a person in criminal activities to their attention, but no information was forthcoming.[35]

---

31 Letter from Lord Boothby dated 19 July 1964; PREM 11/4689, f. 32-43 (National Archives).

32 John Pearson; *Notorious* (London: Century 2010).

33 Ibid.

34 Security Service Report 231/286, 17 July 1964; KV 2/4097 (National Archives).

35 *Hansard*; 22 July 1964, p.30.

On 19 July, the *Sunday Mirror* followed its previous big headline with an equally stirring broadside: "THE PICTURE WE MUST NOT PRINT", claiming that it had in its possession a picture "of the highest significance and public concern."[36] Admittedly, it announced that it would not publish the photo in question, claiming that there were copyright issues and that the image itself was the subject of legal proceedings. The revelations however, gave the Mirror Group the opportunity to push its campaign, highlighting what it saw as the intolerable menace of protection rackets across the West End of London. Sir Joseph Simpson, the Commissioner of the Metropolitan Police, in a political move to placate the politicians as much as anything, had issued "a carefully phrased denial" about the Boothby claims to the press, but this did not stop the *Sunday Mirror* investigators hammering home their point about organised crime in London. And it was clear who they were referring to:

> *Behind the lights which shine so brightly in the heart of London's West End, behind the gaiety and the music in the night, there are men who are afraid – and men who make fortunes out of terror. In the past week we have been making inquiries into the "protection" racket which has now become big business.*
>
> *And we have found that two East End thugs are terrorising hundreds of clubs – including some of the top-name nightspots – and are more feared than any gang bosses the underworld has known. The two gang bosses live like millionaires with incomes of more than £2,000 a week from frightened people.[37]*

The article went on to outline just some of the ways these overlords of crime apparently established their authority:

> *One thug produced a water pistol filled with petrol, sprayed the jacket of an owner who refused to pay, then tossed a lighted match at him.*
>
> *Another "client" was knocked unconscious and a car driven over his legs – as a warning of what was to follow.*
>
> *A man who talked too much was given the "mouth widening treatment" – slashed on the mouth with an open razor.*
>
> *A punter who ran away rather than pay a gambling debt was "operated" on and the muscles removed from his calf.*

36 *Sunday Mirror;* 19 July 1964.
37 Ibid.

Where these stories came from is anybody's guess and they do appear to be somewhat over-the-top and theatrical, although it is interesting to note that the 'mouth widening' incident is undoubtedly a reference to what happened to David Litvinoff, strongly suggesting the twins' involvement; perhaps, by association, the other claims, as outlandish as they may seem, might have had a basis in truth. The *Sunday Mirror* was essentially banging its metaphorical fist on the table:

> *This newspaper does not accept that in 1964 the world's greatest city needs to be held to ransom by a gang of evil men. Why cannot the police and the Home Secretary get the evidence to jail these criminals? It is because the people who could give it are too terrified to speak.*[38]

Unbeknown to all, Leslie Holt was on regular speaking terms with a man linked to the press who was in fact an MI5 informer, referred to only as 'Source', who would regularly report back what Holt was saying. The government had no real choice but to act and were quickly assessing the situation. The Home Secretary was by now in regular communication with the Security Service MI5; the spectre of the Profumo affair was still creeping round the halls of Westminster and talk was of another "minor Stephen Ward scandal."[39] Boothby's sexual proclivities were well known in government and his association with individuals like Ronnie and Leslie Holt was no surprise to some in the Security Service:

> *Boothby is a kinky fellow and likes to meet odd people, and Ronnie obviously wants to meet people of good social standing, he having the odd background he's got; and of course, both are queers. Leslie never suggested that there was any villainous association between the two and they are not likely to be linked by a queer attraction to each other: both are hunters (of young men).*[40]

The Home Secretary held a meeting at the House of Commons on 21 July, with the Chief Whip, the Attorney General, the Solicitor General and others in attendance, to sift through what they knew about the matter. They attempted to work out what the motives were behind

---

38 Ibid.
39 Security Service Report 231/286, 17 July 1964; KV 2/4097 (National Archives).
40 Security Service Report 285/27, 15 July 1964; KV 2/4097 (National Archives).

the rumours and the press stories, falling on three possibilities: that it was a campaign to damage the weak Conservative government, to attack the police for what the Mirror newspapers felt was a failure to address the protection racket situation in London, or a general attempt to denigrate the establishment *per se*.[41] Although it was accepted that the police often stepped back from any incidents involving members of government, it was still generally felt that the promoters of the story should be giving up any evidence they had that the Boothby rumours were true, something which had still not happened up to that time.

On 28 July, as the government were racking their brains as to what to do about the explosive situation, the German magazine *Stern* published their own article about the rumours. Unbound by Britain's libel laws, *Stern* printed the names of those involved, although it didn't know which Kray was involved, and confidently likened this potential scandal to the one of the previous year. What follows is the translation of the full article that hit the House of Commons News Desk that day:

London Boulevard Newspapers were the first to discover that Her Majesty's Minister, Mr. John Profumo, was unable to resist the physical allures of Miss Christine Keeler.

But they did not dare mention the erotically unretarded minister by name. Maliciously discreet, the Daily Mirror stated only that "A Minister" had written a love letter to a well known call girl and that the letter was in the newspaper's possession.

This retailing of secrets lasted a few weeks until John Profumo was compelled to admit that it was he who enjoyed the physical favours of the lovely Christine. It was a perfect scandal.

Profumo resigned, the Conservative Government rocked on its heels, the opposition triumphed.

All this is exactly a year old, not completely forgotten, and now, although the preliminary symptoms are different, the same sort of thing is repeating itself in London.

This time, it is the Sunday Mirror that possesses something it dare not print... the photograph of a Lord sitting on a settee with a well known criminal of degenerate tendencies.

And, exactly as at the beginning of the Profumo scandal when the letter remained unprinted and the letter writer remained unnamed,

41 PREM 11/4689, f.33 (National Archives).

the Sunday Mirror has not published the compromising picture nor named those who sit on the settee.

"Der Stern" knows what and who the picture shows. The man on the sofa is none other than the highly respected Lord Robert ("Bobby") Boothby, once Mr. Churchill's Parliamentary Private Secretary and his neighbour on the settee is one of the homosexual twins Ronald and Reginald Kray, who, just now, rank as rulers of London's underworld.

The brothers began their career as boxers but soon turned their punch-up techniques to private use. They are said to command an army of rogues against whom London's police force is powerless. Their most lucrative business is the collection of protection fees from night club proprietors who pay up in hard cash rather than risk savage beatings up and the taking apart piece by piece of their establishments.

Lord Boothby - so hint the London newspapers – not only maintains intimate relations with these notorious criminals. But his position in society helps the gangsters towards more lucrative customers who prefer gambling halls and "other queer amusements."

In addition – so say the exasperated newspapers – police invest-igation of this is being retarded by the Home Office itself with an indication that the 1957 Commission of Inquiry set up by the Home Office itself recommended a judicious handling of adult homosexuals.

According to British press tradition, it can be taken as reasonably certain that there is a hardcore of truth in all this. It can be thus assumed that Lord Boothby – for years a Tory M.P., at one time a candidate for the premiership, raised by the Queen to the Peerage and since then a member of the House of Lords – will soon be the central figure of a scandal that will overshadow the Profumo affair.

Even in England, the country of male friendships, pleasures in perverse practices find even less understanding than Profumo's normal if extramarital, passions...[42]

For all its rather contemptuous looking down on perceived British sexual mores and florid language, the *Stern* article finally brought the central characters of this explosive scandal into the public eye, and something needed to be done quickly. Boothby had already spoken of taking a libel action against Mirror Group newspapers, but this was

42 PREM 11/4689, ff. 6-8 (National Archives).

deemed undesirable as any information upon which the scandal was based would have to be brought out, and, as much of it was essentially true, Boothby wouldn't have stood a chance. Ronnie Kray, a key player in the situation, was indeed involved in the much-discussed protection business, and yet the police had publicly denied that there was any particular problem with it and that organised crime was on the wane.[43] Not only that, the cross-party involvement of Tom Driberg in the whole affair opened yet another can of worms. Boothby was effectively stuck in a rut and almost left high and dry – unable to serve a libel writ on his accusers and now finding himself in a situation where "there was no advice that Members of the Government could give him on this matter."[44] But, for Boothby, a long-standing Conservative, salvation was just around the corner, and from the most unlikely of sources – Harold Wilson, the Labour Leader of the Opposition.

Wilson's sudden arrival in the story had as much to do with Driberg's situation as anything else. Driberg was one of Wilson's most valuable advisors and, with a general election looming that October, the last thing the Leader of the Opposition wanted was for one of his most trusted (albeit badly-behaved) colleagues to be dragged into the mire, potentially bringing Wilson down with him. Enter Arnold Goodman, top advisor to the opposition and a lawyer of considerable reputation.

It was pretty clear that nobody in politics, Conservative, Labour or otherwise, wanted another scandal like the Profumo affair so close to a general election – these things did nobody any favours and there was an obvious consensus that this story had to be buried before the press, champing at the bit to polish this glorious coup off once and for all, could get any more information that would seal Boothby's fate. Arnold Goodman, Wilson's solicitor and a true Labour lawyer, was seen as just the man for the job; he had tremendous presence, partly owing to his girth,[45] and if anybody could sway those who needed to be swayed, it was him. As John Pearson would later write:

> *He had what politicians called 'bottom'. His pronouncements carried weight. Because of this, people trusted him and he had made himself unofficial spokesman for what was known as 'the Great and the Good' throughout the country... if the English Establishment*

43 *Sunday Mirror*, 19 July 1964.
44 Notes of a meeting held at the Home Secretary's room in the House of Commons, 28 July 1964; PREM 11/4689, ff. 11-12 (National Archives).
45 Satirical magazine *Private Eye* called him 'The Blessed Arnold' and 'Two Dinners'.

had a physical presence in the 1960s, it was Arnold Goodman.[46]

Goodman was fully aware of the fact that going down the usual channels of serving a writ for libel on the *Mirror* was not an option, but he had the unenviable task of having not just to save Boothby's skin, as well as that of Driberg and anybody else connected with the story, but also, at the same time, to leave both major political parties free from any metaphorical egg on their faces. There was so much at stake that, suddenly, Ronnie Kray's significance in the whole situation had been reduced considerably.

John Pearson's book *Notorious* gives the most detailed account to date of how the Boothby affair came about and how it was quashed, and yet the exact way that Goodman achieved this goal, in terms of what he said, is not entirely known. One thing that did happen was that Goodman managed to give Hugh Cudlipp, Editor of the *Sunday Mirror*, every good reason why this story should die off. Both the Prime Minister and the Leader of the Opposition wanted the story buried and Cudlipp had the power to make that happen. Whatever was said, the persuasive Goodman received assurances that the story would no longer be pursued and then went back to Boothby, convincing him that the best thing to do was to write a letter to the *Times* flatly denying everything. Using the *Times* as a sounding board was a sensible idea – that venerable newspaper's letter page was still effectively an establishment institution, and any denial Boothby was prepared to have published there would put more weight behind Goodman's plan to convince Hugh Cudlipp that the 'Great and the Good' were desirous of a quick end to it all. It wasn't something that could easily be argued with.

On Friday, 31 July, Robert Boothby wrote the letter that was meant to blow away this scandal once and for all, and to show he meant business, he delivered it to the offices of the *Times* personally.[47] Under the title "THE SUBJECT OF RUMOURS – ALLEGATIONS DENIED", the letter was published the following day:

TO THE EDITOR OF THE TIMES

Sir – On July 17 I returned to London from France and found, to my amazement, that Parliament, Fleet Street and other informed

46 John Pearson; *Notorious* (London: Century 2010).
47 Ibid.

quarters in London were seething with rumours that I have a homosexual relationship with a leading thug in the London underworld involved in a West End protection racket; that I have been to "all male" Mayfair parties with him; that I have been photographed with him in a compromising position on a sofa; that some people who know of these relationships are being blackmailed; and that Scotland Yard have for months been watching meetings between me and the underworld thug, and have investigated all these matters and reported on them to the Commissioner of the Metropolitan Police.

I have, for many years, appeared on radio and television programmes; and for this reason alone, my name might reasonably be described as "a household word", as it has been seen in the Sunday Mirror. On many occasions I have been photographed, at their request, with people who have claimed to be "fans" of mine; and on occasion I was photographed with my full consent, in my flat (which is also my office) with a gentleman who came to see me, accompanied by two friends in order to ask me to take an active part in a business venture which seemed to me to be of interest and importance. After careful consideration I turned down his request on the ground that my existing commitments prevented me from taking on anything more; and my letter of refusal is in his possession.

I have since been told that some years ago the person concerned was convicted of a criminal offence; but I knew then, and know now, nothing of this. So far as I am concerned, anyone is welcome to see or to publish, any photographs that have ever been taken of me.

I am satisfied that the source of all these sinister rumours is the Sunday Mirror and the Daily Mirror. I am not a homosexual. I have not been to a Mayfair party of any kind for more than 20 years. I have met the man who is alleged to be a "king of the underworld" only three times, on business matters; and then by appointment in my flat, at his request, and in the company of other people.

I have never been to a party in Brighton with gangsters – still less clergymen. No one has ever tried to blackmail me. The police say that they have not watched my meetings, or conducted any investigations, or made any report to the Home Secretary connected with me. In short, the whole affair is a tissue of atrocious lies.

I am not by nature thin-skinned; but this sort of thing makes a mockery of any decent kind of life, public or private, in what *is still supposed to be a civilized country. It is, in my submission, intolerable that any man should be put into the cruel dilemma of having to remain silent while such rumours spread, or considerably to increase the circulation of certain newspapers by publicly denying them. If either the Sunday Mirror or the Daily Mirror is in possession of a shred of evidence – documentary or photographic – against me, let them print it and take the consequences. I am sending a copy of this letter to both.*

Your obedient servant
Boothby

House of Lords, July 31[48]

Reading this letter, one can only be exasperated by the fact that this response to a "tissue of atrocious lies" was exactly that. What the *Sunday Mirror* had been suggesting was fundamentally true, and yet in this polemic, Boothby had denied everything to the point where, if he had been made to stand in a court of law and give his side of the story, he would have been committing outright perjury.

The threat of any legitimate libel action would be catastrophic, Goodman convinced IPC, the publishers of the *Mirror* newspapers, if they failed to produce the much-demanded evidence, which at that time they could not. The payout would be phenomenal and the damage to the company and its shareholders in particular was a harrowing prospect. In addition, Boothby and Ronnie Kray had given permission for the *Daily Express* to finally run the photo of the pair of them at Eaton Square. Ronnie was interviewed by the newspaper, describing Boothby as "a man for whom I have a great deal of respect. It is because of this that I wanted to have the picture taken with him."[49] Both Ronnie and Boothby repeated their stories regarding the nature of their business dealings and previous meetings, and the article as a whole strongly suggested they really did not have anything to hide. As well as the photo of the two protagonists on the settee, the *Express* also ran a second photo, taken the previous evening, of Ronnie and Reggie strolling through the wide courtyard of Cedra Court, a photograph that can go on record as being the first iconic image of the twins.

For IPC, there was really no choice but to admit to making a colossal mistake and settle out of court; Boothby was awarded £40,000

48 *The Times*, 1 August 1964.
49 *Daily Express*, 4 August 1964.

damages[50] and was also guaranteed a very public, front page apology by Cecil Harmsworth King, the Chairman of IPC:

> It is my own view, and the policy of this Group, that when a newspaper is wrong, it should state so promptly and without equivocation.
>
> I am satisfied that any imputation of an improper nature against Lord Boothby is completely unjustified. In these circumstances I feel it my duty to sign this unqualified apology to Lord Boothby and to add the personal regret of myself and the directors of IPC that the story appeared.[51]

And so, what could have potentially been the greatest political scandal of 1960s Britain was avoided. The 'Blessed Arnold', as the conduit of the establishment, had ensured that a tight lid had been put on the Boothby affair, and with *Sunday Mirror* journalists being told in no uncertain terms - from the very top - to drop the story forthwith, that lid would remain tightly sealed for decades to come.

As for Ronnie Kray, and the twins themselves, it was yet another fifteen minutes of fame to add to their growing celebrity. Although Ronnie received no monetary compensation, just a written apology, he would certainly benefit from this whole affair. Throughout his association with Boothby – which is not believed to have ever been a sexual one - he had kept all correspondence with him, going back a long time before the scandal broke, in a brown suitcase which was left at Vallance Road. This, for Boothby, would be a veritable Pandora's Box, and ensured that the Krays would have their illustrious acquaintance on-side in the future.

Leslie Holt would be cast aside by Boothby, who offered his young lover a pay-off of £2,000, taken from the IPC damages, after sacking him with a very curt letter. Holt was furious and threatened to blow the story wide open once again, but soon simmered down.[52] This may have been due to the fact that, according to Holt, who had met the 'Source' in passing, that his distinguished former lover had given him another £200 and "had got Ronnie Kray to threaten him that it would not be a good thing for him to do anything or say anything

---

50 The equivalent of just over £500,000 today.

51 *Daily Mirror*, 6 August 1964.

52 Security Service Report 285/36, 11 September 1964; KV 2/4097 (National Archives).

against Boothby."[53] And the double motivation of money and violence had won the necessary silence. Leslie Holt would go on to make the headlines again in 1979 when he died after being administered a lethal dose of anaesthetic prior to a simple foot operation. Dr. Kells, who administered the fatal drug, had been finding likely targets for Holt's cat-burgling skills and was aware that the police were closing in on his little venture. It was suggested that Kells deliberately killed Holt, but he was acquitted of murder.[54]

However, as always with the twins, no matter how successful they were, no matter how easily they slipped out of trouble, there was always a new problem waiting in the wings, and in the autumn of 1964 that problem made its first appearance on the grand stage that was the Kray saga. The ancient Greeks called it 'Nemesis': for the twins, its name was 'Nipper'.

53 Security Service Report 285/38, 16 October 1964; KV 2/4097 (National Archives).
54 Colin Fry; *The Krays: A Violent Business* (London: Random House 2011).

EIGHT

THE UNTOUCHABLES

Before its closure in 1970, Commercial Street Police Station was home to the Criminal Investigation Department of H-division, the Metropolitan Police area concerned with much of the East End of London. The handsome wedge-shaped building certainly had an illustrious past: in 1888, many of its detectives were directly involved in the hunt for Jack the Ripper and some of those men, such as Chief Inspectors Frederick Abberline and Edmund Reid, have since been immortalised as characters in film and television.[1] Walter Dew, the detective who arrested the murderer Dr. Crippen, also served here in his early days in the force. In the summer of 1964, another notable Commercial Street alumnus arrived in the East End following promotion to Detective Inspector and a transfer from D-division's Paddington Green station: Leonard Read.

On 27 July 1964, Read, who had not been at Commercial Street that long, was approached by Area Chief Superintendent Frederick Gerrard with a 'special job'.

"I want you to get a little team together and have a go at the Krays", said Gerrard.[2]

Leonard Ernest Read was born in Nottingham in 1925 into a Methodist family. He had two older sisters and a younger brother;

1 Abberline has been played by actors on numerous occasions, most noticeably by Michael Caine (*Jack the Ripper*, 1988) and Johnny Depp (*From Hell*, 2001). Reid, portrayed by Matthew Macfadyen, appears in the TV series *Ripper Street*.
2 Leonard Read & James Morton; *Nipper Read: The Man Who Nicked the Krays* (London: MacDonald & Co 1991).

however, on the death of his mother in 1929, the children were split up as their father could not cope with raising them, and so they were sent to live with various relatives until such time as Read Snr was in a position to reunite the family. Academically bright, Leonard Read excelled at school and was also keen on sports, particularly boxing, which, alongside policing, would remain his great love. After joining the Grundy Boxing Club, he won his first medal in 1937 and it was around this time that, owing to his small stature and quick reflexes, Read acquired the nickname by which he would become subsequently known to many – 'Nipper'. Despite success at school, Read had to leave full-time education at fourteen, for, despite passing the entrance exams, his father could not afford the books he would have needed to attend Nottingham High School; and so the young 'Nipper' got a job working for Player's in a wholesale tobacconist's warehouse, feeding tobacco leaves into a great machine that would shred them to make them suitable for cigarette production. It was hardly an auspicious start for the future Assistant Chief Constable of the Nottinghamshire Constabulary.

With the inevitable disruption of the Second World War, Read, aged only eighteen, joined the Navy and served for three years before being demobbed in 1946. It was whilst in the Navy, where he reached the rank of Petty Officer and achieved a varied number of sporting accolades, that he began to seriously think about his future:

> ...I was determined that on my demob I wouldn't go back to Player's, amongst all that dirt and tannin. By law my job was still open to me but I had no intention of returning. My life in the Navy had given me freedom. My education had been broadened. I had met a delightful man, Eric Stealey, a well-spoken and intelligent man who had worked as a shipping clerk in the docks in the East End. We had discussed what future we contemplated after the war and he said that on his discharge he was going to join the police. When I asked him why he said it was an outdoor life, with a certain amount of freedom to make decisions and, of course, it was a career with a pension at the end of it. This was something that was always in my mind.[3]

Read joined the Metropolitan Police in February 1947; his original intention had been to join the Nottinghamshire Constabulary, however, with their minimum height requirement of six feet at that

3   Ibid.

time, Read was too short, and so the Met, with its height restriction being four inches less than that of Nottinghamshire, was the next best thing. After passing his training, he was posted to North West London's D-division, which encompassed Regent's Park, Camden, Marylebone and Paddington and, from thereon, 'Nipper' Read's rise through the ranks of the Metropolitan Police was a steady one.

During his time on D-division, Read showed himself to be a resourceful officer who was soon chosen to work in plain-clothes; he would also use disguises as part of his method of gathering intelligence and assisting in arrests. A move to the CID was a logical step, and Read applied, joining in 1948. He was initially reassigned to St John's Wood, a generally affluent district of North West London not far from his old D-division stomping grounds. After transferring to Harlesden, and then back to Paddington, Read found himself back in St John's Wood when he was promoted Detective Sergeant in 1958. More moves followed a promotion to first class Sergeant, first to Chelsea and then back to Paddington before his promotion to Detective Inspector in 1964, at the age of 39, which saw Leonard 'Nipper' Read get his first taste of the East End at Commercial Street.

As a detective, Read was meticulous in his methods and seemingly immune to corruption, a blight which by the 1960s would bedevil the British police force, and do so for several decades to come. When Frederick Gerrard put him on the Kray case in that eventful summer of 1964, he asked Read if he had any problem with the suggestion, to which Read replied with some irritation, "No, of course not. I don't know them."[4] Everyone in the police knew who the Krays were, but by his own admission, Read forcefully announced that he had never had any personal dealings with them, and thus Gerrard understood that this career detective in front of him was not, and would never be, in the Krays' pockets.

Read gathered a bespoke team of ten officers as part of his squad, taken from different divisions, and most of them, having worked with 'Nipper' at some time, had earned his trust and respect. The whole operation was to be coordinated at City Road Police Station. But first, Read realised he had to actually see what he was dealing with, to try to witness a Kray at first hand. His first successful attempt at 'Kray-spotting' took place at the Grave Maurice pub on Whitechapel Road

4   Leonard Read & James Morton; *Nipper Read: The Man Who Nicked the Krays* (London: MacDonald & Co 1991).

where, according to Read's sources, Ronnie Kray was due to meet journalist Michael Barratt.[5] The ever-efficient detective, dressed in shabby East End workman's attire, found himself a position in the bar where he could see most of the room and especially the entrance, and settled down with a pint, a sandwich and a copy of the *Evening News* opened at the racing page. As it was just after 6.00 p.m. on a weekday, Read was the only customer. Soon after, a car pulled up alongside the wide pavement outside the Grave Maurice. Colin 'Duke' Osbourne got out and walked into the pub, looking around and surveying the scene. He checked the toilets and then went back to the car, at which point out stepped Ronnie:

> *For a moment I could not believe what I saw. His hair was smartly cut and gleaming and his gold-rimmed spectacles firmly in place. He was wearing a light camel coat which almost reached his ankles, the belt tied in a casual knot at the waist. For all the world he looked like something out of the Capone era.*[6]

Barratt, arriving not long after, was (despite wearing a neck brace) frisked vigorously before the meeting with Ronnie could commence in one of the pub's many booths.

It was a mark of how Ronnie Kray saw himself, and perhaps how the twins felt they should be perceived at large, that the simple act of meeting somebody in a pub should have been such a performance. Read appreciated how over-the-top it all was, but at last he could see the sort of thing, albeit a quite dramatic display of it, that he was going to be handling. But with the pervasive influence of the Boothby affair having essentially negated the previous police investigations, Read pretty much had to start from scratch, and he discovered pretty quickly that getting useful information out of anybody regarding the Krays' activities was not going to be easy. In his initial enquiries he discovered that nobody was willing to talk: visits to numerous clubs that he believed were being extorted by the twins promised much, but the owners soon clammed up when the moment came to actually admit that they were victims of protection rackets or, in the case of clubs frequented by the homosexual community, blackmail. David

---

5   Barratt later became a television presenter, most notably on the BBC's regional magazine *Nationwide* from 1969-77.

6   Leonard Read & James Morton; *Nipper Read: The Man Who Nicked the Krays* (London: MacDonald & Co 1991).

Litvinoff looked as though he too could be somebody who was willing to impart crucial information, particularly as Read believed that his horrific 'mouth widening' injury was down to the Krays, but again, the enthusiastic Detective Inspector met with the now infamous 'Wall of Silence':

> *Litvinoff said he had no intention of making any written statement or assisting in any prosecution, maintaining that although he had been attacked he could not identify his attackers.*[7]

◆

Ronnie's outward swagger, as witnessed by 'Nipper' Read, perhaps belied the fact that not entirely everything was going well in the Kray camp. Esmeralda's Barn was not doing as well at it once was, partly due to spiralling debts and partly due to mismanagement (often Ronnie's fault). The Enugu project was still meant to be going ahead, but by the autumn of 1964, even that was about to run its course.

Charlie Kray seemed to be the one brother who had more to do with the Great African Safari, the one who, despite having his own business to attend to,[8] had taken a more active involvement in the actual management of the Krays' interest in the project. After all, it was Charlie who collected the first down-payment from one of the contractors and promptly took it back to England to bolster the Firm's coffers. Unfortunately for all concerned, it was that contractor who put a spanner in the works, swiftly marking the demise of GAS and providing evidence, at least to Leslie Payne's mind, of "the Krays' evident unsuitability for any large scale enterprise."[9]

On another trip to Enugu, during a meeting with Payne, Freddie Gore and the project architect, the contractor who had already made his down-payment approached them demanding a further contract for another 500 homes. Payne advised that they wait a while, but the contractor was adamant and insisted he get a further contract or else he would want his initial £5,000 back. Of course, Payne and the Krays didn't have that money any more. A row ensued with Charlie attempting to smooth things over, but even the elder Kray's charms would not satisfy the angry contractor who now began to demand

---

7   Leonard Read & James Morton; *Nipper Read: The Man Who Nicked the Krays* (London: MacDonald & Co 1991).

8   He had set up a theatrical agency in 1963.

9   Leslie Payne; *The Brotherhood* (London: Michael Joseph 1973).

back his £5,000, warning the British contingent that "my cousin is the chief of police."[10] The upshot of the disagreement was that Payne, Gore and the architect, as representatives of GAS (Charlie was still not officially part of it), were arrested and imprisoned, having been charged with being directors of non-existent companies. This was peculiar as the whole project was registered and legitimate; however, the real issue was the £5,000 which had to be repaid: the contractor had pulled certain strings with the Nigerian authorities to get those owing him put away with no promise of immediate release until the money had been returned. Charlie, as would increasingly become his role in the Firm, now had to organise a damage-limitation operation whilst the other three sat festering in a squalid Enugu jail cell. It took a couple of days, but with Charlie impressing upon them the severity of the whole issue, the twins worked hard back in England to secure the required funds from all manner of sources, with Freddie Foreman footing much of the bill.[11] Eventually, the £5,000 was wired to Nigeria. The boys from GAS were freed and immediately flew home to Britain. The 'Great African Safari' was over.

Further compounding their problems, the Krays had by now lost the Kentucky, which had closed down in April 1963 after the drinking and entertainments licences had been refused. Esmeralda's Barn was wound up in September 1964, owing to unwanted interest from the Inland Revenue and crippling liabilities of £4,400.[12] Payne's long-firm frauds were really the only potential source of substantial money that remained, as the London protection rackets continued to drip-feed useful weekly cash into the Kray pockets. But the Enugu project had also managed to soak up a colossal £60,000 of this money, leaving the Krays in a precarious financial state, especially as they always insisted on living beyond their means. Bills were now piling up at the two Cedra Court flats, especially Ronnie's, and final demands for payment of general rates, furniture items, parking tickets and telephone bills were steadily turning into summonses, many made out to Leslie Payne, the legal owner of Flat 8.[13] In the meantime, membership of the Firm had continued to change, and 1964 would see the arrival of

10 Colin Fry & Charlie Kray; *Doing the Business* (London: John Blake 1993).
11 Freddie Foreman; *Freddie Foreman: The Godfather of British Crime* (London: John Blake 2007).
12 Report by Detective Superintendent Leonard Read, undated (1968); CRIM 1/4900 (National Archives).
13 Many of these can be found on record in MEPO 2/10763, ff.6-15 (National Archives).

a number of new and significant members.

That year, John Alexander Barrie, known as Ian Barrie or 'Scotch' Ian, and John Dickson, referred to as 'Scotch' Jack, had arrived from their native Edinburgh hoping to find the good life in London. Dickson, born in 1930, had been a marine who had served on the HMS *Newcastle* during the Korean War and had received three service medals; after leaving the forces in 1955, he had found work as a rigger for the Scottish Gas Board. But he had found the routine dull in comparison with his former life of travel and excitement in the military, and it was as he began to toy with the idea of moving down to London that he met Barrie, who worked at Salveson's Shipping Company in Leith.

Barrie had been born in Bristol in 1937, but the family had moved to Edinburgh when he was a few months old. He had quite a colourful past: he spent a year employed as a seaman with a whaling company in the Antarctic, and from 1958 to 1961 had served in the Royal Scots Greys. It was during this time that Barrie had an accident when his tank caught fire when it was being serviced, resulting in burns on the right side of his face, his ear, and around the right hand and wrist. Several months of treatment followed at Catterick Military Hospital, leaving Barrie with visible scarring,[14] but as Dickson would recall, "this didn't stop women finding him attractive... he looked tough and we got on well together. He could obviously handle himself."[15]

Barrie had also been thinking of moving to London and so the pair took their first steps into the great metropolis together, first taking accommodation in the somewhat seedy King's Cross area, a popular place for first-time Irish and Scottish migrants to settle. It wasn't all straightforward, as on 18 June 1964, Barrie was charged with 'wandering abroad', essentially vagrancy, and was given a conditional discharge for a month.[16] Unimpressed by the general grime of the district they then moved on to Stoke Newington, not a major improvement, but as its once-impressive houses had now been sublet as bedsits (many on easy terms), they were quickly able to find a place to stay in return for working as window cleaners. It was during this time that they heard from a colleague about a card club in Brick Lane in the heart of the East End:

14 Details from Barrie's pre-trial medical report, 26 August 1968; CRIM 1/4927 (National Archives).
15 John Dickson; *Murder Without Conviction* (London: Sidgwick and Jackson 1986).
16 Barrie's CRO No. was 4953/64; MEPO 2/10922 (National Archives).

We could see this was a very old part of London, and it was also very shabby; the streets were narrow and full of cottage-style houses, some of which were hopelessly overcrowded and little more than slums.[17]

The 20th Century Club was situated above a shop and accessible by a narrow staircase from the street door, and was looked after by Billy Kray, the younger brother of the twins' father. In the eyes of these two strangers from Scotland, Billy was a generous and friendly man and they soon began to socialise with him. An encounter with his infamous nephews was, therefore, soon in the offing. This happened at the Grave Maurice one night. Reggie appeared friendly and took the time to talk to Barrie and Dickson before circulating, but Ronnie was less sociable and gave off an aura of control as he sat in his regular chair whilst the various members of the Firm kept a careful eye on the two unfamiliar faces. In fact, Ronnie was unimpressed that Uncle Billy had brought two strangers to the pub without informing him first. Within a few weeks, however, Barrie and Dickson had won the trust of the Krays and Ronnie offered them both the chance to work for the Firm.

The other new addition was Albert Donoghue. In the autumn of 1964 he had been released from prison and, unaware that his comment about Lenny Hamilton's assault by Ronnie at Esmeralda's Barn two years previously had found its way to the Krays, decided to pay them a visit, expecting that, as an ex-con, they would be willing to help him out a little financially. On 15 September, Donoghue went to the Crown and Anchor on Cheshire Street, just round the back of Vallance Road, after hearing the twins would be there. Sure enough, they were, accompanied by about fifteen Kray familiars, including their Uncle Alf, 'Duke' Osbourne, Bobby Ramsey and Billy Maguire. Somebody said, "Here he is!" and then things began to turn strange. Donoghue went to the bar and greeted a few old mates as he did so.

Then they started drifting away. After a bit no one would come near me. So I knew something was up. I looked around but realized I couldn't get away without making a bolt for it, so I decided to stick it out. I noticed that one or two people were passing in and out of the back room, and afterwards I realised they must have been waiting for the artillery. Suddenly there was a bang behind me and

I felt a pain in my left leg. I turned round and saw Reggie Kray with an automatic in his hand and he was pulling the cocking action again.[18]

Reggie, probably believing that this latest patron of their local had come to inflict a little vengeance for the branding of Lenny Hamilton, had taken the initiative and shot Donoghue in the leg, and it looked as if he was about to do it again. Donoghue began to walk towards him but Ronnie, uncharacteristically the diplomat on this occasion, stepped in, took him outside and, after hearing the true reason Donoghue had come, got a couple of the Firm to drop him off in Bow so he could go to the hospital. Donoghue convinced his chaperones that he could deal with his predicament on his own and went home directly to inspect the injury for himself, only to find that it was not something he could take care of.

At about 10.40 p.m., Donoghue limped into the casualty department of St Andrew's Hospital in Devon's Road[19] to have the wound inspected. An X-ray found a foreign body embedded in his left calf, about five inches above his heel, and that it had fractured his fibula.[20] Under anaesthetic, the bullet was removed and Donoghue's leg was set in plaster before he was admitted to the hospital ward to recover. The bullet, according to the police Scientific Officer who examined it, was "a 32 automatic round, fired, probably in an automatic pistol, through a barrel with six right-hand grooves."[21]

Donoghue was wise enough to cover his tracks and when he gave his statement regarding the incident he claimed he had been drinking in the Black Swan pub on Bow Road[22] that night and that on his way home, on the corner of Bow Common Lane and Devon's Road, he was shot in the leg by a passing driver. He claimed not to know who had done it and went so far as to say, "even if I did know or get to know, I

18 Albert Donoghue & Martin Short; *The Enforcer* (London: John Blake 2002).

19 The hospital was opened in 1871 as the Poplar and Stepney Sick Asylum and changed its name to St Andrew's in 1920. It closed down in 2006 and was demolished a few years later to make way for a modern housing development.

20 Statement by Dr. V. C. Vyas, 28 September 1968; MEPO 2/11404, ff. 1682-3 (National Archives).

21 Statement by Michael Isaacs, 20 November 1964; MEPO 2/11404, f. 1685 (National Archives).

22 Situated almost opposite the former Double R Club, the original pub was destroyed in a Zeppelin raid in September 1916, resulting in the deaths of five members of the landlord's family. Rebuilt in 1920, it was subsequently demolished c.1970 during the widening of Bow Road.

would not tell you."[23] On 3 October he discharged himself, against all advice. The landlord of the Crown and Anchor was interviewed by the police and, obviously understanding what was expected of him by the Krays, denied all knowledge of any trouble involving guns in his pub in seven years as the licensee.[24] It was the staunch way in which Donoghue dealt with his situation that obviously impressed the Krays and therefore, like his brother-in-law Billy Donovan and a number of others before him, this supposed 'loyalty' and understanding of the criminal code resulted in a job offer with the Firm.

Ultimately, Barrie would become Ronnie's right-hand man and Dickson would become his driver; Donoghue would become known as 'Reggie's man'[25] and be responsible for collecting the weekly 'pensions', the protection money from various clubs across London.

◆

Soon after these new men were absorbed into the Firm, word went round that money was now in short supply and that there were "too many people doing nothing, or getting money and not declaring it to the rest of the Firm."[26] The decline of a few major business concerns, and the Enugu fiasco particularly, had bitten deep and so it had been decided that a little extra effort was required by all to reinforce the standing, and thus the financial situation, of the Kray empire.

One of the first targets in this new initiative was the Glenrae Hotel at 380 Seven Sisters Road in the Finsbury Park area of North London. Since 1959 it had been run by Phoebe Woods and her common-law husband Edward Lavender (who was known to all as Woods, strangely enough) and after several major renovations and alterations, the Glenrae Club also opened on the premises in 1963. In September 1964, the usually quiet and respectable club was witness to some trouble in the bar when a number of men, unknown to the proprietors, began fighting, ultimately setting about Mrs. Woods's son, who was injured in the attack. Windows were broken and Mrs. Woods herself was slightly injured when a table was thrown at her by one of the unknown troublemakers. The reason for the fracas was

23 Statement by Albert Donoghue, 15 September 1964; MEPO 2/11404, f. 1681 (National Archives).

24 Statement by George Williams, 10 September 1968; MEPO 2/11404, f. 1686 (National Archives).

25 Albert Donoghue & Martin Short; *The Enforcer* (London: John Blake 2002).

26 John Dickson; *Murder Without Conviction* (London: Sidgwick and Jackson 1986).

never ascertained, but Mr. and Mrs. Woods were in such shock that they closed the club down the following night.

Three weeks later a group of three men, brandishing knives, called at the hotel demanding that the club be reopened. Mr. and Mrs. Woods stalled them by saying they would think it over, just to placate the intruders, but instead went to Highbury Vale Police Station the following day to report what was now happening. That night, a man named Fred Mizen called in, again asking for the club to be reopened and saying that if it did not happen, he would "blow the place up."[27] Edward Woods tried to reason with him, only to be knocked down and beaten by Mizen, who, thankfully, was eventually detained by the owners' son, and arrested when the police arrived.

This appeared to be an uncharacteristic spiral of violence for the Glenrae, but the probable reasons for it would soon become apparent. Phoebe Woods, after some pleading by the former regulars at the Glenrae, had decided to reopen the club on 11 December 1964. The potman, Joe Tullen, had met a man who offered to do the catering for the club when it reopened: it was Sam Lederman. In short, terms were agreed and in light of previous incidents, Lederman also offered "a barman who could look after himself and stop any trouble."[28] The barman turned out to be Billy Exley and, before Mr. and Mrs. Woods knew it, Bobby Ramsey had also been installed as a doorman. Joining the dots, it was, to all intents and purposes, a carefully orchestrated takeover job by the Krays, who now had yet another venue to add to their portfolio of unofficially acquired business premises.

Within a week of the club reopening, Phoebe Woods received a call from Ronnie Kray, whom she was familiar with from the pubs around the East End, asking if she would accommodate him, Reggie and another individual at the hotel, to which she agreed. Ronnie and Reggie took rooms 1 and 2 and, after a week, Ronnie asked if he could defer payment of the bill (which amounted to £46 0s 6d for drinks and £88 1s 0d for board) until after Christmas, an irregular request to which Mrs. Woods again agreed. Gradually, the clientele of the Glenrae began to change, becoming a haunt of the twins, the Firm and their boxing and criminal friends, and thus the whole establishment

---

27 Statement of Edward Lavender/Woods, made at Highbury Vale Police Station, 20 September 1964; MEPO 2/10763 f.38 (National Archives).

28 Statement by Phoebe Woods made at City Road Police Station, 7 January 1965; MEPO 2/10763 f.33 (National Archives).

was now unwittingly under the influence and protection of the Krays and also being 'nipped' into the bargain.

Simultaneously, the Krays were making themselves busy in the West End again. This time the action settled around a small nightclub at 16 Gerrard Street, Soho, called the Hideaway, which was owned on a 50/50 basis by restaurateur Gilbert France (who had part owned it with Frankie Fraser when it was known as the Bon Soir) and Hew McCowan, and it was around the latter man that the next major incident in the Kray story would revolve.

McCowan, as the son of Sir David James Cargill McCowan, Baronet of Dalwhat, was born into wealth and privilege, with a considerable trust fund available to him, and on his father's death in 1965 he would assume the position of 3rd Baronet. He was also a practising homosexual and had acquired convictions for sodomy in July 1953 and gross indecency in November 1955, as well as two other convictions for breaking the terms of probation and driving without a licence with intent to deceive.[29] It is a sign of those times that 'Nipper' Read, in a report on the case that was soon to transpire, felt it necessary to state the following with regards to McCowan's sexuality in relation to his potential reliability:

> ...it is fair to point out that he is not a particularly noticeable homosexual type in that he does not dress in a flamboyant fashion nor does he adopt exaggerated female gestures...[30]

His flat in Great Cumberland Place was an unusual affair, filled with slot machines, and guests would be given a bag of half-crowns to play on them. McCowan would pick up young men and take them home, but the company he kept was not always salubrious and many of these casual acquaintances would steal from the flat. When this happened, McCowan would gladly report back to the police and the boys would ultimately be arrested, making McCowan as good as a police informer.[31]

The story of McCowan and the Krays had begun in July 1964 when Leslie Payne and John Francis, a friend of the Firm who had a number

29 McCowan's CRO No. was 31158/53; MEPO 2/10763 (National Archives).
30 Report by Detective Inspector Leonard Read, 7 January 1965; MEPO 2/10763 (National Archives).
31 Leonard Read & James Morton; *Nipper Read: The Man Who Nicked the Krays* (London: MacDonald & Co. 1991).

of criminal convictions for robbery and assault,[32] visited McCowan unannounced, claiming to be mutual friends with a man named 'Bob Gerald'.[33] The purpose was to interest McCowan in investing in the Enugu project, as had been done with Lord Boothby, promising that, with £250,000 investment, a profit of £3,000,000 could be made in three years. McCowan suggested that any material on the project be forwarded to his solicitors, which was done, but the solicitors, M.A. Jacobs and Sons, advised McCowan to have nothing to do with it. Over time, Francis would occasionally visit McCowan at his flat in Great Cumberland Place and on one occasion, accompanied by one of the twins, McCowan mentioned the club he was about to open which would become the Hideaway. The interest of his guests was aroused.

> *Mr. Franz [sic] said he would like to see the premises and I took him along and showed him. He gave me to understand that with the backing of Ronnie and Reggie Kray and the people they knew, we could make the club an enormous success. I had no idea at the time who the Krays were, nor was I aware of their reputation.*[34]

Francis, who was essentially the Krays' mouthpiece in all this, suggested that the twins could supply the capital and even prominent guests they claimed to know, such as Nat King Cole, Frank Sinatra and others, to make the club a success. A meeting was arranged that November with McCowan, who was accompanied by his friend and financial advisor Sidney Vaughan, at the Grave Maurice, which was rapidly becoming the Firm's pub of choice when it came to important business, and it was here that the subject of protection was first mentioned. The Krays wanted to book a table for the Hideaway's opening night and Francis suggested that McCowan may like to have a couple of men on the door. Reggie then began to push forward, saying, "Well, [when] we go into business with people we provide protection but of course we need some financial incentive."[35] When McCowan exclaimed that such arrangements may not be financially in his best interest, Reggie suggested supplying protection in return for a share of the profit; 25% for the Krays, 25% for McCowan and the remaining

32 Francis's CRO No. was 2200/53; MEPO 2/10763 (National Archives).

33 This was actually Robert Gould who would later be involved in the twins' racket of selling stolen Bonds.

34 Statement by Hew McCowan taken at City Road Police Station, 6 January 1965; MEPO 2/10763, ff. 1-11 (National Archives).

35 Ibid.

50% to remain with co-partner Gilbert France. McCowan politely said such arrangements were not for him and the discussion ended amicably with more drinks at a private house in the East End.

Further meetings took place that month. On one occasion, Ronnie offered Vaughan the tenancy on a flat owned by Payne (which was probably Flat 8, Cedra Court) and another time, during another meeting at the Grave Maurice, the twins had increased their demands to taking 50% of the proceeds of the Hideaway in exchange for their services. The meeting became rather heated, as McCowan flatly declared the proposition as totally unreasonable and Vaughan said, "You're a cunt," to Ronnie because he was so disgusted by the way he had made the demand.[36] True to form, it was Reggie who calmed things down in this instance – Vaughan's direct insult toward Ronnie could have been disastrous for his physical well-being.

The Hideaway opened on Saturday 16 December 1964, but the Krays' table reservation remained empty, and an anonymous phone call was received to cancel the booking during the evening. The following Monday, at around 2.30 a.m., 'Mad' Teddy Smith arrived at the Hideaway, obviously the worse for drink, and began to cause trouble. McCowan had had a previous encounter with Smith a while before at the Cambridge Rooms on the Kingston Bypass, which Smith was looking after for the twins at the time. There had been a disturbance and Smith, half drunk, had thrown McCowan and his party out of the club. For this reason, McCowan was quick to recognise Smith, who, owing to his drunken state, was originally refused entry to the Hideaway. Ten minutes later Smith returned and just before he was ejected from the club again found McCowan and shouted at him, "I'll be back. You know who I am, McCowan. I'll get you."[37] In his drunken, aggressive state, Smith also broke two neon signs behind the bar, causing approximately £5 worth of damage, before he was thrown out onto the street.[38]

It was a while before McCowan or Vaughan met either of the twins again. By the New Year, 1965, the Hideaway had temporarily closed its doors pending a legal wrangle between McCowan and France and this matter was brought up when McCowan and Vaughan met the

36 Statement by Sidney Vaughan taken at City Road Police Station, 7 January 1965; MEPO 2/10763, ff. 12-21 (National Archives).

37 Ibid.

38 Report by PC Currant, 21 December 1964; MEPO 2/10763, f.42 (National Archives).

twins at the Glenrae Club. Reggie conveniently brought up the subject of 'trouble' and McCowan, who had already realised that the source of that trouble was a Kray associate, brought up the Smith incident. After assuring McCowan, quite falsely, that Smith was a *former* employee of theirs, Reggie's next response was perhaps predictable:

> *You see the sort of trouble we can save you. If you had our man on the door, Smith would run a mile. We know everyone in town and they know us. If four of them had come in and smashed the place up you wouldn't have liked it. Anyway, now you're open we would like you to sign an agreement for us to protect you and we would do that for 20% of the takings.*[39]

McCowan was certainly not happy with the way things were going, but agreed to meet the twins again on Wednesday 6 January 1965. But now the penny had well and truly dropped:

> *I now realise of course that this was an out and out protection rack [sic] and an endeavour to extort money from me on the threat to smash my place up if I did not agree to pay.*[40]

Before meeting the Krays, McCowan bit the bullet and went to the police.

Detective Inspector 'Nipper' Read felt there was enough meat to McCowan's story to instigate an immediate arrest and, that evening, 6 January, he took up position opposite the Glenrae Hotel with Detective Superintendent Gerrard and watched as McCowan arrived in a white sports car. After a while, McCowan left the hotel and met the two officers round the corner. Then, at 9.15 p.m., Read, Gerrard and Detective Sergeant Hall entered the Glenrae Club and saw Ronnie and Reggie at the bar with a number of others, including Charlie, with Billy Exley serving the drinks. Gerrard took the twins aside and promptly arrested them for demanding money with menaces. Reggie wanted to say goodnight to his girl (presumably Frances), but was refused, at which he shouted over to Charlie to get him a brief.

In the police car outside, Read sat with the twins on the back seat and had a brief conversation.

"Who's nicked us, Mr. Read?" asked Ronnie.

39 Statement by Hew McCowan taken at City Road Police Station, 6 January 1965; MEPO 2/10763, ff. 1-11 (National Archives).
40 Ibid.

"You've just been told – Mr. Gerrard," Read replied.

"Yes, but I mean who's it down to? Somebody must have put the finger on us. We haven't been out blacking people you know."

"What's this man got the needle to us for? This is definitely not our game," interjected Reggie.[41]

At Highbury Vale Police Station, the twins were searched and Ronnie's problems increased when he was found to have a sheath knife in his hip pocket. When asked about it, his reply was typically casual: "It's just one of those things. That will be a bit more aggravation I suppose... I just have it, you know – it's nothing."[42]

After being taken to City Road Police Station, the Kray twins were formally charged with demanding money with menaces. Appearing at Old Street Magistrates on 7 January, they were held on remand for eight days and their application for bail was refused; the magistrate, Mr. Neil McElligott, commented that

> I am satisfied, so far as I can be at this stage, that there are other persons at large, who are in a position to interfere with witnesses and impede the investigations and would perhaps be in a better position to, were you at large.[43]

That evening, at about 9.30 p.m., Read received a telephone call from Johnny Francis. He knew he was wanted but refused to see Read personally, stating

> I don't want to walk in and get nicked. I don't mind getting nicked for something that's going to get me about 12 months, but if you're putting me with the Krays I must get a right lagging because of the people I am associated with.[44]

Francis begged for a few days grace, citing that he had a family to consider and that he had letters to write to various authorities, including the Council for Civil Liberties, but Read insisted he come to see him. Francis knew that an arrest would be the result if he did, and unable to get an assurance that he would not be tied in with the menaces charge, hung up. Johnny Francis was never caught and

---

41 Report by Detective Inspector Leonard Read, 19 January 1965; MEPO 2/10763, ff.26-30 (National Archives).
42 Ibid.
43 *Daily Mirror*, 8 January 1965.
44 Report by Detective Inspector Leonard Read, 19 January 1965; MEPO 2/10763, ff.28-29 (National Archives).

according to Read years later, the police believed that he had gone to Torremolinos in Spain with a view to moving on to Mexico.[45] In fact, he went to America and became singer Nat King Cole's chauffeur, before working as driver for Angelo Bruno, a liaison which would allow him to be instrumental in the Krays' later dealings with the Mafia.[46]

The McCowan case had come as a little godsend for 'Nipper' Read and his team, just when all avenues of investigation had appeared to hit the now-established 'Wall of Silence', that tacitly understood threat of retribution from the Krays and their Firm against anybody who dare speak out. Due to this, Hew McCowan, as chief prosecution witness, would remain anonymous whilst the twins were on remand, despite applications by the Krays to have his name made public in the resulting press coverage.

Teddy Smith was arrested on 14 January and cautioned by Read. As would be expected, Smith denied all involvement with the Krays until Read reminded him that at one time he had lived with Ronnie at Cedra Court. He did admit one thing, however:

> *The only time I get naughty is when I've had a few drinks, and the next morning I don't remember. I did a club up the other week in Gerrard Street – I think it was the Hideaway. Two fellows took me home afterwards in a cab. It was only a drunken brawl. I got the worst of it. I never remember these things the next morning.*[47]

Having heard enough, Gerrard charged Smith with demanding money with menaces.

With the Krays and Smith in detention, the police searched the Glenrae Club and the flats at Cedra Court for any incriminating evidence. At the latter, they certainly uncovered enough unpaid bills and final demands to suggest that the twins were not always rolling in money. They also found innumerable letters from various individuals, some of whom could not be identified. Naturally, there was correspondence from various members of the Firm and other close associates: Tommy Welch, Mickey Fawcett, Bill Ackerman, Leslie Payne, Freddie Bird, 'Duke' Osbourne, Johnny Davis, 'Limehouse'

45 Leonard Read & James Morton; *Nipper Read: The Man Who Nicked the Krays* (London: MacDonald & Co. 1991).

46 Douglas Thompson; *Shadowland: How the Mafia Bet Britain in a Global Gamble* (Mainstream Publishing 2011).

47 Report by Detective Inspector Leonard Read, 19 January 1965; MEPO 2/10763, f.30 (National Archives).

Willey, Billy Exley, 'Nobby' Clarke, Frank Mitchell, the Nash Brothers, Dr. Blasker and Freddie Foreman, to name just a few of those in regular contact with the twins. But interestingly, the number of celebrities represented was astonishing, showing how much the Krays, two simple East End boys who had chosen the path of villainy, had ingratiated themselves into the world of 'the stars' during their club-owning days. There were many familiar names, as well as their contact details: singers Lennie Peters, Billy Daniels and Lita Roza; composer Lionel Bart, actors Barbara Windsor and Ronald Frazer, boxers Terry Spinks, Kid Lewis and Sonny Liston; the artist Francis Bacon appeared in one address book (he was an occasional visitor to Esmeralda's Barn with his friend Lucian Freud), as did Tom Driberg; and, most impressive of all, Judy Garland.[48]

The visitors' book and members' list of the Glenrae Club certainly showed that the Krays were taking over; guests were signed in by club members, and from the entries over the period of 21 December 1964 to 6 January 1965, the membership of the club reads as a veritable who's who of the Kray circle; Ronnie and Reggie, Charlie, Dave Simmonds, 'Limehouse' Willey, Ian Barrie, Johnny Davis, Bill Ackerman, Billy Exley, Bobby Ramsey, Harry Hopwood, Sammy Lederman, Billy Donovan, John Dickson and Harry 'Jew Boy' Cope. It seems that wherever the Krays went, everybody went.

Ronnie, Reggie and Smith were committed for trial on 1 February 1965, after being refused bail for a second time. It was because of this persistent refusal to grant bail that an old friend attempted to bring the situation to a wider audience: Lord Boothby, perhaps more than aware of Ronnie's little briefcase of incriminating papers, made it known that he was going to bring the matter up during a House of Lords debate. It is very likely that he was asked to do this by the twins, and although he would have known full well that such a matter would be inappropriate for such a forum, he felt compelled to give it a try, for his own security as much as anything. And again, in a statement to the press, Boothby did something that he had become rather good at doing as far as the twins were concerned: he lied.

> *I have not been in touch with the two brothers since last July and hold no brief for them. They did not ask me to put the question. It is simply that I am opposed to a legal situation which permits*

---

48 MEPO 2/10763, ff.8-17 (National Archives).

the Kray twins to be held in custody for nearly five weeks without trial.[49]

On 11 February, Boothby executed his futile gesture. The impropriety of what he was doing was quickly seized on by the House, as can be seen from the somewhat comical transcript of the debate:

> **Boothby:** *My Lords, I beg leave to ask the Question which stands in my name on the Order Paper.*
>
> *To ask Her Majesty's Government whether it is their intention to keep the Kray Brothers in prison for an indefinite period without trial.*
>
> **The Parliamentary Undersecretary of State, Home Office (Lord Stonham):** *My Lords, I understand that a magistrates' court has committed these men in custody for trial at the current session of the Central Criminal Court. Under Paragraph 12 of Schedule 1 to the Administration of Justice Act, 1964, the trial must begin not later than February 28 unless the court otherwise orders. This is not a matter in regard to which my right honourable friend has any responsibility.*
>
> **Boothby:** *My Lords, I would only say, in response to that answer, that I hold no brief at all for the Kray brothers, one of whom I have never met and the other of whom I have met on only two occasions in my life, last July. But I am on the record as having fought continuously—*
>
> **Several Noble Lords:** *Order, order!*
>
> **Boothby:** *Why "order"? I am simply saying that I have fought against imprisonment—*
>
> **Several Noble Lords:** *Ask a question.*
>
> BOOTHBY: *I am going to ask the Lord Chancellor a question, because I am not interested in the activities of the Home Office, which have been characteristic in this case and have done infinite damage to the reputation of this country—*
>
> **Several Noble Lords:** *Order, order!*
>
> **Boothby:** *My Lords, I am going to ask the Lord Chancellor a direct question. It is this: will he take a sharp and a hard look at our system in Scotland, where the procurators fiscal act under the directions of the Lord Advocate and where this kind of situation could not possibly arise?*

49 *Daily Express*, 10 February 1965.

Viscount Dilhorne: My Lords, before the Lord Chancellor answers that question, may I ask the Leader of the House whether it is in accordance with the customs of this House to table a question on a matter in respect of which the Government have no responsibilities at all, as has been stated, and which, according to today's Press, still remains sub judice?

Lord Rea: My Lords, may I ask the Leader of the House whether he would agree that this is a leading question, is not in accordance with the tradition of this House, and is therefore to be regretted?

The Lord Privy Seal (The Earl of Longford): My Lords, I am sorry I was detained and was not here at the beginning of this part of Question Time. If I may give a direct answer first to the noble Viscount, Lord Dilhorne, I am informed that it is the responsibility of the Peer who asks the question. The Table try to give advice but have no authority from the House to censor questions. That is the official answer. Therefore, it rests with the Peer to ask the question, and it rests with the Government whether they choose to reply to it.

Lord Conesford: My Lords, are all the Ministers aware that those who care most about human freedom have no desire whatever that the executive Government should interfere with the Judiciary in the administration of criminal justice?

The Earl of Longford: I certainly agree with the noble Lord.

Lord Boothby: My Lords, if this kind of question is not allowed to be put on this kind of occasion in one or other House of Parliament, then we might as well pack up.

Several Noble Lords: Order, order!

The Earl of Longford: My Lords, I think the noble Lord will regret that intervention when he reads it in cold blood.[50]

The trial took place at No. 2 Court of the Old Bailey, presided over by Judge Carl Aarvold. Ronnie was defended by Peter Crowder QC, with Reggie represented by Paul Wrightson QC[51] and Smith by Kenneth Richardson. During the trial, on 8 March, one jury member had to be removed from his position for expressing views about the case, and proceedings continued with eleven jurors.[52] On 16 March, Peter

---

50 *Hansard*; House of Lords Debates; 11 February 1965, Vol 263, cc271-3.

51 It was Wrightson who had been on the prosecution during Reggie's trial for demanding money with menaces back in 1959 and Reggie had been impressed by him enough to have him on his side on this occasion.

52 *Daily Express*, 10 March 1965.

Byrne, who was giving evidence for Reggie, admitted that he had been threatened by Hew McCowan and consequently attacked by several men at his home. The scrutiny applied to Byrne, a postcard seller, dragged out the fact that he had been convicted at Oxford Assizes in January 1962 for "attempting to get money from a probation officer at Oxford by making allegations accusing the officer of homosexual offences."[53] Such information about Byrne would point him out to any jury as an unreliable witness. In fact, later, Byrne would admit that his claims against McCowan were bogus.[54]

Strangely, Sidney Vaughan claimed that McCowan had hired somebody to threaten him too, worried that Vaughan would turn against him in the case. The matter of alleged tickets for a flight to Dublin for Vaughan and his family, procured in order to make sure Vaughan could not attend the trial as a witness, were discussed in court and much of this kind of muck-raking about the apparent double-life of Hew Cargill McCowan was doing the chief prosecution witness no favours at all.[55] Peter Crowder QC, on the last day of the case, alluded to McCowan's irregular behaviour by stating that he was "a most abnormal person" and "perhaps a bit mental."[56] Crowder made it quite clear to the jury in his summing up that the Krays and Smith were little more than victims of a frame-up by McCowan, who, it was revealed, had at one time boasted to Vaughan that he was "working with the police to get the Krays."[57]

The trial ended on 18 March. In his summing up, Judge Aarvold stated that "the case had its unpleasant details of homosexuality, people being put under pressure, the pressure of violence, and the so-called protection of clubs." He also singled out McCowan for consideration, saying "He is a man with homosexual tendencies, you may well think. Does that make him a man who cannot be believed or not?"[58] It appeared that a lot hinged on the discrediting of McCowan to bolster the Krays' cause.

The jury, apparently "looking tired and strained",[59] obviously struggled with what was a rather messy case. After deliberating for

53 *Daily Mirror*, 17 March 1965.
54 Leslie Payne; *The Brotherhood* (London: Michael Joseph 1973).
55 *Guardian*, 13 March 1965.
56 *Guardian*, 18 March 1965.
57 *Daily Mirror*, 17 March 1965.
58 *Daily Mirror*, 19 March 1965.
59 Ibid.

over three and a half hours, a unanimous decision was unforthcoming. A further fifteen minutes did not turn up the required verdict either way and so a retrial, planned for the following week, was scheduled. In fact, what had happened was that the jury had been compromised. The threat of a jury being interfered with is always a very real one, and many precautions are taken, particularly in big cases, to limit the possibility of such things happening. In this case, however, it was not enough, and the Firm had been busy. Many years later, Reggie came clean about the rigged jury in the McCowan case:

> At the end of those trials, it was suggested that we had got at the jury so as to get an acquittal. Well, let's imagine that a man found himself in the dock when totally innocent, discovered that perjured evidence was being used against him by the police, and realized that the only way out was for him to corrupt a jury. Would he do so through his friends, or would he suffer the consequences of a long jail sentence passed on him because of fabricated evidence?
>
> On more than one occasion I have found myself faced with this moral dilemma, I've acted in accordance with the will to survive, and so did corrupt some members of a particular jury.[60]

For his public readership all those years later, Reggie makes it clear that he and his brother were innocent of the charges against them and that he was justified in bribing or threatening jury members. They most certainly were not innocent of those charges, but it does show the criminal mindset, particularly that of villains as prominent as the Krays: the willingness to erase any knowledge of guilt when 'on the record', and the self-delusion that it falls down to police harassment or vendettas against them. This was not the first time the Krays had taken this attitude and it wouldn't be the last.

After some delay, the retrial began on 29 March. The new jury were advised by McCowan's representative, John Matthew, to disregard anything from the previous trial and to keep an open mind.[61] But this trial was a very different animal from the preceding one. First, using money 'nipped' from the now vulnerable Boothby, the twins were able to employ a private detective, George Devlin, to dig up as much dirt on McCowan as possible, including his convictions for sodomy and gross indecency. Additionally, Sidney Vaughan and Peter Byrne had

60 Reggie Kray; *Born Fighter* (London: Arrow Books 1991).
61 *Daily Mirror*, 30 March 1965.

been 'convinced' by members of the Firm that they would be better served representing the defence, leaving McCowan, with his rapidly diminishing reputation and integrity, as the remaining prosecution witness.[62]

On 5 April, the case against the Krays and Smith collapsed. At the close of evidence for the defence, the presiding judge, Mr. Justice Lyell, spoke earnestly to the jury, impressing upon them that the case now rested on the evidence of McCowan:

> *If all of you agree that McCowan is not a reliable witness upon whose evidence you can act with every confidence, and that, in consequence, you cannot be sure of the guilt of the accused or any of them, it is open to you at this stage to tell me you do not wish to hear any more and return a verdict of not guilty in favour of each of these defendants.*[63]

After the jury deliberated for a few minutes, this is precisely what happened. The Kray twins and 'Mad' Teddy Smith were free. Costs were applied for but were turned down, potentially damaging the Krays' finances again, but the important thing was that they had defied the police, and the full might of the British justice system, and prevailed.

Obviously, this was cause for celebration and family, friends, assorted well-wishers and, of course, the press, assembled outside the modest 178 Vallance Road to greet Bethnal Green's most famous, and infamous, sons. 'Cannonball' Lee was there to offer his old boxing stories to anybody who would listen, Violet beamed proudly to one and all, probably relieved that her precious boys had been vindicated (as she probably always believed they would be), and brother Charlie was there to add support and, famously, to be photographed with his younger siblings in a visually significant display of Kray harmony, complete with three-way handshakes. The whole scene was one of joy and relief, all played out against the simple, unified cottages of Vallance Road and the grim, functional railway arches beyond. The press waxed lyrical about the Kray family unity:

> *FIRST for Reginald there was the excitement of a reunion with his pert and pretty 19-year-old fiancée, Frances Shea. As the new beige*

---

62 John Pearson; *Notorious* (London: Century 2010).
63 *Guardian*, 6 April 1965.

Jaguar which brought them back home from the Old Bailey slid to a standstill outside the pink-curtained Kray house, Frances came to the door for a bear hug from her man. She wore fluffy mule slippers and cuddled Mitzi, the family Pekingese. Reginald slipped an arm tightly round her waist. They smiled into each other's eyes. And he said: "We hope to marry very soon - yes, maybe next week."

NEXT came Mum, Mrs. Violet Kray. She drew both sons into her arms and could only say: "Wonderful, wonderful."

AUNTIE MAY from next door ran out to give them a kiss. THEN out bounced Grandpop Jimmy Lee, a spry 89-year-old in cap and braces, giving his grandsons a shadow-boxing welcome.

"They've been kept like wild animals in a cage all this time all for nothing," he said; Grandpop added: "As Jimmy Lee I was known as the Southpaw Cannonball. I was a bantam-weight champ and I've watched my grandsons grow up as boxers. They're good lads."

There were kisses and congratulations for the twins from their sister [sic], who lives in the house on the other side of Grandpop. And back-slappings from the man next door to her.

"Knew it would work out this way." he said. "A dead liberty it was they took with you."

Then the twins went into their own home - with their father, Mr. Charles Kray, to meet Mum. As the news spread more friends arrived in a regular stream - all with the thumbs up sign.

"A couple of real nice boys, Ron and Reg," some of the callers said as they left the house.[64]

That evening, the twins appeared on television for the first time. Interviewed on BBC News about the repercussions of the McCowan case, the short piece of footage[65] offers a fascinating, albeit brief, glimpse of the Kray twins in their prime. In dealing with the various questions put to them, it is noticeable that the twins speak in turn, almost as if one knows what the other was about to say (unless one considers they had been briefed on which questions they were meant to answer) and they never look at each other, as if they don't need to. The only time they disengage with the interviewer is when their representative speaks and they both turn to him. The other significant element is the voices of the brothers themselves; Reggie talks as one

64 *Daily Express*, 6 April 1965.
65 This clip is available on Youtube at www.youtube.com/watch?v=D1Qc_8DoUCs.

would imagine an East Ender would, the sort of cockney accent one would associate with coming from a 'geezer', but Ronnie's voice is soft, lisping and in some ways, slightly effeminate, as different from that of a controlling, violent career criminal as one could imagine:

> *Interviewer: How much has this trial cost you?*
>
> *Ronnie: It's cost us roughly £8,000.*
>
> *Interviewer: And how do you feel about that?*
>
> *Reggie: I don't suppose anyone likes the idea of spending that money for no reason at all, you know?*
>
> *Interviewer: Does it leave you broke, or –*
>
> *Ronnie: It doesn't leave us broke, but at the same time it's a lot of money to have to pay out when one is innocent.*
>
> *Interviewer: A lot of people have got the impression from this trial that clubland, London, is very tough. Do you think it is? You run a couple of clubs...*
>
> *Reggie: Well, in all clubs you get the occasional drunk, you know, and they have to be slung out, that's why there's doormen and that. I suppose it's like nightclub land all over the world really, it's just the same. I don't suppose it can be that bad or people wouldn't go to them really, would they?*
>
> *Interviewer: Ronald, what do you think about clubland in London?*
>
> *Ronnie: Well I think most clubs are very respectable, you know, and I don't think there's any trouble at all in them. Except occasionally.*

The acquittal left the police crestfallen, for this was their chance to come down hard on the Krays, with results, and it had all come to nothing. This was a significant moment for the twins and the Firm. As 'Nipper' Read would later remember:

> *Well, of course they went back to the East End like heroes... And what they were saying to their followers and the public was, "Well, this is us, we told you we could walk on water; we told you that the police were impotent to prosecute us; we told you that we've got good, powerful influential friends, like Boothby, like Driberg, and that they will support us.*[66]

And in a way, Read was right. Fleet Street had been told to steer clear of anything that could result in trouble from the Krays; anyone

---

66 *The Krays: Lords of the Underworld*; Channel 4 UK, broadcast 23 June 1997.

caught up in the Firm's affairs was under no misapprehension as to what the 'Wall of Silence' was meant for; and the British legal system had found the twins infinitely resourceful in avoiding prosecution. And to top it all, all of this was splashed across the press, complete with photographs, in a way that did not make waves and only served to highlight the Krays' public profile.

They would never be more powerful than they were at that moment.

NINE

THE PUBLIC EYE

Throughout those high-profile and trying times of 1964 and early 1965, Reggie was still officially dating Frances. Marriage had already been discussed, despite the fact that it was not always a smooth relationship, for Frances and her fiancé were very different people: he was a confident East End male, blessed with charm and drive that hid any intellectual shortfalls, and an outward reputation of wealth and success that barely hid a dangerous side; she a sensitive, intelligent young woman at the start of a life that, as the Swinging Sixties cranked into gear, promised opportunities unheard of by a previous generation. But Frances was also rather shy around the Kray family, a trait noticed by Maureen Flanagan, who had been Violet Kray's hairdresser since 1961:

> *Frances, for all her beauty, seemed quite timid. We chatted briefly, but you could see she was a shy, nervous thing. At one point she got up and attempted to make us all tea while I got on with Violet's hair. She was clattering around, nervously picking things up, putting them down, frowning a little bit. She didn't seem to be in any way domesticated. Just making tea for three people was too much it seemed.*[1]

Reggie, as an unreconstructed man of his era, was probably more than happy for Frances to be undomesticated. In his world she would

---

1   Maureen Flanagan with Jacky Hyams; *One of the Family: 40 Years With The Krays* (London: Century 2015).

not need to work, and he had soon convinced her to give up her job; as far as he was concerned, she was on a pedestal and no future wife of a Kray would have to work long hours to attain the lifestyle he had in mind for them. This also meant that she would rarely go out with her friends, as Reggie's suspicious nature dictated that he always needed to know where she was and who she was with, which ultimately meant that she would spend much of her social life accompanying him to West End night clubs.

When she was at Vallance Road without Reggie, Frances "seemed to live on her nerves",[2] as Flanagan put it, constantly referred to the clock, and asked when her beloved would be home. Much of this could be taken as Frances's concern for Reggie when he and Ronnie were out on 'business', for the aura of danger that followed Ronnie around always meant that she would never truly know what the brothers were up to or what the result of a night out could be. The strange relationship between Frances and Ronnie has been discussed often. It is no mystery that Ronnie, the dominant twin and the one who was more focused on the Krays' becoming true gangsters had little time for women other than his mother and other members of the close family, and saw them as a drain on the manly pursuits of villainy. With Frances so close to Reggie, she was a threat to all this and, perhaps fundamentally, a threat to their unique bond as twins.

Simply put, Reggie was extremely possessive of Frances, and had fixed ideas about what role his fiancée should play in his life. It didn't matter that she was not keen on the club-hopping, where she would be left alone with people with whom she had little in common whilst Reggie circulated and conducted his business. It didn't matter to him that they were never alone: more often than not, Ronnie was around, as were any number of the Firm. Reggie did what Reggie did, for the twins were always used to getting what they wanted when they wanted it, a state of mind that rarely left room for the opinions and needs of others. For Reggie, the balance came from the gifts he would shower on Frances, or the nice holidays they would take together. The fact that they never shared a room, let alone a bed on these trips was Reggie's way of showing respect for his woman, to prove to her and her family that he was a man of honourable intentions.

The double life that Reggie was living and the growing sense of restriction that Frances felt as the relationship continued sometimes

2   Jacky Hyams; *Frances: The Tragic Bride* (London: John Blake 2014).

caused arguments, some of which led to temporary break-ups. Nervous she may have been around the Krays, but when she and Reggie were alone she was able to express her personal views about him more readily and was probably one of the few people who could actually do so. She would chastise him for always walking in front of her, or bemoan the fact that they rarely had time alone together without Ronnie or the Firm. During one holiday, she told him that, when they were abroad, he was a 'nobody',[3] unknown outside of his native London. Reggie may have found her honesty refreshing at times, but Frances was underlining a few issues that did not make for a strong union; it seemed that Reggie, through force of will, was making it strong, and on his own terms. And even when they did separate, albeit briefly, there was no way Frances could see another man without the threat that any new suitor would feel the wrath of a disgruntled and highly jealous Kray, and thus Reggie would remain her only option.

Reggie's insecurity has been discussed before. Mickey Fawcett occasionally worked as a driver for Reggie and on a few occasions was given the job of driving Frances home after a date. One time, she confided in Fawcett, "I suppose he's told you that I mustn't talk to anyone. It's ridiculous. All my friends, I'm not supposed to talk to them – because he gets annoyed."[4] Sometimes, Reggie would literally spy on Frances and on one occasion, as he sat unnoticed in a car opposite her house in Ormsby Street, he watched as a man dropped her off in his car. The number plate of the vehicle was taken down and a car dealer friend found out the name and address of the owner. Mickey Fawcett was instructed to give the man a solid beating, only to find that the very mention of the name Kray reduced the man to a gibbering wreck: no violence was needed.[5]

By these controlling tactics, Reggie Kray always made sure that Frances was his alone, even when they were apart.

One spanner in the works was Frances's family. For sure, older brother Frankie was pretty much on side, but it was Elsie Shea who had grown to mistrust the Krays and to have serious misgivings about her daughter's relationship with Reggie. And it is not hard to see why: Reggie may have ingratiated himself to Mr. and Mrs. Shea early on with

3   Jacky Hyams; *Frances: The Tragic Bride* (London: John Blake 2014).
4   Ibid.
5   Mickey Fawcett; *Krayzy Days* (Brighton: Pen Press 2013).

his charms, polite manner and obvious respect for their daughter, but what the twins got up to in life was no real secret any more. Since Frances and Reggie had been dating, there had been two charges of demanding money with menaces, suggestions of attempted burglary, nightclubs raided and closed down by the authorities and a scandal involving a peer of the realm. Add to that Frances's complaints about the lifestyle she was being drawn into, and one imagines that mother Elsie was not happy. Their occasional separations showed that, sometimes, Frances would voice these concerns to Reggie, channelling her mother; and yet any attempt at severance would be doomed.

For Reggie, at least, with his driven mind, marriage for him and Frances was a given, and given the circumstances of their relationship, this young, bright, often nervous young woman had very little say in the matter. In fact, when asked during the BBC interview in April what he intended to do after the McCowan case, Reggie effectively put his cards on the table:

> Well, I'd like a bit of family life now, you know, I intend to get married in the near future – I did before this case, but it's been put back over the case and... just get married as soon as possible.[6]

The elation felt by all after the McCowan acquittal had obviously produced a shift in Frances's feelings and, as was noted by the press, she appeared happy and relaxed now that Reggie had been freed and, in the family's eyes, vindicated. Marriage was imminent and Reggie started to make it happen.

◆

Business with the US Mafia had, in the meantime, been continuing apace. The initial meetings between the Krays and Angelo Bruno had proved productive and with the Krays being the 'go-to' people to organise protection for the growing number of West End Mafia-backed clubs, relations were good. A small hiccup had occurred in late 1964 when Ronnie, obviously keen to strengthen links with what he probably saw as a passport to the criminal big time, had flown to New York on a tourist visa[7] to meet Bruno, Meyer Lansky and other members of the Mafia aristocracy. Unfortunately for Ronnie, on arrival

---

6   www.youtube.com/watch?v=D1Qc_8DoUCs.
7   Valid from 16 October 1964 to 16 October 1968. Ronnie's occupation was listed as 'general dealer'.

in the States, US Immigration officials refused him entry and stamped his visa with the word 'INVALIDATED'.[8] With all the recent interest in the Krays' activities, and the suddenly enhanced profile of Ronnie in particular following the Boothby affair, one can only assume that somebody in authority had passed information to the US that marked Ronnie out as undesirable.

This situation had threatened to undermine the relationship between the American and East London crimelords; however, the twins had been doing well minding the West End clubs. The Colony Club in Mayfair had been fronted by actor George Raft, who, because he was a movie hero of the twins, received no small amount of respect from them, and theirs was a flourishing friendship. This would have helped Raft's Mafia connections to remain, for a little longer at least, sympathetic to the Krays. Add to this the famous acquittal in the McCowan case, which demonstrated that the Firm over in London was more than capable of handling any serious police action with aplomb, and the Mafia could see that they had no real need to jettison the Krays just yet. And so it was that the Firm were able to consider Leslie Payne's next 'big thing'.

It all began in Piccadilly in early 1965 when Payne, crossing the busy London thoroughfare, had his way blocked momentarily by a large black Buick Riviera. In the brief moment before Payne was able to cross over, one of the windows of the car partially opened and an American voice told him to "ring Nash", as they had a business proposition to put to him.[9]

The deal was tempting. Backed by the US Mafia, $2,000,000 worth of negotiable Bearer Bonds had been stolen from various banks in North America and Canada and somebody needed to cash them in outside of America for obvious reasons; whoever did so could, of course, take a tidy cut from the proceeds. Payne explained what Bearer Bonds were to Charlie Kray who was (on account of the previous business disasters) by this time the only brother Payne felt comfortable talking to:

> *Bearer Bonds are like shares, issued by most American corporations and utilities, but without registered owners. The person who holds one in his hand is legally the owner – just like money – and they had coupons which the owner could clip, send in and get his dividend.*

8   John Pearson; *Notorious* (London: Century 2010).
9   Leslie Payne; *The Brotherhood* (London: Michael Joseph 1973).

They are devised to make it easier for investors to hide their wealth from the Inland Revenue and to deal in securities without the publicity of stock exchange trading, but this anonymity makes them splendid material for criminal dealings.[10]

Payne was soon making himself busy and flew to Montreal, returning with a sample of $80,000 worth of stolen bonds, for which the New York syndicate had been happy to accept $5,000 on account once they were sold on. Payne disposed of the bonds through a broker friend and the Krays received their cut from the profits, apparently £10,000.[11] The Krays' involvement in yet another Mafia-backed project would increase their standing further and spread their influence wider, as, in addition to London, these bonds, as they were procured over the next few years, would be sold on in mainland Europe.

And whilst Leslie Payne was orchestrating a project that would be beneficial both materially and psychologically, the Krays were refusing to lie low as far as the media in Britain were concerned. When they were interviewed after their acquittal, they announced, "It's the quiet life for us now, Peace and quiet - right away from the West End. That's all we want now, today, and every day."[12] But Reggie and Ronnie Kray could never find the quiet life, if indeed they ever wanted it, and one thing they did in the first half of 1965, more than anything, secured their immortality and enhanced a public fascination that has continued indefinitely.

The twins were fascinating characters, whatever their proclivities and manner of business, and the highbrow press were beginning to notice. Two journalists from the *Sunday Times*, Lewis Chester and Cal McCrystal, interviewed the twins for a full-page article which was careful not to make waves nor to make careless comments about their true activities. But it was Francis Wyndham, another *Sunday Times* journalist, who helped raise the Krays to a level unprecedented by any British criminal figures before them.

The well-connected Wyndham was spellbound by the twins, as many in the upper echelons of society often were, and Reggie and Ronnie demonstrated their peculiar reverence for the 'Great and the Good'; this mutual respect ultimately led the twins to introduce Wyndham to the modest family life at Vallance Road, something

10 Ibid.

11 Colin Fry & Charlie Kray; *Doing the Business* (London: John Blake 1993).

12 *Daily Express*, 6 April 1965.

they did when they were particularly taken by somebody. Wyndham agreed to write a big article for the *Sunday Times Magazine* and, needing classy photographs that would befit the glossy supplement that was proving perfect for the burgeoning Swinging Sixties,[13] he commissioned photographer David Bailey for the job.

Bailey, as the most prominent photographer of that vivacious decade, had photographed many of the popular icons of the day, including the Beatles, Michael Caine, Twiggy, Jean Shrimpton, Andy Warhol and Francis Bacon. He had shot for *Vogue* magazine, and when he was given the job of capturing the country's most feted villains on camera, he chose the quiet, stark environs of that most illustrious magazine's studios to do the job. It would turn out to be a significant decision.

All three brothers were present at the shoot. A number of shots from Bailey's contact sheets reveal that a triple portrait of the Kray brothers was considered: in one, Charlie, positioned between the twins, looks on handsomely into the distance in a semi-dramatic manner, whilst Ronnie and Reggie, flanking the central figure in a more upright stance, look out over the photographer's head with almost dead expressions. Most shots feature the twins alone, as if the inclusion of Charlie upsets an obvious choice of subject matter. A number of images were captured of Ronnie, directly engaging with Bailey's lens, with Reggie, almost secondarily, emerging from behind his brother's right shoulder. But one in particular from that little run of shots stands out.

Ronnie stares with his customary menace at the camera, in control, every bit 'The Colonel' and almost daring the photographer, and thus the viewer, to challenge him. Reggie, leaning out from behind, is a worthy back-up man, his customary inquisitive look almost asking, "What are you looking at?" and suggesting that, should you manage to get past his brother, he is there to make sure you get no further. In their sharp suits and ties, with their air of authority mixed with threat, these two men could not be anything other than dangerous and Bailey captured this: he was no fool and knew exactly what he was dealing with:

> They'd fucking nail you to the floor, crucify you, but you've got to
> understand that everything is time and place. People say, "How

13 *The Sunday Times Magazine*, the first colour supplement of any newspaper in Britain, first appeared in February 1962.

could you like Reg?" And I knew what he was, but I did like him. He didn't do anything to me. Ron I avoided, cos a slip of the tongue and you could be fucking dead.[14]

Ultimately, the powers-that-be at the *Sunday Times* perhaps felt that there was already too much about the Krays in the media and Wyndham's article was never published in the pages of their vibrant colour supplement. The photo of the twins would have to wait until the end of the year before it appeared (with Wyndham's revamped word-portrait) in *David Bailey's Box of Pinups*,[15] a lavish book of thirty-six portraits of the movers and shakers of the 1960s: the Kray twins were now almost a part of the pop-culture of that most fascinating decade, staring out of the pages of Bailey's book, aligned with their more legitimately illustrious peers: Michael Caine, John Lennon and Paul McCartney, Terence Stamp, Mick Jagger, David Hockney, Lord Snowdon, Andrew 'Loog' Oldham... It is a defining portrait: if the Kray twins had been American, artist Andy Warhol would have turned the stark black and white image into one of his large pop-art screenprints, just as he did with Marilyn Monroe, Chairman Mao, Elizabeth Taylor and the Krays' old friend, Judy Garland.

With the eventual publication of this portrait, Reginald and Ronald Kray would become part of an elite number of public figures who would be defined by, and wholly recognisable from, one iconic image.

◆

The date had been set, 19 April 1965, for the East End wedding of the year, when 31-year-old bachelor Reginald Kray would marry his 21-year-old fiancée Frances Elsie Shea at St James the Great Church on Bethnal Green Road.[16] In a show of continued loyalty to those he respected, Reggie had asked Father Richard Hetherington to conduct the service; however, the response was undoubtedly not what Reggie had expected: Father Hetherington, a staunch supporter of the twins and a man who had often gone out of his way to furnish them with glowing character references to help them in their hour of need, refused. Years later, John Pearson spoke with Father Hetherington

14 Interview with Michael Hodges for *Time Out*; www.timeout.com/london/art/david-bailey-interview.
15 David Bailey; *David Bailey's Box of Pinups* (London: Weidenfield and Nicolson 1965).
16 The church, which still stands, was closed in 1981 and redeveloped into flats two years later.

about his decision; his reply was characteristically forthright. "I'd known Reg since he was a boy, but when they came and asked me to marry them, I said I couldn't. I told them that I hoped they would not go through with it." When he was asked why, the reply was, with the benefit of hindsight, alarmingly prophetic:

> *Because they simply had no idea of what marriage was about. Not merely was there not the faintest hope of either of them finding any happiness together, but I could see them causing serious harm to one another.*[17]

But the wedding went ahead in spite of Father Hetherington's advice, and the service would be conducted by the younger Father John Foster, who, only a few months before, had been a witness for the twins during the McCowan case, adopting a role he seemed to have inherited from his predecessor. Other dissenters had come in the shape of Frances's parents, who by now were totally dead-set against their daughter committing herself to a Kray; but the wedding was going to happen, nobody could stop it, and, of course, it would be done Reggie's way. If Frances had wanted a quiet, modest affair, then her wishes had been completely disregarded.

The scene at Vallance Road that morning was buzzing, as one would expect before any wedding. Maureen Flanagan tended to Violet's hair whilst Reggie paced around the kitchen, nervous and edgy, constantly concerned that something had been forgotten. Violet, of course, was confident that all was going to be perfect, and constantly reminded Reggie that there was nothing to worry about, whilst all the time trying to keep Ronnie, who was beginning to bristle with disapproval at the whole scenario ahead, from saying the wrong thing. "Wot's he want to get married for?"[18] had become Ronnie's latest mantra and one can detect not only the obvious dissatisfaction with his twin's forthcoming nuptials, but also an almost childlike fear of change and loss. At one point, Reggie and Ronnie disappeared upstairs and Flanagan was on tenterhooks waiting for the possible fraternal flare up, which, as it turns out, didn't happen. Violet had seemingly worked her magic on the increasingly disgruntled Ronnie.

---

17 John Pearson; *The Cult of Violence* (London: Orion Books 2001).

18 Maureen Flanagan with Jacky Hyams; *One of the Family: 40 Years With The Krays* (London: Century 2015).

Over one hundred telegrams had arrived at Vallance Road, including good wishes from Judy Garland, Lita Roza, Joan Littlewood and Lord Boothby.[19] Guests began to assemble outside the church, including former boxers Terry Allen, Terry Spinks and Ted 'Kid' Lewis, actress Diana Dors, singer Lennie Peters and David Bailey, who pulled up in a blue Rolls Royce and wearing a blue velvet suit for his role as photographer, something he had agreed to as a present for the couple.[20] Tom Driberg was also said to be in attendance.[21] A "large group of large men" also lingered on the pavement: one newspaper mentioned the names of people like "Big Pat" and "The Dodger",[22] demonstrating that many of the Firm were (inevitably) in attendance.

The Kray family were driven the short distance from Vallance Road in impressive cars, with Grandad Lee managing to pitch in with his usual, "I was once known as the Southpaw Cannonball," when approached by the waiting press.[23] Reggie, perhaps to calm his nerves, walked to the church and as the families and friends settled in the pews of St James the Great, the congregation awaited the arrival of the bride. One thing that did not go unnoticed was the attire of Elsie Shea: defiantly showing her disapproval of the whole thing, she had deliberately worn black for her daughter's wedding. Another element of the wedding that was noticeable was the sheer number of guests on the groom's side of the church compared to that of the bride. The Krays had certainly made sure that this would be the East End event of 1965 and filled the pews accordingly, whilst the Shea family, none too enamoured by the whole affair, had kept their guest list relatively modest.

Ronnie, despite the obvious displeasure he felt at potentially 'losing' his twin brother to Frances, was on his best behaviour, kissing the bride and executing his duties as best man with little problem. But Ronnie could always be relied on to 'perform' at the least opportune of moments, and this he did as the congregation began to sing the first hymns during the wait for Frances's arrival. As the organist began playing 'Oh Perfect Love, All Love Excelling', it became apparent that not enough people knew the words and thus a non-committed murmur

19 *Daily Mirror,* 20 April 1965.
20 This would be the only wedding Bailey ever photographed in his career.
21 John Pearson; *Notorious* (London: Century 2010).
22 *Daily Express*, 20 April 1965.
23 Ibid.

issued from the congregation. Ronnie, perhaps driven by loyalty to his brother's desire for a perfect day, despite his own misgivings, sensed that the assembled guests were not giving their all, rose up and began strolling down the aisle. In a truly misjudged attempt to inject some life into the proceedings, he hissed "Sing, fuck you, sing!" until the congregation reached the desired level of enthusiasm. What the guests actually felt about this has never been recorded.

However, the wedding, for all its outward display of success and happiness, was not to everybody's taste. Maureen Flanagan's husband, when he discovered that his wife could have attended, said he was relieved she hadn't: "There were a lot of horrible guys there", he said.[24] Albert Donoghue, who could not be there as he was at that time serving a short prison sentence in Brixton Prison following a pub fight,[25] said, after seeing the photos, that

> *Where most people's wedding photos are filled with Mum, Dad, Auntie Mary and other young couples, these were dominated by big flat-noses wearing buttonholes. The reception was packed with scar-faced thugs. She could not have missed them. It was obviously a happy occasion for some, but Frances was getting the drift of what was going on even then. She tried to look happy. She managed a smile, but what's a smile? You can sit in a dentist's chair and open your mouth, and it looks like you're smiling, but you're in agony.*[26]

The reception itself was held at the Glenrae Hotel. Despite the problems ensuing from the McCowan case and their arrest there, the Krays still held sway over Phoebe Woods's little North London venue and one can imagine that, as a result of holding the reception there, they could still show they were in business whilst effectively 'nipping' the proprietors for drinks and food in the meantime. In fact, Phoebe Woods had made a remarkable about-turn after 'Nipper' Read and Fred Gerrard had arrested the twins at the Glenrae the previous January. As Read would later recall:

> *Once the Krays were arrested, Phoebe Woods became hysterical, screaming with relief, and literally threw herself at my feet saying*

24 Maureen Flanagan with Jacky Hyams; *One of the Family: 40 Years With The Krays* (London: Century 2015).

25 On 9 March 1965 he received a six month sentence for malicious wounding and twelve months for causing grievous bodily harm, running concurrently; CRIM 1/4900 (National Archives).

26 Albert Donoghue & Martin Short; *The Enforcer* (London: John Blake 2002).

how glad she was that things were over, how all her customers had been driven out of the club and how there were bills for the rooms and drink amounting to over £100 outstanding...

The next morning she was at Old Street Magistrates' Court, dressed to the nines and looking like a different woman. She wore a fur piece and high heels. Her hair was smartly done and she was smiling and confident. She offered to stand bail, insisting that the management of the club by the Krays was an arrangement with which she and her husband were perfectly satisfied.[27]

The Firm had obviously been busy in the twins' absence.

The cracks in Reggie and Frances's already long relationship began to reappear immediately. The honeymoon, in Athens, was not an entirely happy affair. Lured by the promise of fine Mediterranean weather and exotic locations, the newlyweds found a country still reeling and battered from the Greek Civil War,[28] they were not keen on the food, and both quickly missed the home comforts of East London. Photographs taken at the time reveal a tense couple strolling around the dishevelled city of Athens in smart, almost formal attire, totally unbecoming of two young people enjoying a sightseeing holiday on the continent. And the marriage was not consummated during that gloomy week in Athens, as Reggie would often, it has been said, spend the evenings drinking alone whilst Frances sat in their hotel room.[29] The honeymoon lasted eight days, and, on returning to London, Reggie continued to strive to give his new wife the sort of life others with similarly humble backgrounds could only dream of; the first thing he did was find a flat in Marble Arch, lavishly furnished, as their new marital home.

On 29 April, the day after Reggie and Frances returned from their ill-fated honeymoon, Hew McCowan's Hideaway club reopened; only this time it had a new name, El Morocco, and the club was now being run under the auspices of the Krays. The twins had got more than they had originally wanted as far as the Gerrard Street venue

---

27 Leonard Read & James Morton; *Nipper Read: The Man Who Nicked the Krays* (London: MacDonald & Co 1991).

28 The Greek Civil War of 1946-49 had left the country in ruins and Greece suffered from social and political problems for many decades afterwards. Soon after the honeymoon, in July 1965, the resignation of Greek Prime Minister Georgios Papandreou instigated what became known as the Apostasia crisis, when King Constantine II installed a replacement in what was effectively a 'Royal Coup'.

29 Jacky Hyams; *Frances: The Tragic Bride* (London: John Blake 2014).

was concerned and the opening night, co-hosted by friend Freddie Foreman, was used as an excuse to celebrate the twins' acquittal three weeks previously. It was attended by family, friends, members of the Firm and their partners, and of course, a number of celebrities, including the actors Edmund Purdom, Victor Spinetti and Adrienne Corri. The Kray propaganda machine made sure that everybody realised what a star-studded event it would be, even going so far as to promise the presence of celebrities like The Beatles, who, of course never attended.[30] It had worked and the club was filled to capacity. There was, however, one guest who had certainly not been invited, and who found himself unwittingly in the lion's den that night: Leonard 'Nipper' Read.

Read, keen as ever, had decided to check out this gathering and positioned himself outside in a telephone box, so as to update the intelligence that had so far been gathered about the Krays' activities. One of the guests, George Devlin, the private investigator who had been employed by the twins to investigate McCowan during the trial, noticed Read and went over to speak to him. Read gave a feeble excuse for being where he was and Devlin knew it straight away. "That's bullshit. I know what you're doing," he said. "If you want to see who's here, why don't you come inside, it's no problem."[31] Reluctantly, Read accepted the strange invitation and his arrival in the club was met with an unsurprisingly frosty response. Ronnie was visibly furious, although Reggie appeared to be unfazed. In time, as the atmosphere became more uncomfortable, Read left. Unfortunately, the following day, the *Daily Express* carried a photograph of Edmund Purdom with the Krays and mistakenly labelled the actor as Read.[32] The suggestion that Read had had his photo taken with the twins at El Morocco has often been repeated since and, years later, Read was quick to extinguish the story once and for all. He was also quick to point out that there had been no investigation into the incident and that he had not been suspended from his duties on the Kray case as a result. What happened is that he was offered some 'time off' and enrolled on a six month Intermediate Command Course at Bramshill in order

30 Chris Lambrianou and Robin McGibbon; *Escape From the Kray Madness* (London: Sidgwick and Jackson 1995).
31 Leonard Read & James Morton; *Nipper Read: The Man Who Nicked the Krays* (London: MacDonald & Co 1991).
32 *Daily Express*, 30 April 1965.

to facilitate his future promotion to Chief Inspector:[33] the Kray investigation, thanks to the setbacks that the police had experienced over the previous year, had wound down to little more than a trickle, but this was certainly not the last the Krays would hear from 'Nipper' Read.

It was also at this time that a very unusual proposition was made to the Krays, and in this instance it did not involve any active criminal enterprise. In 1965, Vince Cable, politician and one-time deputy leader of the Liberal Democrat Party,[34] was president of the Cambridge University Union and had invited Alfred Hinds, an East End burglar and safe-cracker who became known as 'Houdini' Hinds for his numerous escapes from detention, to speak during a debate entitled "The Law Is An Ass", due to take place at the Cambridge Union Society on 18 May. Supporting him was to be Reggie Kray, with barrister Alistair Sampson and television comedy writer Harvey Orkin opposing the motion. This looked to be a most unusual debate and Cable reported that Reggie was enthusiastic: "Mr. Kray told me that he would be delighted to come down and speak and that he was bringing his brother and some friends."[35]

As it happens, Reggie and his inevitable entourage never made it inside the hallowed walls of Cambridge University. It was a sign of his 'prestige' at that time that the Cambridge Union would ask him to take part in their debate, but Reggie must have had second thoughts. The twins were not exactly intellectual by nature, but they certainly knew their own minds, and for all we know Reggie could have excelled in a public arena such as this. That said, the whole situation may have been somewhat intimidating, being as it was outside the Kray comfort zone of London villainy. Could Reggie have had misgivings because he was advised not to draw any more attention from the press to himself, his dealings with the law, and his associates?

◆

33 Read was promoted to Chief Inspector in March 1966 and transferred to West End Central Police Station.

34 Cable was a member of the Labour Party until 1982, when he joined the Social Democratic Party. He unsuccessfully stood for Parliament in the general elections of 1970, 1983, 1987 and 1992 before being elected as the MP for Twickenham in 1997. He became acting leader of the Liberal Democrats in 2007 before being replaced by Nick Clegg. He lost his seat in the general election of 2015.

35 *Daily Mirror*, 5 May 1965.

After Leslie Payne had delivered the first consignment of stolen bearer bonds from Canada, the Krays assigned a party of men to make a second pick-up, with Charlie Kray and Payne fronting the team. They were backed up by Charlie Mitchell, the bookmaker and moneylender who had been involved in the beating of the unnamed man from Adams Casino Enterprises in 1962; Bobby McKew, an old friend of Charlie Kray; and Gordon Anderson, a Canadian citizen who had been a part of the machinations behind the ill-fated Enugu project. The deal was that the Krays would take 50% of the proceeds from any sale of these bonds, an arrangement that was too good to pass on. Unfortunately, on this particular occasion, all involved were stopped by immigration at Montreal. In short, somebody who knew what was going on had spoken out and the Canadian authorities were determined not to let the group past customs.[36] It was never determined who gave the tip-off that stopped Charlie Kray and his associates entering Canada, but it was only through the intervention of Montreal Mafia boss Don Ceville (who was coordinating the initial robberies that acquired the bonds in the first place) that the party were able to leave the country and return home as quickly as they did.

It was only a brief headache, however, and Payne believed that this had been "a spasmodic, reflex action by the Canadian immigration authorities and not a systematic drive to prevent communication between criminal groups in the two countries".[37] Sure enough, the following week, a Canadian associate arrived in London with $50,000 worth of bonds which were soon cashed successfully in Germany, and so the plan was still on. Throughout 1965, the movement of stolen bonds across the Atlantic continued apace. They were being sold on across Europe, in Geneva, Paris, Amsterdam and Hamburg; the number of individuals now involved in this highly lucrative project was growing all the time, and new contacts were being made. One new associate was Alan Bruce Cooper, an American who would quickly replace Leslie Payne as the twins' business ideas man and ultimately steer them in directions that the comparatively careful Payne would have stayed clear of.

Cooper was by all accounts an unassuming man, something which probably helped him to deal with highly dangerous people without getting hurt. He was 5 feet 7 inches tall, with a "sad moustache, sparse

36 Colin Fry & Charlie Kray; *Doing the Business* (London: John Blake 1993).
37 Leslie Payne; *The Brotherhood* (London: Michael Joseph 1973).

hair and a faint stutter"[38] and lived with his attractive wife Beverley on Campden Hill in London's prestigious Holland Park. Born in America, Cooper's father had been a driver for the infamous gangster 'Lucky' Luciano, the Sicilian-born mobster who was considered to be the father of organised crime in the USA[39] and young Alan's first taste of criminal life came whilst he was serving in the American Army during World War Two – he spent seven years in Fort Worth Prison after being convicted of bank robbery. Alan Cooper had a lot of fingers in a lot of pies worldwide and rarely stood still as far as business was concerned: many of his domestic and international financial dealings, both legitimate and illegal, were done through his private bank in Wigmore Street in West London, and he was once thought to have operated a gold-smuggling ring in the Far East. He was also believed to be an arms dealer.[40] In fact, there were many rumours about Alan Cooper. Initially, it was his job to organise the forging of registration certificates which made the stolen bonds negotiable, but he soon began to use his strange charisma on the twins, and Ronnie in particular could see the benefits, and was excited by the criminal potential of this enigmatic American. Reggie and Charlie were less impressed, and Reggie certainly felt there was something not right about this newcomer to their affairs. But Ronnie, as dominant as he was by this time, was certainly up for any scheme Cooper could come up with.

One of Cooper's early ideas was the incredibly ambitious, and dangerous, plan to fleece a group of influential men from the Congo out of a large sum of money on the pretence that he, with the Krays' backing, would enable them to spring a high-ranking African official from detention. 'Scotch' Jack Dickson was commandeered by Ronnie to attend a meeting with himself, Cooper and the three men behind the plot at the Hilton Hotel in Hyde Park. As Ronnie and Dickson sat and listened, Cooper gave the men every reason to believe the Kray Firm were more than capable of the job, which involved some considerable high-powered weaponry. The idea, of course, was a scam, for Cooper intended to go to the Congo, collect a considerable down-payment

---

38 John Pearson; *The Profession of Violence* (London: Weidenfeld & Nicolson 1972).
39 Charles 'Lucky' Luciano was for many years the head of the Genovese crime family and, along with associate Meyer Lansky, was a major force in setting up the National Crime syndicate. He died of a heart attack in 1962.
40 John Pearson; *The Profession of Violence* (London: Weidenfeld & Nicolson 1972).

for the job and then leave with the money, with no intention of ever fulfilling his side of the deal. Before he knew it, Dickson was ordered to accompany Cooper to Africa and keep an eye on him in case this turned out to be a ruse to dupe the twins too; and as Ronnie Kray was giving the instructions, Dickson had no choice in the matter.

At the meeting in Africa a few weeks later, Cooper explained to his contacts what he and the Kray organisation could bring to the operation, which, as well as the impressive weaponry, also included a helicopter standing by in Gibraltar. Dickson, as a mute observer, had his misgivings as he had a strange feeling that this meeting was not necessarily the first between Cooper and the Africans. A down-payment of £75,000 was mentioned before Cooper was asked if the twins would be coming over, to which he confidently replied, "Of course they will, assuming we can make a deal. The plan would not work without them."[41] The up-front payment was agreed by the Africans, on the proviso that they could see the helicopter in Gibraltar beforehand.

At that point the deal had effectively failed. Although Cooper assured them there would be no problem with their request, there was no way the Africans were going to see any helicopter, or even the Krays for that matter. As they all shook hands and went their separate ways, Cooper admitted it was a failure and that the twins would be "very disappointed" that no money had changed hands. And he was right: when Dickson returned to Vallance Road and told them what had happened, Reggie lost his temper with Ronnie, shouting, "I told you that fucking Yank was no good. I don't know why the fuck you trust him!"[42]

Alan Cooper, despite being instrumental in the ongoing success of the stolen bearer bonds racket, would prove to be somewhat unreliable when it came to pulling off the big schemes he offered the twins. Maybe the reservations that Reggie, Charlie and Jack Dickson had were not born of nerves and paranoia after all.

---

41 John Dickson; *Murder Without Conviction* (London: Sidgwick and Jackson 1986).
42 Ibid.

*Covering letter to Violet Kray which accompanied the death certificate of
daughter Violet who died prematurely soon after birth*
(Private collection)

EDWARD J. HIGGINS,
GENERAL

Read 'THE WAR CRY'

THE SALVATION ARMY
(WILLIAM BOOTH, FOUNDER)

WOMEN'S SOCIAL WORK

COMMISSIONER CATHERINE BOOTH,
Leader of
The Women's Social Work

Headquarters:
280 MARE STREET, HACKNEY,
LONDON, E. 8

THE MOTHERS' HOSPITAL,
LOWER CLAPTON ROAD,
CLAPTON, LONDON, E.5
Telephone: 1050 CLISSOLD

26ᶜ September 1929.

Dear Mr. Kray,

I enclose the certificate of the baby's death.

Yours faithfully

C. P. Giles.

R.M.O

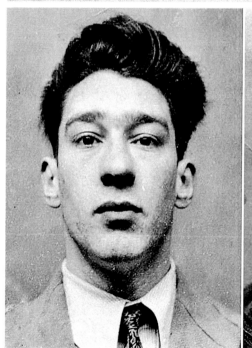 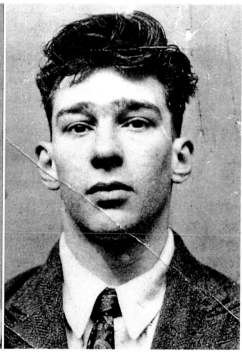

*Early mugshots of Ronnie (left) and Reggie.
Their similarity here is striking, although they would gradually look different as they got older*

List of exhibits, including weapons, used in the assault case against the twins, Patrick Aucott and Thomas Organ in 1950

CRIMINAL APPEAL ACT, 1907.

R. v. *Thomas Organ & others*

LIST OF EXHIBITS.

Number or other identifying mark on Exhibit.	Short description of Exhibit.	Produced by Prosecution or Defence.	Name and address of person retaining Exhibit.	Directions of the Judge of the Court of Trial.
1.	Piece of Bicycle Chain	Pros.	Police	
2	Cosh	..	..	
3	Two chains with wooden handles	..	..	
4	Statement by Ronald Kray	..	Court	
5	Statement Reginald Kray	..	..	
6.	Statement by Aucott	..	..	

Sch. II.—No. 30.

LIST OF EXHIBITS.

Signed

North London

Clerk,

Magistrates Court.

The Coach and Horses pub, Mile End Road, prior to demolition, the scene of one of the Krays' earliest high-profile battles

Cedra Court, Cazenove Road, Stoke Newington, in 2015
(Laura Prieto)

Esmeralda's Barn Ltd.

Directors:
ALD KRAY (Managing)
REGINALD KRAY
J. PAYNE (Secretary)
CHARLES KRAY
ALFRED KRAY

50, Wilton Place, Knightsbridge,
London, S.W.1

Telephone:
BELgravia 3040
3039

ee about office Re Solisitor   PHone

answer Letters to USA   WRITE

PHone HARRLy ST. DOCTOR   RE. House PHone

VISA   SEE

CHA CHA

LETER. TO, PUT.
VISA TRouBLE
CHA...

A police raid on Cedra Court in January 1965 unearthed all manner of items, including this list of reminders written by Ronnie on Esmeralda's Barn notepaper. 'CHA CHA' was the nickname of one of the Firm's associates, South African Anton Kumala

Sunday Mirror

July 12, 1964 No. 67

PEER AND A GANGSTER: YARD PROBE

he most exciting

The most intriguing

ean Shrimpton

By **NORMAN LUCAS**

A TOP level Scotland Yard investigation into the alleged homosexual relationship between a prominent peer and a leading thug in the London underworld has been ordered by Metropolitan Police Commissioner Sir Joseph Simpson.

The peer concerned is a household name and Yard detectives are inquiring into allegations that he has a "relationship" with a man who has criminal convictions and is alleged to be involved in a West End protection racket.

The Yard investigation, being conducted by Detective Chief Superintendent Fred Gerrard, head of No. 3 District CID of the Metropolitan Police, takes in the activities of a well-known team of East End gangsters.

IN MAYFAIR

I can reveal that the investigation embraces:

1 Inquiries into Mayfair parties attended by the peer and the East End thug.

2 The private week-end activities of the peer and a number

Public men at seaside parties

of prominent public men during visits to Brighton.

3 The relationships that exist between the East End gangsters, the peer and a number of clergymen.

4 Allegations of blackmail against people who know about these relationships.

One man who promised to make statements to Yard detectives about the "unusual circumstances" surrounding people now being investigated has left the country. Before he went, he told detectives that his life had been threatened.

For several months, Yard men have been watching meetings between the peer and the underworld thug. Details of these meetings have been the subject of reports by officers to the Commissioner.

I understand that, within the next forty-eight hours, the Commissioner will meet the Home Secretary, Mr. Henry Brooke, and give him details of the reports and of the instructions he has now given to Detective Chief Superintendent Gerrard.

Investigations I have made during the past three weeks show that the thug concerned has been involved in a protection racket in London's clubland that has cost club proprietors thousands of pounds.

BUSINESS DEALS

Detectives who have probed this aspect of the thug's activities are also inquiring into deals that have been made during the past few months with a solicitor and barrister who have been guiding the thug in his private business deals.

I understand that they are anxious to know whether the lawyers' fees have been paid in cash or by cheque and whether the fees charged are in line with standard fees laid down by the legal profession.

WRITES ON PAGES 14 and 15

Although there was never believed to be any sexual relationship between Ronnie Kray and Robert Boothby, Norman Lucas's front page exposé threatened to create the biggest political scandal of the 1960s

Reggie and Ronnie appear on BBC television discussing the McCowan case and their plans for the future

The Lion pub in Tapp Street, seen here in the early 1970s. Also known as 'Madge's', or 'The Widow's', it was a significant Kray meeting place

The Blind Beggar pub, Whitechapel Road, the day after Ronnie shot George Cornell. The car in the foreground is the one Cornell had borrowed and which was used by his wife Olive to attend the scene after she heard about the shooting
(Trinity Mirror / Mirrorpix / Alamy Stock Photo)

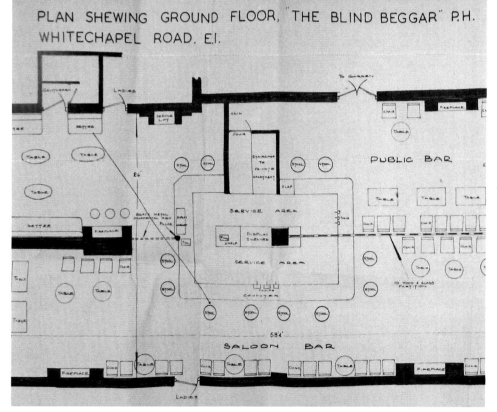

PLAN SHEWING GROUND FLOOR, "THE BLIND BEGGAR" P.H. WHITECHAPEL ROAD. E.I.

PUBLIC BAR

SALOON BAR

Police plan of the Blind Beggar crime scene, complete with a line showing the trajectory of the bullet that killed Cornell

Reggie on the phone at Vallance Road after being released from police custody in August 1966
(Trinity Mirror / Mirrorpix / Alamy Stock Photo)

Above:
The notorious booby-trapped briefcase, now kept at Scotland Yard's famous Crime Museum, which was to be used to kill a man in late 1966
© *Museum of London /*
Courtesy Metropolitan Police Service, The Crime Museum

Left: Jimmy Evans, the target

Right: Squire 'Split' Waterman, who designed the briefcase

Right:
Police photograph of
Frank Samuel Mitchell
– the 'Mad Axe Man'

Below:
The spot near
the Elephant's Nest
pub at Horndon where
Albert Donoghue
and Teddy Smith
picked up Mitchell

The Carpenter's Arms, Cheshire Street, in the 1960s

Above: A rare photograph of Jack McVitie taken during his National Service days, c. 1951.

Right: The house in Evering Road, Stoke Newington, where Jack McVitie died, pictured in 2015. (© Laura Prieto)

The faulty gun used by Reggie in his first attempt at killing McVitie: the poor condition is down to it having been submerged in the River Lea for nearly two years before it was found by police divers

© Museum of London /
Courtesy Metropolitan Police Service, The Crime Museum

tv BBC-2

8.35

THIRTY-MINUTE THEATRE

The Top Bunk

by

TED SMITH

with

BRIAN COBURN
as Big Bill Bishop
PATRICK WESTWOOD
as Bonkey Stone
JOHN MOORE
as James Smithers
DOUGLAS BLACKWELL
as first Prison Officer
ANTHONY HALL
as second Prison Officer
Designer, Fanny Taylor
Producer, GEORGE SPYNTON-FOSTER
Directed by BRIAN MILLER

Two old lags who share the same cell
have got prison life down to a fine
art. They are upset when an outsider
a public school type and a first timer
is made to live with them, and bowled
over when he reveals a sinister side
to his nature, which makes him the
natural leader, entitled to the position
of prestige—the top bunk.

COLOUR

7.30 p.m.

OUTLOOK

for Monday:

MIDDLE AGE

Five programmes on the problems
of the mid-life period

4: Health Hazards—Women

In this programme, the ' change of
life ' and some of its associated
problems. Also a quick look at breast
cancer and the right way to conduct
a self-examination.

Director, SALLY DAVIS
Producer, ROGER OWEN

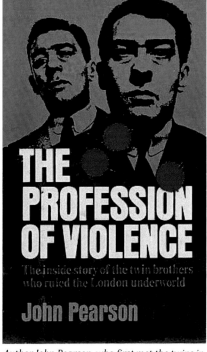

Author John Pearson, who first met the twins in late 1967: his book about them, The Profession of Violence, would be published in 1972

Ronnie and Reggie pose for photographer David Bailey with their pet pythons 'Read' and 'Gerrard' in early 1968

Leonard 'Nipper' Read (centre front in the grey coat) poses triumphant with his team outside their Tintagel House headquarters following the Krays' convictions in March 1969 (Keystone Pictures USA / Alamy Stock Photo)

TEN

TROUBLE BREWING

To say that Reggie and Frances's marriage was not going well was an understatement. In fact, it had started shakily and only grew steadily worse. The Marble Arch flat may have had all the appeal of good living, but true to form, Reggie would be out all hours of the day and night on 'business', leaving Frances alone and isolated from her family and close friends.

Frances kept a diary at this time – not so much a journal as a collection of notes and thoughts – and it is from these scattered writings that a peculiar picture of her marriage to Reggie becomes apparent. It appears she was in Ibiza, Spain from 6 June until 14 July 1965, followed by two weeks in an undisclosed hotel, before a stay in Torremolinos from 2 August until 13 August. On returning to England from this extended Iberian sojourn, she booked into the Alexandra National Hotel in Finsbury Park for a while before returning to the Marble Arch flat.[1] What is remarkable about this is that, only a couple of months after her marriage to Reggie, this extended period abroad had been spent alone. Indeed, Frances appeared to spend an awful lot of time alone. It was a most curious situation: when Reggie wasn't showering her with material things or showing her the razzmatazz of London, he was taking on married life at an abusive and in many ways alarmingly destructive level. Frances' diaries reveal incidences of bitter cruelty, verbal abuse and life in a constant environment of

1   Jacky Hyams; *Frances: The Tragic Bride* (London: John Blake 2014).

197

fear. Reggie kept guns and knives in the flat, and went out nightly, only to return in the early hours of the morning drunk and aggressive. He angrily berated Frances about her parents and whenever she argued back, he would deliver his customary response, "Shut your mouth," or worse.

When they both realised that living in the West End was not helping the situation, they spent a brief - and for Reggie, probably excruciating - period at the Sheas' house in Ormsby Street before the couple moved into Reggie's recently redecorated flat at 1 Cedra Court. This may have been closer to home, but it was also closer to Ronnie, and the proximity to her husband's difficult and often resentful brother made life even harder for Frances. Mickey Fawcett could certainly see it:

> She was not welcome as far as Ronnie was concerned. With the one exception of the twins' mother, Ronnie thought women were, in general, vile, dirty creatures, but he particularly loathed Frances. She came between the brothers... Ronnie did see the end of their partnership in Frances and never lost an opportunity to get at her.[2]

With Ronnie now so close by and influencing his twin as before, things got even worse. Reggie would disappear upstairs to Ronnie's flat and return in the small hours extremely drunk. If Frances remonstrated with him about what he was up to and why she was always being left alone, he would become drunkenly abusive, blaming her for her own unhappiness and again bringing her parents' dislike of him into the argument. He would rant, swear, and verbally berate her when he was in this state, but he apparently never hit her. This would go on until he passed out; the next morning, he would be loving, attentive Reggie again, and, for him at least, the events of the night before would be forgotten. But Frances could not forget and the accumulation of incidents and the unhappiness she felt with her new life led her to take solace in the medicine cabinet. With Ronnie's noisy parties above her going on into the early hours of the morning, she began to take sleeping tablets to help her get through the night. Medication to help her deal with her situation would be something that would soon play an increasing part in her life.

Why was this so? Why was this sensitive and obviously intelligent young woman so neglected and ill-treated by the very man who put her

2   Mickey Fawcett; *Krayzy Days* (Brighton: Pen Press 2013).

on a pedestal and smothered her with gifts to the point of suffocation? Father Hetherington's prediction, for Reggie at least, appeared to be incredibly accurate: Reggie Kray had no idea what marriage meant. Before marrying Frances, he had had a number of liaisons with girls, but none of these brief relationships went any further than a one night stand or a few dates at the very most. There was no commitment at all, for the only true commitment Reggie had was to his twin brother and the business they had created around themselves. By the mid-1960s, the brothers Kray had forged a sprawling, often chaotic, criminal enterprise which, along with the diverse infantrymen of the Firm, took a tremendous amount of drive and sheer legwork to maintain. It meant long nights out oiling the machinery of business with drink at innumerable large and small social gatherings. It meant responding to any crisis that manifested itself with methods that would be hard to justify to anybody not embroiled in that world. The 'normal' world was not an option.

But Reggie, like Ronnie, was also somebody for whom being told what to do, or how to do it, was anathema. Mickey Fawcett once described Reggie as "the most selfish bastard you've ever met."[3] The pair of them always strove to get what they wanted or to justify what they felt was correct; with Frances, who could be relied on to break out of her shyness with her husband and remonstrate with him like any wife could, Reggie was faced with somebody who openly challenged everything he was about. Any man who spoke in such a way to him would more than likely feel his wrath, possibly with physical force, the great leveller as far as the twins were concerned. With Frances, there could never be a broken jaw or a slashed face, but, once fuelled by more than a few gin and tonics, Reggie's anger and frustration over being criticised for what he was doing, or for being told to leave his perceived responsibilities aside, would erupt in non-physical ways.

Reggie undoubtedly loved Frances, but his personality, his lifestyle and his reputation were so set in stone that, had he dropped it all to conform to married life, he would, at the very least, lose his brother and all they had strived for, or, at the very worst, cease to exist. For Ronnie, as a highly active practitioner of the still-illegal 'love that dare not speak its name', commitment of a kind that would alter his chosen lifestyle was never going to happen. He was free to devote himself to

3   Jacky Hyams; *Frances: The Tragic Bride* (London: John Blake 2014).

villainy, and would remain unfettered by anybody else's needs: as far as he was concerned, Reggie should have been thinking along the same lines, not getting himself bogged down with serious relationships.

But Reggie's heavily suppressed bisexuality, specifically the homosexual side of it, could also have been a contributing factor in his behaviour toward his wife. In 2002, Frankie Shea announced to the press that Reggie was actually in love with him and back in the late 1950s had made overtures to that effect. The resolutely heterosexual Frankie left Reggie's employ as a driver as a result and as an act of vengeance, Reggie took his sister as his bride.[4] This all sounds fanciful stuff but the homosexual dilemma within Reggie could have had something to do with the fact that he could not interact with Frances sexually. For sure, he could demonstrate his love in a - some may say - shallow way by inundating Frances with gifts and treats, but when it came to physical manifestations of love, specifically sex, Reggie just could not manage it. Both Mickey Fawcett and Albert Donoghue have mentioned in their memoirs how Frances told them that Reggie had never laid a finger on her in that way. One imagines that, as a relatively normal young woman, she wanted her husband to make love to her, but that he could not, or would not, oblige. Later, Reggie caused Frances no end of distress when he attempted what she referred to in her diary as an "offence regarding s", believed to be anal sex.[5] Whatever Reggie's psyche permitted and forbade regarding sexual relations with his own wife, it appeared complicated, strongly suggested some repressed hang-up, and ultimately created yet another barrier to the happiness and success of the Kray marriage.

By the autumn of 1965, Frances had effectively left Reggie and was living with her parents at Ormsby Street. In September, she took the first steps to get treatment for her increasingly troubled emotional state. She received help from Dr. Lewis Clein, the Harley Street consultant psychiatrist who had treated Ronnie on the recommendation of Dr. Morris Blasker, the twins' own medical 'Mr. Fix It', many years previously. Frances was already taking anti-depressants as prescribed by her own NHS doctor, and so Dr. Clein changed her medication and suggested a short recuperative stay in a private hospital called Greenways in Fellows Road, Hampstead. After

4   *East London Advertiser*, 18 January 2002.
5   Jacky Hyams; *Frances: The Tragic Bride* (London: John Blake 2014).

one week at Greenways in October, Frances returned to her parents and apparently seemed to be better. But Dr. Clein was very aware of the problems this young woman was having, and described her as "a severe depressive."[6]

◆

"I hate drugs – I always have."[7]

So said Reggie Kray in the 1980s; however, in 1965, the twins extended their constantly exploring fingers into the murky waters of drug-smuggling. Whether this was more at the behest of Ronnie than his more careful brother is unclear, but that year, a Pakistani gambling club owner who paid the twins protection money was asked at a meeting in a pub to do a little job for them:

> Ronnie told me that I had to go to New York and collect a suitcase of drugs from the Pakistani Embassy. The drugs was hashish. I had to sell the drugs to certain people over there and I could keep 25% of the profits. They offered me the job because they trusted me and because I was a Pakistani and could do better business with the Pakistani Embassy. I knew the job was genuine, because I saw the President of Pakistan's son, Tahir Ayub, with them in the pub. I had also sold a lot of drugs for them in London. They used to get other people to deliver the drugs to me. I don't know who these people were. Up to that time I had sold up to 2,000 lbs. weight of hashish for them. Ronnie had told me to sell the stuff. He also told me that the stuff was not his but that he was selling it for a friend.[8]

The drug business had been another new project introduced by Alan Cooper. The American was certainly bringing new ideas to the Kray table and with Ronnie more than enthusiastic to follow his exciting schemes, Cooper was fast becoming a worthy replacement for Leslie Payne in Ronnie's eyes. Payne had begun to have less to do with the Krays after being arrested - and subsequently acquitted - on a charge of fraud that year, and was happy to take a back seat in their affairs, leaving Cooper to continue organising the sale of the stolen bearer bonds:

6   Ibid.
7   Reggie & Ronnie Kray, with Fred Dinenage; *Our Story* (London: Sidgwick and Jackson 1988).
8   Statement by unnamed man, taken at Central Office, New Scotland Yard, 18 May 1968; MEPO 2/11387, ff.853-4 (National Archives).

As the deals progressed, it became more apparent that the Krays contributed little but gaping pockets to the arrangements. This was about the time I drifted away from them and my place as their brains was bid for by Cooper...[9]

As the loose membership of the Firm continued to shift, new faces were coming forward. Cornelius 'Connie' Whitehead, an Eastender born in 1937, was becoming a regular presence within the Firm, and an occasional driver for the twins. He had a number of convictions, including two for dishonesty and one for assaulting a police officer, and, as well as having numerous jobs as a docker, a porter and a labourer,[10] he was not averse to a little pimping on the side. In fact, in 1963, Whitehead had been a suspect during the investigation into the murder of prostitute Gwynneth Rees, in what later became known as the 'Jack the Stripper' murders.[11] Whitehead, known for knocking his girls about, had had an altercation with Rees and she had left him, only to be found dead a short while after; however, there was insufficient evidence against Whitehead, who (for a short time at least) appeared to be the best suspect for the murder.[12]

Ronald Bender, from the Isle of Dogs, was also moving into the ranks at this time, a handsome man who had risen to the position of Acting Sergeant during his National Service and who had worked for the Dock Labour Board since 1960. For the preceding couple of years, however, he had missed a lot of work owing to a back injury,[13] and was now acquiring his income as an increasingly useful member of the Firm. Lenny Hamilton was a good friend of Bender and described him as "a big, strong man. He wasn't violent and if he couldn't do you a good turn then he certainly wouldn't do you a bad one."[14] Significantly, up to that time, Bender did not possess a criminal record, probably the only member of the Firm who didn't.

Alfie Teale, working as a bit-player in the Krays' operations, had introduced the Firm to his mother's club, the '66' in Upper Street,

9   Leslie Payne; *The Brotherhood* (London: Michael Joseph 1973).
10 MEPO 2/11388 (National Archives).
11 These murders, also known as the 'nude murders' or the 'Hammersmith nude murders', involved the deaths of six to eight women, all prostitutes, in 1964 and 1965. The killer was never apprehended.
12 TruTV Crime Library; *Jack The Stripper: Death of a Good Time Girl*; www.trutv.com/library/crime/serial_killers/unsolved/jack_the_stripper/2.html.
13 MEPO 2/11388 (National Archives).
14 Lenny Hamilton & Craig Cabell; *Getting Away With Murder* (London: John Blake 2006).

Islington. One night, Ronnie and Dickie Morgan paid a visit, only to be told by Alfie's brother David, who was minding the door, to go away; he didn't realise who they were. Alfie was horrified and quickly managed to get Ronnie and Morgan into the club before telling David what he'd inadvertently done. Despite David's embarrassment, Ronnie saw the funny side of it and even went as far as to complement David on his professionalism.[15] From then on, Ronnie, and therefore other members of the Kray gang, used the '66' often, and thus David Teale was quickly drawn into the Kray circle. The Teale brothers would be drivers and an extra presence at meetings, sometimes armed at the twins' behest, and later, their other brother, Bobby, would join the ever-expanding and contracting ranks of the Firm.

Eric Mason was another regular associate who, in several prison sentences, had served on the quarry party at Dartmoor Prison and who had apparently been the last person to be given the cat o' nine tails at Wandsworth Prison in the mid-1950s. After leaving Dartmoor, he had approached the twins for help and had received money and new clothes, as many had done before him. He soon became a regular at the Krays' social gatherings and, in 1963, opened his own small club called the Brown Derby in Kingly Street, Soho.[16] The Brown Derby thus became another West End Kray bolt-hole, joining such other establishments as the Colony, La Pigalle, the Starlite and the Astor Club, amongst others. The West End had always been considered a sort of 'no man's land' as far as London gangs were concerned: the Nash brothers were still on good terms with the Krays and a tacit understanding regarding territory and business interests ensured that when the North and East London overlords came together in the West End, mutual respect would prevail. The Richardsons of South London, however, posed a different problem. The Nashes and the Krays maintained their equilibrium through a dialogue that went back many years, but the Richardsons, isolated by the great swathe of the River Thames and backed by such notorious associates as George Cornell and Frankie Fraser, were seen as a potential threat to any peace in the West End. The Richardson brothers thought otherwise, but they were smart, conducting their criminal empire south of the river in a manner that avoided unwarranted attention from the law.

15 Bobby Teale with Clare Campbell: *Bringing Down the Krays* (London: Ebury Publishing 2012).
16 Tony Lambrianou with Carol Clerk; *Inside the Firm* (London: Smith Gryphon 1991).

Charlie Richardson later likened their operation to "a creature of stealth, stalking his prey with great cunning", and the Krays as "bulls in china shops, setting off alarms and continually bodging things up."[17]

The Richardsons made large amounts of money from their scrap metal business, but had branched out into protection and long-firm fraud, plus a highly successful enterprise installing and managing fruit machines called Atlantic Machines, which was run by Eddie Richardson and Frankie Fraser. Many of their machines were placed in West End venues; some, like the Astor, Pigalle and The Stork,[18] were frequented by the Kray Firm, and the very fact that Richardson-owned machines sat in certain clubs ensured the proprietors automatic protection, which undoubtedly diluted the Krays' (and other gangs') potential influence in the area.[19] And they were ambitious, as Charlie Richardson's involvement in the diamond mining operation in South Africa attested. The problem was that, as the 1960s progressed, the Richardsons began to show an interest in opportunities outside their 'manor'. They had a protection interest in a small East End minicab firm and two of their associates, Brian Mottram and Billy Stayton, were running long-firms in Hackney Road and on the Essex coast at Southend-on-Sea. They were nothing if not driven, and backed themselves with a powerful reputation for meting out 'discipline'. In the words of Ronnie Kray:

...they were a mightily powerful and feared organisation. Feared because if anyone crossed them, the Richardsons were ruthless in their retribution. Some of the methods used by the Richardson gang made the Kray twins look like Methodist preachers...

Even our guys were scared stiff they'd fall into the Richardson's hands. None of them went south of the river unless they had to, and then they'd scurry back as quick as they could when their business was finished...

There was sort of a truce between us and the Richardsons, based on the premise that they would stay south of the river and we would stay on the other side. But it was always an uneasy truce and I had the gut feeling that something or someone would force us into a

17 Charlie Richardson: *The Last Gangster: My Final Confession* (London: Century 2013).

18 Frankie Fraser with James Morton; *Mad Frank – Memoirs of a Life of Crime* (London: Sphere Books 1994).

19 Paul Willets; *The Look of Love: The Life and Times of Paul Raymond, Soho's King of Clubs* (London: Serpent's Tail 2013).

full-scale war.[20]

A potential flashpoint had come sometime previously, one night at the Astor Club, when Eric Mason found himself entangled in an altercation with Frankie Fraser. The background behind the incident, like the timing, is unclear,[21] as the story differs in the telling between Mason and Fraser; however, the outcome was potentially explosive. The night ended with Mason being taken under duress to Atlantic Machines' headquarters in Tottenham Court Road and being set upon in the cellar by a number of men, including Fraser. 'Mad' Frank lived up to his nickname by attacking Mason with an axe:

> *I must have put me hand up to ward off a blow, and the chopper... must have gone through me hand... my hand was pinned to my head with the chopper. And somebody was trying to chop my hand off... and I heard somebody say "Chop his hands off, he'll never fight again," that was the words; and I realised my brain must have been damaged as I couldn't speak. I was trying to mouth something... and I felt quite a lot of blows, and one thing and another, and the next thing I knew, I woke up on a bit of waste ground. An old boy, a tramp or somebody, had stumbled over my body – that saved my life, because he must have told somebody and they took me to hospital. The next thing I knew, it was two days later, when I come to. I had 370 stitches in me, three fractures in me skull...*[22]

According to Leslie Payne, who was present at Vallance Road when Mason had recovered sufficiently to see the twins about the incident,

> *[Mason] was in a terrible mess, all twisted up where he hadn't healed properly, with one leg trailing, and his left arm hunched up under his shoulder, and said, 'Look what they did to me.' Ronnie replied, 'Yeah, well, Fraser took a bit of a liberty with you, but it's not really our problem now, is it?'*[23]

The twins had been a little unhappy with Mason for some time as they disapproved of him using their name to exert influence in his own business ventures. Uncharacteristically, they took no retribution,

20 Reggie & Ronnie Kray, with Fred Dinenage; *Our Story* (London: Sidgwick and Jackson 1988).

21 It is believed to have happened either in late 1964 or early 1965.

22 Eric Mason, interviewed by Liam Galvin; www.youtube.com/watch?v=BbYBcEMsX98.

23 Leslie Payne; *The Brotherhood* (London: Michael Joseph 1973).

although they had a collection and gave Mason £40, and with that, he was effectively off the Firm. Soon after, Mason took his business to the north of England.

The Mason/Fraser incident had all the makings of a Kray/ Richardson equivalent of the Cuban Missile Crisis, but like that most worrying of historical confrontations, the twins' refusal to step up to the plate and let it pass avoided any potential tit-for-tat bloodshed. The *détente* would not last for long, however, and as 1965 drew to a close, the Krays, and particularly Ronnie, as ever 'The Colonel', would start to perceive the Richardsons as a major threat. Albert Donoghue watched from the front line as Ronnie began to obsess about the south Londoners' success:

> *The idea that Charlie Richardson was becoming stinking rich drove Ronnie into a blind jealousy – blind because he should have seen we could copy the Richardsons. But no. Just because he couldn't match them, all he wanted to do was smash them and take over their empire. He believed that if the Firm didn't soon crush the Richardsons, they would quickly crush the Firm.*[24]

In December 1965, a meeting was held between the Krays and the Richardsons at the Astor Club, a kind of diplomatic conference intended to neutralise the risk of any impending trouble in what was looking to be a very contentious issue: what to do with the West End? Albert Donoghue recalled a summit between the two gangs which also included the Nash brothers and members of Freddie Foreman's firm,[25] organised to set out lines of demarcation. Whether these meetings were the same event is unclear, but the result of both was that the Richardsons, keen to do their own thing without having any restrictions put on them by any unwritten code of conduct, rejected all suggestions, and thus any part in any multi-gang accord. Things got heated and no progress had been made. Ronnie was apparently furious.

It has been said that it was also at a meeting at the Astor Club that George Cornell, present as Richardson 'muscle', uttered his famous put-down about Ronnie Kray being a 'fat poof'. Ronnie later said that this was at a meeting at the club with a couple of important American Mafia representatives. The idea, according to Ronnie, was that the

---

24 Albert Donoghue & Martin Short; *The Enforcer* (London: John Blake 2002).
25 Ibid.

Richardsons would be introduced to the twins' Mafia-led projects and the meeting was called to work out just who was going to do what.

> *Cornell, of course, couldn't resist sticking his oar in, time and time again, even though it was strictly none of his business. The negotiations were actually between the Krays and the Richardsons – the others were there purely for protection, to keep a watching brief. But Cornell was doing his best to stir things up. He said we were fannying [talking a load of rubbish]. Then he did a very stupid thing. In front of all those people – our own men and top men from the other side – he said, "Take no notice of Kray. He's just a big, fat poof."*[26]

Many commentators have taken this as gospel, but some have challenged the assumption. On balance, the alleged insult on Ronnie's sexuality in all likelihood probably did happen, somehow, somewhere. Unquestionably, George Cornell was a strong character, some would say an arrogant man at times, and it is fair to assume that on occasion, when the subject of Ronnie Kray came up in conversation and Cornell wanted to show his disdain for his old acquaintance, 'fat poof' would have made an ideal put-down.

Frankie Fraser always maintained that the insult never happened; he believed that the contretemps took place at a later meeting at the Stork Club when the Krays, intent on getting a slice of a porn-film racket that the Richardsons were about to get involved in, were told to leave well alone. Fraser wasn't at the meeting himself, but has often stated that although insults were traded between Ronnie and Cornell, 'fat poof' wasn't one of them.[27] Interestingly, in his memoir, Mickey Fawcett claimed that the 'fat poof' story was a tale created by the Firm, as a smokescreen "to hide the truth of a feud gone desperately wrong."[28] Tony Lambrianou certainly went along with the 'fat poof' story, describing the alleged insult as "a direct challenge."[29]

Many believe that Cornell would never have said it to Ronnie's face: such insolence and such a public denigration of Ronnie's pride and status would probably have resulted in instant retaliation. But a good

26 Reggie & Ronnie Kray, with Fred Dinenage; *Our Story* (London: Sidgwick and Jackson 1988).

27 Frankie Fraser with James Morton; *Mad Frank – Memoirs of a Life of Crime* (London: Sphere Books 1994).

28 Mickey Fawcett; *Krayzy Days* (Pen Press 2013).

29 Tony Lambrianou with Carol Clerk; *Inside the Firm* (London: Smith Gryphon 1991).

example of Cornell's feelings towards Ronnie's sexuality can be seen in this revealing story from John Barry, former owner of the Regency Club:

> *[Cornell] came into the Grave Maurice pub, you know, one day and Ronnie's with his little boys, you understand? He come in on his own. The Firm were there, if you like, all the crew, they went to get him a drink and he went "Nah, nah, nah, I don't drink with you and your little poofs", and had his drink and walked out.*[30]

There was certainly no love lost between Cornell and Ronnie, and Billy Webb would claim that Cornell told him that he would have loved to get Ronnie on his own and "tear him apart with his bare hands."[31] It does appear that the number of accounts which state that the famous insult was uttered (regardless of how often, when and where, and to whom) adds weight to the suggestion that Cornell really did say it, or at least words to that effect. The real issue is that, if he did indeed insult Ronnie face-to-face at a meeting, with others present as witnesses, only those who were there could confirm it, and all the main protagonists have now passed on.

What is clear is that, in late 1965 and early 1966, an attempt was being made at a compromise between the major-league London gangs over what was going to happen in the West End and the Richardsons, successful, driven and ruthless, were not about to have their thriving enterprise watered down or messed about with by anybody else. 'The Colonel' mobilised his 'troops' for what he could see as an impending battle. Albert Donoghue recalled:

> *The twins cut a list up. We were each given the name of a member of the Richardson firm, so that when it really came off, our job was to take this one particular person out to kill him. So me and Connie Whitehead were given Brian Mottram, one of the Richardsons' long-firm men. 'Take Mottram out', was the command. Once we'd done him, we would probably be given another one. Scotch Jack and Ian Barrie were given Frankie Fraser; Ronnie Kray and Nobby Clarke were going to have Charles Richardson, though if it had actually come to it, Ronnie would have wanted Fraser too. Reggie was going to have Eddie Richardson. George Cornell was also mentioned, but*

---

30 Interview featured in the TV documentary *The Notorious Kray Twins* (Aubrey Powell Partnership Production 2001).

31 Billy Webb; *Running With The Krays* (Edinburgh: Mainstream Publishing 1993).

he wasn't top of the list.[32]

It was all a case of 'wait for the command'. The order could come as a result of some incident or perceived imminent threat, or, worryingly, spontaneously from Ronnie when he was in one of his darker, volatile moods. The Firm were very much aware that when 'The Colonel' felt the time was right, even if it wasn't, they would be going to war.

◆

At 75 Rushey Green in Catford, South London, sits the former Savoy Ballroom, a once handsome dancehall now in use as a furniture showroom, with the Right Now Jesus centre occupying the first floor. In the 1960s, it was a dancing and gaming club, first known as The Witchdoctor, then Mr. Smith's, and in the first half of that vibrant decade it had seen gigs by such illustrious performers as the Rolling Stones and Gene Vincent, who both played there in 1964.[33] It was a licensed club with facilities for dining, cabaret and gambling, the games offered being Blackjack, American dice and Roulette; it was licensed until 2.00 a.m. The club used fruit machines supplied by Atlantic Machines and as a result, even though there was not sufficient evidence for the police to make a criminal case of it, Mr. Smith's effectively fell under the protection of the Richardsons.

On the night of 7 March 1966, Eddie Richardson, accompanied by Frankie Fraser, Jimmy Moody, Billy Stayton, Henry Rawlings and Ronald Jeffrey, all key members of the Richardson firm, were socialising in the club, having arrived at 10.00 p.m., and were sitting in the raised seating area known as the balcony restaurant. Also sitting nearby were a group of men who ran their own operations in the area, a gang headed by brothers Billy and Harry Hayward. Billy Hayward was there with Henry Botton, William Gardner, Peter Hennessey, Richard Hart and a few others.[34] Unbeknown to all, some of the men in the club, most significantly Hart, were armed.[35] The evening turned into the early hours of the following morning and

32 Albert Donoghue & Martin Short; *The Enforcer* (London: John Blake 2002).
33 The Who played there in April 1966, as did Desmond Dekker three years later; www.derelictlondon.com/music-history-landmarks.html
34 Report by Detective Superintendent Cummings, 5 July 1966; MEPO 2/10933 (National Archives).
35 Frankie Fraser with James Morton; *Mad Frank – Memoirs of a Life of Crime* (London: Sphere Books 1994).

officially, drinks would stop being served at 2.00 a.m.; however, by 2.45 a.m. the two factions were still present, the regular customers having long since left. There was an air of foreboding and the bar staff were of the opinion that trouble was brewing, as the Hayward group wanted more drinks. Eddie Richardson did not want to flout the licensing laws any more than they already were and decided that everybody had had enough and that the club should finally close, and as a result, words were exchanged between the two groups. Suddenly, Eddie Richardson and Peter Hennessey were having a stand up fight, or 'straightener', on the dance floor and, within moments, other fights began to break out. Frankie Fraser takes up the story:

> Dickie Hart had produced a gun and slipped away from the raised dais where the tables were and from a distance of about thirty feet he's firing a 45 revolver at random more or less. He could have hit anybody – friend or whoever. One bullet hit a chair leg and another the roof, and a third hit Harry Rawlings in the shoulder and arm and busted an artery. In seconds, Harry was bleeding to death. Literally seconds, you could see it. I told Hart, who was still waving the gun, that Rawlings was very seriously injured and we had to get him to a hospital. He said all right but then he went and fired another shot.[36]

Fraser was shot in the leg whilst trying to subdue Hart and the fight spread as the brawling factions piled out of the back door of the club onto Farley Road. More shots were fired, one hitting Eddie Richardson. Jimmy Tippett, the doorman that night, managed to get the gun off of Hart and placed it in the handbag of the girl he was with, but before he left, somebody must have retrieved the gun.[37] Hart was shot during the chaos, the identity of the gunman unknown. When the police arrived, alerted by local residents, they found Fraser slumped in somebody's back garden incapacitated by a shattered thigh bone. Hart was found lying by the back door of the club with a bullet wound to the chest.

All involved were arrested for affray and the injured men, Richardson, Fraser, Rawlings and Hart, were taken to Lewisham Hospital. They were admitted at 4.00 a.m., but Hart died seven minutes later, the

36 Frankie Fraser with James Morton; *Mad Frank – Memoirs of a Life of Crime* (London: Sphere Books 1994).
37 Interview with Jimmy Tippett; *Gangsters: Faces of the Underworld* (Revelation Films 2014).

cause of death being "haemothorax and a gunshot wound to the chest."[38]

Like the Pen Club shooting in 1960, this was another appalling result of gangland violence run amok. With many of the Richardson gang now locked up on a charge of affray and Fraser also being charged with the murder of Hart,[39] this spelt the beginning of the end for the Richardson gang and, on the face of it, the Krays build-up to a battle with their south London rivals suddenly became unnecessary. The big problem was that Dickie Hart was a friend of the Firm. Although associated with Hayward's gang, it is possible that he was one of the Krays' spies south of the river. The Hayward brothers, Billy and Harry, and their 'team', had been attempting to stymie the Richardsons' expansion and so by default were allies of the Krays. Hart was not a member of the Firm as such, but he was certainly somebody whose life the Krays respected. And now he was dead.

The Richardsons were now effectively washed up; war had been averted, it seems, although at a cost. However, there was one member of the Richardson gang who was not at the shooting: George Cornell.

38 Report by Detective Superintendent Cummings, 5 July 1966; MEPO 2/10933 (National Archives).
39 Fraser was charged on 29 April 1966 and appeared in court on 20 June, pleading 'not guilty' to the murder. He was acquitted, but was sentenced to five years imprisonment for the affray.

ELEVEN

"LOOK WHO'S HERE..."

Author's note: To avoid repetitive citations, all statements, timings, reports, names and other associated information in this chapter are drawn from MEPO 2/11406, MEPO 2/10922, MEPO 2/10923 (the Metropolitan Police files referring to the Cornell murder -1966 and 1968 - held at the National Archives) unless otherwise stated. Only specific quotes from these reports are individually referenced.

◆

The murder of George Cornell by Ronnie Kray, in the Blind Beggar pub in Whitechapel on the night of 9 March 1966 has surely gone down in history as one of the most notorious British gangland executions of all time. Every book on the subject of the Krays has to mention it; many books on British crime give it page space; and people still visit the pub today as a minor East End tourist attraction. Bar staff are often asked about an alleged bullet hole that is supposedly concealed by a strategically placed picture, and it is often the first port of call for East End gangster tours.[1] But what is interesting to note is that there have been few first-hand accounts of what actually happened inside the pub that evening. Apart from newspaper reports from the Kray trial and fleeting accounts by Ronnie Kray and the barmaid who witnessed the shooting, little is known about how a quiet Wednesday

---

1   Britmovie Tours use this as the starting point for their Gangster Tour, hosted by actor Stephen Marcus, who played the character of Nick the Greek in the 1997 movie *Lock, Stock and Two Smoking Barrels.*

night turned into a night of very public murder.

Reggie's later killing of Jack McVitie and the fate of Frank 'The Mad Axeman' Mitchell have been well covered in the media: in these two cases, there were multiple witnesses, mainly from the Firm, who publicly gave their accounts in memoirs, interviews and in court; and, as we shall see, it is not too difficult to assemble a rounded portrayal of those events.[2] But the real story of the Cornell murder – from the moment the Blind Beggar opened that evening, through the untimely death of Cornell in West London later that night, to the subsequent police investigation – has sat hidden in the files of the Metropolitan Police since 1966. The statements of the people present at the time of the shooting, the medical teams and police officers who responded, Cornell's friends and family... all of these reveal, harrowingly, what really happens when somebody is murdered by gunshot, and the repercussions which follow. Those police files on the Cornell shooting, lodged between 1966 and 1968 and only opened to the public by the National Archives at the beginning of this century, have never really been mined effectively: Craig Cabell[3] has used their content and, even so, his account of the death of Cornell is incomplete. Cabell made a number of deductions based on the information available, and drew conclusions with which, with due respect, this author cannot agree. James Morton, in a book specifically written for the National Archives,[4] could only give them so much space, likewise Martin Fido.[5] By looking more closely at these files and contemporary newspaper reports, and by drawing upon the memoirs of the key players (Ronnie Kray, the barmaid and Jack Dickson; Ian Barrie has always remained resolutely silent about his time with the Krays) and peripheral characters (Bobby Teale, Albert Donoghue and, of course, Reggie Kray), the real story can now be told in full for the first time. But first, it is worth considering why this most open of murders happened in the first place.

As discussed in the previous chapter, the well-worn explanation for the shooting is that it was an act of revenge, a disproportionate gesture by which Ronnie repaid Cornell's earlier description of him as a 'fat

---

2 For instance, in 2000's *The Krays: Unfinished Business*, author Martin Fido published a number of then recently-released reports and statements which allowed him to put together a most comprehensive account of what happened to Jack McVitie.

3 Craig Cabell; *The Kray Brothers: The Image Shattered* (London: Robson 2002) and Lenny Hamilton & Craig Cabell; *Getting Away With Murder* (London: John Blake 2006).

4 James Morton; *The Krays: Crime Archive* (London: National Archives 2008).

5 Martin Fido; *The Krays: Unfinished Business* (London: Carlton Books 1999).

poof'. Regardless of its merits as a trigger for gangland retribution, this alleged insult is only one of several reasons put forward over the years.

Leslie Payne talked about an incident involving an East End warehouseman from whom Cornell had been demanding protection money. In the hope that the twins could get the south Londoner off his back, the warehouseman gave them £2,000 after they suggested he pay them to kill Cornell. The twins went to see Cornell in the assumption that he would know what was good for him and back off, leaving the twins with a handy £2,000 which the warehouseman would be foolish to ask to be given back. Cornell simply ignored the threat and went back to the warehouseman and beat him up for causing trouble. This would have been seen by the twins, and particularly Ronnie, as a humiliation, a sign that they did not have the control everybody believed they had, and that Cornell was making them look foolish.

Payne certainly believed that somebody was going to get killed at some time or another:

> *I think Ronnie had been dreaming and planning a murder for years and years. There was nothing subtle about his intentions; if someone annoyed him, he would always say: "I wish I had him in some lonely barn in the country. I'd pour two gallons of petrol over him and set the bugger alight." It is a remarkable tribute to his self-confidence that he could make his debut as a murderer in such an astonishingly public way, walk away from the body and the shocked drinkers, and make no effort at all to cover up the mess.*[6]

But of course there is also the idea of a wider feud, and other interpersonal issues (picked up by Tony Lambrianou and later Mickey Fawcett) which some say had been building for years. At least two former associates, Lenny Hamilton and Bobby Teale, suggested that the rivalry was set in motion in the early 1960s, with a fistfight outside the Brown Bear pub in Leman Street, Whitechapel, which Cornell dramatically won, making him apparently the only person ever to knock Ronnie Kray out. Interestingly, John Pearson recounted a conversation Ronnie had once had with his friend Wilf Pine,[7] about why the situation built up as it did: if true, Ronnie mentioned the

6 Leslie Payne; *The Brotherhood* (London: Michael Joseph 1973).

7 Pine, once described as one of only two Englishmen to be allowed into the Mafia, was a minder for rock band The Move in the 1960s and went on to co-manage Black Sabbath in the 1970s. Ronnie Kray's book *My Story* is dedicated to him.

alleged fight, although in a different venue to that mentioned by Hamilton, and the famous insult. Pearson himself believed that it was "the nearest Ron ever came to giving anyone a proper answer."[8] Apparently, in Ronnie's account, the alleged fight happened in the Green Dragon Club. Ronnie was on his own, and already drunk by the time he arrived. He found Cornell in attendance and some of the old antagonism that had once existed between the Bethnal Green boys and the Watney Streeters was rekindled. After an exchange of insults, the pair had a fight, and here Ronnie takes up the story (as told to Pine):

> I'll be honest with you, Wilf, Cornell kicked the shit out of me that night... Afterwards of course, I wanted to go after him, like the next morning, but Reg put a block on it. "Don't go getting involved," he said. We were getting a good pension off the place from Bill Ackerman who ran the Green Dragon at the time. So Reg told me, "Ron, don't fuck it up by going for Cornell, it just ain't worth it."

> So I didn't do anything about it. But over the years, every time I saw Cornell he gave me a sneer and said something sarcastic. Yeah, once he did call me a fat poof, and a couple of other things I won't repeat. But it was always a case of wrong place, wrong time for me to retaliate and it meant that Cornell was somehow always on my mind. I don't know if I was afraid of him or what, but as the thought of that beatin' kept on coming back to me I suppose I might have been. Fear can make you do funny things.

> Then, after I heard about the Richardson's fight at Catford, I wasn't at my best. I don't know that my pills weren't working, and when I was told that Cornell was just around the corner at the Beggar, I could see him coming round to Vallance Road and making a name for himself by trying to kill all of us unless I stopped him...

> And that is how Cornell got killed. And you know, Wilf, the funny thing is that it worked. After that I didn't have to remember being beaten by him anymore. Even now when I think of him, all I can see is his fucking head spurtin' blood instead.[9]

The fracas at Mr. Smith's club in Catford the night before Cornell's shooting, which involved the Richardson gang and which resulted in the death of Dickie Hart, appears to have been a catalyst for the subsequent murder. There are two issues here: the death of Hart

---

8   John Pearson; *Notorious* (London: Century 2010).
9   Ibid.

could easily have been something worth avenging – an eye for an eye – in the mind of somebody like Ronnie Kray. Hart was not a part of the Kray Firm, as has often been said, but he was a member of Harry Hayward's south London gang, which had been trying to block the Richardsons' expansion; the code of 'the enemy of my enemy is my friend' would surely have applied. Also, the police operation after the Mr. Smith's affair led to the sweeping up of most of the Richardson gang; in other words, the Krays' supposed South London rivals were seriously depleted and there was hardly anybody left to hit back at. If revenge was going to be the order of the day, there was really only one 'last man standing' prominent enough to warrant such retribution, one of the few Richardson associates who was not actually at Mr. Smith's that night – George Cornell.

The oft-repeated idea that Cornell was drinking on the Kray 'manor' with impunity only twenty-four hours after the death of Dickie Hart has also been seen as the final straw. Perhaps it was (to Ronnie at least), but claims that Cornell was deliberately ignoring the boundaries and making a provocative show in the East End are basically wrong. Cornell, as an Eastender by birth, was a frequent visitor to the area. Some of his siblings still resided there (his brother Joseph lived in Hereford Street, only a minute's walk from the Kray house at Vallance Road), and he was a regular visitor to the pubs, including the Blind Beggar. As a friend of Patsy Quill, who ran the pub, he would often drop by for a drink and a chat and in fact had done so only two days before his death. Thus the idea that Cornell was doing anything provocative by sitting in a pub on Kray territory does not hold water.

What must be considered is the build-up of animosity between George Cornell and Ronnie Kray that had been going on for several years. If Ronnie disliked or mistrusted somebody, then they would get little leeway if they were perceived by him to have done something wrong, or had taken liberties. Cornell had obviously aroused Ronnie's displeasure on several occasions and did not seem to care, cranking up the feud at any given opportunity. Put this together with any of the other incidents and put George Cornell in the immediate area and all one has to do is add one more vital ingredient to create the explosive mix: Ronnie's mental health.

As Leslie Payne had observed, Ronnie, owing to his unstable mental state, with its characteristics of paranoia and violence, would probably have killed somebody sooner or later. When his moods were at their blackest, he could be capable of tremendous brutality, and his reaction to events often depended on how effective his medication was. He often fantasized about inflicting bloody retribution on his perceived enemies, sometimes to the extent of planning to have them executed. He already had a list of potential victims. The problem was that Ronnie drank quite heavily, and alcohol was never a good combination with drugs like Stemetil; he had been drinking for some time at the Lion pub when he heard that Cornell was in the Blind Beggar. If Wilf Pine's account is correct, Ronnie certainly implied that he was having some issues with his medication on that fateful night.

The conclusion is that a whole series of perceived slights, insults and misdemeanours by Cornell, going back years, had seen to it that he was marking himself out to be a good candidate for Ronnie's first murder. The death of Dickie Hart may have exacerbated the issue and the fact that Cornell happened to be close by in the Blind Beggar, when Ronnie was somewhat worse the wear for drink, probably clinched it. Whatever excuses people try and give, George Cornell died at the behest of an unpredictably dangerous, homicidal man who just snapped into violent mode, as he was prone to do, because he was in the wrong place at the wrong time. As a result, Cornell left behind a widow, an eight-year-old son and a six-month-old daughter who would never remember her father.[10] If Ronnie had received the same news about Cornell's whereabouts a day later, or even an hour later, it may all have been very different.

◆

Wednesday, 9 March 1966 was all set to be another run-of-the-mill weekday evening at the Blind Beggar when William Ivor Richards, the nineteen-year-old barman, opened up at 5.00 p.m. The 'Beggars', as most people referred to it, was a large pub which, on account of its position close to the busy junction of Whitechapel Road and Cambridge Heath Road (Mile End Gate), attracted a range of clientele: it had its regulars as well as passing trade, and could become extremely busy at weekends. As was common in those days, the Blind Beggar was split into several bars. The entrance doors on the left side led into the long saloon, with its two fireplaces and ladies' toilet on the left side, the bar on the right and the gents' in the far corner. On the other side of the pub, accessible by the right hand entrance, was

10 William was born in 1958, daughter Rayner in 1965.

the public bar. With the counter on the left side, this was smaller than the saloon, as the far end was separated by an arch leading to what was invariably called the snug or 'dark bar' and the gents' and ladies' toilets for the public bar. A wrought iron arch led to the left from here back into the saloon. In all bars, tables and chairs and sometimes stools were situated against the walls, and there were the customary stools positioned around the bar itself.

For four years, the licensee at the Blind Beggar had been Patrick 'Patsy' Quill, who owned a number of other pubs in the East End with his brother Jimmy, and he employed several bar staff: assistant manager Edwin Wood; William Richards (whom everybody knew as 'Ivor') and his brother David; John Keating, a huge comical man whose nickname was 'nut-nut';[11] Frances Sanders, a mother of three who had separated from her husband and who had known the Quills for nearly ten years; and occasionally, Jimmy Quill.

Patsy Quill kept a respectable house and, whether his customers were villains or not, he made sure that everybody knew how to behave. For this reason, the Blind Beggar was a kind of no-man's land for the criminal fraternity and all knew that they could drink there in what was essentially neutral territory. Ronnie Kray did not like the Beggars and hardly ever went there, preferring the Grave Maurice down the road, but Reggie was an occasional early evening visitor, and was usually alone.[12] Ronnie described the pub as

> ...a big ugly building in a very poor part of London. Not the sort of place you'd want to take a lady friend for a quiet drink or a business contact to clinch a big deal. It was simply the kind of pub where the poor people in that part of London would go for a drink to drown their sorrows, to have a knees-up on Saturday nights and pretend they were feeling happy.[13]

Billy Ambrose, who had been injured in the Pen Club shooting, was a regular customer with his friends and family and, of course, there was George Cornell, an old friend of Patsy Quill from the Watney Street days. As has already been stated, Cornell used the Beggars often, but was usually alone when he did so.

11 Mrs X with James Morton; *Calling Time on the Krays: The Barmaid's Tale* (Little, Brown and Company 1996)
12 Ibid.
13 Reggie & Ronnie Kray, with Fred Dinenage; *Our Story* (London: Sidgwick and Jackson 1988).

When Ivor Richards opened up the pub on that fateful Wednesday in March 1966, waiting for him at the door was seventy-year-old Isaac Kramer, sometimes known as 'Ginger Ike' and, as the first customer of the evening, he bought a pint of bitter in a jug (the first of three he consumed that night) and sat at a table close to the saloon bar door. About an hour or so later he was joined by Henry Wardle, a clerk, and, at 7.00 p.m., another friend, William Quinn, a clerical officer.

At about 7.30 p.m., William Amass entered the saloon. A nineteen-year-old instrument maker, Amass was alone, and after ordering a pint of Red Barrel, sat at the bar, quietly minding his own business. Soon after, he noticed several men come to the bar; it was George Cornell and friends.

At the time of his death, George Cornell was living at Masterman House, New Church Road, Camberwell, with his wife Olive and their two children. He had already been out for much of that day and had been drinking for a while with brothers Ron and Billy Webb and their cousin in the Old Basing House pub on Kingsland Road, Haggerston.[14] He left them stating he was going to visit Jimmy Andrews, a friend of theirs who was recovering in the London Hospital from a devastating gunshot wound to the leg,[15] and they agreed to meet again the following day in the Ten Bells in Spitalfields,[16] an appointment Cornell would never make. He returned home at about 4.30 p.m., where he stayed until about 6.30 p.m. When he left, he didn't tell Olive where he was going, or what time he would return, but she was not too worried as he would usually call her at a later hour so they could meet in their local pub. Although Cornell had a car at his disposal (a 1965 Vauxhall Victor, borrowed from a friend), he did not drive that night; he had arranged with fellow south Londoner and bookmaker Albert Wood to visit Andrews, and Wood picked Cornell up in his own car, a Zephyr Six.

After the visit, which lasted about an hour or so, they decided to stop off at the nearby Blind Beggar for a drink, and as they did so they were spotted parking in front of the pub by John Dale, William Wylie (a Scotsman known as 'Jock') and Henry Isaacs. These three men had

---

14 Billy Webb; *Running With The Krays* (Edinburgh: Mainstream Publishing 1993).

15 Andrews would subsequently have to have the leg amputated.

16 At 84 Commercial Street, this pub is famous for its alleged associations with the victims of Jack the Ripper; between 1975 and 1988 it was renamed the 'Jack the Ripper', blatantly cashing in on its infamy.

recently left the 20th Century Club on Brick Lane and, with Isaacs driving, they had intended to have a further drink at the Hayfield pub on Mile End Road; however, when they saw Cornell, whom Dale knew, Dale suggested a change of venue. On entering the saloon bar, Cornell, Wood, Dale, Isaacs and Wylie settled at the far end of the bar. Cornell and Wood sat on stools on the corner, Dale stood by Cornell next to the ironwork arch that led to the small snug area of the public bar, and Isaacs and Wylie stood nearby.

At about 8.00 p.m., there was a bit of movement in the saloon as Isaacs and Wylie, who had not intended to stay long, left Dale, Cornell and Wood to their drinking and chatting. Over by the main door, Isaac Kramer and Henry Wardle left William Quinn to his own devices. An unemployed young man, Rodney Parker, came in and ordered a pint, drank it alone and then went off to Murphy's next door. In the public bar an old regular, seventy-seven year-old Thomas Slarke, known to all as 'Pop', came in and ordered a pint of mild. By now, barman Ivor Richards must have been looking at his watch – not only was the pub pretty quiet, with little to do, but Frances Sanders, the barmaid, was running late. She should have started at 7.30 p.m., at which point Richards would normally go off to his parents' house for supper; but Sanders, looking after three children with the help of her cousin, often arrived a little late. She eventually dashed in at about 8.10 p.m., and after going upstairs to drop off her coat and stopping for a brief exchange with Patsy Quill's wife Frances, came back down to start her shift. Richards left and, with it being so quiet, Sanders set about cleaning some ashtrays. 'Pop' Slarke had done a bit of sweeping in the public bar as a favour, so she gave him a ham roll, before serving a group of three people (who were never identified) who had just entered the public bar. It was looking to be a very uneventful night.

◆

Famously, at this time, the twins and assorted members of the Firm were having one of their regular drinks at The Lion in Tapp Street. Jack Dickson and Ian Barrie were the first of the second-string to arrive, but Ronnie Kray was already there and appeared to have made an early start on the drink. Reggie came in with Albert Donoghue and gradually, various members of the Firm turned up. Perhaps feeling that there needed to be more of a presence, Reggie phoned David Teale's flat in Moresby Road, Clapton, and asked him and his brothers,

Alfie and Bobby, to join them: they weren't too keen (they had all settled in for a night of TV), but they realised that if they didn't go, Reggie would send somebody round to collect them anyway, so they made their preparations to join him.[17]

It was about 8.15 p.m. when Ronnie got the message that George Cornell was in the Blind Beggar. Some accounts suggest that a phone call was received on the bar phone, but Albert Donoghue, who was there, stated that one of Ronnie's informers came into the pub and told him where Cornell was. Ronnie announced that he was going elsewhere and called out, "Who's got a car with them?" When nobody answered, he called out for Connie Whitehead, whom he considered an irritant, but he hadn't arrived, so Ronnie barked, "Ain't that bastard here yet? He's always late getting here when I want him – he's always poncing around with other bastards."[18] He was obviously in a dark mood. Jack Dickson was asked directly if he had a car and with no choice but to say yes, was commandeered with Ian Barrie to follow Ronnie out of The Lion. Before they left, Reggie asked Ronnie what was going on, and received the reply, "I'm going to see if that bastard Cornell is in the Beggars." Reggie, obviously aware that trouble was brewing said, "Let's talk about it first," but Ronnie, true to form, was having none of it. He'd made up his mind. "There's nothing to talk about," he said. "I'm going to do the bastard."[19]

As Ronnie and his two companions left The Lion, Reggie turned to Albert Donoghue and said, "Cornell's round the Beggars, and he's going round there. I hope he doesn't do anything stupid."[20]

Once Ronnie, Dickson and Barrie were in the car, Dickson asked where Ronnie wanted to go, and he replied that he wanted to go to the house in Vallance Road.[21] On arriving, Ronnie got out and went inside, whilst Dickson and Barrie chatted about what a "fucking bad mood"[22] Ronnie was in. Before long, Ronnie emerged, jumped back into the car and told Dickson to head for the Blind Beggar. They drove down

---

17 Bobby Teale with Clare Campbell: *Bringing Down the Krays* (London: Ebury Publishing 2012).

18 John Dickson; *Murder Without Conviction* (London: Sidgwick and Jackson 1986).

19 Reggie Kray; *Born Fighter* (London: Arrow Books 1991).

20 Albert Donoghue; *The Enforcer* (London: John Blake 2002).

21 Some accounts say that Ronnie got Dickson to stop at the Grave Maurice pub, as if he was looking for Cornell in there; however, Dickson makes no mention of this in his memoir and, after all, he was there.

22 John Dickson; *Murder Without Conviction* (London: Sidgwick and Jackson 1986).

Vallance Road before turning left into Whitechapel Road and as they approached the Blind Beggar, Ronnie told Dickson to go straight over the traffic lights at the corner with Cambridge Heath Road then do an immediate U-turn and go back across the lights before parking outside the bank that sat directly opposite the pub. Dickson mentioned that he wouldn't be able to stay there, but Ronnie told him aggressively, "I want you to stay here! I shall only be a short time."[23] Just before Ronnie and Barrie left the car, Dickson saw Ronnie hand Barrie a gun: this was not unusual, as Ronnie had a habit of getting members of the firm to look after weapons for him, but as Barrie gingerly pocketed the weapon, Dickson could see he was not happy – his face had gone white. As the two men left the car and strolled across the road to the Blind Beggar, Dickson sat waiting, oblivious to the events which would unfold over the next few minutes.

As Ronnie Kray made his preparations to confront his nemesis, two more customers entered the Blind Beggar: Michael Flannery, a 27-year-old sales rep and his friend Raymond Drury, a technical sales executive. After ordering their pints, they established themselves at the bar in the snug, not too far away from Cornell, Dale and Wood, who were on the other side of the bar beyond the ironwork arch into the saloon. William Quinn, now alone, went to the bar for another drink and, spotting Cornell at the other end of the bar, decided to stand him a pint; he waved a pound note at Sanders to attract her attention. Cornell knew Quinn and, rather than accept a drink, he bought Quinn one instead: Quinn thanked him, waved the note again and said, "Well, I'll keep this now."[24] After a while, Quinn went to the toilet, passing Cornell and his companions and, thanking him on the way back, slugged back the remains of his drink and left, going to the Grave Maurice nearby to meet his wife. Presently, a young couple in their mid-twenties (whose names were never ascertained) came in, bought a drink and sat near the saloon door.

Frances Sanders had just put a record on the turntable behind the bar. She later claimed that when things were quiet, she would put music on, usually the latest chart hit she was keen on, to the point of playing it over and over again: "George'd just recovered from Gene Pitney and 'I'm Going To Be Strong', and now he thought he was going to get the Walker Brothers singing 'The Sun Ain't Gonna Shine

---

23 John Dickson; *Murder Without Conviction* (London: Sidgwick and Jackson 1986).
24 Statement made at Arbour Square Police Station, 12 March 1966.

Anymore'[25] for weeks."[26] It was at that moment, at approximately 8.35 p.m., that Ronnie Kray and Ian Barrie walked into the saloon bar. They strode purposefully towards where Cornell was sitting, but nobody present took any notice of what seemed like two more drinkers arriving on a quiet night. At that moment, John Dale was walking to the toilet in the snug bar. Cornell noticed Ronnie, however, and said, "Look who's here," put his hand in his pocket as if to get some money out, and muttered, "Let's have a drink." According to Ronnie, years later, "Nothing was said. I just felt hatred for this sneering man... his eyes told me that he thought the whole thing was a bluff."[27] And then a shot rang out.

Ronnie had removed a 9mm automatic from his coat and, with arm slightly bent, fired it at Cornell from a range of about six feet. Ian Barrie then fired two shots from a .32 automatic over the bar towards the area where Michael Flannery and Raymond Drury were sitting. Fortunately, on hearing the initial gunshot, both men had dived onto the floor. One of Barrie's shots had passed perilously close to the barmaid's head before she ran back down the bar towards the cellar door.

Dale had not reached the toilet when he heard the first bang and dived onto the floor of the snug with Flannery and Drury. Without any delay, he picked himself up and dashed through the public bar and out the door, pushing it so hard that he cracked a pane of glass. Just prior to that, George Stephens and his companion Anita Varnes had walked into the public bar, heard the gunshots and walked straight out. Albert Wood had also dived onto the floor by the bar at the sound of the first gunshot. In the cloud of smoke, George Cornell had recoiled off of his stool and landed on his right side next to Wood. Blood was pouring out of a hole in Cornell's forehead and he was groaning. When Wood regained his composure, he peeked over the bar and saw Ronnie and Barrie leaving; he then stood up and walked out of the saloon bar through the snug and was about to leave via the public bar door when he realised he had left his coat on one of the chairs near where

---

25 Originally recorded by Frankie Valli, the Walker Brothers' version reached the top chart position in the UK on 17 March 1966 and stayed there for four weeks. It was the group's biggest selling record and their second number one hit.
26 Mrs X with James Morton; *Calling Time on the Krays: The Barmaid's Tale* (Little, Brown and Company 1996)
27 Reggie & Ronnie Kray, with Fred Dinenage; *Our Story* (London: Sidgwick and Jackson 1988).

he had been sitting. Perhaps through shock more than anything else, he walked back past Flannery and Drury, collected his coat and after looking down at Cornell, strode out of the public bar.

Frances Sanders had jumped down the stairs of the cellar in abject terror. She was worried that the gunmen would come after her and had moved so quickly that she had literally slid down the steps and hurt her back. She spent mere minutes in the cellar until she was aware that all was quiet upstairs back in the bar – all she could hear was the Walker Brothers record, which had stuck in a groove, repeating the same lines over and over.

At this point, Ivor Richards returned from his supper break. He had entered through the public bar and, seeing some broken glass on the floor of the snug bar, thought there had been a fight. The group of three men, sitting by the door apparently unfazed by what had occurred, said, "The barmaid's down there," indicating the cellar, but when Richards moved round the bar he saw Sanders on the stairs leading to the flat above the pub, and Patsy Quill already on the phone to the emergency services (Quill had been watching television and his wife was in the bath when they heard the shots). Flannery and Drury were still in the snug bar. The three unidentified men remained in the public bar along with 'Pop' Slarke. William Amass, who had been in the saloon gents' toilet when he heard the three shots, saw the result and went over to the young couple sitting near the saloon bar door.

"Am I drunk?" he said to them. "No. You were in the range of fire,"[28] the young man replied and, without saying another word, the couple finished their drinks and walked out.

Patsy Quill asked Frances Sanders what had happened. Her first reaction was to tell him straight that Ronnie Kray had shot Cornell, but his reaction said much about the situation they now found themselves in: "Well, you might just as well be six feet under," he said.[29] Together, Quill and Sanders went round to where Cornell was lying and surveyed the sorry scene, whilst Richards kept vigil at the door waiting for the emergency services. Cornell was lying on his right side at a forty-five degree angle to the bar. A pool of blood and matter from his head wound was rapidly expanding beneath him. Occasionally he groaned, proving to all that he was at least still alive. Quill and Sanders applied clean bar towels to Cornell's head in some vague attempt

28 Statement by Amass made at Arbour Square Police Station, 9 March 1966.
29 Statement of Det. Inspector Edward Tebbell, 2 July 1968.

to stem the flow of blood; "The smell was foul," said Quill later, "a mixture of blood, gore and gunpowder."[30] As he cradled Cornell's head in his arms, Quill became aware of somebody standing next to him; 'Pop' Slarke had emerged from the public bar and was looking down dispassionately at the terrible scene before him. "Fuck me," he said, "I guess he won't be drinking any more booze, will he?"[31] Slarke may have been in shock, or his time as a First World War veteran may have hardened the old man to such scenes,[32] but his throwaway comment was darkly comical under the circumstances.

The fact that George Cornell was still alive was in itself miraculous, for it transpired that the 9mm bullet from Ronnie's gun (variously described as a Luger or a Mauser)[33] had entered Cornell's forehead three-and-a-half inches above the bridge of his nose and one-and-a-half inches to the right of the midline, had travelled in a horizontal path through his skull and brain and exited the back of his head one-and-a-half inches lower than it entered. The bullet then continued its trajectory to the back of the snug bar, where it hit the wall sideways between the ladies' and gents' toilet doors, about eight feet up, and had finally come to rest on the floor. The embossed wallpaper and plasterwork was damaged where the bullet had struck.[34]

The emergency services were incredibly quick to respond; in fact, Jack Dickson later claimed that even as he drove Ronnie and Ian Barrie back to The Lion police sirens could be heard. At 8.38 p.m., mere minutes after the shooting, Poplar Accident Station received a call of 'man shot' and an ambulance, manned by Henry King and Leonard Tarron, proceeded to the Blind Beggar. Simultaneously, police patrol cars began getting messages from station incident response units: PCs Francis Davidson and Kenneth Gerreli, attached to Commercial Street Police Station, were driving in their patrol car when they got the message about the shooting, as did PC Robert

---

30 Laurie O'Leary; *Ronnie Kray – A Man Amongst Men* (London: Headline 2001).

31 Ibid.

32 Slarke, who was born in 1888, had fought for over two years in the battlefields of France as a Private in the 19th London Regiment during the First World War and had been shot in the chest in August 1918, earning him a trip home and a stay in the Military Hospital in Kingsland Road, Hoxton. (From the military records of Thomas Alfred Slarke, Private 611870, held at the National Archives). He died in 1974.

33 In *Our Story*, Ronnie calls it a Mauser, but Albert Donoghue believed it was a Luger which looked quite new.

34 This is probably the origin of the legendary bullet hole that is often inquired about by visitors to the pub today.

Bartlett, who was from Bethnal Green Station. These three officers were the first officials at the scene and all reported seeing Cornell on the ground being tended by Sanders. They also ensured protocol was observed and importantly, as there had obviously been more people in the pub when the shooting occurred (evident by the amount of unfinished drinks on the bar and tables), everybody still present was ordered not to touch any glasses, bottles or surfaces, pending forensic examination.

At around 8.45 p.m., Police Sergeant John Nairn, accompanied by Detective Constable Anderson, arrived at the pub. They too saw Cornell on the floor and Nairn noticed that he appeared to be struggling for breath and had begun to vomit. Blood was also coming out of his mouth, as well as from the head wounds. As a senior officer Nairn took charge, instructing all present to remain on the premises whilst the other officers took their particulars, and reiterating that nothing should be touched. The ambulance arrived whilst Nairn was coordinating procedure. Henry King immediately examined the body of Cornell, placing bandages over his head wounds, before he and driver Tarron placed Cornell on the stretcher and removed him from the pub. Nairn secured the area where Cornell had been lying with chairs and, as he left, he took note of the licence plate numbers of all the cars parked out front.

Accompanied by PC Bartlett, Cornell was admitted to the casualty department of Mile End Hospital in Bancroft Road at 8.49 p.m., where he was examined by Dr. Jaivant Lal:

> I examined him and found that he had a penetrating wound to the forehead which had brain tissue protruding. He was comatose, his eyes were closed and I found that his right eye had lateralisation. He vomited and I saw that he could not project it. I caused the oral cavity to be sucked out in order that he could breath.[sic]. His heart was quite strong and death did not seem to be eminent [sic]. An airway tube was inserted into his mouth by the anaesthetist.[35]

There was one problem: the Mile End Hospital had no facilities for neural surgery, considered the best course of action for Cornell, and so he was transferred to Maida Vale Hospital where the necessary procedure could be performed. Cornell was still alive and thus it was deemed a possibility, albeit a slight one, that his life could be

35 Statement by Dr. Jaivant Lal made at Arbour Square Police Station, 12 March 1966.

saved. Before being sent to Maida Vale, Sergeant Nairn arrived and made a search of Cornell's jacket, looking for any papers which could confirm his identity. Nothing of the sort was found, although Nairn took possession of a notebook filled with names and phone numbers, whilst approximately £70 in cash was taken into possession by the hospital authorities.

In the meantime, the police work at the Blind Beggar was gathering momentum. Howard Jones, senior photographer from New Scotland Yard's photographic section, took seven photographs of the scene: a view of the saloon bar from the entrance, a view from the other end showing the crime scene, a close-up of the bar where Cornell and his friends had been sitting, a view of the public bar and a close-up of the bar itself, a view of the snug bar showing the torn plaster where the 9mm bullet had ricocheted off the wall and, most horrifyingly of all, a close-up of the pool of blood, tissue and vomit that marked where Cornell had fallen.[36]

At 9.00 p.m., Detective Sergeant James Hunter, assisted by Detective Sergeant Osbourne, began the painstaking task of gathering evidence from the scene of crime. Together they collected a considerable amount of material: a significant number of blood and tissue samples from within and around the large pool of blood on the floor; several cigarette butts from the floor by the bar; a .32 calibre bullet found lying in the main pool of blood; two spent .32 calibre cartridge cases and a single spent 9mm cartridge case; a piece of flesh from the door of the gents' toilets in the snug bar; and a tuft of hair from the floor near the ladies' toilet in the snug bar.[37]

At 9.15 p.m., as the ambulance raced across London, Cornell's wife Olive received a phone call from Albert Wood. "I have some bad news. George has been shot."[38] After telling her it happened in the Blind Beggar, Wood hung up and Olive immediately flew into a panic. She called her friends Mrs. Collins and Johnny Longman, told them what had happened and asked them to accompany her to the pub. Olive took the car that Cornell had borrowed from a friend, the Vauxhall Victor, and drove to pick up Mrs. Collins. From there they went to Johnny Longman's in Walworth and he followed them to the Blind Beggar. On arrival, the two women were initially refused entry into

36 Statement of Howard Jones, taken 10 March 1966.
37 Statement of Det. Sgt. James Hunter, taken 28 June 1968.
38 Statement by Olive Myers, taken at Arbour Square Police Station, 14 March 1966.

the pub, but Olive was allowed in once her identity as Cornell's wife had been established. In fact, she was not allowed to leave until the police had satisfactorily ascertained her name and address and those of her companions. On being told that Cornell had been transferred to Maida Vale Hospital, she was taken there by Longman; the Vauxhall Victor she had been driving was left outside the pub. When Olive arrived at Maida Vale, she was refused access to her husband who was already being prepared for emergency surgery.

The house surgeon was Dr. Raymond Newcombe, MB, BS, FRCS (Ed), and his report gives us a picture of the last moments of George Cornell:

> There was profuse blood loss from the wound at the back of the head, and the origin of the blood loss appeared to be within the skull, and therefore, could not be stopped by pressure alone. A sample of blood was taken from a vein at the left elbow, and an intravenous infusion was set up into a vein at the right elbow.
>
> The patient was also bleeding from the back of the throat, and had appeared to have inhaled a considerable quantity of blood into the lungs. He was given a blood transfusion of two bottles of blood to overcome his blood loss, and he was transferred to the operating theatre. Mr. Lindsay Morgan, Consultant Neurosurgeon, was present. The patient was placed on the operating table, and the scalp was shaved. Antiseptic solutions were applied to the scalp in preparation for an operation, but at this stage at 10.29 p.m. Dr. J Collis, the anaesthetist, reported that the heart had stopped. Cardiac massage by the normal closed technique was immediately commenced, and continued until 10.35 p.m. without obtaining any further heart beats. It was considered that the brain damage together with the fluid inhaled into the lungs, together constituted a condition from which survival at that time, after cardiac arrest, was impossible.
>
> Patient was declared deceased at the time of the cardiac arrest, namely 10.29 p.m. His wife was informed.[39]

Ronnie Kray had finally fulfilled his own warped destiny. Scotland Yard's Murder Squad were now on the case, and Detective Superintendent James Axon now had the enormous headache of leading an investigation into a very public murder – an investigation

39 Statement by Dr. Raymond L. G. Newcombe, taken at Arbour Square Police Station, 14 March 1966.

with which no witness was prepared to fully cooperate, as he would soon discover.

◆

As the Teale brothers drove into gloomy Tapp Street for their unscheduled meeting with the Firm at The Lion, the claustrophobia of the daunting railway arch was punctuated with the shapes of people milling about vacantly under the dim neon lights. There was something not right about the situation and the Teales could sense it immediately. They got out of the car and were approached by Reggie and Charlie 'Nobby' Clarke, who asked, "What motor are you going in?" Reggie replied, "I'll go with these", indicating the Teale brothers. Once they were in the car, Reggie said, "Come on kid, we've got to get off the manor." David Teale pulled the car away and for a while there was silence until Reggie was asked what was going on. Calmly, he said, "Ronnie has just shot Cornell."[40]

It appears that the Teale brothers had arrived not long after Ronnie, Jack Dickson and Ian Barrie had returned from their fateful trip to the Blind Beggar. They had only been away for fifteen minutes and the Lion was still busy, with about thirty to forty people in the bar. Ronnie went straight up the stairs, and Barrie and Dickson went to the bar for a drink. Barrie was obviously in a state of shock and couldn't bring himself to say what had happened. Reggie came over and asked them where they had taken Ronnie; the Blind Beggar, they told him; Reggie asked what had happened. Barrie whispered something in Reggie's ear, at which Reggie dashed upstairs to see Ronnie. At that moment, somebody came into the bar and shouted, "There has been a shooting in the Whitechapel Road!"[41] The assembled throng now began putting two and two together and, unnerved, started drifting out of the pub.

After hearing Ronnie's account of what had happened, Reggie, with a reaction teetering between panic and exasperation at his brother's careless violence, immediately began making moves to get everybody out of the Lion and away from the East End. Albert Donoghue, who was making a phone call, was told, "Scrub the call. Get off the manor. We're moving."[42] As Reggie commandeered the Teale brothers' car, Ronnie was once again driven by Jack Dickson, and various other

40 Bobby Teale with Clare Campbell: *Bringing Down the Krays* (London: Ebury Publishing 2012).

41 John Dickson; *Murder Without Conviction* (London: Sidgwick and Jackson 1986).

42 Albert Donoghue; *The Enforcer* (London: John Blake 2002).

members of the Firm abandoned the pub for different vehicles which sped off in different directions. Ultimately, the disorganised convoy hit Cambridge Heath Road, struck north to Hackney and continued carefully along Lea Bridge Road towards Walthamstow. According to Albert Donoghue, the first port of call was the Stow Club, a gambling club managed by 'Limehouse' Willey on the High Street in Walthamstow. In the upstairs poker room, 'Nobby' Clarke was given two guns to dispose of and various people were sent off to get clean clothes for Ronnie, Barrie and Dickson. Then the group decamped to the Chequers pub at 145 High Road, owned by 61-year-old ex-policeman Charlie Hobbs, who had been introduced to the Krays by Willey two years before. The twins and their associates had been using the Chequers on and off in those two years, and Hobbs usually set aside a private bar for them whenever they visited: this mutual arrangement, along with the pub's location outside the Kray manor, must have made the Chequers the logical place to lie low that evening.

Once inside, everybody was ushered into the private bar and drinks were bought. Ronnie, who had appeared calm and now actually seemed in quite a good mood, had gone upstairs to scrub the gunpowder marks off his hands and change his clothes; comically, he wore some of Alfie Teale's clothing which was way too small for him. Ian Barrie loosened up and began to speak about what had happened. Reggie was not particularly happy with what Ronnie had done and repeatedly mumbled that Ronnie should have organised things better. The radio was put on so the crowd could listen to any news bulletins about the shooting. They didn't have to wait long; the first report claimed that a man had been shot in Whitechapel and that the police had set up roadblocks in the immediate area. Then, at around midnight, came the news that the injured man had died in hospital. "Ronnie started cheering," claimed Donoghue, "and all the little wets joined in so they wouldn't stand out as dissenters."[43] Bobby Teale apparently heard Ronnie say, "Always shoot to kill. Dead men don't talk."[44]

Eventually talk turned to where everybody could go once the Chequers closed. The first choice was the home of Roland Tarlton, a Chequers regular, whose living room had a genuine bar installed,

43 Albert Donoghue; *The Enforcer* (London: John Blake 2002).
44 Bobby Teale with Clare Campbell: *Bringing Down the Krays* (London: Ebury Publishing 2012).

which would ensure a regular supply of much-needed refreshment. This made do for a short while until Tarlton's wife returned home from working a late shift and promptly flew into a rage, saying in no uncertain terms that these strangers were not welcome in her home, especially with a baby sleeping in the next room. It was Reggie who said to David Teale that they go to his house at 51 Moresby Road, although it wasn't so much a suggestion as an order. Despite living with his wife, Christine, and two young daughters in a small house with only two rooms, Teale could not convince Reggie that it was a bad idea, and so began one of the more bizarre episodes in the Kray story, and one that would demonstrate the madness of Ronnie Kray in particular.

◆

The morning after the shooting, the press naturally reported the sensational details, with the popular *Daily Mirror* devoting almost the entire front page to the story. Many reports focused on the gang war that was perceived to be growing at the time, suggesting that the Mr. Smith's incident and the Cornell shooting, even if they were not linked, were still indicative of a menace that was getting out of hand. Amid all the press attention, the Blind Beggar was still undergoing examination and was now blessed with a constant police presence at the front. At 10.30 a.m. on that morning, 10 March, the ironically-named PC Frederick Luger from Limehouse Station visited the Blind Beggar for the purpose of taking measurements of the interior of the pub in order to produce accurate plans of the scene, a practice that had been undertaken by select officers for many decades. Around this time, the pub's cleaner, Michael Lynch, no doubt trying to do his job as best as possible under the circumstances, found a damaged 9mm bullet on the floor of the snug bar, which he handed to Patsy Quill. This was the bullet that killed Cornell.

John McCafferty, Senior Experimental Officer at the Metropolitan Police Laboratory, examined the bar of the Blind Beggar for further clues. He found the mark on the back wall of the snug bar caused by the 9mm bullet, and discovered two examples of damage to the bar furniture. The first was a hole in a chair leg, the other an entry and exit hole in the top of a stool, both of which were consistent with having been made by .32 calibre bullets. Interestingly, of the three bullets fired only two were ever found, although all three spent cartridge cases were retained.

At 11.30 a.m. that same day, at Westminster Public Mortuary Dr. Keith Simpson of Guy's Hospital, a Harley Street physician and professor of forensic medicine at London University, conducted the post-mortem on the body of George Cornell. By all accounts he was a healthy man, with no abnormalities to any of his organs and no sign of disease. The head wound was examined in detail and it was noted that his palate was shattered and his stomach was empty save for some mucus and blood. Unsurprisingly, cause of death was given as 'Firearm wound of the head.' The following day, accompanied by Detective Superintendent James Axon, Olive Myers, Joseph and James Cornell (George's brothers) and ambulance attendant Henry King identified George Cornell's body. Interestingly, the death was registered twice, under the names Cornell and Myers.[45]

In the meantime, Scotland Yard's fingerprint department had been working hard. The only confirmed people remaining in the bar of Blind Beggar immediately after the shooting were Patsy Quill, Frances Sanders, Michael Flannery, Raymond Drury, William Amass, 'Pop' Slarke and Ivor Richards, and all of them had been questioned thoroughly that evening. But it was important for the police to ascertain the identities of anybody else who had been in the pub that night, particularly the men who had been with Cornell when he was shot. Fortunately for the police, half the people who had been in the pub that night had criminal records and thus their fingerprints were on file, and so, through the painstaking task of dusting every glass and bottle in the pub for fingerprints, the names of the mystery drinkers quickly became known; they were John Dale, Albert Wood, Henry Isaacs, William Wylie and William Quinn. And with a better understanding of who could have potentially seen the shooting, and most importantly the gunmen, witnesses were summoned to give statements.

The most important statements were given by Sanders, Flannery, Drury, Wood and Dale: these were the people closest to the incident, and thus their recollections were vital, and yet nobody was able, on paper at least, to identify the two gunmen. Michael Flannery, who later appeared in court, gave a description of the man he saw wielding a gun:

---

45 Officially George was a Myers – his wife Olive took the name, as did his two children, but as he was known to many, including the emergency services, as Cornell, he was registered under both names in separate entries.

I would describe the man who had the gun as aged 30-35, about 5'9", stocky build, I would say about 12-12½ stone, wearing a blue raincoat, a college boy haircut, dark hair greying, slightly frizzy. He had a Roman shape nose and gave the impression of being slightly Italian appearance... I think I might recognise the man with the gun again but I'm not sure.[46]

A couple of points notwithstanding (the description of the hair specifically), it was a fair description of Ronnie Kray. Both Flannery and Drury were able to describe Albert Wood quite accurately, as he had passed them a couple of times after the incident before leaving the pub. John Dale offered no description of the men, but Albert Wood, probably closer to the gunmen than anybody, gave accounts that were reasonably good descriptions of both Ronnie and Ian Barrie:

1st man, age about 30 years – about six foot tall –round face – dark hair – it was short and loose – well built – wearing a dark, blackish raincoat – no hat – appeared well dressed. He wore a collar and tie. I would know this man again.

2nd man, age about 30 years – 5'10" to 5'11" tall – mousey coloured hair, not brushed back but loose – normal build that is slightly thinner than the first man. I would know this man if I saw him again.[47]

John Dale's statement, taken on 12 March, did not give much away other than what he himself was doing that night; however, it later transpired that he made a crucial admission after the statement was signed. In a later report, written by Detective Inspector Edward Tebbell, all becomes apparent:

After he had signed the statement I said, to him, "I believe you can tell me the name of the man who shot George". He said, "No, but George was like an uncle to me. If I knew it would be no good telling you. I shall get a gun and shoot him myself."

I said, "That would be stupid. It is best for you to tell me" and he replied, "I think you already know".

I said, "I may have a good idea but it is essential you name the man yourself without any lead from me". John Dale was ashen white and obviously frightened but after what seemed some minutes

---

46 Statement of Michael Flannery, taken at Commercial Street Police Station, 9 March 1966.
47 Statement of Albert Wood, taken at Arbour Square Police Station, 14 March 1966.

hesitation he said, "All right, it was Ronnie Kray".

Superintendent Axon returned to the room and I said to John Dale, "Tell Superintendent Axon the name of the man who killed George Cornell" and he said, "It was Ron Kray".

Mr. Axon asked him if he would put that down in writing and he said, "No and I shall not identify him. It is more than my life is worth. I shall be scared to leave here tonight". He was allowed to remain at Arbour Square Police Station that night until handed over to the care of his father.[48]

The same report by Tebbell also sheds light on the testimony of Frances Sanders, the barmaid. Nowhere in her original statement, taken on 9 March, did she claim to have known the identity of the two gunmen, but in Tebbell's report he spoke of a meeting with Sanders, on the same day as the Dale confession, which saw this most crucial of witnesses open up.

I said to her, "Mr. Axon and I believe there are a few mistakes in the statement you made to me on the night the man was shot in the pub".

She immediately started crying and practically collapsed. After some time she partially recovered and Mr. Axon said to her, "Just tell us tonight if there is anything you know".

She was still sobbing and said, "I am sorry Mr. Tebbell, there were two white lies. I recognised the man who done the shooting as a man who had been pointed out to me in the pub as Ronnie Kray. I didn't know the other man who was behind him."[49]

The grapevine is a fast-growing plant, and it is likely that through local street-talk the police knew almost immediately who had shot Cornell. The admissions of Dale and Sanders on 12 March 1966 would have clinched it for them, had the pair not been too frightened to include these facts in their original, signed statements. Without such cast-iron material, there was no reason to arrest Ronnie, for, *officially* at least, he was not the man in the Blind Beggar that night.

Nonetheless, several alternative candidates were questioned by the police, perhaps as a process of elimination as much as anything. A number of local villains, particularly those with protection racket

48 Statement of Det Inspr. Edward Tebbell, taken at Bethnal Green Police Station, 2 July 1968.
49 Ibid.

records, were asked to account for their whereabouts on the evening of 9 March and all gave a satisfactory account of themselves. It was thought that Cornell was implicated in a south London protection racket involving a number of businesses, and that the various directors were interviewed to see if there may have been any connection between the threats made against them, George Cornell's possible involvement, and the shooting. However, the businessmen had never even heard of Cornell and that particular avenue of inquiry came to a dead end.

As far as word of mouth was concerned, Ronnie Kray shot George Cornell dead, but with the reluctance of witnesses to make that fact legally recognisable, the police really had nothing concrete to go on. Olive Myers, now widowed with two young children to support, made her feelings very well known on 14 March when she went to Vallance Road to have it out with the Krays. She admitted to having an argument with Violet and Charlie Snr, whom she described as 'aggressive', but what she failed to admit was the fact that, in her anger, she threw a brick through their window, for which she was fined £1.

The press were quick to make the link between various recent incidents in light of the murder of George Cornell; the gun fight at Mr. Smith's and the disappearance of Tommy 'Ginger' Marks in January 1965[50] were considered grave examples of what was happening in underworld London. "Gang war flares in East London",[51] said the local press; the *Daily Express* spoke of "Guns for hire"[52] and, with the police seemingly unable to find the killer of George Cornell, the shooting in the Blind Beggar was deemed the apex of gangland violence, "part of an underworld war which has been going on for months."[53]

---

50 Marks was accidentally shot dead on Cheshire Street by Freddie Foreman, the intended target being George 'Jimmy' Evans who was with Marks at the time. Foreman's brother George had been having an affair with Evans' wife and in late 1964, Evans had gone to George Foreman's home and shot him in the groin as he answered the door. The intended killing of Evans in Cheshire Street was an act of revenge. Evans escaped, but Marks, killed on the spot, disappeared. His body has never been found, but Freddie Foreman later revealed that it had been disposed of at sea.
51 *East London Advertiser*, 11 March 1966.
52 *Daily Express*, 24 June 1966.
53 *Daily Mirror*, 10 March 1966.

TWELVE

ERRORS OF JUDGEMENT

The Teale brothers, Alfie, David and Bobby, were really no different from any other young men who found themselves drawn into the mixture of violence and glamour that constituted the Krays' world. Alfie and David were already established as part of the twins' inner circle, and the younger Bobby was regularly impressed by his brothers' stories about gangland London. Working on the Isle of Wight, Bobby Teale's world was a million miles away from the exciting life his brothers led. He had met the twins when they had visited Colin 'Duke' Osbourne in Parkhurst Prison and had stopped by Bobby's home, which he shared with his wife Pat and their children. The marriage, however, was floundering and in early 1966 it collapsed altogether; Pat and her family instigated divorce proceedings and Bobby's solicitor's fees – to the tune of £2,000 – were paid for by Reggie. This, one imagines, was a convenient way of getting the young Teale brother on side as a member of the wider Firm.

> *"Leave her behind," he'd tell me. "Women, what do they know?"*
> *Reggie was only too pleased to stump up the money to buy me out*
> *of a marriage that was no longer working. His own marriage had*
> *failed, so why not mine?*
>
> *That part of my life was over: a wife, children, a home of our own.*
> *I was back running with the pack. I was on the prowl again. I came*
> *back to wicked old London, to be part of the big Kray party.*[1]

---

1   Bobby Teale with Clare Campbell: *Bringing Down the Krays* (London: Ebury Publishing 2012).

Alfie had already warned his younger brother about getting in too deep, but when it came to the Kray twins, saying 'no' to any of their offers or suggestions was never an option. Besides, Bobby was excited about being back in London, and the prospect of working alongside his two brothers as part of the Firm was incredibly exciting. But he was soon to realise that, as Alfie had warned, getting 'in too deep' would have serious consequences.

The decision by the twins to decamp to David Teale's flat in Moresby Road following the murder of George Cornell instigated a course of events which would be considered surreal if they had not been so terrifying. For one, Ronnie, flying high after committing his status-raising execution, was very much 'The Colonel'. From the minute he arrived at Moresby Road, he treated the place like his own, asking David Teale if his wife, Christine, could get up and make him something to eat, even though it was past 1.00 a.m. Ronnie wouldn't accept 'no' for an answer to anything, even if it meant walking through an occupied bedroom to have a bath at some ungodly hour of the morning. Also, the little flat was now the temporary home to a number of members of the Firm, all of whom had been instructed to stay put whilst the heat following the Cornell murder died down. 51 Moresby Road, home to David, Christine and their young children, was now occupied by a group of total strangers, some of them armed, many of them as trapped in the situation as the Teales were, and all at the behest of a totally dominant and unpredictable Ronnie Kray. It would turn out to be an extremely stressful, and painful, fortnight.[2]

Reggie was extremely angry about Ronnie's shooting of Cornell. The two argued violently, adding further friction to the Teale home. Various members of the Firm would run back and forth with clothes and refreshments and, of course, the constant threat of interest from the police kept the atmosphere electric. The darker side of Ronnie's character manifested itself during this difficult period. Bobby Teale recalls seeing Ronnie's now-famous list of people he wanted killed; this was something that was constantly revised, scrapped and rewritten as the days went by, and it included Leslie Payne, who by this time was noticeably distancing himself from the Kray Firm. His frequent absence from the twins' activities had caused them to be highly suspicious of him, as he knew so much about their business

2   A detailed account of the 'siege' at David Teale's flat can be read in *Bringing Down the Krays*, and readers are advised to seek out the book for a fuller picture of events.

that he could not be anything other than a gift to the police should he be coerced into talking.

One day, when the Teales' eleven-year-old brother Paul visited, Ronnie took a rather alarming interest in him and sat him on his knee. Soon he was trying to take Paul upstairs to bed for a 'lie down', but, in what could have been a major flashpoint, he was blocked by Bobby Teale. Bobby even armed himself in case Ronnie looked about to get his wish, and was more than ready to empty an entire chamber of bullets into 'The Colonel'. The tiny flat now stank of booze, tobacco and sweat. Ronnie maintained constantly that the police would not attempt a full-scale raid as David and Christine's children were there, effectively acting as human shields. In fact, the only person who seemed happy with the situation was Ronnie himself.

After the incident with his brother Paul, Bobby Teale cracked, and in doing so, began what should have heralded the almost instant destruction of the Kray empire. On the premise of visiting his mother, he went to a telephone box near Cedra Court and phoned New Scotland Yard. Initially, Teale lost his nerve and hung up, but after visiting his mother, went back and got through to Superintendent Tommy Butler:

> Taking a deep breath, I said the seven words that would change the course of the rest of my life. "I have some information about the Krays." [3]

After Teale had made his initial approach to the police, and following a number of clandestine meetings with Butler and other officers, it was clear that Moresby Road, and those who were allowed to come and go, were under the watchful eye of Scotland Yard. Bobby Teale, using the codename 'Phillips', had said that Ronnie had killed George Cornell, that he was in hiding in his brother's flat and that there were children present who were potentially being used as human shields. The fact that the Krays may well have had a number of officers 'in their pockets' who could pass information back to the Firm was a constant worry. But for those two difficult weeks, Ronnie Kray felt he was safe and did everything he could to stay put.

Most people were permitted to come and go for various reasons, whether it was to collect supplies or to act out some semblance of normal life, just so as not to arouse suspicion. Ronnie himself even

3 Bobby Teale with Clare Campbell: *Bringing Down the Krays* (London: Ebury Publishing 2012).

managed the odd visit to a pub, although he kept clear of the usual Bethnal Green and Whitechapel haunts. Violet Kray visited on at least one occasion with fresh clothes, and was visibly worried. She mentioned the incident where Olive, Cornell's widow, had visited Vallance Road and broken a window, but Ronnie was quick to say that the stories she may have heard about what he had done in the Blind Beggar were malicious gossip – and she probably believed him. Reggie, of course, was a frequent visitor, but he was still unhappy with Ronnie; and, of course, since Frances was now living with her parents, he had problems of his own to contend with. And all the time, Bobby Teale was doing something that he felt was right, but which he knew full well could result in his death if he underestimated the influence and power of the Krays and the Firm. He had broken the 'Wall of Silence' and rejected the old criminal mantra, 'Thou shalt not grass.'

◆

When the 'siege' at Moresby Road eventually ended, much to the relief of everybody concerned bar Ronnie Kray, the Firm went their separate ways and laid low for a while. The twins spent a few weeks with their old mentor Billy Hill in Tangier, an experience enjoyed by both brothers, who had been careful to travel under false names and passports. Reggie seemed happy, despite his marital problems back home. He even spoke of settling in Morocco and setting up a small club there, away from the crises unfolding in London. He invited a hostess from the Latin Quarter Club in Soho to join him, and neither Frances, nor his life in the East End, were mentioned. Ronnie, always at home in exotic locations, enjoyed the young Arab boys.[4]

But the trip was cut short. Despite the apparent inaction of the police, things must have been happening in the background, and, working on information sent to Morocco by the British authorities, the Tangier police sought out the twins and had them extradited as undesirables. Despite flying back under their real names, there was no arrest on their arrival in London over the Cornell shooting, or over any information Bobby Teale had been supplying, and so, seemingly off the hook again, the Krays got back to work. Ronnie quickly regained his confidence:

4   John Pearson; *The Profession of Violence* (London: Weidenfeld & Nicolson 1972).

You could see it. Everybody knew what he'd done but no one was saying anything. It made him feel even more in command. He really was untouchable. In the meantime his madness seemed to be getting worse.

He started talking to himself, just muttering: 'Yeah, right,' all the time as if he was in conversation with someone else. Or else he was constantly reminding everyone: 'I'm the governor round here. I'm the Colonel. Fuck the police, fuck the government.'[5]

Throughout the siege, the twins had been organising visits to Dartmoor Prison to see Frank Mitchell. They had kept up their correspondence with the 'Mad Axeman' since their days at Wandsworth, sending him money and paying the occasional visit. Since September 1962, Mitchell had been at Dartmoor and, far from being the ultra-violent scourge of the prison system, had calmed down considerably:

At Dartmoor he responded well to treatment and had been involved in no violence, or prison offence of any kind, since April 1962. Sanction was therefore given in May 1965, after 6½ years' imprisonment, for him to be employed on an outside working party.

For many years this has been the usual practice for very long-term prisoners at Dartmoor who have reached a later stage in their sentence, or whose release is under consideration in the case of life sentences.

The object of outside working parties is to test the trustworthiness and develop the responsibility of a prisoner in conditions of less than maximum supervision when his eventual return to the community is contemplated.[6]

The only problem was, Mitchell had not been given a release date. Albert Donoghue, who, along with 'Limehouse' Willey, 'Fat' Wally Garelick, Charlie Kray, Billy Exley, Alfie Teale and 'Big' Pat Connolly, had been one of the many members of the Firm who had been sent to see Mitchell throughout 1966, many under aliases, said:

According to Frank, the governor had said he would urge the Home Office to give him a date. Whether it was immediate or a couple of

5   Bobby Teale with Clare Campbell: *Bringing Down the Krays* (London: Ebury Publishing 2012).
6   Statement by Home Secretary Roy Jenkins; *Guardian*, 14 December 1966.

years ahead didn't really matter. All Frank wanted was a date to focus his mind on. But months went by, nothing was heard back from the Home Office, and so the governor had nothing to tell Frank. So Frank is raging because now he feels the governor's promise isn't worth the paper it isn't written on.

Then in flies the good fairy: Ronnie Kray.[7]

Ronnie promised Mitchell that he would get him out of Dartmoor and whilst at liberty, find a way of getting the Home Office to give him the much-wanted release date. It was a blatantly stupid idea – how could anybody expect to escape from prison, a crime in itself, and go back after a period on the run expecting to be released on a date earlier than would have been expected? But trivialities like this were of no concern to Ronnie Kray, who, after making the promise to Mitchell, would have made his mind up; and when Ronnie made his mind up, there was no going back. Mitchell, believing the Krays to be men of their word who had his best interests at heart, would be looking forward to the fulfilment of that promise, like a child looking forward to Christmas.

In the meantime, the twins were cautiously avoiding Cedra Court[8] and found separate homes; Ronnie, still keeping away from the East End, where Superintendent Tommy Butler – having now taken over from Detective Superintendent James Axon - was undoubtedly still making his enquiries into the Cornell case, moved into a bungalow in Chingford with Ian Barrie. This was nothing less than an imposition on the actual residents - 'Nobby' Clarke, his wife and their twelve cats - but there was little the scared couple could do. Reggie got a flat with Bobby Teale in Manor House in North London, not far from the Glenrae Hotel. For Teale, this was a huge risk, as he was now having regular meetings with his Scotland Yard contact, Detective Sergeant Joe Pogue, and keeping the police abreast of the movements of the Krays. Unfortunately for Teale's blood pressure, it became apparent that somebody within Scotland Yard was passing information back to the Firm, as Ronnie brought the matter up in a meeting and even repeated the informant's codename, 'Phillips'. Bobby Teale must have thought he was living on borrowed time.

With the regular stream of information now coming from 'Phillips',

---

7   Albert Donoghue; *The Enforcer* (London: John Blake 2002).
8   They would both move out of Cedra Court for good later that year.

it was only a matter of time before the police pounced on the Krays. Seemingly constantly on the move at this point, the twins had, by the summer of 1966, started living above A. Adams barber's shop at 471 Lea Bridge Road, Leyton, and, with information garnered from Teale, the police picked a moment when it was understood that the Firm would be in attendance there. That moment was 1.50 a.m. on 4 August when a team of officers broke into the flat whilst the Krays and assorted friends were having a drinking party. Ronnie, Reggie and Ian Barrie were taken into custody, with Ronnie and Barrie being detained at Commercial Street Police Station, and Reggie going to Leyton.

An identification parade was held by Detective Inspector Lyons at Commercial Street at 12.25 p.m. the following day in the presence of Detective Superintendent Butler, Detective Inspector Edward Tebbell and Mr. S. Wray, clerk to Ronnie's solicitors, Sampson and Company. Both Ronnie and Barrie seemed anxious and Ronnie remarked to Butler, "Why is it every time there is a big job in the East End the law picks on us?" Barrie said nothing. Fourteen men participated, with Barrie standing seventh in line, and Ronnie twelfth.[9]

Two witnesses were called to identify the men they had seen in the Blind Beggar on the night of the Cornell shooting; Cornell's drinking companion Albie Wood, and another man named Robertson (who may have been any one of the five unidentified customers in the pub at the time of the incident). The barmaid, Frances Sanders, was called to attend but never turned up after losing her nerve. Neither Wood nor Robertson gave a positive identification.[10] Reggie, held at Leyton, was not required to be part of any parade, but was detained in case anything transpired with Ronnie and Barrie. In all, Ronnie was held for thirty-six hours, Reggie for forty, before they were released to no small amount of publicity. Photos were taken of the twins in the living room at Vallance Road later that day, again offering the media iconic images of the gangster twins enjoying a cup of tea in their little East End home.

Ronnie seemed to take it all in his stride, as he did with any police interference:

> *They looked after me all right. I had sausages and mash – and*
> *another time – pie, beans and chips. And there was tea when I*

---

9   MEPO 2/10922 (National Archives)
10 Ibid.

wanted it. Mr. Butler told me that if they wanted to see me again, he'd get in touch.[11]

Reggie played the victimisation card:

It's getting a bit strong, the coppers involving us in all this. Our Mum has been very worried about all this. It's her birthday today – she's fifty-six. So we'll be having a little drink, and cheer her up.[12]

Despite the inconvenience, it was yet another chance for the Krays to show that the police were powerless to bring them down and to prove to the public that they were the victims of yet another round of harassment. It was by now common knowledge that Ronnie had shot Cornell and the police were receiving anonymous letters stating as much. One, dated 9 August said, "Keep plugging at it. Ronnie Kray did the shooting."[13] Another missive, undated and written entirely in capitals, read:

SIR

YOU HAD THE RIGHT ONES FOR THE MURDER OF GEORGE CORNELL THE KRAY TWINS DONE IT. PEOPLE IN THE BLIND BEGGER [sic] KNOW. YOU CAN EXPECT ANOTHER MURDER IN EAST END SOON THEY WILL BE THE GUILTY ONES. WATCH THEM.[14]

But until witnesses spoke out, there was little the police could do. Within a week of the abortive identification parade, Ronnie, probably buoyed-up by yet another triumph against the law, decided to get his own back.

Detective Sergeant Leonard Townshend, aged 42, was a police officer with twelve years' experience behind him. Married with three children, he had been attached to Hackney Police Station (G Division) since February 1966, and during his career had received three commendations and bore no defaults on what was a spotless service record.[15] On 9 August, Townshend had come across Ronnie in the

---

11 *Daily Mirror*, 6 August 1966.
12 Ibid.
13 MEPO 2/10922, f. 11Q (National Archives).
14 MEPO 2/10922, f. 9C (National Archives).
15 Report by Detective Chief Inspector E. Fletcher, 15 September 1966; MEPO 2/10680 (National Archives).

Baker's Arms pub at 75 Northiam Street, Hackney[16] and in the course of events had made an offer of assurance that the Krays could use the pub as a bolt-hole, free from police interference, if an 'arrangement' could be made. Ronnie, accompanied at that time by Ian Barrie, Harry 'Jew Boy' Cope, Teddy Smith and 'Nobby' Clarke, either thought this could be beneficial to the Firm's operations or quickly realised that he now had an excellent opportunity to put one over on the police, and a meeting was arranged for the evening of 11 August. Enter George Devlin, the private investigator who had helped the twins to discredit Hew McCowan eighteen months earlier; Devlin rigged Ronnie with a hidden microphone and concealed tape recorder so that the meeting could be recorded. On the night, Devlin, accompanied by his new assistant Diana Langlands, went to the Baker's Arms to observe the unfolding events. From the transcript of that meeting in the back room of the pub (part of which is published here for the first time), it was clear that Townshend, now accompanied by Detective Constable Peter Barker, was looking to gain financially from the situation, unaware that Ronnie was setting a trap:

> Townshend (LT): You need a little place to work quietly, don't you?
>
> Ronnie Kray (RK): Yes.
>
> LT: It was quite by chance I stumbled in here the other day and found you. Now obviously this is your little hide-away.
>
> RK: Yeah.
>
> LT: I don't necessarily want to spoil it for you.
>
> RK: No, no.
>
> LT: But it must be worth something I suppose – and that's the whole idea obviously.
>
> RK: Well, tell me the truth – what, do you want information or what?
>
> LT: No, I don't want any information from you.
>
> RK: Come to the point.
>
> LT: You can use this pub; it's on my manor, you can use it.
>
> RK: It's on your manor?
>
> LT: Yes.
>
> RK: What is this, Well Street?

16 Closed in 1971 and demolished in 1974. The whole of Northiam Street is now covered with recently-built housing.

LT: Hackney.

RK: Hackney?

LT: Yes. Now I don't want – I'm not going – I won't come back here again.

RK: No.

LT: A little bit of rent.

RK: Yea, how much?

LT: Well, there are two of us in it – a pony a week each.

RK: A pony a week. Well, I'll have to discuss it with my brother.

LT: Certainly.

RK: Because everything I do, I do it with him. You know.

LT: Yeah, yeah. I put it at a weekly amount because...

RK: How can I give you the money? I can't give it to you myself.

LT: Give it to him.

RK: Who – the governor? What in an envelope?

LT: Yeah.

RK: Give it to him in an envelope.

LT: That's fair enough, isn't it?

RK: Hmm.

LT: Now I put it on a weekly basis for the very simple reason this – If I ask for a lump sum there is no guarantee to you, is there?

RK: No.

LT: So if we – as long as I leave you here and you are left alone.

RK: Yes, we'll be left alone. But will any of the other police know about it?

LT: Nobody else will know.[17]

The 'governor' was publican Eric Marshall, who now found himself as the go-between in Ronnie's plan. The arrangement was that Marshall would take delivery of an envelope of money once a week and pass it on to Townshend at a time when the Krays were not using the pub; the first drop was arranged for the following night, Friday 12 August, which the twins duly honoured. Also on that day, the tape of the conversation between Ronnie and Townshend was delivered

---

17 Transcript of conversation between Leonard Townshend and Ronnie Kray, 11 August 1966; MEPO 2/10680 (National Archives).

to New Scotland Yard at 11.00 a.m. by Jacob Sampson, the Krays' solicitor, and Devlin. The recorder itself was given to old friend Geoff Allen for safekeeping. Two days later, on the Sunday, Townshend rang Marshall at the pub to enquire if the envelope was in his possession, but Marshall told him that as it hadn't been collected quickly, the twins had taken it back. The telephone conversation was recorded, adding more incriminating evidence against the officer:

> *Eric Marshall (EM): Well, what do you want me to do? You wanted me to meet you outside, didn't you? Or do you want to pick it up in here?*
>
> *LT: No, I did prefer – look, I'll tell you what to do. If you can get them to give it to you, I'll tell you where to drop it, shall I?*
>
> *EM: Well.*
>
> *LT: You know the Duke of Wellington in Morning Lane?*
>
> *EM: Yes.*
>
> *LT: You can pop it in there.*
>
> *EM: Yes I will. What after we've shut? I can probably come round before we shut, it depends on how busy we are.*
>
> *LT: Yes, I'd be obliged if you pop it down. The guv'nor.*
>
> *EM: Leave it with the guv'nor?*
>
> *LT: Yes, leave it with the guv'nor. Tell him it's for Len. He'll understand that all right.*[18]

The rearranged collection was set for the following morning, after the twins had left the envelope with Marshall. The venue had been changed at the eleventh hour, for on that day, Monday, 15 August, Townshend was apprehended accepting the envelope containing £50 from Marshall at the Triangle on Mare Street, Hackney, and immediately suspended from duty.

As far as the Kray twins were concerned, it was a particularly cunning plan: assisted by Devlin, who had more than shown his worth during the McCowan case, Ronnie had made an uncharacteristic subtle strike at the police, and all he needed to do now was to let the internal investigation procedures of the Metropolitan Police take their course. It could have only added to his feelings of power.

◆

18 Transcript of conversation between Leonard Townshend and Eric Marshall, 14 August 1966; MEPO 2/10680 (National Archives).

The Regency was a tatty little club-cum-restaurant, owned by two brothers who paid protection money to the Krays. It was OK for a quiet drink after hours in the week. Local villains felt safe there, knowing nearly everybody who walked through the door. But Saturday was a different matter. Then the place attracted young Jack-the-lads who didn't know the score, would-be tough guys who liked getting tanked up and having a fight to impress their birds and the Old Bill. The Regency on a Saturday was a place any self-respecting gangster avoided.[19]

For some time, the Krays had been 'nipping' the club in Amhurst Road, Stoke Newington, which had been owned by brothers Anthony and John Barry since 1960. It was popular with a number of underworld characters and was considered a neutral venue; the twins and their associates had been using it for many years, having become more active in the area since the acquisition of their flats in nearby Cedra Court. When it was considered that the time had come to finally cut a full protection deal with the Barrys, Albert Donoghue, Dickie Morgan and Ronnie Hart were sent to let them know what the twins wanted.

Ronald Joseph Hart, born in Bethnal Green in 1942, was a distant cousin of the twins[20] and had lately been ingratiating himself into the Firm. He had recently been released from prison, and like many before him, went to the twins for help on his release. Reggie later remembered that

He came knocking on the door at Vallance Road one day and said, 'Hello, I'm your cousin. I want to join your gang.' We'd never met him before but our checks showed he seemed to be reliable – another mistake – and so we took him on. He was our cousin but he had the habit of calling us both 'uncle'.[21]

Hart was a young man with boyish good looks who admired the twins' way of life, and he enjoyed the sort of work that the twins could now offer him; this was probably provided more out of some family

19 Chris Lambrianou and Robin McGibbon; *Escape From the Kray Madness* (London: Sidgwick and Jackson 1995).
20 It has never been explained in what way Ronnie Hart was actually related to the twins. His parents were Thomas Joseph Hart and Mary Ann Burling, who had married in Stepney in 1937.
21 Reggie & Ronnie Kray, with Fred Dinenage; *Our Story* (London: Sidgwick and Jackson 1988).

loyalty than a real desire to make Hart a valid, useful member of the Firm. A visit to an established club, with two trusted members of the gang, in order to exert the Kray influence, must have been a very appealing prospect to the young Ronnie Hart. When the three men arrived at the Regency, neither of the Barry brothers was present, but one quick phone call and John Barry obediently arrived. Donoghue said that the twins wanted £50 a week for protection and although Barry wasn't best pleased with the demand, he capitulated, on the promise that the frequent 'nipping' would cease. Later, the Barrys asked for the protection rate to be dropped to £20, to which the twins agreed, but when they stopped paying, the Firm were sent round again to boost the price back up to £50. The Regency was now part of the Krays' portfolio of protected clubs, which meant that they had no small amount of control over what went on inside it. As Albert Donoghue later explained:

> The 'moral' of this story is that protection is a circular racket. Any trouble in the Regency, we were causing it. Then we were paid to stop it. When the Barrys dared to appeal, we made it clear the trouble would start again... If the Firm had its claws into you, there was no way you could get free.[22]

The Regency Club, now firmly in the grasp of the Krays, would go on to play an important part in their future. One incident, involving Ronnie, has become quite notorious in Kray lore.

It has never been definitively stated when the incident of 'The Magic Bullet'[23] occurred, when Ronnie attempted to shoot villain George Dixon in the head, only for the gun to fail. A number of people who witnessed it have written about it, including Leslie Payne, and considering that he had drifted out of the Kray circle by 1967, one must assume it happened prior to that. Payne, Lenny Hamilton and Mickey Fawcett, amongst others, have described the incident, and all claim they were there, and that it happened at the Regency, except Hamilton, who says it happened at the Green Dragon Club. On that weight of evidence, we must assume, with all due respect to Hamilton, that everybody else was right. Ronnie himself said it happened at the Regency.

22 Albert Donoghue; *The Enforcer* (London: John Blake 2002).
23 A term coined by Colin Fry in *The Kray Files* (Edinburgh: Mainstream Publishing 1998).

Dixon had been barred from the club; Ronnie claimed it was down to his heavy drinking and because Dixon was making disparaging remarks about Ronnie's sexuality. On that particular night, as Ronnie, Reggie, Charlie and Leslie Payne were having a meeting, Dixon arrived and remonstrated with Ronnie for barring him.

> *Ronnie stood up, turned round and put a little pistol to Dixon's head. Nobody could move or speak; the hammer click on the dud shell sounded like the gun itself going off. We leapt up, wrestled the gun away; and asked Ronnie what did he do it for?*
>
> *'Well I told the so and so never to come in here didn't I?'*
>
> *Charlie came up and explained that he'd said Dixon could come again. So Ronnie just went over to Dixon and said, 'You should have told me Charlie said all right. You could've got hurt.'* [24]

The famous aftermath of this alarming incident has been widely quoted; Ronnie, with his customary sense of humour, apparently gave Dixon the bullet which should have killed him.[25]

But it wasn't only George Dixon who was getting on the wrong side of the twins. On 5 November 1965, Jack McVitie had been released from prison after serving his sentence for possessing explosives and carrying an offensive weapon. Apart from the occasional minor motoring offence, he had managed to keep himself out of trouble and had also begun living with Sylvia Barnard, with whom he had had his third child.[26] Barnard describes McVitie's seemingly hum-drum life when they were together:

> *For a living he gambled and bet. He did a couple of odd jobs for different people... During the time I knew him, he didn't have a regular job. For a few months, he was signing on at the Labour Exchange, for quite a while, in fact...*
>
> *I know about most of his day-time activities and mostly about his night-time activities too. Most days I was with him during the day-time. He used to go to the Betting Shop around the corner but he wasn't out all the time. He used to stay in. He was never out all the*

24 Leslie Payne; *The Brotherhood* (London: Michael Joseph 1973).

25 In *Our Story*, Ronnie claimed that he'd given the bullet to his driver, 'John, from Canning', to pass on to Dixon with the message that "he must have nine lives, like a cat." Some accounts claim that Dixon subsequently wore the bullet round his neck on a chain.

26 Statement by Sylvia Barnard, 15 October 1968; MEPO 2/11404 (National Archives). The sections which mention the existence of a child have been heavily redacted and there is an FOI exemption on this information until 2050.

time and he was never in all the time. He did decorating at home
and used to do odd jobs around the place, like mending his car and
so on.[27]

Since meeting Reggie in prison, Jack McVitie had always wanted to work for the Firm and was now available; accordingly, when the Krays wanted a small-time crook who owned a van to do a little job for them, McVitie's name came up. The plan was for him to drive to a warehouse in Kent, pick up a load of merchandise, and bring it back to the East End, for which he would be paid £200, with £50 up-front for expenses. The Krays, however, did not entirely trust McVitie; he was an impetuous, unpredictable joker who, since acquiring his freedom, had become dependent on drugs, as well as developing a serious drinking habit. Jack Dickson was given the job of tailing McVitie to make sure he did the job properly, but on the way back from the pick-up, McVitie must have realised he was being followed and drove so fast that Dickson lost him in traffic.

The job was done as arranged and the goods delivered, but when members of the Firm checked, they discovered that some of the merchandise was missing: McVitie had sold some of it on the way back and never came to collect the rest of his fee. When he heard, Ronnie erupted, "The bastard has double-crossed us. Who the fuck said we could trust him?"

Poor Jack the Hat. That was one bad mistake he should never have
made. No one ever double-crossed the Firm and got away with it. I
think we all knew it would only be a matter of time before they did
something about it. There was some talk of shooting him in the legs
in case it got around how easy it was to double-cross the Firm. But
they soon stopped looking for Jack the Hat because they knew it
wouldn't be long before he turned up. He was such an idiot. He kept
going round the clubs telling people that he had turned the Kray
gang over and that they didn't do anything about it.[28]

The next target for the Krays was Charlie 'Nobby' Clarke, good friend to their brother Charlie and a long-standing member of the Firm. This time, however, it was the usually cautious Reggie who dished out the punishment.

27 Statement by Sylvia Barnard, 15 October 1968; MEPO 2/11404 (National Archives).
28 John Dickson; *Murder Without Conviction* (London: Sidgwick and Jackson 1986).

Reggie's marriage was an utter mess by this time; his regular visits to Frances at her parents' home were not always straightforward and sometimes she would not speak to him. Adding to Reggie's frustration was the fact that on 22 March 1966, Frances had changed her name by deed poll back to Shea,[29] a sign, in her mind at least, that the marriage was as good as over and that she felt strongly enough about it to disassociate herself from her husband's notorious name. Significantly, in June 1966, Frances made it known to Reggie that she intended to get an annulment on the grounds of non-consummation. Surprisingly, Reggie offered to make the petition himself, and Frances, keen to make it happen as quick as possible, agreed. But Reggie just dragged his feet, and by all appearances had knowingly taken control from his wife in order to ensure the annulment never happened. It never did.[30]

Frances' frustration with the whole situation boiled over in a letter she penned to Reggie on 23 June, but which he never received:

> I am not in the least interested in seeing you ever again in the whole of my life and I really mean that. I am only interested in getting the papers through and getting my annulment. Don't ever try to contact me not ever again because I have had enough of the life I have had to lead so far. I am keeping myself occupied at the moment & I don't want any interference from you ever again so just get out of my life & leave me alone & let me forget the past.
>
> *Frances*[31]

In a further, undated letter, Frances seemed to rail at the treatment her husband had given her in the past, citing obvious incidents of verbal abuse;

> Your low breed, sickly mouth ugly face sicken me. If I remember words of this effect from your mouth "F---- OLD BATTLEAXE" which are only suitable for your type of creatures. CRAWL BACK TO THE GUTTER. Get some 'F----- OLD B/AXE' to be a dumb blond, old, slave for yourself. Get a ROBOT – a stupid woman void of humanity. I'm finished with you forever and don't come crawling back gutter snipe. Have the decency to let me live my type of life and you can stink in yours unless you want a ghost to haunt you.[32]

29 HO 282/66 (National Archives).
30 Note of a meeting in Romney House, 9 April 1969; HO 282/66 (National Archives).
31 HO 282/66 (National Archives).
32 Ibid.

Frances was clearly at the end of some sort of tether in the summer of 1966, as these letters attest. The aggression in the language, as well as the ominous reference to a ghost haunting her husband, seemed to hint at a woman rapidly losing her self-control in the face of tremendous emotional pressures. But the raging emotions on both sides affected Reggie too. He had now begun to drink heavily – often neat gin – and frequently enough to render him extremely intoxicated more nights than not. It coloured his judgement and made him more volatile, if it did not render him incapable. And so it was that, soon after McVitie's little indiscretion, Reggie focused his attention, whilst drunk, on 'Nobby' Clarke. In his memoirs,[33] Jack Dickson claimed that Reggie was convinced that this loyal associate had been working with McVitie on the scam; however, in a statement made in 1968, he says Reggie blamed 'Nobby' for the breakup of his marriage to Frances.[34] Whatever Reggie's motives, alcohol had caused his usually suspicious nature to tip over into bitter paranoia and Clarke warranted punishment.

Accompanied by Dickson, Ronnie Hart and 'Fat' Wally Garelick, one of the Firm's peripheral members who had been helping with the machinations behind the sale of the stolen Canadian bearer bonds, Reggie went to Clarke's home. It was early in the morning and still dark and the streets were almost deserted. With bleary eyes, Clarke's wife answered the door and was told by Reggie to go into the kitchen to make a cup of tea as he wanted a private word with her husband. When Clarke appeared, Reggie pushed Dickson away and told him and Hart to "fuck off";[35] outside, the two men heard a gunshot as Reggie shot Clarke in the leg. Mrs. Clarke stormed out of the kitchen screaming, "You bastard! You have shot my husband!"[36]

A quick getaway was needed. The deafening sound of the gunshot had woken the neighbours and lights were coming on and curtains were twitching. Garelick, waiting in the car, was quickly joined by the other three and as the car sped off, Reggie muttered, "That will keep the cunt quiet."[37] Reggie was obviously a well-known face in the

33 John Dickson; *Murder Without Conviction* (London: Sidgwick and Jackson 1986).
34 Statement by John Dickson, 24 September 1968; MEPO 2/11404, ff.1288-1291 (National Archives).
35 Ibid.
36 John Dickson; *Murder Without Conviction* (London: Sidgwick and Jackson 1986).
37 Statement by John Dickson, 24 September 1968; MEPO 2/11404, ff.1288-1291 (National Archives).

East End and could not risk being identified, but, if anybody did see him, the 'Wall of Silence' remained intact in this instance. Ultimately, Clarke kept silent too, as he knew what was good for him, and the wound, which was not life threatening, was patched up by the ever-loyal Dr. Blasker. But it was a close call; if Reggie's bullet had hit its target, Clarke could have joined George Cornell as another villain dispatched by the Krays. Charlie was livid that a good friend of his had been drawn unnecessarily into such violence and even Ronnie berated his twin, seemingly oblivious to his own track record. Reggie may not have joined his brother as a killer on this occasion, but his mental condition, through his drinking and his painfully unhappy marital situation, was making him trigger-happy. Soon after came another incident where Reggie's volatile state resulted in violence with firearms, and this time, Jack McVitie was involved again.

Maybe part of Reggie's frustration was born out of trying to keep the Kray enterprise afloat. Money was again becoming tight and numerous clubs in London were being indiscriminately targeted by the twins in a desperate attempt to make some extra cash quickly. Jack Dickson, seemingly at the centre of things in 1966, was instructed to go and take a look at a club that had recently opened in Stoke Newington; it was apparently doing well and Reggie felt there could be rich pickings involved. But Dickson was not so enthusiastic; he had been going to the club for a while and was on good terms with the owner and so, after the reconnaissance mission, where he was accompanied by Ian Barrie, Dickson reported back that the club was only small and not worth bothering about. The attempt to save the owner from unnecessary trouble failed, as the twins were adamant that something could be made from the club. They wanted £1,000.

Eventually, Reggie and a few members of the Firm paid the club a visit, insisting that they were going to get what they wanted. They had not been there long before Jack McVitie walked in, bold as brass and obviously feeling no shame or fear over his previous indiscretion with the twins. Reggie asked McVitie to summon the owner over, at which point he got excited, sensing that he may be asked to help with a little muscle. The owner was apologetic, saying, "I'm sorry that I couldn't help you with the money, but as you can see there's not a lot of business here. This is only a little sideline that I have."[38]

---

38 John Dickson; *Murder Without Conviction* (London: Sidgwick and Jackson 1986).

Suddenly, McVitie began to punch and kick the owner brutally, before being dragged out of the club by Dickson. As the two men argued outside, they heard a gunshot. Inside, the owner was bleeding from the beating that McVitie had given him and from a gunshot wound in the leg, courtesy of Reggie Kray.

"If we tell you to pay up, we are not fooling around," shouted Reggie, "This is just a warning."[39]

The usual precautions were taken; Reggie lay low for a little while in a safe-house and the gun was disposed of. The reliable Dr. Blasker attended to the club owner's wounds and the 'Wall of Silence' ensured that nobody contacted the police. The twins, however, did not receive any money from the club, as the owner, reluctant to face financially crippling protection payments or physically crippling repercussions for non-payment, closed down the establishment.

◆

Sorry I didn't meet you last Saturday. If you want those pills, I'll see you this Saturday, 22nd October. I'll get them this Friday. I will meet you outside the Odeon Cinema at 3pm. Be there.

PS: If you want to answer back, write to me. Please answer if you are not coming.[40]

The above handwritten note, sent from Tottenham in North London by somebody with a Greek-sounding name, was posted to Frances Shea on 17 October 1966. By all accounts, it suggests that Frances was taking street drugs, a dangerous, unregulated way for her to assuage her anxieties and depression. She must have now been desperate to escape the mental prison she found herself in; her estranged husband, for all his dalliances with other women during the separation, was not going to let go easily, and the fact that Frances had changed her name back to Shea must have seemed little comfort when, in reality, escaping her situation was beginning to appear almost impossible.

On 17 October, Frances's father found her unconscious and barely alive in the house in Ormsby Street, the result of an overdose of barbiturates. It is unclear whether the pills she had taken were prescribed officially or acquired illicitly with suicide in mind; however, it appeared that what Frances had done was more than a

39 John Dickson; *Murder Without Conviction* (London: Sidgwick and Jackson 1986).
40 Jacky Hyams; *Frances: The Tragic Bride* (London: John Blake 2014).

cry for help: she really had tried to kill herself. She was admitted to St Leonard's Hospital in Nuttall Street, Hoxton, and naturally, on hearing the news, Reggie sped round there to see his wife. He was refused admission, as Frances was far too frail to accept any visitors, and promptly went back to Vallance Road, railing against the Shea family as he disappeared into the bottom of a gin bottle.

After three days, Frances was discharged. She apparently said afterwards, "I've been defiled. I'm useless. What is there left for me to live for? I deserve to die."[41]

All this must have been unbearable for Reggie. Pressure was building from all angles: his wife was looking to kill herself, his twin brother was looking to kill anyone who upset him, the general violence around the Firm was increasing and the desire to keep the financial situation ticking over healthily, with the various unsolicited attempts to squeeze money out of unsuspecting club owners, was adding to the emerging friction. The Canadian bearer bond racket was still ongoing and had become a big operation, but the Krays spent money as quickly as they earned it; they had expensive tastes and men had to be paid their 'pension', and, as 1966 was drawing to a close, the twins, seemingly losing their grip for the first time, were stumbling across unusual ways of making money and maintaining their prestige. Alan Cooper, the enigmatic American, began to find his way towards the centre of this chaotic picture.

That October, plans were tentatively made for a 'contract' to be taken out against a particular man, and Cooper was deemed the right person to approach to help pull it off. The proposed victim was Jimmy Evans, the small-time villain who had shot Freddie Foreman's brother George in the groin over an affair some time before. Evans was the original target when Foreman accidentally killed 'Ginger' Marks in Cheshire Street in January 1965; Evans escaped, and thus vengeance was not seen to be done. It is probable that the Krays put the contract out on Evans as a favour to the highly respected Foreman. Conveniently, it was known that Evans was due to appear at the Old Bailey in the coming months.

At a meeting with the twins, Charlie Kray and Tommy Cowley in the Crown and Anchor pub in Cheshire Street, Cooper was told of the plan. A fee of £1,000 was agreed so that Cooper could approach the people to whom he intended to give the job with a realistic pay offer.

41 John Pearson; *The Cult of Violence* (London: Orion Books 2001).

It was also decided that no knives or guns should be used, and that any link with the Krays was to be strictly avoided at all costs. This was the big league, contract killing, an old Mafia approach which Ronnie certainly must have relished. But how could this be done? The answer came from an unexpected source: an associate of Cooper by the name of Squire 'Split' Waterman.

Waterman had worked as a toolmaker before the war and had initially been refused military service owing to his occupation being on the reserve list. Eventually he did serve in the Royal Fusiliers before being invalided out of active service owing to shrapnel wounds acquired during the Allied invasion of Italy. An enthusiasm for speedway racing saw him become one of Britain's top speedway riders of the post-war years, finishing second in the World Speedway finals in 1951 and 1953.[42] He acquired his nickname 'Split' after ripping the seat of his racing leathers in a fall, when his colleagues referred to him as 'Split Arse'.[43] After retiring from the sport, he went into business in sheet metal working and plastic injection moulding, making plastic goods for companies such as Woolworths and Airfix. He also had a sideline in arms dealing and, via Cooper, whom he had first met in 1964,[44] he had supplied the Krays with various weapons including two sub-machine guns. His skill in construction would supply the answer to the problem: how to kill Jimmy Evans in the Old Bailey, in public, without anybody knowing?

The answer was something that would not have been out of place in a James Bond film: a briefcase that contained a secreted syringe which, with the surreptitious pulling of a small ring, would deliver a lethal dose of hydrogen cyanide when jabbed against the leg of the victim. Waterman called it "a beautiful piece of craftsmanship."[45]

The man chosen to do the deed was Eugene Paul Elvey (usually called Paul), an electrician with (obviously) no qualms about killing, if the price was right. He had several meetings with the Krays, Cooper, Waterman and Tommy Cowley; on one occasion, at the White House Hotel, Waterman demonstrated how the mechanism of the briefcase worked by knocking it against the side of an upholstered armchair,

---

42 R. Bamford & G. Shailes; *A History of the World Speedway Championship* (Stroud: Tempus Publishing 2002).

43 Trevor Davies; *Warzone Speedway* (Trevor Davies Publishing 2008).

44 Statement by Alan Bruce Cooper, 17 July 1968; CRIM 1/4927, ff. 1-21 (National Archives).

45 Leonard Read & James Morton; *Nipper Read: The Man Who Nicked the Krays* (London: MacDonald & Co 1991).

and then his own leg.[46] Reggie apparently expressed his approval and said that it was "just what they wanted."[47] Elvey later took possession of the briefcase at a meeting outside the Grave Maurice pub in Whitechapel Road.

As with many plans with which Alan Cooper was involved, the assassination of Jimmy Evans in the foyer of the Old Bailey failed, mainly owing to Elvey's incompetence. A photo of Evans had been supplied, but this was obviously not enough:

> *I should say I went 2 days running. The idea of doing this at the Old Bailey, seemed to me, to be rather ludicrous to start off with but I had to make some sort of effort, or some sort of show. By this time, we had the name of the man, and a photograph and his address. I understood he was attending the Old Bailey, something to do with a conspiracy, I am not sure in what capacity. I understood there was some danger of his going to prison shortly and that there was some urgency.*
>
> *On both occasions I visited the Old Bailey, I saw the man whom I understood was the intended victim. On the first occasion I was there, I did not use the briefcase. There were two main reasons. The first main reason, one reason was that there was a little bit of doubt we had spotted the right man. The photograph we had was not so good. The second reason was that my nerve failed me. I hesitated on the second occasion for much the same reason as the first occasion. After the second occasion, this person walked some distance, and we followed him by car. He ultimately went to his home address. I think he got there before us because we lost him. After that incident, the briefcase stayed in my possession and I used it as a briefcase. I cannot recall what happened to the hypodermic syringe.[48]*

Evans had made a lucky escape and the plan was never repeated. It has never been officially determined how quickly death would have come if Elvey had been successful in his task, as the strength of the hydrogen cyanide solution used was never established. The bore of the needle and whether the needle hit a blood vessel or mere muscle tissue would also have affected the speed of death.[49] But had the lethal

---

46 Statement by Eugene Elvey, 19 July 1968; CRIM 1/4927, ff.36-49 (National Archives).

47 *Daily Mirror*, 18 July 1968.

48 Ibid.

49 Statement by Francis Camps, (date unrecorded, probably July 1968); CRIM 1/4927, ff. 26-29 (National Archives).

dose of poison been successfully administered, the contract would have been fulfilled with practically no way of tracing it to the Krays. Francis Camps, the noted pathologist, was later asked his opinion on the effectiveness of the briefcase and stated:

> *This mechanism in the suitcase, in conjunction with hydrogen cyanide, is a viable method of killing somebody. If the suitcase were used by putting the point of the needle into the body of someone, he would not necessarily know anything about it, provided the needle was sharp. If the mechanism had been used and had resulted in death, in my opinion, this is not something that would be readily detected on examination. It could be accepted as death from natural causes.*[50]

---

50 Statement by Francis Camps, (date unrecorded, probably July 1968); CRIM 1/4927, ff. 26-29 (National Archives).

THIRTEEN

"THAT DOG WON"

The time had nearly come to spring Frank Mitchell from Dartmoor. Winter was on its way and, as Mitchell's escape hinged around his being part of the prison Honour Party, it was vital that the plan was executed before the outdoor work was wound up for the season. 27-year-old Discipline Officer Derek Brisco had been in charge of the outdoor working party since October, and had originally expressed his disapproval at Mitchell's inclusion in it as, some time before, he had heard of a possible plot by Mitchell and several others to escape. The powers that be, however, assured him that the escape plan had been ditched and that Mitchell should continue as part of the Honour Party as a way of treating him leniently so as to get him his release date.[1] Brisco explained the usual routine:

The system of taking the 'Honour' party to Bagga Tor was that we would be collected from near the prison gate by a private mini bus owned by Mr. Finch of Princetown, and this would convey us to the end of the road leading to Bagga Tor. On occasions I would ask the driver to stop the vehicle in Peter Tavy and I would call at the Post Office and buy eggs, sauce and peas with my subsistence money received as I worked with the outside party...

On reaching the end of the road we would have half-a-mile to walk to our hut. Beyond this point work could take us the extreme

---

1   Statement by Derek Brisco, 15 December 1966; MEPO 2/10805, ff. 2-5 (National Archives).

distance of a mile and three quarters.[2]

On occasion, Mitchell would stay at the hut with the cook and help to prepare the communal meal for the party whilst the other four or five inmates, accompanied by Brisco, would continue working. This meant that sometimes, Mitchell and his companion could be alone for anything up to three-and-a-half hours at a time. Sometimes there was a long wait in the hut for the transport bus to arrive to take them back to the prison, and Brisco was not averse to allowing Mitchell and another inmate to go for a walk, as long as they didn't take too long. Consequently, Mitchell took full advantage of the freedoms the working party offered, and the prison officers in charge were satisfied that he would not abuse his privileges, possibly because they feared he would revert to his violent ways if challenged.

Much has been said about what Mitchell used to do when outside the prison walls: he would wander off and feed the local horses and, unbeknown to the guards, would visit local pubs for a drink, usually accompanied by a fellow convict. In fact, the accounts of some of the local people are testimony to just how much 'The Mad Axeman' could get away with. One local farmer, George Dore, spoke of how one day Mitchell approached him about borrowing a horse to ride on, just to pass the time, to which Dore agreed.[3] At the Elephant's Nest pub in Horndon, Roy Turner was offered £5 by Mitchell to buy his old Vauxhall, and probably would have sold it if Mitchell's offer had not been way below Turner's asking price of £20.[4]

There were two pubs close to where the Honour Party used to work; the Elephant's Nest, previously mentioned, and the Peter Tavy Inn at Peter Tavy. According to Edgar Roberts, the licensee of the latter, Mitchell had been frequenting his pub at least once a week from October to early December and was always accompanied by a second man, believed to be a fellow trusted convict by the name of Whelan. Naturally, in conversation with Roberts, the two visitors would give false stories as to who they were and why they were in the area:

> *I understood that Mitchell was a transporter with three lorries and he was hoping to get a contract up at the new reservoir which is*

---

2   Statement by Derek Brisco, 15 December 1966; MEPO 2/10805, ff. 2-5 (National Archives).

3   *Guardian*, 19 December 1966.

4   Ibid.

> *proposed at Hillbridge. Mitchell always appeared to have plenty of money and it was he that actually paid for the drinks. We have received £5 notes from Mitchell and on Friday, 2nd December, 1966, we changed a £10 note for him.*
>
> *Most times Mitchell would purchase bottles of drink to take away with him, it varied from cider and beer to bottles of gin, Whisky and Vodka, also cigarettes. On the average Mitchell would spend £5-£4 but on one occasion the amount spent was over £9.*
>
> *Mitchell and his friend used to remain on my premises for about 45 minutes. I never saw them with transport of their own, but I only saw them arrive walking from the direction of the village.*[5]

Mitchell and Whelan had also been frequenting the Elephant's Nest since the end of September, sometimes up to twice a week. The first time they visited, they downed a few pints of bitter and after discussing what they should take away with them, bought bottles of "Vodka, Gin, Whisky, Martini, Beaujolais and a bottle of 1962 Blue Nun wine" at a cost of £11.[6]

Incredibly, at about midday on 29 November, Mitchell ordered a cab from the Elephant's Nest so that he could visit a pet shop in a nearby town centre. The cab driver suggested Tavistock and en route they stopped at Peter Tavy so Mitchell could dash into a shop and use a public telephone. Once at Tavistock, Mitchell went into a pet shop and purchased a finch which he carried out in a small box, and the cab returned to Hillbridge at about 12.50 p.m. The driver was, of course, none the wiser as to the significance of his customer, for Mitchell had told him that he was in charge of digging trenches for a 'government department', and as the two men parted company, Mitchell paid the 16 shilling fare with a £1 note and some loose change – a generous tip indeed.[7]

Thanks to the Krays' generosity, Frank Mitchell had money to burn, regularly leaving these two Dartmoor pubs with the modern equivalent of, on average, over £100 worth of booze. And yet the prison authorities had no idea and, according to Derek Brisco, not

5 Statement by Edgar Roberts, 15 December 1966; MEPO 2/10805, ff. 9-10 (National Archives).
6 Statement by Bernard Land (licensee of the Elephant's Nest), 15 December 1966; MEPO 2/10805, ff. 14-15 (National Archives).
7 Statement of Clifford Down, undated (December 1966); MEPO 2/10805, ff. 18-19 (National Archives).

once did they detect the smell of alcohol on Mitchell's breath. The astonishingly liberal regime that Mitchell exploited would mean that any escape would be incredibly easy.

Throughout the latter part of 1966, Mitchell continued to receive regular visits from assorted members of the Firm. It was undoubtedly on these occasions that money and information regarding the escape was exchanged. There was also a small hideout on a deserted farm on the moor where Mitchell would leave the bottles of drink, as well as food for the moorland ponies. It was also possible that money was left there for him to collect.[8] On 11 December, three men, a 'Mr. Walker' (actually Wally Garelick), a 'Mr. Bishop' (Teddy Smith), and 'Big' Pat Connolly made the final visit.[9] They were seen by a number of local residents and stood out as they were driving a large grey three-litre Rover saloon – the presence of the huge Pat Connolly also stuck in people's minds. One witness, a farmer from Kingred Farm, Peter Tavy, felt decidedly uneasy about the three men; he watched them for a short while as they were stuck behind a flock of slow-moving sheep. Once the car had moved on, the witness, with no small degree of perception, said to his brother, "What's the London underworld doing down here?"[10]

By now the plan was fully formed: Mitchell would be collected from the moor at an agreed spot and taken back to London where he would be held in a safe house. Whilst the authorities searched for this most dangerous of escaped convicts, 'Mad' Teddy Smith, who always thought of himself as a bit of a wordsmith, would dictate letters for Mitchell to write, expressing his regret that he had not got a release date and that, on the proviso that he was offered one, he would give himself up. It was also felt that the publicity given to the letters, if published in the national press, would sway public sympathy for Mitchell's plight.

Yes, ludicrous as it sounds, that was the deal the twins had persuaded Mitchell to believe. He didn't think it was ludicrous because to him, Ronnie was a God.[11]

8   *Guardian*, 19 December 1966.
9   Prison Visits list; MEPO 2/10805, f. 21 (National Archives).
10 Statement by David Hill, 30 December 1966; MEPO 2/10680, f.33 (National Archives).
11 Albert Donoghue & Martin Short; *The Enforcer* (London: John Blake 2002).

But the springing of Frank Mitchell was also a large public relations exercise. Ronnie Kray was known throughout the underworld as a character of great generosity. Many former convicts could attest to his donations of money, clothes and places to stay, although such profligacy had caused a downturn in the profits of a number of Kray-owned enterprises. But for Ronnie, this was all important, as much about his public image as a benefactor to the trusted criminal as it was his reputation as a man to be feared. When the underworld got to hear that the Krays had 'Big' Frank Mitchell, the 'Mad Axeman' - the legend – on their side, the image-enhancing benefits would also be considerable.

But as the final preparations for Mitchell's escape were being finalised, Ronnie had a little, perhaps not unforeseen, problem to contend with. On 24 November, Sergeant Leonard Townshend had been summoned to appear at Old Street Magistrates' Court on two charges of corruption, in contravention of Section 1 (1) Prevention of Corruption Act, 1906. The two counts were for attempting to gain £50 from Ronnie Kray on 11 August 1966 in order to show favour, and for accepting the said monies from Eric Marshall on 15 August.[12] It was inevitable, once the committal hearing was underway, that Ronnie would be required to give evidence. He, along with Ian Barrie, Teddy Smith and Harry Cope, had already made brief statements about the night in the Baker's Arms on 11 August, but, for Ronnie, that was as far as he was prepared to go, and he had already told Geoff Allen that "he did not propose to appear at the Police Court hearing, nor would he give evidence." He was also alleged to have said, "I did this because the law are always verballing people, now it's our turn."[13] Whatever the law made of Townshend's case, Ronnie Kray was not going to play ball.

◆

On Monday, 12 December 1966, Albert Donoghue and Teddy Smith made the 235-mile journey from London to Dartmoor in a grey Humber Hawk, specially hired by Billy Exley from Auto Hall in St Martin's Lane.[14] Donoghue and Smith had only visited Mitchell once

12 Report by Detective Chief Inspector E. Fletcher, 27 April 1967; MEPO 2/10680, f.23A (National Archives).
13 Report by Detective Sergeant J. Barrett, 12 December 1966; MEPO 2/10680, f.18B (National Archives).
14 Statement by William Exley, undated (1968); CRIM 1/4900, ff. 80-93 (National Archives).

and it was thought best that two individuals whose names had barely graced the Dartmoor Prison visitor's book would be suitable for the pick-up, in the interests of security. The idea was that Mitchell would meet them at a pre-arranged spot, by a telephone box not far from the Elephant's Nest pub.

Mitchell had gone out with the Honour Party as usual that morning and the group were working on repairs to an old fence. The weather was bad and so, for much of the time, the group stayed in their hut playing cards. Officer Brisco recalled the subsequent events:

> We had a cup of tea about 3.30 p.m. at this time Mitchell asked if he could take some bread to the horses which were near the gate where we picked up the transport, this wasn't unusual he had done it many times before and often Whelan went with him.
>
> When we arrived at the gate at about 4.20 p.m. the transport was there, but Mitchell wasn't. I didn't think anything was wrong as some two hundred yards along the road from the gate is a track leading to the place where the horses are kept and sometimes Mitchell waits there.
>
> We got into the van and drove down there and he wasn't there. I had a look for him and went to the place where the horses were, but I could not see him anywhere. I got into the van and had the driver go to the telephone kiosk in Peter Tavy. I did not have any change and it took several minutes to get a reverse charge call to the Prison.[15]

(Brisco would later admit that the timings in this original statement were erroneous – he actually last saw Mitchell at 11.00 a.m.[16] – and Albert Donoghue's later account[17] says that he and Smith were due to meet Mitchell at midday. This fits correctly with later timings for Mitchell's arrival in London given by Donoghue and Jack Dickson.)

Donoghue and Smith had parked the Humber by the telephone box and Smith went inside, pretending to make a call; they didn't have to wait long before Mitchell came strolling down the road. He got straight into the car. Smith drove whilst Donoghue supplied Mitchell with a change of clothes donated by Tommy Welch, who was of a similar size. As he removed his clothing, Mitchell produced

---

15 Statement by Derek Brisco, 15 December 1966; MEPO 2/10805, ff. 2-5 (National Archives).

16 Martin Fido; *The Krays: Unfinished Business* (London: Carlton Books 1999).

17 Albert Donoghue & Martin Short; *The Enforcer* (London: John Blake 2002).

a large home-made knife and Donoghue had to use all his powers of persuasion to convince Mitchell that not only was it unnecessary, but also totally undesirable. If the police were setting up roadblocks already, an offensive weapon would be the last thing they would want to be caught with. The unwanted clothing (a pair of wellington boots, two pairs of socks, two shirts, a pair of overalls and a green anorak)[18] were rolled up into a bundle and thrown out of the car window, along with the knife, outside Okehampton.

The long drive back to London went without a hitch, and Mitchell's escape was not reported on the radio news until the car had reached Fulham in South West London. From there, Donoghue phoned Reggie, using the code "That dog won" to indicate that all was well.[19] Mitchell was driven through his old stomping ground of the East End before their destination, Priscilla Road in Bow, was reached, where he was going to be put up temporarily by the elderly parents of the long-suffering 'Nobby' Clarke. But when the Clarkes got cold feet, an alternative hiding place was suggested and so Mitchell was on the move again; their destination was 206A Barking Road, East Ham, a small ground-floor flat in a 1950s low-rise block owned by Kray friend Lennie Dunn (also known as 'Books', as he ran a bookstall on Whitechapel Market). 'Nipper' Read remembered Dunn as a strange, almost pathetic character:

> He was by turns nervous, servile and timid and could then display a violent temper. He had known the Krays for years – who didn't in the East End? – and had gone out of his way to scrape an acquaintanceship with them. He was typical of those who hero-worshipped them. He frequented pubs where they drank and boasted of his acquaintance. The truth was they never really noticed him, but to be in the same room was sufficient. Eventually he was identified as a camp follower and he let them know that he would do virtually anything for them.[20]

About eighteen months previously, Dunn had told the Krays that they could use his flat for meetings.[21] At the Krays' behest, Dunn

18 Report by Bryan Culliford, Principal Science Officer, Metropolitan Police, 10 January 1967; MEPO 2/10805, f.51 (National Archives).
19 Albert Donoghue & Martin Short; *The Enforcer* (London: John Blake 2002).
20 Leonard Read & James Morton; *Nipper Read: The Man Who Nicked the Krays* (London: MacDonald & Co 1991).
21 Statement by Lennie Dunn, undated (1968); CRIM 1/4900, ff. 36-50 (National Archives).

was now about to share his home with the 'Mad Axeman' and a revolving group of minders from the Firm which essentially boiled down to Albert Donoghue, Jack Dickson, Billy Exley and on a couple of occasions, Connie Whitehead.[22]

Mitchell, in his childlike way, was excited to be free. He wanted to start writing his letters straight away and he was keen to see his heroes, the Kray twins, especially Ronnie. But that was never going to happen. On 13 December, Sergeant Townshend appeared at Old Street Magistrates' Court on the two charges of corruption, to which he pleaded 'not guilty'. Ronnie was required urgently as "the essential witness"[23] and a warrant, compelling him to attend court, was issued that day. Through a friend, he found a flat in Finchley, North West London, and effectively barricaded himself in, intending to stay out of the way until the Townshend case had run its course and the warrant expired. This meant that there was no way he would be able to visit Frank Mitchell in East Ham any time soon. In fact, not even Reggie made much of an effort to see Mitchell, much to the giant man's dismay. This was not a good state of affairs, for all involved; for the time being, Mitchell was trapped in the flat, with only the hand-picked members of the Firm for company. He was an unpredictable character and everybody was aware that he had to be kept 'sweet' as the repercussions of an angry Frank Mitchell did not bear thinking about. His minders were happy to indulge his peculiar habits; he bathed and brushed his teeth several times a day and was prone to spontaneous demonstrations of his physical prowess, particularly press-ups or bouts of arm-wrestling. He was obsessed with keeping fit. Sometimes he would be happy to play cards, or have a drink and listen to music, but other times he would sit and brood. These were awkward moments for the Firm and it was not difficult to detect the growing frustration within Mitchell as the first few days passed. As Albert Donoghue rightly observed, "The twins had hooked him out of Dartmoor, without thinking what they would do with him a couple of stages on."[24]

The one occasion Reggie came to visit Mitchell was, apart from showing his face, to facilitate two things: to discuss the letters he was going to write and to get him a girl. It appears that Ronnie Kray had

22 *Daily Express*, 27 June 1968.
23 *Daily Mirror*, 14 December 1966.
24 Albert Donoghue & Martin Short; *The Enforcer* (London: John Blake 2002).

already begun to push Teddy Smith's plan of writing to the media when, on 16 December, he phoned Dennis Darling, an old prison friend of Mitchell, and said, "We want you to contact the newspapers, and try and arrange a deal for Frank. If the Home Office give him a date of release he will give himself up."[25] Darling did as requested, first contacting the *Sunday Pictorial* newsdesk. They seemed uninterested, so he got in touch with the *News of the World* and a meeting was arranged at a pub in Holborn. There, Darling met two men who called themselves 'Mr. Earle' and 'Mr. Charles'; however, they could not help as they were in no position to contact the Home Office directly about Mitchell's situation. Darling quickly reached a dead end and the idea fizzled out. The next move was for Mitchell to write his letters and see if their publication would do the trick.

After a couple of days, Teddy Smith sat down with Mitchell to write the letters that he was to send to the media. It took a lot of time and a lot of paper, as Mitchell was barely literate, and, as Smith dictated the content of these letters, the 'Mad Axeman' laboriously wrote out his case, twice: once for the *Daily Mirror* and once for *The Times*.

> *19/12/66*
>
> *Sir,*
>
> *The reason for my absence from Dartmoor was to bring to the notice of my unhappy plight. To be truthful I am asking for a possible date of release. From the age of 9 I have not been completely free, always under some act or other.*
>
> *Sir, I ask you where is the fairness of this? I am not a murderer or sex maniac nor do I think I am a danger to the public. I think that I have been more than punished for the wrongs I have done.*
>
> *I am ready to give myself up if I can have something to look forward to. I do not intend to use any violence at any time should I be found, that is why I left a knife behind with my prison things.*
>
>

Yours sincerely
Frank Mitchell

>
> *P.S. I have not been in touch with the News of the World nor with Mr. Danny Darling.*[26]

---

25 Statement by Dennis Darling, 17 December 1966; MEPO 2/10680, ff.42-43 (National Archives).

26 Letter published in the *Daily Mirror* and *The Times*; 21 December 1966.

It is interesting to note that he mentions Dennis Darling and the aborted *News of the World* deal. Darling's statement of 17 December, made at the offices of the Flying Squad at Scotland Yard, actually made a tantalising link between the Krays and Mitchell's disappearance: it mentioned Reggie as a fellow prisoner at Wandsworth and named the man who phoned the previous day as 'Ronnie'. Also, witnesses had come forward about the Rover (licence plate UPM 533) that Pat Connolly and his companions had used on their last two visits to Dartmoor. 'Fat' Wally Garelick had been visited at his home in Stepney by Detective Superintendent Edward Harris and Inspector Swain on 13 December, and taken to Arbour Square Police Station for questioning; Garelick, perhaps surprisingly, gave the names of practically everybody who had visited Mitchell, even revealing their aliases, but was careful not to implicate any of them in the actual escape.[27] Two days later, using Garelick's information, Pat Connolly was spoken to at Stoke Newington Police Station by Harris. Connolly was less cooperative, but still gave names which confirmed Garelick's statement. When asked how often he visited Mitchell, he replied, "Lots of times – the twins send us down there. They look after lots of slags."[28]

The Rover was quickly traced and sweepings from the floor were analysed for anything that could connect it to the clothing discarded by Mitchell on his escape.[29] Nothing was found, and the Krays were probably blissfully unaware at this stage of how close these leads could have come to bringing the police to their door.

With the first letters sent, it was now apparent that Mitchell needed something else to occupy himself: a woman. After all, he was a powerful man with strong needs and it was felt that, as he quickly became more agitated by his confinement in the flat, some female attention would calm him down. Tommy Cowley was a regular patron of Winston's nightclub in Clifford Street, Mayfair, and knew many of its hostesses, and so he was brought in to see if he could recommend one of the young ladies for the job of being Mitchell's 'companion'. Cowley knew just the woman, an attractive, "plumpish" blonde from the North of England named Patricia Watson. Until now, this key

27 Statement by Wallace Garelick, 13 December 1966; CRIM 1/4900 (National Archives).
28 Statement by Detective Superintendent Edward Harris, undated (1968); ibid.
29 Report by Bryan Culliford, Principal Science Officer, Metropolitan Police, 10 January 1967; MEPO 2/10805, f.51 (National Archives).

player in the Mitchell affair has been known as Lisa Prescott, and she was known to all involved as 'Lisa' or 'Liza'. Her flatmate knew her as Lisa Polowski, and so in the interests of clarity, from here on in she will be known just as Lisa.[30]

Lisa came to London from Leeds in the early 1960s and began working as a nightclub hostess and cigarette girl, first at the Bagatelle Club, and later Winston's and its sister-club, Churchill's in New Bond Street. She also worked in other clubs which shared management with Winston's, namely the Savoy in The Strand and The Minstrel in Beak Street, Soho.[31] She was married – Polowski was believed to be her married name - but had been separated from her husband for a while, and despite suggestions made later, she had no children.[32] The desire for anonymity, and thus an alias, came with the job; Lisa herself made it clear what she did for a living:

> *Being a hostess consists of entertaining men at the club and afterwards. I am paid for entertaining men afterwards.*
>
> *A club hostess is a polite word for a prostitute. I was not prepared to go to bed with virtually anybody for a sum of money. I had to like the men first before I went to bed with them...*
>
> *If I liked a person and I spent the night with them, my fee was £25 or more.*[33]

In the summer of 1966, Lisa had moved into a flat in Craven Terrace, Bayswater, with friend and fellow hostess Valerie Fiske. On the night of 19 December, Lisa and Fiske shared a cab to their respective clubs and Lisa alighted at Winston's; it was the last the two would see of each other until Christmas Eve. Reggie, Donoghue and Cowley were waiting for Lisa at Winston's to put their proposal to her.

> *Tommy asked me to do him a favour. I said yes because I thought I could leave before he did. ... The next thing I knew I had my coat, and I was sitting in a taxi outside the club, Reggie Kray and Tommy and Albert were in the taxi. Tommy said I would be as good as*

---

30 Statement of Patricia Watson (Lisa), undated (1968); CRIM 1/4900, 52-72 (National Archives).

31 Lisa's background information here comes from an undated statement (1968) by Valerie Fiske; MEPO 2/11404, ff. 1558-1563 (National Archives).

32 Statement of Patricia Watson (Lisa), undated (1968); CRIM 1/4900, 52-72 (National Archives).

33 Ibid.

gold, and Reggie said that if I did this I would have the respect of everyone in the East End. I did not know what it was I was expected to do, and I think I went in fear more than anything else.[34]

After a quick stop by Vallance Road, Lisa was taken to Lennie Dunn's flat; it was 3.00 a.m. on Tuesday, 20 December. Donoghue made the initial introductions and although it was now the early hours of the morning, Lisa and Mitchell had drinks and spoke for over an hour. Amongst other things, she told him about her baby and baby-sitter,[35] a white lie that give her a reasonable excuse for having to return to her flat if necessary. When everything seemed to be in order, Lisa and Mitchell went into the bedroom together and closed the door behind them. She would remain at Lennie Dunn's flat, except for one quick visit home, for the next four days.

Mitchell made full use of his new companion, who described him as a "ruthless and demanding lover whose primitive passions electrified me."[36] As far as Mitchell's temperament was concerned, the arrival of Lisa, and the fact that the 'Mad Axeman' could vent his vast libido, had noticeably calmed him down, for the moment at least. The couple got on better than anybody had hoped, but this did not mean that Lisa was entirely happy with the situation. She had quickly realised who Mitchell was, thanks to the reports of his escape that were now a regular feature on the television news, and she was painfully aware of the element of danger in the whole situation. On two occasions she tried to escape, the first attempt failing after she tripped on an electric fire in the dark and made a noise: "I got a spanking from Frank Mitchell after that",[37] she later said. "It was not very hard, but it was hard enough for me."[38] The second time, she tried to leave through a window, but Mitchell caught her: "He said if I tried to escape he couldn't protect me."[39]

Lisa was allowed one visit to her Bayswater flat, under the watchful eye of Billy Exley, to pick up fresh clothes; since arriving, she had nothing to wear other than the black cocktail dress she was in when

34 *Daily Mirror*, 27 June 1968.
35 *Daily Express*, 27 June 1968.
36 Leonard Read & James Morton; *Nipper Read: The Man Who Nicked the Krays* (London: MacDonald & Co 1991).
37 *Daily Mirror*, 22 April 1969.
38 Statement of Patricia Watson (Lisa), undated (1968); CRIM 1/4900, 52-72 (National Archives).
39 *Daily Express*, 22 April 1969.

she had left Winston's. Her flatmate, Valerie, was out and so Lisa left a note, one approved by the Firm, under the television set, saying, "Half the rent is here, and I will be away for a few days",[40] giving nothing away.

On 20 December, Mitchell wrote a second letter, guided by Teddy Smith and assisted by Lisa, which was sent again to the *Mirror* and the *Times*:

> *20/12/66*
>
> *Sir,*
>
> *It is obvious I have moved since posting my last letter. I am sorry that my absence has caused certain people to think badly of men like Mr. Roy Jenkins who I am sure is trying to use modern methods of dealing with prisons. What Mr. Jenkins has said is true --- treat people like animals and they will react like animals. But treat them like human beings and they will act like human beings. When I was in prison I received some kindness from some members of the staff. I would like to thank those officers who offered to bring me back to Dartmoor. When Mr. Malone was Governor of Dartmoor I had hope to carry on despite the hardship of life in Prison because I felt sure I would one day get a date of release.*
>
> *I have read with interest what has been written since I sent my last letter. I can only repeat my appeal to the humane thinking people of this country. If I must be buried alive give me some reason to hope.*
>
> *Trusting in the goodness of others.*
>
> > *Yours sincerely*
> > *Frank Mitchell* [41]

Despite these letters, nothing seemed to be happening. The issue of Mitchell's escape was being debated in the House of Commons almost every day; however, much of the discussion revolved around the controversy surrounding the concept of the Honour Party and the risks involved when high-maintenance prisoners, such as Mitchell, were allowed on it. The Conservative MP for Tavistock, Michael Heseltine, was deeply concerned about safety to his constituents, noting that the proximity of a firing range close to where the Honour Party worked could only increase the risk of escaped convicts

40 Statement of Patricia Watson (Lisa), undated (1968); CRIM 1/4900, 52-72 (National Archives).
41 MEPO 2/10680, ff.36-39 (National Archives).

acquiring firearms.[42] Robert Mark, Chief Constable of Leicester, had been preparing a report[43] which Parliament was keen to see, yet there was no talk of offering Mitchell his much-wanted release date, or even the ethics of doing so. Unfortunately, with Parliament due to go on Christmas recess on 21 December, the question of Mitchell's proposal was going to have to take a back seat until mid-January 1967. The plan to secure the promise of a release date was being scuppered by political inertia.

With that, things started to get fractious at the Barking Road flat. Despite the benefits of having Lisa around, Mitchell was again becoming increasingly frustrated. For Lennie Dunn, Albert Donoghue, Jack Dickson and Billy Exley, it was like walking on egg-shells. Donoghue was around most days, reading Mitchell's moods, which swayed between confidence that the authorities would capitulate to his demands and utter despair.

> After the first week, Lisa's charms could still keep him happy in bed, but they could no longer tranquillize his mind. During the night one of the guards woke up to see Frank standing over him with a knife. This incident was instantly reported to the twins who soon had a lot more to worry about.[44]

This was one issue that contributed to Mitchell's anger; the fact that more than a week had passed and the twins had still not come to see him (beyond Reggie's sole token visit). With his child's mind, Mitchell could not understand how his two heroes, particularly Ronnie, who had made all the big promises (and up until now had honoured them), seemed to want nothing to do with him. Ronnie's situation was explained, but to no avail. Then Mitchell made a statement which signalled an ominous change in the whole escapade: he said that if the Krays didn't visit him soon, he would visit them. He knew their family address in Vallance Road and when he made this threat, he meant it. He was now aware that he had exchanged one prison for another and was desperate to do something beyond the walls of Lennie Dunn's little flat, whether it was seeing the Krays, visiting his own family or doing something as simple as having a few drinks in a pub.

42 House of Commons debates, 20 December 1966; *Hansard*, vol. 738, cc.1195-1254.
43 As part of the Mountbatten inquiry into prison security, set up in 1966 following the escape of spy George Blake from Wormwood Scrubs.
44 Albert Donoghue & Martin Short; *The Enforcer* (London: John Blake 2002).

None of this was practical. East London was under complete police surveillance in case Mitchell attempted to see his family and old friends, and even the Royal Marines were involved in the nationwide hunt for him. He was effectively the most wanted man in the country, standing a conspicuous six foot three in height, with his picture slapped all over the media. Venturing into the outside world was something Frank Mitchell could never do without dire consequences for all involved. The authorities had let him down, the twins had let him down, and now the 'Mad Axeman' was getting truly mad with it all. And then he started announcing that he wasn't going back to prison. For the Krays, the solution had to be drastic, for there was no way that Frank Mitchell would go down fighting: he knew the names of all involved and had, on one occasion, even threatened to tell all if a confrontation with the police ever occurred.[45] But in his current state of mind, Mitchell had become too dangerous to contain; "To unleash him on the public was as irresponsible as taking the muzzle off a crazed Rottweiler and letting it loose in a playschool", Albert Donoghue once observed.[46]

On 23 December 1966, a meeting was held in neutral territory – the Hackney home of old Kray family friend Harry Hopwood – to discuss what to do with Mitchell, and Freddie Foreman was brought over from Lambeth. Accounts differ, however, as to who was present at this important meeting: Donoghue claimed it was himself, Foreman, Hopwood, Reggie and Charlie Kray.[47] Foreman later denied the presence of Reggie and Charlie, saying that only himself, Hopwood, Donoghue and Ronnie Kray were there, although Donoghue and Hopwood were in a different room when the real discussions took place.[48] It is important to note that when Foreman made those claims, long after the event, Ronnie was already dead, and thus he may have felt it necessary to protect the two surviving Krays in a way only the criminal underworld could, by being economical with the truth. Foreman's account is also problematical because Ronnie was very much in hiding at the time.

Harry Hopwood would later say that Charlie Kray had given him

45 John Dickson; *Murder Without Conviction* (London: Sidgwick and Jackson 1986).

46 Freddie Foreman; *Freddie Foreman: The Godfather of British Crime* (London: John Blake 2007).

47 Albert Donoghue & Martin Short; *The Enforcer* (London: John Blake 2002).

48 Statement by Harry Hopwood, 20 August 1968; MEPO 2/11404, ff. 1196-1207 (National Archives).

£5 to take the day off so the meeting could take place at his flat, and that Charlie, Reggie, Tommy Cowley, 'Nobby' Clarke and "some other people I had not seen before who were strange faces" were at the meeting.[49] Everybody arrived at different times.

Donoghue claimed that he and Hopwood were sent to another room whilst Reggie, Charlie and Freddie Foreman knocked out their plans for Mitchell in the kitchen, and subsequently, when they emerged, the idea was broadcast that Mitchell was to be taken "down to Kent to a farm where he'll spend Christmas with Ronnie" before being sent abroad.[50] It is fair to say that there was no way this was actually going to happen: the 'Mad Axeman' was going to have to disappear.

The timing was crucial. With Christmas imminent, Mitchell would have become utterly unmanageable in the hideout if he was stuck there over the festive period. Those who were protecting him would have families of their own to be with and their absence would have attracted unwanted suspicion and domestic friction. In fact, the day before the meeting, Billy Exley was already losing his patience with the situation and was beginning to voice his anger; Jack Dickson was looking forward to a few days back in Scotland; and Lennie Dunn, who wasn't going anywhere, had made it known that he hadn't yet received the £500 he was promised by the Krays for the use of his flat. Worst of all, Mitchell was now utterly frustrated and had begun to aggressively vent his dissatisfaction with the twins and their plan:

> I had more fucking freedom in Dartmoor. At least I wasn't cooped up – I could get out and see a bit of sunshine. How long do they think they can keep me here? I want to see Ronnie. He's fucking letting me down – if he doesn't get here fast I will be looking for him. He was supposed to have me out of London days ago.[51]

And so the plan to solve the Frank Mitchell problem, devised at lunchtime, was executed in the evening. It meant Albert Donoghue, who had Mitchell's trust as one of the men who had collected him from Dartmoor, having to let Mitchell know that he was being taken to the country in a van, where he would stay with Ronnie over Christmas. The only snag was that Lisa would not be going with him. This was a

---

49 Statement by Harry Hopwood, 20 August 1968; MEPO 2/11404, ff. 1196-1207 (National Archives).
50 Albert Donoghue & Martin Short; *The Enforcer* (London: John Blake 2002).
51 John Dickson; *Murder Without Conviction* (London: Sidgwick and Jackson 1986).

major issue for Mitchell, for not only did he and Lisa get on well, but Mitchell had fallen in love with her. He obviously thought that their relationship, born out of a casual attempt to distract and pacify him, was destined to continue, although Lisa, despite being fond of and not a little sorry for Mitchell, certainly did not love him. She also knew that what she was involved in was temporary and that she would have her own life to return to once it was all over. This meant that when Mitchell heard of the plan for Lisa, he was not best pleased and became visibly distressed. Albert Donoghue had to use his best powers of persuasion to make Mitchell see the sense in the idea:

> Well the only way to do this is to think what's going to happen if you get a stoppo on the way down. If the Old Bill pull you, you're going to go right into one, and she's going to be involved. She'll either be hurt or nicked. You don't need that. So what we'll do, we'll set you off first, and I'll follow up with Lisa half an hour later. We'll get you there all nice and safely, you'll be with the Colonel and Merry Christmas.[52]

Mitchell seemed happy with that and set about packing for the journey. He was also happy to be told that it was Ronnie himself who would be picking him up, at 8.30 p.m. prompt. When the time came, Mitchell had changed into a new set of clothes and was ready with his belongings. He was told that a van was waiting outside for him, just round the corner in Ladysmith Avenue. To Mitchell, the fact that a van was being used immediately rekindled the idea of taking Lisa with him, as he felt there would obviously be enough room for both of them. His suggestion made Lisa extremely anxious, for she most certainly didn't want to go, and she looked at Donoghue for some way out of the scenario. The trusted Donoghue, getting nervous himself, tried one more time to convince Mitchell that all was well and that Lisa would follow on:

> Frank, I will find out where you are going and I will have her with you in twenty-four hours. She must let her flat-mate know where she is going. Please trust me. Come on, let's go now, he is waiting.[53]

Mitchell spent a while saying goodbye to Lisa and they kissed. Lennie Dunn came out of the back bedroom and they bade him

52 Albert Donoghue & Martin Short; *The Enforcer* (London: John Blake 2002).
53 John Dickson; *Murder Without Conviction* (London: Sidgwick and Jackson 1986).

farewell as Lisa then sat on the settee and cried.[54] As Mitchell left, he looked sad, probably because he was leaving his beloved behind, but for Lisa, Dunn and Jack Dickson, who stood watching as the big man strolled out the door of the flat with Donoghue, it was a blessed relief. As they left, Dunn was told to turn out all the lights in the flat and Lisa was told to go to the back bedroom.[55]

As Donoghue led Mitchell round the corner into Ladysmith Avenue, a policeman appeared, walking his beat. This must have been a terrifying moment for all; Mitchell tensed up but managed to control himself. The slightest interest from the officer could have sparked a calamitous reaction from him, but they passed each other without issue, and, breathing a sigh of relief, turned into Ladysmith Avenue where they saw Jerry Callaghan, an associate of Freddie Foreman, standing on the pavement. Nearby, double-parked and with the engine running, was a dark van. Callaghan opened the back doors and it was immediately apparent that two men, Foreman and Alfie Gerrard, were already inside, sitting on the left-hand wheel arch. Foreman politely greeted Mitchell, asked him to sit on the opposite wheel arch, and then told Donoghue to go round the front to tell Callaghan how to get to the Blackwall Tunnel.[56] Donoghue, for some reason, actually got into the passenger seat of the van; it is possible he misunderstood Foreman's instruction, but as Callaghan climbed into the driver's seat and slammed the door, there was a barrage of gunfire from the rear of the van as it moved down Ladysmith Avenue away from Barking Road. Apparently, Mitchell had quickly worked out that there was something amiss and made a sudden lunge toward the driver's seat, at which point Foreman and Gerrard began shooting him earlier than they had planned. For Donoghue, stuck in the front seat and apparently unaware up to that point what exactly was meant to happen, it was a harrowing experience:

> *They just keep popping the man. He comes off the casing on his knees, then he falls back, and these bullets are going all over him. Then he goes still and one of the guys, Foreman, leans over and puts three more shots in around the heart. You can see the shirt*

54 *Daily Express*, 22 April 1969.
55 *Daily Mirror*, 27 June 1968.
56 It was suggested during the 1969 Mitchell trial that the driver was actually Ronnie Oliffe; however, Freddie Foreman strenuously denied that he was there. Donoghue only mentions Foreman, Gerrard and Callaghan in relation to the Mitchell shooting.

jumping...

He's been lying quiet for a while. He's got to be dead. Then all of a sudden there's a groan, and he lifts his head up again. I don't know what they call it – after death, the body relaxing or gas escaping – but then there's another groan. So Gerrard says, "He ain't fucking dead, give him another one, I'm empty."

...Yeah, I'm pleased to hear one guy's empty – at least I've only got one gun to deal with now – but then Foreman goes and puts the gun right up behind Frank's ear and Pop! Pop! That's the last two shots that's fired into him.[57]

Four, maybe five, muffled gun shots were heard in Lennie Dunn's flat, the first batch of shots fired as the van pulled away. Lisa, on hearing the bangs, exclaimed, "Oh God, they've shot him – I've had it now!"[58] She wanted to run out into the street, but Dickson and Dunn convinced her not to; Dunn tried to put the noises down to a car backfiring, with little conviction. And then Donoghue returned. The van had turned right out of Ladysmith Avenue into Central Park Road and then immediately right up Kimberley Avenue. On reaching the junction with Barking Road, Donoghue had got out and walked away in silence, thoroughly expecting a shot to the back of the head which, thankfully, never came. He flapped his coat in the breeze to get rid of the smell of cordite before going inside and, seeing the excited state of the people there, confidently brushed aside any talk of gunshots. Lisa went sobbing into the bedroom, convinced that Mitchell was dead. It was an awkward situation, as now Donoghue had to call Reggie Kray and let him know the deed had been done, in a way that would not distress Lisa any further. When he got through, he simply said, "That dog won," the code he used to signify that something had gone according to plan. Famously, Lisa later claimed that Donoghue had said, "The dog is dead."[59]

Then it was all hands on deck. The first job was to clear Lennie Dunn's flat of any traces of the 'Mad Axeman' or anybody else who had been there during those tense eleven days. Anything belonging to Mitchell that had been left behind was taken away to be burnt, and all surfaces of the flat were wiped down to get rid of fingerprints. Once

57 Albert Donoghue & Martin Short; *The Enforcer* (London: John Blake 2002).
58 *Daily Mirror*, 29 June 1968.
59 *Guardian*, 29 June 1968.

the work was done, Connie Whitehead arrived to take Donoghue and Lisa to see Reggie at Sammy Lederman's flat. Before they left, Donoghue told Lisa she was going to see Reggie for a 'debriefing' and that on no account was she to mention shots – to do so would have suggested that she knew too much. Lisa may have been upset, but she had her wits about her enough to know what was good for her. In the car, Whitehead was laughing and joking and it was obvious that he had no idea what had just happened. To Lisa, however, it appeared as if he knew full well what had taken place and was finding it amusing; fearing that this giggling villain was about to take her to her own demise, she turned to Donoghue and said, "When it's my turn will you do it? Cos I think you'll do it quick."[60]

As it turned out, Lisa had her chat with Reggie:

> Reggie told me that Frank Mitchell had gone against them and joined another group but not in those words and that he was going by boat somewhere and if I ever said anything to anyone, ever, however far in the future, they would find out. I can't remember the exact words but he meant that he would kill me but I can't remember – he did not say those words. I now remember what he said: he said that they would get me.[61]

She was also given a carrier bag with money in it, apparently £100, but there seemed less and a while later, she would receive another £30.[62] It was, of course, 'hush money', for if Lisa started talking, it would mean the end for many people, and thus the 'Wall of Silence' was thrown up one more time. That night, they all went to a party in Evering Road, Stoke Newington, in a basement flat belonging to Carole Skinner,[63] where Donoghue and Lisa ended up sleeping together:

> A naughty thing to do with a lady, but I had to calm the girl down. You can imagine the state she was in. And that was that. Next day she went back West and carried on with her little life.[64]

The following morning, Lisa was picked up by Connie Whitehead, who, ominously indicated the repercussions of her talking to anybody

---

60 Albert Donoghue & Martin Short; *The Enforcer* (London: John Blake 2002).

61 Statement of Patricia Watson (Lisa), undated (1968); CRIM 1/4900, 52-72 (National Archives).

62 *Daily Mirror*, 22 April 1969.

63 Statement by Billy Exley, undated (1968); CRIM 1/4900, ff. 80-93 (National Archives).

64 Albert Donoghue & Martin Short; *The Enforcer* (London: John Blake 2002).

about the affair by drawing his finger across his throat.[65]

By all accounts it was a cold, ruthlessly planned killing, born out of desperation and, above all, a sheer lack of consideration for the long-term repercussions of springing such a notorious criminal as Frank Mitchell. Nobody, it seems, was thinking straight. When Mitchell finally disappeared from their lives for good, the twins, who had authorised the execution, dealt with it in their typically different ways. Apparently, Reggie, on hearing the news of Mitchell's death, shed a tear: was it genuine sadness, or relief, or just a manifestation of Reggie's emotional state around that time that caused this uncharacteristic emotional display? Ronnie, now in hiding above a curio shop in Fulham, responded differently to death. Donoghue went to see him to tell him what had happened: "Ronald wanted to know all the details about Mitchell, how he acted, how he took it. I told him everything I saw, I told him it a few times. It seemed that whenever he got drunk on the days after that he wanted to hear it all over again."[66]

A few weeks later, Donoghue was sent over the water to Freddie Foreman's Southwark pub, the Prince of Wales,[67] and handed over £1,075, believing it was payment from Ronnie for killing Mitchell. Foreman always vehemently denied this, claiming that the execution was a favour to the twins and that he didn't need to kill anybody for financial reward. Suggesting that the money was actually payment from various joint club ventures that he had going with the Krays, Foreman later described Donoghue's claim, that he "handed over £1,000 after Mitchell's disappearance", as "an insult."[68]

But what happened to Frank Mitchell? Obviously, for some considerable amount of time, he was believed to be still alive and on the run. Records show that Interpol were working on locating Mitchell abroad well into the 1970s[69] and, in the 1980s, the twins themselves put forward their own ideas. Reggie called the plot "brilliantly clever"[70] and Ronnie was particularly vocal about the

---

65 Statement of Patricia Watson (Lisa), undated (1968); CRIM 1/4900, 52-72 (National Archives).

66 *Daily Express*, 23 April 1969.

67 At 23 Lant Street.

68 Freddie Foreman; *Freddie Foreman: The Godfather of British Crime* (London: John Blake 2007).

69 MEPO 2/10805 (National Archives).

70 Reggie & Ronnie Kray, with Fred Dinenage; *Our Story* (London: Sidgwick and Jackson 1988).

whole Mitchell affair; he called it the "greatest coup, the most brilliant stunt ever pulled by the Kray twins", and showed nothing but disgust for people like Donoghue, Dickson and Exley whom he claimed later told "unforgiveable lies."

> *As for Frank Mitchell, the man they called the Mad Axeman. He wasn't mad, he wasn't an axeman, and he isn't dead either. Like many others he has good reason to thank the Krays. One day he will reappear and then the world will know the truth.*[71]

In fact, Ronnie was telling the lies. In his own memoir, published in 1993,[72] he even claimed, inconsistently with his previous assertions, that some 'Greek men' and Billy Exley killed Mitchell. From a legal standpoint, only Albert Donoghue, Freddie Foreman, Alfie Gerrard and Jerry Callaghan would ever know the truth of what happened in the back of that van on Ladysmith Avenue. The issue of what happened to Mitchell's body, in the absence of anybody else to speak out, would remain purely with Freddie Foreman. On Donoghue's evidence, Foreman was later charged (along with Reggie and others) and tried for the murder of Frank Mitchell, but he was acquitted in April 1969. Three decades later, Foreman explained the fate of the 'Mad Axeman': his body was driven down to the south coast at Newhaven and with the help of some sympathetic fishermen who had helped Foreman's team with assorted cross-channel smuggling runs over the years, Frank Mitchell's lifeless body was wrapped in chicken wire, weighted down and thrown overboard at sea, away from the fishing lanes.

> *We had been told by American contacts that bodies weighted down in this way would never find their way to the surface but would slowly be disposed of by crabs and other deep-sea dwellers. Many people prefer burial at sea...*[73]

The life of Frank Samuel Mitchell was a tragedy from the moment he stole that bicycle as a child. From then on he had travelled through practically every correctional system available in Britain, including those used for prisoners considered criminally insane. He had been

---

71 Reggie & Ronnie Kray, with Fred Dinenage; *Our Story* (London: Sidgwick and Jackson 1988).

72 Ron Kray, with Fred Dinenage; *My Story* (London: Sidgwick and Jackson 1993).

73 Freddie Foreman; *Freddie Foreman: The Godfather of British Crime* (London: John Blake 2007).

birched and flogged in some of Britain's toughest prisons and had become as good as institutionalised, some would say irreparably damaged, by his prolonged exposure to the penal system. Even if Mitchell had been given his release date and had managed to experience real freedom, there is no guarantee that he would not have reoffended, such was the nature of his mind. Despite the attentions of his family and friends on the outside, Mitchell probably had no future; respect came to him from the underworld and those with whom he shared the regimes of prison life. The Krays were seriously out of their depth when they swiped him off Dartmoor on that blustery December afternoon: they thought they could save him, and that his allegiance to them would serve them well in the future, but they failed to think it through beyond the bare essentials.

And thus another life was lost.

FOURTEEN

RELEASE ME

Reggie and Ronnie Kray may have thought that the springing of Frank Mitchell would be a masterstroke, but in reality, it was an unmitigated disaster. How could the murder of somebody who was meant to be given hope be anything but a cataclysmic failure? Members of the Firm had put themselves in serious jeopardy too: Billy Exley was already growing disenchanted with his association with the Krays, and Albert Donoghue had been convinced, for a moment at least, as he walked away from that gunsmoke-filled van, that he was about to have his head blown off. Lennie Dunn spent the next few months sleeping with a gun under his pillow in fear of his life, and Lisa's memories of her four days with Mitchell, culminating in his obvious demise, would stay with her for a long time; "I lived in fear for 17 months", she later said.[1] She told her flatmate that she had been with a wealthy man during that time, since this appeared to explain the money that she was now spending freely over the Christmas period; but other than that, she refused to talk about what really happened.[2]

As 1967, the apex of the Swinging Sixties, cranked into gear, the Krays were anything but swinging. Not that they were ever truly part of that significant era in the way most people would consider it - free love, rock music, the counterculture, the esoteric – little, if any, of this

1 Statement of Patricia Watson (Lisa), undated (1968); CRIM 1/4900, 52-72 (National Archives).
2 Statement by Valerie Fiske, undated (1968); MEPO 2/11404, ff. 1558-1563 (National Archives).

figured in the criminal enterprise of the Krays. Certainly, Ronnie was openly homosexual and was very casual with his relationships, but then he was no different during the austere 1950s and didn't need the cultural sea-change of the 1960s to make him any different. One could say he was ahead of his time in that respect. But, outwardly, the Kray twins were strictly 'establishment', from their choice of West End nightclubs and schmoozing with the rich and famous, down to their constantly formal attire of smart suits, tightly-knotted ties, pristine white shirts and polished shoes. David Bailey, himself a pillar of '60s culture, had made them part of the burgeoning 'scene' by way of his striking photographic portrait, and yet, whilst bright colours and paisley were becoming common in fashion, the Krays, and their Firm, looked more like chairmen of the board. When the Beatles' pioneering, lysergic, 'Strawberry Fields Forever/Penny Lane' single was beaten to the top of the charts by Engelbert Humperdinck's crooning ballad 'Release Me' in February 1967, one can imagine that the Krays would have found the latter title more to their tastes.[3] And yet Reggie had previously attempted to get into the music business in 1965 when he became briefly involved in the management of a pop group called the Shots, who missed the hit parade with the song 'Keep a Hold Of What You've Got.'[4] The band's lack of immediate success caused Reggie to lose interest, and he quickly moved on.[5]

The Krays may not have been about peace and love, but they were infamous when it came to giving to charity. Many of their donations had been given publicly, with the press in attendance, a way of demonstrating to all that they had their hearts in the right place and possessed the money and influence to be seen to be doing the right thing. However, in November 1966, Reggie, probably accompanied by members of the Firm, had attended a charity gala in Cardiff in aid of the Aberfan Disaster Fund with no publicity at all, doing something quite laudable in the process. In October that year, a colliery spoil heap in the village of Aberfan, near Merthyr Tydfil, collapsed onto a nearby school, killing 116 children and 28 adults. The disaster sparked a

---

3   Despite being considered one of the greatest pop singles of all time, this was the first Beatles single not to reach number one in the charts since their second single 'Please Please Me' in 1963.

4   Released on 8 October 1965 on Columbia Records (DB 7713).

5   In *Born Fighter*, Reggie claimed the group disbanded soon after he let them go; however, they actually changed their name to The Smoke and in 1967 had a controversial minor hit with 'My Friend Jack' which was refused airplay by the BBC on account of its drug references. It reached number 45 in the charts and was covered by Boney M in 1980.

major national outpouring of grief and a fundraising committee was immediately set up to assist the families and communities that had suffered. There were many contributions from companies, organisations and private individuals, as well as charity sports events and gala nights.[6] Although it was unannounced at the time, Reggie presented the fund with £100, the equivalent of £1,286 today, and on 2 January 1967 he received a letter from the committee thanking him for what was "the largest single amount given by any individual to our appeal."[7] This appeared to be at odds with the way the Krays' charitable arm typically operated – the usual publicity opportunity was waived – but it is also known that they helped quite a number of East End organisations with little fanfare. John Pearson later suggested that the Aberfan money, as with all their finances, undoubtedly came from the 'proceeds of crime',[8] possibly explaining the surreptitious nature of the donation, although, of course, with Ronnie in hiding, attention would be the last thing the twins really wanted at that time.

Ronnie, still wanted as a witness in the Sergeant Townshend corruption case, had been served an arrest warrant on 16 January 1967. He had to remain in hiding and be more careful than before, but all the prolonged isolation was not good for him; he drank to excess and his illness, with its dark moods and paranoia, began to take him over again.

> The curtains were kept drawn and he never ventured out. Instead he got the Firm to bring in stocks of food and gin and bottled beer so he could stay hidden there for weeks on end. Codes were invented for the telephone and letters. He played Italian opera on the gramophone and had a fresh boy every night. During the day he would be busy working out who needed murdering.[9]

After the flats in Finchley and Fulham, Ronnie then moved into Lennie Dunn's place in Barking Road for several weeks. In the end, Dunn had received a mere £10 for harbouring Mitchell, but Ronnie gave him £100 for his own stay.[10] It could not have been easy for the

---

6   The fund eventually raised £1,606,929 (£27.8 million in 2015, if adjusted for inflation) from around 90,000 contributors, although there was later much controversy as to how it was all managed.

7   *Daily Express*, 7 October 2010. (The letter from the committee was in the possession of John Pearson, who put it up for auction with other material relating to the Krays in 2010).

8   Ibid.

9   John Pearson; *The Profession of Violence* (London: Weidenfeld & Nicolson 1972).

10 *Daily Express*, 27 June 1968.

already frightened bookseller.

Then, on 30 January, Frances Shea made a second attempt on her life. Locking herself in the front room of her parents' home, she turned on the gas fire and swallowed a large quantity of barbiturates. Her father found her in the nick of time and again she was taken to St Leonard's Hospital. Recovering from barbiturate poisoning, she remained there for eight days before being discharged on 7 February. The Sheas felt utterly helpless; Frances, having made two suicide attempts in as little as four months, seemed intent on ending it all. She was now a shadow of her former self, thin, haunted and pale. It was thought that a change of scenery may help, to get her away from Ormsby Street with its bad memories and constant threat of visitation by Reggie, or observation by members of the Firm who had been asked to keep watch on Frances's movements. She moved into brother Frankie's flat in Wimbourne Court, a modern high-rise development on the Wenlock Estate in Shoreditch. There, Frankie and his common-law wife Lily, known to all as 'Bubbles', could keep an eye on her. Frances adored their daughter, also called Frances: this attempt at 'happy families' would perhaps take the strain off the Sheas and, of course, hopefully turn Frances's troubled life around.

In fact it was soon to be all-change for the Sheas and the Krays. Both Ormsby Street and the stretch of Vallance Road that the twins and their families had called home since 1939 were now under compulsory purchase orders. Tower Hamlets Council were about to undertake a major slum-clearance program across the borough and great swathes of the East End, much of which had miraculously survived the Blitz, were bulldozed and replaced by modern developments throughout the late 1960s and well into the following decade. 178 Vallance Road may have been Violet Kray's pride and joy, and kept immaculate on the inside, but it still had problems with structure and sanitation; its rickety outside lavatory and lack of bathroom made it the kind of dwelling that was crying out for replacement with high-rise concrete modernity. The twins' cousin Rita remembers:

> None of us owned the properties so from the point of view of renting, all it would mean to us would be that we'd be paying our rent to a different landlord. But from an emotional view it was going to be a terrible wrench for all of us.

Each house was small, decaying, damp and overrun with rats and mice, but every brick held a memory.[11]

In many ways, the end of an era was approaching.

◆

By the beginning of 1967, all three Teale brothers found themselves detained as guests of Her Majesty. Bobby and David were in Wormwood Scrubs and Alfie was at Wandsworth, for on 4 October 1966 they had been sentenced at the Old Bailey to three years' imprisonment for demanding money with menaces; however, their convictions were by no means conventional. There had been a police set-up.

The previous summer, Bobby Teale had become friendly with a man named 'Wallace' who ingratiated himself with what initially appeared to be some form of business proposal. 'Wallace' seemed to be homosexual, although he never made any advances to any of the brothers. During a convivial meeting at his flat in Dolphin Square, by the Thames Embankment, he lent them £900, against which they signed a receipt and promised to pay the amount back within a month. The Teale brothers then stayed overnight at the flat, sleeping on the sofas and floor.

Well, about seven thirty the next morning, the doorbell goes. I can't remember who opened the door, but it wasn't Wallace. He wasn't even in the flat. In marched three plain-clothes policemen – with Wallace behind them.[12]

It transpired that 'Wallace' had told the police that the Teales had been keeping him hostage and that he had had to escape via the rubbish chute. Alfie and David were completely flummoxed by what was going on, but Bobby certainly began to realise what was happening: the police – using 'Wallace' as a plant – were getting Bobby Teale, now a major informer, off the streets and, taking no chances, bringing his brothers with him to be on the safe side. For Bobby, the frustration was excruciating: he could not tell his brothers the real reason for their incarceration, and, to all intents and purposes, despite the real background of the arrests, Scotland Yard had done literally nothing with the information they had been given regarding

11 Joe Lee, Rita Smith and Peter Gerrard; *Inside the Kray Family* (London: Carlton 2008).
12 Bobby Teale with Clare Campbell: *Bringing Down the Krays* (London: Ebury Publishing 2012).

the Krays' involvement in Cornell's death, save for the identity parade shambles in August 1966.

The problem for the police was that they had an important informant who was giving information about Ronnie Kray killing George Cornell, but there was little else they could do with him, as those who had actually witnessed the shooting were refusing to go on the record. It was apparent that, thanks to their insiders in the police, the Krays knew of the existence of 'Phillips', and it was only a matter of time before Bobby Teale would be exposed to grave danger. Taking the Teales out of the Kray orbit was merely a way of ensuring their safety, although it did not ensure the safety of their families. But, for the moment at least, the Teale brothers were looked on sympathetically by the twins, who would supply them with gifts during their sentences.

By now the Lambrianou brothers, Chris and Tony, and occasionally another brother, Nicky, were skirting around the fringes of the Firm. Tony was certainly now becoming active with the Krays: not a fully recognised member of the Firm, but another side player in its activities. During the early days of the twins' involvement in the West End, the up-and-coming Tony would frequent clubs such as the Pigalle, the Bagatelle and Churchill's, as well as more local haunts like the Regency and the City Club in Angel, North London. Before long, Tony Lambrianou would be well acquainted with the various members of the Firm and those who knew him would often remark, "You should be with the twins."[13]

The twins, or Reggie at least, were interested. Not long before he married Frances, Reggie paid a visit to Pellicci's Cafe in Bethnal Green Road, accompanied by Ronnie, 'Big' Pat Connolly, Teddy Smith, Tommy Cowley, Sammy Lederman and Harry 'Jew Boy' Cope, and noticed Tony Lambrianou sitting with a friend, Timmy Reynolds. Reggie, recognising Tony as the friend of his future brother-in-law, made an approach, saying, "Don't forget us, come and see us,"[14] and promptly paid Tony's bill. Reggie Kray was obviously on the lookout for some fresh faces in the Firm and perhaps, with Tony's reputation,[15] he could see somebody who would make a useful addition.

13 Tony Lambrianou with Carol Clerk; *Inside the Firm* (London: Smith Gryphon 1991).
14 Ibid.
15 By 1967, Tony Lambrianou had six convictions including shopbreaking and assault with intent to rob. He was released from his last prison sentence in November 1966; MEPO 2/11388 (National Archives).

Chris Lambrianou had the least to do with them, but the Krays knew of him through his friendship with Eric Mason. Mason's earlier attachment to the Firm, and his willingness to use their name in his own business dealings, had cast those around him in the reflected light of the Krays, something they were not particularly happy with. Chris enjoyed the perks of being erroneously associated with the infamous East End villains, taking satisfaction from the respect it gave him and full advantage of the drinks and meals that were bought for him by those in awe of the twins. Partly through his association with Mason, he had recently moved out to Birmingham and was making a great success of club protection and other crime there, as well as in other locations in the Midlands and the North, such as Liverpool, Manchester and Leicester. A chance meeting with Ronnie Bender, an old acquaintance from years before, led Chris briefly, for the moment at least, into the Krays' world. Bender had obviously told the twins about Chris's Midlands connections and he was summoned to meet with them at The Lion in Tapp Street.

Resourceful as ever, Charlie Kray was masterminding the opening of a nightclub in Leicester with a partner, Trevor Raynor, and Reggie and Ronnie wanted to know if Chris could use his influence there to ensure that the club, called Raynor's, was a success. "Do you think you could introduce a few people who might spend a few quid? If you do that, we'll put you in for your corner," Reggie said to him.[16] Chris saw potential in the idea and went with it, but, nonetheless, his feelings about the meeting were mixed. Present in The Lion was Connie Whitehead, whom Chris had known from his Borstal days, but Whitehead merely nodded at him and made no effort to interact any further, and Chris's comments regarding that evening were interesting:

> I liked some of the things I saw in the Widow's that rainy February night. If somebody was skint, for example, it didn't mean he couldn't drink all night long. Those with money, including the twins, stuck pound notes and fivers in a glass on the bar and each round was taken out of there. It seemed like a good system to me.
>
> I was impressed with the courtesy and politeness of Ron and Reg, too. There was, I felt, a sense of honour and decency and straightness about what they were doing.

16 Chris Lambrianou and Robin McGibbon; *Escape From the Kray Madness* (London: Sidgwick and Jackson 1995).

But I didn't see a lot of respect among their so-called henchmen,
only fear. I saw a lot of Jack-the-Lad stuff going on, too, and it made
me think that I didn't want any part of it.[17]

Chris Lambrianou, perhaps with the fresh perception of an outsider with his own concerns to manage away from London, realised early on that if he became part of the Firm, he would never be totally in control of his own financial gains. He could sense that all was not well within the Kray organisation, and thus he would go on to maintain a sensible distance as much as he could.

By this time, the Krays were also beginning to use the Carpenter's Arms on Cheshire Street, just a short walk from Vallance Road, for their meetings and social gatherings. This now famous pub has usually been described as the one the twins 'bought for their Mum', so much so that it has become part of East End lore; nearly every account of the pub describes it as at least belonging to the twins, and yet there is little or no evidence that the Krays actually had any legal ownership of it.[18] In later years, Charlie Kray claimed that Harry Hopwood had called him asking for a loan of £2,000 because the twins needed it to buy a pub.[19] It was all very rushed but the money was found and within a few weeks the Krays 'owned' the Carpenter's Arms.[20]

What is certain is that, in March 1967, Michael Hatfield, the husband of Harry Hopwood's daughter Janet, became the licensee.[21] It is likely that the twins did indeed want a pub to call their own, and the only way they could get one was to provide the necessary finance and have somebody else installed as the legal tenant, because their criminal records would have precluded them from being granted a licence.[22] In this indirect way, the Krays now had a pub and – regardless of any other name on any legal agreement – as they had effectively paid for it, it was their establishment with their rules. It also meant that they,

---

17 Ibid.

18 Records of Truman's Brewery are held at the London Metropolitan Archives; unfortunately, the records of the licensees of specific pubs in the East End go no further than the 1950s.

19 Charlie Kray & Robin McGibbon; *Me and My Brothers* (London: Grafton 1988).

20 In *Me and My Brothers*, Charlie also claimed, obviously erroneously, that it was the Carpenter's Arms in Cambridge Heath Road.

21 Statement by Janet Hatfield, 9 September 1968; MEPO 2/11404, f. 1214 (National Archives).

22 Freddie Foreman had a similar arrangement at his pub (The Prince of Wales) in Lant Street, Southwark where his wife was actually the legal licensee, although Foreman was very much in charge.

their family and friends, and members of the Firm, could drink there 'on the house' when they felt like it, an arrangement which caused the Hatfields to move on after less than a year, having "finished up penniless."[23]

◆

Early 1967 appears to have been a happier time for Frances Shea, now settled in Wimbourne Court with Frankie and 'Bubbles'. In March she renewed her passport, a prelude to a number of overseas trips, probably with friends, which included a ten-day cruise around the Canary Islands.[24] Reggie was still trying to have some involvement in Frances's life – it was probably he who financed those little breaks – and, on one occasion, he called Dr. Clein in order to get him to recommend another stay at Greenways for her, but when Clein consulted the Sheas, the proposition was flatly turned down. Despite this, the situation between the estranged couple was beginning to look brighter; Reggie's visits to see Frances at her brother's flat were not as uncomfortable as those when she was living with her parents, and with the case against Sergeant Townshend opening at the Old Bailey on 17 April, the continued and enforced absence of Ronnie from the East End must have made Reggie's life easier when it came to giving up valuable business time to see his wife. On those visits, there were signs that Reggie was back to his old romantic self and, throughout May, it was beginning to look as though reconciliation was in the offing.

On 5 June, Frances went to see Dr. Julius Silverstone, the consultant psychiatrist at Hackney Hospital. She seemed much better and told him that she was due to go on holiday with her husband;[25] she asked for some tablets to ease her in-flight nerves (which Silverstone duly prescribed)[26] and the following day, she and Reggie went to a travel agent to book a trip to Ibiza. It will never be understood how willingly or happily Frances was going along with these travel ideas; was she doing it merely for a quiet life, or did she really feel that she and Reggie could save their marriage and have a future together? For Reggie, it would have been a much needed move towards stability. Ronnie's

23 Statement by Harry Hopwood, 20 August 1968; MEPO 2/11404, ff. 1196-1207 (National Archives).
24 Jacky Hyams; *Frances: The Tragic Bride* (London: John Blake 2014).
25 *Daily Mirror*, 14 June 1967.
26 Ibid.

killing of George Cornell was now a major shadow over the twins' life and the escalating violence that surrounded the Krays always threatened to trigger renewed police interest; if directed in the right way, at the right people, this could lead to arrest and, with murder on the charge sheet, that guaranteed long-term imprisonment. Reggie was no fool, he was often cautious, but his excessive drinking and troubled mind were causing him to be reckless and dangerous. Reconciliation with Frances could rekindle Reggie's latent dreams of distancing himself from the criminal life so embraced by his powerful twin, moving on into legitimate business, playing happy families.

At about 10.00 a.m. on the morning of Wednesday, 7 June, Frankie Shea brought a cup of tea to his sleeping sister, leaving it on the bedside table, before going out. At 2.00 p.m. he returned to find Frances still in bed, apparently sleeping, with the cup of tea remaining untouched. She would not wake up, so Frankie called a doctor; on his arrival, the doctor confirmed what Frankie must have been thinking all along – Frances was dead.

Reggie called by the flat later that morning. He rang the doorbell and got no answer:

> I saw the window open and I was going to climb through, but I hesitated. I did not want any conflict with my in-laws.
>
> I then drove off to Kingsland Road, where I normally get my hair cut and while I was waiting in the chair for my turn, I had a strange premonition of a funeral in procession. Somehow I knew it was the funeral of Frances. I could see it all before me.
>
> When I left the barber's, I went back to the flat in Shoreditch and one of the friends of Frankie Shea, my brother-in-law, came towards me as I pulled up in the car. He told me in faltering words that something had happened and that Frances was dead.[27]

Reggie's premonition seems fanciful stuff, but his reaction to Frances's death was anything but. He was by turns devastated and bitterly angry; devastated because he had lost, without warning, the only woman he had ever loved (after his mother) and angry because he felt that Frances had taken her own life as the result of the continued pressure from her parents to reject him. He blamed the Sheas for the whole sorry debacle and, in his darkest moments, conspired to have them killed. These nadirs usually came in drink, which Reggie took

27 Reggie Kray; *Born Fighter* (London: Arrow Books 1991).

to with renewed vigour in a desperate attempt to blot out the pain of his loss. He was mixing the gin, sometimes up to a bottle a night, with Valium. Quite frankly, he became a mess.

The inquest into Frances's death took place at St Pancras Coroner's Court on 13 June 1967, with Reggie and Charlie in attendance. Recording a verdict of 'suicide whilst of unsound mind' and death from barbiturate poisoning, it was reported that Frances "had killed herself with an 'enormous' overdose of drugs".[28] It was mentioned that Frances suffered from a personality disorder, not news to those who had treated her over the years; however, there were a few further revelations. Reggie was stunned to hear that Frances, suffering from depression at the age of thirteen, had made a suicide attempt even then.[29] Also, Frankie mentioned that 'Bubbles' took sleeping tablets, and revealed that, often, some would go missing.[30] Even when bottles of Frances's own pills were hidden to regulate her intake, she would invariably find them.

There was apparently no suicide note, or at least there was no mention of one at the inquest. On the previous occasions, Frances had penned one, and Reggie was suspicious that a member of the Shea family had found one this time and hidden it.[31] A photocopy of a suicide note does survive in the National Archives which Jacky Hyams suggests may actually be the last one.[32] The writing is visibly shaky and is often difficult to read, and, whether it was the final note or not, it does show the tortured mind of this troubled young woman:

> Dear Mum and Dad and Frankie
>
> I'm sorry I've had to do it so this way but do me one favour and don't grief [sic] too much over me after all, it's useless now and you have the baby to compensate for me.
>
> I was dying in any case you know when it comes there's nothing any doctor can do for you then. I wish it wasn't me that had to bring disaster on the family – if I'd had the guts I would have drowned myself – it all happened since I had that relapse [it was an

28 *Daily Mirror*, 14 June 1967.
29 Jacky Hyams; *Frances: The Tragic Bride* (London: John Blake 2014).
30 *Hackney Gazette*, 16 June 1967.
31 Reggie Kray; *Born Fighter* (London: Arrow Books 1991).
32 HO 282/66 (National Archives). The letters written by Frances were submitted to the Home Office in 1969 when Elsie Shea was applying to have Frances's final resting place moved.

unnatural trance?] and I've had to keep on as long as possible for your sake. I'm sorry, I've told Bubbles some of the unusual things that have happened to me. Please don't grief [sic] for me – it's been a hard enough job for me to keep alive these last 7 weeks that's why I've always been so fidgety. Please forgive me as my last wish. I couldn't go on any longer and you know I'm not the person to give in if there's any chance of survival which there wasn't. Please love me always think there's always Frances to [compensate?].

Please forgive me

> *Love and xxx*
> *Frances*

In spite of all his outward displays of grief, which were considerable, Reggie could still be relied upon to show gross insensitivity and selfishness. Totally disregarding the desolation felt by the Shea family, he insisted on commandeering everything he had ever given Frances, including clothes and jewellery, some of which he later gave away to members of his own family. He insisted that Frances should be buried under the name Kray, despite his late wife having reverted to her maiden name and against the wishes of the Sheas. He also decided that she would be buried in her wedding dress, wearing the ring she had worn at the 'East End wedding of the year' two years previously. When Frankie consulted the funeral directors, Hayes and English of 148 Hoxton Street, the negotiations were interrupted by Reggie and "a priest whom Mrs. Shea described as 'crooked' and who later gave evidence in his favour at his trial";[33] this was undoubtedly Father Hetherington, who, despite refusing to marry Frances to Reggie, could not refuse the invitation to bury her. Reggie had bought Plot B8 in the north-eastern corner of Chingford Mount Cemetery,[34] intending that, one day, he and his family would join Frances by her final resting place.

The Sheas did manage one small victory, however. Before the funeral, Elsie Shea convinced the funeral directors to dress Frances in a slip and a pair of tights which covered her entire body and ensured that no part of her wedding dress made contact with her skin. The wedding ring was also switched with one that Frances wore as a girl. Apart from that, the ostentatious funeral, which apparently

33 Note of a meeting in Romney House, 9 April 1969; HO 282/66 (National Archives).
34 Frances's grave was No. 70685, curiously the same one used for Charlie Kray's son Gary, who died of an AIDS-related illness in 1996.

cost £2,000, was entirely the way Reggie wanted it. The Sheas were ignored during the proceedings, their modest floral tributes dwarfed by the sheer number of wreaths from the Kray family and everybody associated with them. Ronnie, still in hiding, did not attend, but police officers mingled with the mourners in the hope of catching up with him, something which Reggie and the rest of the Kray entourage found in bad taste.

But, for some, bad taste came in the form of Reggie's insistence that Albert Donoghue check the name cards on the floral tributes and make a note of anybody who had not sent anything. This did not go unnoticed by the Sheas, who were appalled, and Donoghue himself thought it was too much. "It was sick," he later said.[35]

Maureen Flanagan later remembered a conversation she had with Violet Kray not long after the funeral which, on the face of it, sounded quite thoughtless. Violet said:

> My Reggie's a broken man. We all loved her. But I knew she couldn't be a wife. She couldn't cook. She couldn't even make a cup of tea properly. Or wash a shirt. You saw her Maureen. She should never have married him. My Reggie needs a girl to look after him. Like I've always done.[36]

But Violet was right on one count, just as Father Hetherington had been back in April 1965 when he refused to conduct the wedding: Frances should not have married Reggie. In fact, it is hard to imagine who would have made a suitable wife for Reginald Kray at that time in his life. Who would have had the strength of character and thick skin to weather the ups and downs of life with a Kray? But the failure of the marriage was down to more than just personal circumstances and Frances's mental health. Violet Kray's unguarded comments to Maureen Flanagan indirectly summed up one element of it – Reggie could never move out of the shadow of his mother, a pivotal influence on his life. It was her doting nature and her refusal to see any wrong in her 'lovely boys' that was partly responsible for shaping their attitude to the world. As Flanagan stated in a documentary interview in 2015,[37] and as has been stated here earlier, the twins were spoilt rotten: they

35 Jacky Hyams; *Frances: The Tragic Bride* (London: John Blake 2014).
36 Maureen Flanagan with Jacky Hyams; *One of the Family: 40 Years With the Krays* (London: Century 2015).
37 *The Krays: Kill Order* (Metrodome Distribution DVD, 2015).

got what they wanted when they wanted it, and to hell with what anybody else wanted. It didn't matter if it was Hew McCowan, the Barry brothers or Frances Shea: when it came down to it, only the needs and ideals of the Krays mattered. This was hardly a recipe for a mutually contented marriage.

Reggie's latent homosexuality must also have been a contributing factor to the lack of empathy he showed to his young wife. His only apparent attempt at consummating the marriage, when he attempted to have anal intercourse with Frances, was a traumatic experience for her. Albert Donoghue once said that Reggie asked him how to 'touch a woman.'[38] Finally, there is, of course, the often mentioned relationship between Reggie and Ronnie. Ronnie was vocal about where Reggie's loyalties ought to lie and would make his displeasure known at every turn if he thought his brother was neglecting the business for something as unimportant as a girl. Reggie, torn between the strong filial bonds of being a twin and doing right by his wife, was in a no-win situation.

Frances must have certainly felt something for Reggie at some time, particularly in the early stages of their relationship, but it is fair to say that, with the pressure from home and Reggie's increasingly dubious activities, love may have dwindled. One must remember how young she was when they first met, and, from the moment Reggie suggested they date, she would never have another partner; whatever her feelings toward him, she would never be able to move on. She was not stupid, far from it, but to say that Frances was inexperienced is putting it mildly, and she did not have the benefit of love and loss behind her to enable her make strong decisions of her own – particularly in the face of such a formidable character as Reggie Kray.

Reggie obviously loved Frances, that much is clear, but his personal life, his habits, his sexual frustrations and his unique relationship with his mentally sick twin brother conspired to leave him unequipped for a conventional relationship. In some ways he was like the awkward, hormonal teenager who falls for the girl and tries desperately, often unsuccessfully, to come to terms with the new feelings he cannot completely control. Despite his often cruel behaviour towards her, Reggie put Frances on a pedestal and would continue to do so until he joined her in that little plot in Chingford Mount. Unconditionally and

38 Interview featured in the TV documentary *The Notorious Kray Twins* (Aubrey Powell Partnership Production 2001).

unthinkingly, Reggie Kray loved his wife - he just didn't know how to.

◆

With the death of Frances still biting deep, Reggie went into a kind of breakdown. Drink and pills, taken to excess almost every night, turned him into a monster almost as volatile as Ronnie. When drunk and drugged, his anger boiled over into increasingly unpredictable behaviour, but, unlike Ronnie, whose acts of violence were often spontaneous, Reggie could store up a grudge and release retribution when the time was right. A week or so after the funeral, Frankie Shea came close to losing his life when Reggie got it in his head to kill him. Frankie's old friend Tony Lambrianou managed to talk Reggie out of it and calm him down before the damage was done.[39] Another man, named Frederick, was not so lucky. Reggie had heard that he had been making disparaging comments about Frances and, in a drunken rage, Reggie went with a couple of members of the Firm to Frederick's flat, and, after crashing through the front door, shot him in the leg.[40] And so the ever-reliable Dr. Blasker received another late-night patient.

In his West London hideout, Ronnie wasn't doing too well either. His illness was becoming more pronounced as he wallowed in a fug of alcohol, cigarette smoke, Dr. Blasker's unregulated medication and the shallow thrill of a different procured boy each night. Blasker, having known the twins since their teens, could see how Ronnie's mental state had deteriorated over the years, despite his medication:

He has gradually got worse and worse. He has told me that if he did not take the drug for as little as two days he feels an uncontrollable desire to attack perfectly innocent people. From what I know of him this is perfectly true.

To take this a little further, if he was annoyed or irritated in even the slightest degree he would be very likely to lose all control of himself and commit the most serious attacks on people up to and including murder. At these times he would quite likely do things and take risks which to a normal person would be incredible.[41]

Then, on 18 July 1967, Detective Sergeant Leonard Townshend was cleared in a second hearing at the Old Bailey of the corruption

39 Tony Lambrianou with Carol Clerk; *Inside the Firm* (London: Smith Gryphon 1991).
40 Reggie & Ronnie Kray, with Fred Dinenage; *Our Story* (London: Sidgwick and Jackson 1988).
41 Statement by Dr. Morris Blasker, undated (1968); MEPO 2/11404, ff. 1689-1693 (National Archives).

charges levelled against him. The jury were advised to deliver the 'not guilty' verdict by Mr. Justice Waller in the absence of any evidence for the prosecution.[42] With Townshend's acquittal, the warrant against Ronnie expired and at last, after almost a year in hiding, 'The Colonel' was back.

Now should have been the time for the Krays to get back on their feet and consolidate their superiority. That summer, the last vestiges of the Richardson gang - including Charlie Richardson, who had originally escaped arrest by being in South Africa when the Mr. Smith's affair took place - had been rounded up and sentenced to heavy jail-terms at the Old Bailey in what became known as the 'Torture Trial'. Chief Superintendent John du Rose had set up a special team to crack the Richardsons once and for all and, as a result of the highly organised and watertight operation, numerous witnesses had come forward to give evidence of brutal assaults and sadistic torture methods involving humiliation, cuttings, beatings and, most notoriously, electrocution. Had he not been killed the previous year, George Cornell, as one of those complicit in the violence, would have found himself in the dock and duly convicted. After forty-six days of drama, the trial had ended on 8 June 1967. As Charlie Richardson was sent down for twenty-five years, to join his brother Eddie, Frankie Fraser and others in some of the toughest prisons Britain had to offer, Mr. Justice Lawton, the presiding judge, must have relished these words as he spoke them:

> One is ashamed to live in a society with men like you. There is no known penal system to cure you... You must be kept under lock and key. You terrorised those who crossed your path... and you terrorised them in a way that was vicious, sadistic, and a disgrace to society...
>
> It must be made clear to all those who set themselves up as gang leaders that they will be struck down by the law as you will be struck down.[43]

The demise of the Richardsons, and Justice Lawton's dire warnings for anybody else of their ilk, was the catalyst for a new offensive against organised crime in London. The Krays were still considered to be at the top of the pile, for all their troubles of late, and as far as Scotland Yard were concerned, they had got away with it for too long.

42 *Daily Express*, 19 July 1967.
43 Brian McConnell; *The Rise and Fall of the Brothers Kray* (London: David Bruce and Watson Ltd 1969).

Now was the perfect time to have one more go at them.

In the summer of 1967, 'Nipper' Read had been promoted to Detective Superintendent and assigned to Scotland Yard's Murder Squad. For Read this was "what being a detective was all about, and everyone who was, or wanted to be, a detective had the Squad in his sights. This was Scotland Yard and these were the people who had given Scotland Yard its international reputation, making them the envy of law enforcement agencies all over the world."[44] In a preliminary meeting with Commander Ernie Millen, Read found out that rather than being posted to some provincial district, he had been assigned to C1 (Central Office). Read was delighted and was buzzing so much from this news that he didn't really take in Millen's comment that "You're going to do a special that is, at the moment, top secret."[45]

After the news of his posting to C1 had sunk in, Read began to ponder what the 'top secret' assignment was. A few days later, in a meeting with Assistant Commissioner Peter Brodie, he found out, and initially he was not best impressed.

"Mr. Read, you're going to get the Krays."

> *As soon as he uttered the words my heart sank, and the pleasure of my promotion evaporated. I could hardly believe what I was hearing. Although I had taxed my brain trying to figure what the 'special' might be, I'd never even considered the Krays. Not them again, I thought. My God, I'd had enough of the difficulties and problems they had posed the last time around. I didn't need them again.*[46]

Nonetheless, the powers that be wanted another high-profile success against organised crime and believed that Read was the man for the job. But Brodie did extend an olive branch to the now piqued Detective Superintendent by telling him that he could go about the investigation in any way he wished, as long as he got the result. Read perked up and asked if he could pick his own team; he had a mental list of excellent and trusted detectives he had worked with in the past, and Brodie agreed that if they were available, they would be on the team. Then came the issue of where the investigation was going to be based. Read, an incorruptible police officer if ever there was one,

44 Leonard Read & James Morton; *Nipper Read: The Man Who Nicked the Krays* (London: MacDonald & Co 1991).

45 Ibid.

46 Ibid.

was concerned about 'the enemy within', the unfortunate presence of corrupt officers who could compromise the secrecy and sensitivity of the operation, and who might even be in the Krays' pockets as paid informers. The investigation would not, therefore, be based at Scotland Yard; but the lines of communication still needed to be in place, and so Read was told that he would be reporting to John du Rose.

Du Rose, who would become head of the Murder Squad in 1969, enjoyed the highest success rate for solving provincial murders, earning him the affectionate nickname of 'Four Day Johnny' due to the speed with which he and his team closed a case. As Chief Superintendent, he had worked on the Jack the Stripper murders, had been a major force in bringing to an end the ten-year reign of Maltese vice racketeers the Messina brothers in 1959, and was now riding high after bringing down the Richardsons. In a meeting with Read, du Rose agreed that the Kray investigation should be conducted away from Scotland Yard itself and it was arranged that Read's team would be based at the offices of the Metropolitan Police in Tintagel House, a modern block situated on the Albert Embankment. Although his name had recently been painted on the door of his new Murder Squad office at Scotland Yard, 'Nipper' Read would hardly see it for the next two years.

As their eventual nemesis busied himself assembling his bespoke investigative team, the Krays were entering a new period. The absence of the Richardsons from the London crime scene had been a Godsend for the twins; the distractions of their troubled year so far may well have allowed the South London brothers, had they been at liberty, to capitalise on the situation and make inroads into mutually desirable pastures, particularly in the West End. With nobody of any real significance to tread on their toes, the Krays were still a major force, at least in the eyes of the world outside the Firm. Kray-run protection in London still flourished and, despite their friend George Raft being deported as an undesirable with criminal associations, relationships with the North American crime syndicates were still positive, even though the trafficking of stolen bonds had abruptly stopped in April 1967. In spite of the apparently growing disorganisation and unpredictability, there was still nobody in London to touch the Krays.

With Ronnie Kray back in the saddle, he decided to make his mark in the way only he knew how; by having somebody killed. The target plucked from his notorious list would be Leslie Payne.

By now, Payne, increasingly concerned about the growing incidents of violence, was well out of the Krays' financial operations. The twins were irritated by the fact that he independently continued to do business with people they also did business with, and also with those who would not work with them. They did not like the fact that here was a man who knew many secrets, who was no longer under their wing and, for that reason, he was dangerous. Would he speak out about all the financial frauds that he had instigated for the Krays if he were approached by the police, as well as talk about other incidents he was party to? A simple solution would be to get rid of him. The twins had three meetings to discuss how to do it.[47]

Of all people, it was Jack 'the Hat' McVitie who got the job. Keen to ingratiate himself with the Firm one more time after his earlier indiscretions, McVitie jumped at the chance, no doubt also drawn by the handsome £500 fee he would receive for killing Payne. Ronnie sorted it all out and in a meeting at the Grave Maurice he handed McVitie £100 as a down payment,[48] the rest promised once Payne no longer posed a problem.

When the day came, Billy Exley drove McVitie to Payne's house in Tulse Hill. The plan was to knock on the door and when Payne opened it, to shoot him there and then. It transpired that McVitie lost his nerve and could not go through with it. Stupidly, he kept the money and gave the twins some limp story about Payne's wife answering the door and saying he wasn't in.

McVitie's major problem was his drinking and drug-taking. In the two years since leaving prison, he had effectively become addicted to both. It made him unpredictable and prone to reckless behaviour. If the twins had tacitly let him off over the abortive Payne execution (perhaps thinking a repeat attempt was in the offing), they were soon to become increasingly concerned by his behaviour and how it reflected on them. Having taken the £100, McVitie would apparently get drunk in the pubs and clubs and loudly boast that he had "turned the Krays over and they've done bugger all about it. I tell you, they're getting soft. They'll have to watch it."[49]

47 Leslie Payne; *The Brotherhood* (London: Michael Joseph 1973).
48 Statement by Cornelius Whitehead, 14 October 1968; MEPO 2/11404, ff. 1398-1400 (National Archives).
49 Reggie & Ronnie Kray, with Fred Dinenage; *Our Story* (London: Sidgwick and Jackson 1988).

One evening, accompanied by his partner Sylvia Barnard, McVitie turned up at the Regency Club with a double-barrelled shotgun, apparently "looking for someone."[50] John Barry managed to diffuse the situation and get McVitie to leave, but it was a wholly unsatisfactory matter; an associate of the Krays was making trouble in a club which fell under their protection. Another club incident earlier in the year also incurred the displeasure of Freddie Foreman, as it took place at his own night club and casino, the 211 in Balham:

> *McVitie, who was losing money that night, pulled a knife on my croupier. Then, when he realised I was on my way upstairs to speak to him, he threw it under the table...*
>
> *I came up behind McVitie and asked him what the problem was: 'Misbehaving again, Jack? Come with me, I just want to talk to you.'*
>
> *He looked at me and replied, 'What, and get a fucking bullet in the head?' I told him I'd go downstairs and that when I got back in 10 minutes I didn't want to see him there. When I returned to the casino, he'd left.*
>
> *He'd also gone to the Starlight Club, where Micky Regan and I had some roulette and blackjack tables, held up the place and made all the guys drop their strides. All told, McVitie was a bit of a nut.*[51]

When somebody upset Foreman, they upset the Krays. McVitie had cheated Ronnie Kray out of £100; in addition, the twins had dealings with a factory out in Essex that produced drugs and the distribution of these illicit narcotics had become another string to the Krays' bow. McVitie had bought some purple hearts from Ronnie and had never given him the money, an issue that Ronnie was not willing to forget. Messages were sent from Ronnie demanding a meeting, all of which were ignored, and McVitie appeared to be disregarding the wishes of those who gave him work, and ripping them off into the bargain. Gradually, he was building up an unenviable portfolio of stupidity and disrespect as far as the twins were concerned. And yet, one night in October at the Regency, he dined with Reggie and a couple of other boys from the Firm and must have laid on a sob-story, because, regardless of what McVitie owed him, Reggie gave him £50. When

50 Statement by John Dickson, 14 September 1968; MEPO 2/11404, ff. 1281-1287 (National Archives).

51 Freddie Foreman; *Freddie Foreman: The Godfather of British Crime* (London: John Blake 2007).

Ronnie heard this, he went mad.[52]

Finally, just like Frank Mitchell, McVitie began making threats against the Krays, instantly causing them to reassess their attitude to him. One night at the Regency, he was told by Jack Dickson that the twins knew that he was shooting his mouth off about them in public and, after looking a little concerned, drew upon reserves of bravado: he stated that from there on in, he would always carry a double-barrelled shotgun with him when he went out, to protect himself from villains who were "going around giving the East End a bad name and taking liberties with people."[53] Dickson assured McVitie that he was probably the biggest offender in that regard, and that he would be best advised to keep out of trouble, but McVitie was now on a roll:

"I don't care," he said. "One day it will be me or them, and as I have told you before, I am tooled-up. If they try to take me I shall most probably take one of them with me."[54]

Word got back to the Krays and decisions had to be made. Reggie was already thinking about it:

> Now when a guy like McVitie is making threats about you and walking around with a shotgun, if you ignore it you're asking for trouble. Not only that, all the other villains are looking at each other and saying, 'What's happening to the Krays? They're letting this McVitie make 'em look like soft prats.' It's a matter of honour, what the Eyeties call 'face'. If you show you're weak, the others start to close in on you like sharks.
>
> We had to make an example of McVitie.[55]

52 Reggie Kray; *Born Fighter* (London: Arrow Books 1991).

53 John Dickson; *Murder Without Conviction* (London: Sidgwick and Jackson 1986).

54 Ibid.

55 Reggie & Ronnie Kray, with Fred Dinenage; *Our Story* (London: Sidgwick and Jackson 1988)

FIFTEEN

JACK 'THE HAT'

Saturday, 28 October 1967 was an ordinary day for Sylvia Barnard. She had been alone with her daughter at the home she shared with Jack McVitie, in Hartland Road, Stratford, for most of it. McVitie was out, and as the afternoon wore on, Sylvia got ready to go to her sister's in Dagenham. At about 4.30 p.m., McVitie returned from wherever he had been and had his dinner, and at around 7.30 p.m., Sylvia bade him goodbye and left with her daughter to see her sister.[1] Up to that point it had been a rather pedestrian - one might even say dull - day, but its significance would be revealed later; Sylvia had seen Jack McVitie for the last time.

In the meantime, it was party time at the Carpenter's Arms. It had been the twins' thirty-fourth birthday only four days before and the celebrations had extended into the weekend; the little Cheshire Street pub was now buzzing with friends and family. With Reggie and Ronnie were their parents, brother Charlie, Connie Whitehead, old friend Geoff Allen, Ronnie Bender and Ronnie Hart. 'Scotch' Jack Dickson, Albert Donoghue, Sammy Lederman and Harry 'Jew Boy' Cope fleshed out the representation of the Firm. The women included, interestingly, Carol Thompson, a red-head who had become Reggie's companion, and accompanying Ronnie Bender was 'Bubbles', Frankie Shea's common-law wife, as the two had recently begun an affair.[2]

---

1   Statement of Sylvia Barnard, 15 October 1968; DPP 2/4583 (National Archives).
2   According to Ronnie Hart, Bender had been told to befriend 'Bubbles' in order to feed her information to see if any of it got through to Frankie Shea; sometimes it did, sometimes not, but Bender and 'Bubbles' fell for each other. Statement by Ronnie Hart, 3 September 1968; DPP 2/4583 (National Archives).

303

Charlie was with his wife Dolly, Whitehead was with his wife Pat and Geoff Allen was accompanied by a girlfriend called Annie. Hart was with his girlfriend, Vicky James, who later became his wife.[3] Ronnie Kray had invited two young men along, Trevor Stone and Terry Clulow: Stone was a masseur and Clulow would eventually become one of the croupiers at the Colony Club. They were both seventeen-years-old and had known each other since their school days in Bethnal Green.[4]

By all accounts it was a happy occasion and, by the time Chris and Tony Lambrianou arrived, the party was in full swing:

> *A juke-box in the corner of the long, L-shaped bar belted out the hits of 1967: the Beatles, the Stones, Dusty Springfield, the Everly Brothers. Members of the Firm were there, suited and booted, all drinking, with smiles on their hard faces. The wives and girlfriends were there, too: all dolled up and smelling nice.*[5]

That night the Lambrianous were entertaining another pair of brothers, Alan and Raymond Mills, noted characters from West London's Ladbroke Grove area. Ray Mills had been living in Birmingham for about two years[6] and had become friendly with Chris Lambrianou, although he had never met Tony; Alan knew Tony but had never met Chris. It was a chance for the four men to get properly acquainted and, at some point, introduce the Mills brothers to the Krays.

Their evening had started at about 7.00 p.m. in the Brown Bear[7] in Leman Street, Whitechapel, and after a few drinks there, Tony Lambrianou made a quick phone call to find out where the twins could be found. Finding out it was the Carpenter's Arms, they made their way there. They arrived to a happy house where for several hours a pot of ten pound notes, a 'whip' for drinks, had been liberally plundered, and the Mills brothers met the Krays. At 11.00 p.m., the pub was due to close and a number of people began to drift off; for

---

3   Tony Lambrianou with Carol Clerk; *Inside the Firm* (London: Smith Gryphon 1991).
4   Statement of Trevor Stone, 20 July 1968; MEPO 2/11404, ff. 1259-1260 (National Archives).
5   Chris Lambrianou and Robin McGibbon; *Escape From the Kray Madness* (London: Sidgwick and Jackson 1995).
6   Statement of Raymond Mills, 17 October 1968; 2/11404, ff. 1470-1472 (National Archives).
7   Tony Lambrianou, in his book *Inside the Firm*, mistakenly calls it the White Bear, an error that has been repeated several times by other authors since. The Brown Bear, at 139 Leman Street, still exists as a pub.

many, the night was still young, as there were always opportunities to extend a party at any number of clubs. There was also talk of a party at 97 Evering Road, Stoke Newington, at the flat belonging to Carole Skinner, a young lady who had been a cloakroom attendant at the El Morocco club, and whose boyfriend, George Plummer, worked at the Green Dragon Club.[8] 'Big' Pat Connolly, after splitting up from his wife, was renting a front room from Winnie Harwood a few doors away at No. 113.[9] Many of the Firm were frequent guests at Skinner's parties, which were held almost weekly, and it was where Albert Donoghue spent the night with Lisa after the death of Frank Mitchell:

> *Various people started coming to these parties including Wally [Garelick], [Connie] Whitehead, Ronnie Hart, [Ronnie] Bender, Albert Barry [Donoghue], Scots Ian, Scots Jack, Tommy Cowley, Tony Cronin, Pat Connolly, Sammy Lederman, Billy Exley, Tommy Flanagan, Ronnie and Reggie Kray.*[10]

Carole Anne Skinner - known as 'Blonde' Carole to distinguish her from Reggie's new red-headed girlfriend - was 27-years-old and had been living at 97 Evering Road since 1963. After four years of marriage, she had separated from her husband, Colin, in 1964 when he went to prison; since Colin's release, he had kept in touch, mainly to visit their two children, but the separation was permanent and since 1966, Carole had been seeing club houseman George Plummer on a regular basis.[11]

Opposite 'Blonde' Carole's, at No. 76, lived Kathleen 'Kitty' Collins, who shared a top-floor flat with her three sons; her husband was at that time serving a sixteen-year prison sentence, and she knew Skinner well as they occasionally worked together at El Morocco and would babysit each other's children. Collins was a frequenter of the local clubs, including the Regency, and had been casually introduced to the Krays through Winnie Harwood the previous year. When unaccompanied, she tended to steer clear of the twins and their associates, a number of whom she knew well by sight; Jack 'The Hat' McVitie was one of them, and she described him as somebody "who

---

8   Statement of Kathleen Collins, 14 May 1968; MEPO 2/11404, ff. 1459-1462 (National Archives).

9   Ibid.

10 Statement of Carole Skinner, 13 May 1968; MEPO 2/11404, ff. 1158-1160 (National Archives).

11 Ibid.

used to speak to everyone in general, and liked to dance with any of the girls all the time. He was very happy go lucky."[12]

As often as not, she generally kept her social life away from the Krays, and often frequented the Coach and Horses on Stoke Newington High Street, a pub usually known as 'Blondie Bill's'. She also had a crowd of friends who were all regulars at the Old Blue Anchor pub in Whitechapel Road, which they commonly called 'Coleman's'[13] after the owner.[14] It was common for them all to drink there on a Friday and Saturday night and, when the pub closed, to buy drinks from there to take back to somebody's house for a party. On the night of Saturday, 28 October, it would be Collins's turn to play hostess, albeit in an unexpected way.

As the Carpenter's Arms emptied, a number of people decided to go to the Evering Road party. Reggie said that he was going for a meal with his Carol. Chris and Tony Lambrianou had left a little earlier with the Mills brothers, keen to see some other pubs before closing time, and so they went to the Queen's Arms on Hackney Road, before Tony suggested moving on to the Regency. Chris was none too keen; having taken some speed (amphetamine) earlier on, he was feeling more ambitious and wanted to venture into the West End,[15] but Tony convinced him and they soon arrived at the Regency and went downstairs to the jazz club, which was typically busy. Chris's reservations returned:

> I knew I'd made a mistake. The place was jam packed with people I didn't know and I didn't feel comfortable. I'd come out for a good old Saturday night, and I wasn't going to get it at the Regency. I thought about walking out, but Tony was getting the drinks in.
>
> Suddenly a face I did recognize came towards us, beaming from under the familiar brown trilby. It was Jack McVitie.[16]

Chris introduced McVitie to the Mills brothers, bought him a lager,

12 Statement of Kathleen Collins, 14 May 1968; MEPO 2/11404, ff. 1459-1462 (National Archives).
13 According to Kelly's Post Office Directory, the Coleman family had been running the Old Blue Anchor, at 133 Whitechapel Road, since 1938. It still operates as a pub, although in 2000 it was renamed Indo.
14 Statement of Kathleen Collins, 2 October 1968; MEPO 2/11404, ff. 1419-1422 (National Archives).
15 Chris Lambrianou and Robin McGibbon; *Escape From the Kray Madness* (London: Sidgwick and Jackson 1995).
16 Ibid.

and they chatted good-naturedly for a while, unaware that a different, and more sinister, conversation was taking place in Tony Barry's office. Reggie Kray had obviously not gone for a meal with Carol and instead, accompanied by Ronnie Hart and Ronnie Bender (and their partners), they had gone to the Regency. Reggie was looking for McVitie.

The club doorman contacted Barry via the intercom, stating that Reggie wanted to speak to him. Barry arrived at his office and walked in with Reggie whilst Bender and Hart waited outside. In the office, Reggie pulled out a gun, a .32 Mauser automatic and said, "I am going to do Jack," and that he was going to 'do' him downstairs.[17] Reggie was visibly irate and was full of hatred for McVitie, referring to him as a "fucking cunt";[18] in fact Reggie was intoxicated and did not seem to be the same cheery man who been enjoying the company in the Carpenter's Arms only a few hours before. He bit his lip anxiously.[19] Tony Lambrianou later said that something had happened to Reggie between leaving the Carpenter's and arriving at the club[20] and Reggie also intimated that he had had a row with Ronnie.[21] Barry was alarmed at Reggie's intentions:

> I mean he showed me a shooter and when he said he was going to 'do' McVitie I presumed he was going to use it. I pleaded with him not to do anything in the club because there were innocent people downstairs and I didn't want anyone hurt or upset. It was just I did not want any trouble in my club.[22]

Reggie opened the office door and called Hart and Bender in and they chatted briefly. There was talk of 'Blonde' Carole's party and Hart mentioned that the Lambrianous were downstairs; according to Barry, Bender or Hart went down to fetch Tony Lambrianou.[23] When he arrived, Reggie asked if McVitie was downstairs and when Tony confirmed this, Reggie apparently said, "Get him drunk, we want to

17 Statement by Anthony Barry, 9 October 1968; MEPO 2/11404, ff. 1434-1439 (National Archives).

18 Ibid.

19 Tony Lambrianou with Carol Clerk; *Inside the Firm* (London: Smith Gryphon 1991).

20 Interviewed in *The Krays – The Final Word* documentary (DVD; WMV 2001).

21 Ibid.

22 Statement by Anthony Barry, 9 October 1968; MEPO 2/11404, ff. 1434-1439 (National Archives).

23 In *Inside the Firm*, Lambrianou claimed it was Barry himself who called him upstairs, although Barry said it was either Hart or Bender, he could not be sure.

take him round Carole's."[24] Tony Lambrianou said, "OK," and went back downstairs to his table. What happened next has been described in different ways by different witnesses and it is worth briefly mentioning the sources when depicting the subsequent events of that evening.

Unlike the Cornell shooting, which involved only a few active participants and a number of unwitting witnesses who were all in one single location when it happened, the events leading up to the demise of Jack McVitie were spread across many hours and many places and, most importantly, were described by a number of people who had to be careful what they said later on. The longest statements on the affair came from Ronnie Hart, who, later running the risk of conviction for a serious crime, tended to underplay his involvement, and thus his account must be approached with a certain amount of caution. Anthony Barry, somewhat exasperated by the unfolding events, appeared to be very honest in his approach. Chris Lambrianou, feeling similarly shocked by what was to happen later, set out his account quite thoroughly, and Bender, later to suffer greatly for his involvement, also made attempts to set the record straight, although none of these witnesses can be relied on entirely. Tony Lambrianou, undoubtedly bound by the criminal codes he held dear, described events and the involvement of others with one eye on his loyalties, and his account must also be considered with more care.

After Tony Lambrianou left the office, Barry recalled either Hart or Bender (again he could not remember which) pulling a large knife, about twelve inches long, from the waistband of his trousers. Hart, unsurprisingly, claimed it was Bender.[25] And although Hart said that Bender took the knife out of the Regency with him, Barry stated that he was given both the knife and Reggie's Mauser to look after, putting them in the letter tray on his desk before locking the office door behind him once everybody had left. Judging from what happened a little while later, weight must be given to Barry's account. Reggie, Hart and Bender left the Regency for the Evering Road party, and whilst Reggie and Hart took their partners, Bender went alone after having an argument with 'Bubbles' Shea who "didn't want to go to a Kray party."[26] When Barry went downstairs, he saw Jack McVitie there

24 Statement by Anthony Barry, 9 October 1968; MEPO 2/11404, ff. 1434-1439 (National Archives).

25 Statement by Ronald Hart, 11 October 1968; DPP 2/4583 (National Archives).

26 Martin Fido; *The Krays: Unfinished Business* (London: Carlton Books 1999).

talking with the Lambrianous and the Mills brothers.

In the meantime, Carole Skinner had been in the basement sitting room at Evering Road, waiting for George Plummer to arrive from the pub with the party guests. It was now between 11.30 p.m. and midnight and she was idly watching television when the doorbell rang. Going upstairs to answer it, she was confronted by the Krays and a group of people looking for a party. With the twins were Carol Thompson, Ronnie Bender, 'Big' Pat Connolly, Ronnie Hart and Vicky James, Connie and Pat Whitehead, Geoff Allen and Annie, Trevor Stone and Terry Clulow. Skinner was a little surprised to see them, particularly when Ronnie said, "Weren't you expecting us?" and despite saying that she was already expecting company, the new arrivals went into the flat and downstairs to the rear living room.

I couldn't really turn them away. I didn't try. I had been used to having them in my flat for parties and so on and I saw no reason to turn them away. It wasn't a question of not daring to turn them away, it just wouldn't have been right to turn them away.[27]

The group commandeered the television set and turned the channel over to watch a boxing match. That night, BBC2 were broadcasting, live by satellite from Los Angeles, the fourth quarter final in the eliminating tournament for the World Heavyweight Championships between Jerry Quarry and Floyd Patterson. They had missed most of it, but they caught the end of the fight - with Quarry winning on points - which ended at 11.56 p.m.[28] During the fight, Skinner had gone over the road to Kitty Collins's place at No. 76 and asked if she and George could bring their party there. Collins was not particularly in the mood, but she eventually agreed,[29] and when Skinner went back over to her flat she met George Plummer and several of the guests outside and told them to go straight over the road.

Ronnie Hart and Connie Whitehead were told to go back to the Regency and collect more drink for the party and whilst there, on the orders of Reggie, Hart was to sort out the gun. The orders were that Anthony Barry should bring the gun to Evering Road himself; why

27 Statement of Carole Skinner, 22 October 1968; DPP 2/4583, ff. 133-136 (National Archives).
28 Statement by John Brown (BBC research analyst), 27 September 1968; DPP 2/4583, f. 91 (National Archives).
29 Statement of Kathleen Collins, 2 October 1968; MEPO 2/11404, ff. 1419-1422 (National Archives).

Reggie wanted Barry to perform the errand is not clear, although it may have just been a case of Reggie playing the old Kray trick of having somebody else do the dirty work, ensuring that another potential witness against him could be relied upon to go 'on side' or shoulder the blame if the worst came to the worst. At the Regency, Barry protested, but he realised that "it was beyond my power to refuse to do what I was asked to do in the circumstances". He capitulated, believing that "it was more than my life was worth to refuse",[30] drove to Evering Road with the gun, and handed it to Reggie at the door of No. 97. Hart took the knife back with him.

All the while, Carole Skinner was going back and forth between the two parties, and on one occasion, whilst she was cutting lemons in her kitchen, Ronnie Bender walked in and surreptitiously took something out of his pocket and placed it on top of a kitchen cabinet.[31] A number of guests, including Geoff Allen, had already called it a night and Ronnie Bender left to give Pat Connolly a lift somewhere. The last time Skinner was there, she saw the men standing in a group chatting, at which point Ronnie Kray called Vicky James over. Skinner heard Vicky say, "Well, what shall I tell her?"[32] and, with that, the two women went over to Kitty Collins's party. Carol Thompson went over a little later, and Connie Whitehead was told by Ronnie to take his wife home and come back later.[33] It was apparent that the women were being strategically removed from the flat.

Jack McVitie was on his way. The very mention of a party had whetted his appetite for a long night out and he drove the Lambrianous and the Mills brothers over to Evering Road in his cream and blue Mark II Zodiac, a clapped-out vehicle with a damaged headlight and defunct windscreen wipers. The journey took only a few minutes and McVitie, who was somewhat drunk on Bacardi and Coke,[34] parked on Jenner Road, opposite No. 97.[35] It was about 12.30 a.m.

The five men climbed the stairs that led to the front door of No. 97. Positioned at a ground floor window was Ronnie Hart who had been

30 Statement by Anthony Barry, 9 October 1968; MEPO 2/11404, ff. 1434-1439 (National Archives).

31 Statement of Carole Skinner, 22 October 1968; DPP 2/4583, ff. 68-71 (National Archives).

32 Ibid.

33 Statement by Ronald Hart, 11 October 1968; DPP 2/4583 (National Archives).

34 Tony Lambrianou with Carol Clerk; *Inside the Firm* (London: Smith Gryphon 1991).

35 This part of Jenner Road, along with No. 76 Evering Road, no longer exists, having been redeveloped for housing in the 1970s.

instructed to keep a look out for McVitie's arrival and, on seeing him, he called down that he was coming. Ronnie Kray told Terry and Trevor to turn up the record player and make more noise, which they duly did.[36] Hart opened the front door, and McVitie, followed by Chris and Tony, and then the Mills brothers, walked through the hallway and began to descend the steps to the basement rooms where the party was being held. Jack 'The Hat', true to type, was champing at the bit, shouting, "Where's the party, then? Jack's here."[37]

What happened next has been recounted innumerable times. The unique nature of this event, essentially witnessed by individuals who were at risk of prosecution for even so much as being in the same room, and many of them villains with long criminal histories, has resulted in dissimilar accounts riddled with contradictions and inconsistencies. Many of these contradictions were the direct result of people trying to save their own skin at a later date, or fibbing because they felt the need to uphold the criminal code of loyalty, 'Thou shalt not grass.' Those who were in any position to relate what happened in that basement sitting room were the Kray twins, Chris and Tony Lambrianou, Ronnie Hart, Ronnie Bender, Alan and Ray Mills, and Trevor Stone and Terry Clulow. Of those, Ray Mills claimed to be too drunk to remember anything much and only Terry Clulow would go on to steadfastly deny everything.[38]

In 1999, researcher, author and broadcaster Martin Fido was granted access to the Metropolitan Police Files on the Kray case prior to their release. In looking at the events surrounding McVitie's death, Fido, an experienced analyst of historical material, said:

> *The familiar scenario essentially combines and abridges two unreliable sources. Ronnie Hart, like any Queen's Evidence witness, was more or less bound to minimise his own involvement and maximise the details that would give the crown the conviction it sought. Reggie Kray, like nine out of ten impenitent professional murderers, was at pains to make his victim look as despicable as possible.[39]*

36 Statement by Trevor Stone, 13 October 1968; MEPO 2/11404, ff. 1475-1483 (National Archives).
37 Chris Lambrianou and Robin McGibbon; *Escape From the Kray Madness* (London: Sidgwick and Jackson 1995).
38 Statement by Terence Clulow, 20 July 1968; MEPO 2/11404, ff. 1261-1263 (National Archives).
39 Martin Fido; *The Krays: Unfinished Business* (London: Carlton Books 1999).

But Fido was also able to use material he found in later appeal statements given by Ronnie Bender, Chris and Tony Lambrianou, and a new confession by Trevor Stone in 1969, to produce what he called a "different scenario" from that which has often been repeated. Having looked at all the differing accounts, whether from official statements or memoirs, it is difficult to disagree with Fido's conclusion, although here we can add the account given by Alan Mills (as independent a witness as there was to the events in the flat that evening).

Jack McVitie was the first to enter the sitting room, followed by the Lambrianou brothers. The Mills brothers were still in the hallway outside when Ronnie Kray, with characteristic spontaneity, walked over to McVitie and smashed him in the face with a sherry glass, just below the eye. According to Tony Lambrianou, Ronnie said, "I've had enough of you, you fucking cunt. Keep your mouth shut. Now fuck off,"[40] before casually walking over to the side of the room by the record player. McVitie began to walk off, slamming his fist into his hand and cursing the twins. With that, Reggie, gun drawn, grabbed McVitie from behind, put the gun to his head and pulled the trigger; nothing happened. There was no shot when Reggie tried again and he cursed the gun, shouting that he had been given "a fucking duff 'un."[41]

Chris Lambrianou walked out into the hallway, shocked by the realisation that he and his brother had been used as patsies to bring McVitie into a perilous situation. He started up the stairs to leave the house, but met Bender and Whitehead returning from their driving chores, whereby Bender convinced Chris to come back down and have a drink with him. When Chris said there had been some trouble downstairs, Bender seemed unconcerned, saying, "Don't take any notice of them fighting, they are always hitting somebody on the chin."[42] Bender, Whitehead, the Mills brothers and Tony Lambrianou were soon in the sitting room. When Bender asked Ronnie what was going on, Ronnie said, "I'll give him challenge me," and punched McVitie in the face.[43] The aggression against McVitie continued as the twins and Ronnie Hart began to attack him with their fists and it was at this time that McVitie hit the window, breaking a pane of glass.

40 Tony Lambrianou with Carol Clerk; *Inside the Firm* (London: Smith Gryphon 1991).
41 Ibid.
42 Ronnie Bender's appeal statement as quoted by Fido in *The Krays: Unfinished Business* (London: Carlton Books 1999).
43 Ibid.

Outside, sitting on the stairs, Chris Lambrianou began to cry. There was a chaotic coming and going around the hallway as people walked in and out of the room, and somebody shouted out that nobody was to leave the house. At one point, one of the twins came out and, seeing Chris Lambrianou upset on the stairs, asked what the matter was. "I didn't come here for this," was all he could say[44] and Connie Whitehead was told to take Chris home. To save face, Chris said he was going home to fetch another gun.

McVitie was trying to fight his way away from the window, where he was effectively cornered. In the melee, Ronnie Kray tried to stab McVitie in the back with an ordinary table knife, but it proved useless. It was most likely Ronnie Hart who retrieved a large carving knife from the kitchen - almost certainly the one that Bender had put there in full view of Carole Skinner earlier - and passed it to Reggie. Terry Clulow ran from the room as Ronnie Kray and Ronnie Hart grabbed hold of McVitie. Alan Mills saw the knife in Reggie's hand and what follows is his version of the shocking events that followed:

The two of them held McVitie by his arms from behind and then Reggie Kray stabbed him in the stomach two or three times. McVitie fell on the floor in front of the window, sort of curled up and sort of on his side. As Reggie Kray was stabbing McVitie Ronnie Kray said, "Go on Reg. Kill him."

Then Reggie Kray went over, leaned over McVitie and pushed the knife somewhere into McVitie's neck. I saw him do this once. I didn't hear McVitie make a sound. I thought McVitie must be dead by then.[45]

In Ronnie Hart's later account, Reggie apparently impaled McVitie through the neck and twisted the knife in one final act of violence, although no other statements or latter day reminiscences by those present mention this; again, Hart's evidence, as we have already said, specifically in relation to the immediate events surrounding the murder, should be regarded with caution.

The Mills brothers had seen enough and quickly left the house. Trevor Stone had followed Terry Clulow out of the room during the first plunges of the knife, as did Tony Lambrianou. Reggie had gone

44 Chris Lambrianou and Robin McGibbon; *Escape From the Kray Madness* (London: Sidgwick and Jackson 1995).

45 Statement by Alan Mills, 5 October 1968; DPP 2/4583, ff. 1463-1469 (National Archives).

berserk and Ronnie Bender ran over to him and tried to wrestle the knife from his grasp. In the scuffle, Reggie cut his hand badly. Bender fetched a towel for Reggie to wrap the wound, after which, some form of blame-game ensued, with Ronnie Kray telling Reggie that the cut on his hand was not Bender's fault but Ronnie Hart's, for supplying him with the knife that did it in the first place.[46]

The defunct gun and knife were wrapped in the towel and then came the pressing issue of what to do with McVitie's body. It was lying doubled up on the floor with a huge pool of blood beneath it. Spots of blood could be seen on the walls, skirting boards and fire surround and the twins themselves were heavily bloodstained. They began to leave the room, accompanied by Hart. Looking at the body, Bender pleaded for some guidance.

"What can I do with it Ron?" he said. Ronnie's reply was probably born as much from ignorance as it was desperation:

> He said, "Chuck it somewhere, chuck it over the Railway somewhere". I said, "Where?" He said, "Put it over the Railway at Cazemove Road, opposite Coral's." I said, "Yes, yes, I will do it." I wanted to get them out of the house, and the Kray twins and Ronald Hart went up the stairs and presumably then left the house.
>
> I then went into the kitchen, got myself a drink, and so far as I know, I was the only one left in the basement of the house.[47]

Bender's statement, made under oath as part of an appeal procedure, differs greatly from Tony Lambrianou's recollections in his memoir, which, in turn, differs from his own appeal statement given in 1969.[48] In his memoir, Tony claimed to have walked out of the room as the stabbing started only to return in time to see Reggie make the final thrust into McVitie's throat. He then said he was there when the order to dispose of the body was given. In his appeal statement, he claimed to have gone upstairs and encountered Carole Skinner's two young children whom he pushed back into a bedroom. After what seemed like an age, Tony went to the sitting room where he saw the Krays and Hart about to leave Bender with the body of McVitie which "was lying under the window with his legs underneath him and with half

---

46 Ronnie Bender's appeal statement as quoted by Fido in *The Krays: Unfinished Business* (London: Carlton Books 1999).

47 Ibid.

48 Anthony Lambrianou's appeal statement made from Durham Prison, as quoted by Fido in *The Krays: Unfinished Business* (London: Carlton Books 1999).

his stomach hanging out, his head was almost severed and his eyes were open."[49]

Chris Lambrianou gives a different version of events in his memoir. He had indeed gone home, driven there by Connie Whitehead, and, feeling that he could not leave his brother at Evering Road alone, collected his gun (a Webley .38) and got a taxi back to the house. The Lambrianous felt that they should be armed in case McVitie turned on them for bringing him to the party for a beating (or worse), although obviously, as he pocketed his gun, Chris was unaware that the firearm was now redundant. When he knocked at the door of 'Blonde' Carole's house, Bender, apparently alone, opened the door. He told Chris what had happened to McVitie and Chris couldn't believe what he was hearing. Enough was enough, and at that point he was all ready to just walk away when, at that moment, Tony appeared; he had apparently left the house entirely and had been loitering outside. Bender pleaded for help.

"Chris, please help me. I don't know how to deal with this. I don't know what to do. I didn't know anything like this was going to happen. I walked right into it. I only came here for a quick drink with them," he said.[50] The Lambrianou brothers could not leave Bender with his predicament and the three men went back downstairs to where McVitie's lifeless body lay in a pool of blood. His face was ashen and his trademark brown trilby was lying a few feet away from him. Chris Lambrianou, in the absence of any suggestions by the others, began to take charge. His first decision was for all the glasses lying around the room to be washed, to clean away any fingerprints. He found some socks in a drawer which belonged to Carole Skinner's two children, and they were worn over the hands to ensure no further prints were left behind. He also crept into the children's bedroom and gingerly removed the eiderdown from the bed in which they were sleeping and took it downstairs. And then, with the worst timing imaginable, Carole Skinner and George Plummer came home.

The party at Kitty Collins's flat had finally wound down; Vicky James and Carol Thompson had left after an hour and a half, and eventually the other guests had begun to drift away, leaving Collins, Skinner and a very drunk Plummer, who was so intoxicated he had to be helped

---

49 Ibid.
50 Chris Lambrianou and Robin McGibbon; *Escape From the Kray Madness* (London: Sidgwick and Jackson 1995).

down the stairs.[51] When Skinner and Plummer let themselves into No. 97, they were about to go downstairs when they were met by Ronnie Bender, wearing the children's socks on his hands.

"Where are you going?" he said. He looked understandably worried.

"We're going downstairs," replied Skinner.

"You can't go down there at the moment," said Bender. "There's been a little bit of trouble down there. We're just tidying up the mess."

Skinner protested, "But I live here," but Bender was adamant that the couple stay upstairs and told them to wait a while in the ground floor bedroom. As they began to move to the bedroom, Skinner caught sight of Chris Lambrianou coming up the stairs from the basement. In his sock-covered hands he held a washing-up bowl full of blood-stained water, which he was taking to the ground floor toilet for disposal.[52] The clean-up operation had well and truly started, with Chris mopping up the mess around McVitie's body, a vile mixture of blood and some solid matter which was later described by both Lambrianous as being like liver.[53] Then, with Skinner and Plummer safely in the bedroom, the very serious task of getting McVitie's body out of the house became an imperative.

The three men placed McVitie on the large eiderdown and wrapped his body in it, twisting the ends like a sweet wrapper. After moving him out of the room, they took up the blood-spattered carpet, which did not cover the entire floor, and folded it up. It would have to be destroyed; in fact every surface of the room would have to be thoroughly cleaned to remove any traces of blood or other incriminating marks.

There were a number of abortive attempts to get McVitie out of the house. His car had been moved from Jenner Road and parked in front of No. 97, but the small journey from house to car was treacherous, as a number of taxi-drivers were passing on their way to a nearby bagel shop. When a convenient gap presented itself, McVitie's body was put on the back seat; the original idea of putting him in the boot was rejected when it was realised there was too much junk in it to accommodate the body. With the body apparently safe in the car, the

---

51 Statement of Kathleen Collins, 2 October 1968; MEPO 2/11404, ff. 1419-1422 (National Archives).

52 Statement of Carole Skinner, 22 October 1968; DPP 2/4583, ff. 133-136 (National Archives).

53 Tony Lambrianou said that when they moved McVitie's body, the liver fell out and had to be burnt in the fire. Chris reckoned the liver had been 'skewered out'.

three returned to the house and Skinner was told she could come back downstairs:

Down in the basement, I went into the living room. My carpet was there but it was all folded up in the middle of the room. The window of the room was broken. The floor of the room was wet. I went into the kitchen. I noticed the kitchen table had been pulled over to the sink. There were bottles and glasses stacked up on the table. The floor of the kitchen was very wet. We all started to wash the bottles and glasses that were piled up on the table.[54]

As the cleaning operation continued, Connie Whitehead and Vicky James arrived. Connie said the whole flat would need to be scrubbed from top to bottom. In the meantime, Chris and Tony Lambrianou and Ronnie Bender had decided what was to happen to the body. It was agreed that throwing it over the railway bridge on Cazenove Road, as Ronnie Kray suggested, was a stupid idea and it was suggested that it would be better off being dumped over the river, well away from Kray territory. Chris went to fetch his car from outside the Regency; Tony had volunteered to drive McVitie's car into south London, followed by his brother and Bender.

McVitie's Zodiac was little more than a death trap; one of the headlights didn't work, making it a prime target for any curious police patrol car that may be passing, so Tony's mission was made all the more risky, as was Chris and Bender's job of following him, as they would be forced to react if the Zodiac, with the dead body in the back, was pulled over. It was a tense drive, through Clapton and Hackney, down to Whitechapel and the Commercial Road and then to the Rotherhithe Tunnel. At one point, a police car pulled out of a side road, coming between the two cars. It was a terrifying few minutes during which Chris eased off the accelerator to distance himself from McVitie's Zodiac and the police car, all the while feeling for his Webley pistol in case Tony was pulled over. To the relief of everyone, the police car turned off into Dalston Lane and thankfully, there were no other problems until Chris and Bender lost Tony just prior to reaching the Tunnel. On the south side, they drove around the immediate neighbourhood looking for him until suddenly they caught sight of him walking along the road. He had left the car in St Marychurch Street, in front of the church of St Mary's Rotherhithe, a quiet back

54 Statement of Carole Skinner, undated (1968); DPP 2/4583, ff. 69-80 (National Archives).

street still sprinkled with confetti from the previous day's weddings.[55]

With the body now dumped, it was time to get out of the area as quickly as possible. Bender wanted to be dropped off in Poplar, apparently to see Charlie Kray, a decision that did not sit well with Chris Lambrianou; Charlie had nothing to do with the McVitie incident, but Chris was in no mood to question Bender and dropped him at the junction of Commercial Road and Burdett Road before driving Tony back to his flat in Bethnal Green. Chris then went to Euston Station to pick up a girlfriend who was known, affectionately or otherwise, as 'The Squirrel'.[56] They stopped by Evering Road on the way back to check on progress, although the young lady was not permitted inside whilst Chris helped with the final stages of clearing up.

Chris Lambrianou has always been circumspect about the death of Jack McVitie. He later described himself as "a coward"[57] for letting it happen and had this to say about the events of the early hours of 29 October 1967:

> *Poor Jack the Hat. Many thought he was a dog, a lairy, loud-mouthed trouble-maker. But, to me, he was a puppy, a likeable guy who loved life. Yes, he was a hard man, a villain. But he was also a clown, the sort of bloke who would fall down and go to sleep where he was. He did not deserve to die the way he did, set upon by a crazed pack, and butchered like an animal.[58]*

◆

Reggie and Ronnie Kray, after shamelessly leaving Ronnie Bender to deal with the mess of McVitie's demise, went with Ronnie Hart to Harry Hopwood's flat in Hackney. The old Kray family friend, whose home had already been used to hatch the plot to murder Frank Mitchell, now found himself entertaining the blood-spattered twins and forced to deal with a situation with which he again had no connection. The Krays, as was their way, had dragged the innocent into their misdemeanours yet again.

---

55 Some accounts suggest that the car had run out of petrol and had spluttered to a halt where it was left, although the following day's events, when the car was taken away, do not bear this out.

56 Freddie Foreman & Tony Lambrianou; *Getting It Straight: Villains Talking* (London: Sidgwick and Jackson 2001).

57 Interviewed in *The Krays – The Final Word* documentary (DVD; WMV 2001).

58 Chris Lambrianou and Robin McGibbon; *Escape From the Kray Madness* (London: Sidgwick and Jackson 1995).

Hopwood and his wife were in bed when the doorbell rang between 1.00 and 2.00 a.m.:

> *Ronnie and Reggie Kray, on my doorstep, were covered in blood. I didn't notice anything of that kind about Hart. There was no conversation on the doorstep. They just walked in, into the passage, and then through into the front room. Ronald said that Reg had just done McVitie in, could they clean up? I took Reg upstairs into the bathroom. I noticed Reginald had a cut on his hand. I don't remember which hand. The cut was across the palm. I showed him where the towels were and I left him running the bath and I went downstairs. Downstairs, Ron and Ronald Hart were standing in the front room and Ron Kray asked me: "Where's the best place to get rid of these?" He meant a gun and a knife.*[59]

Hopwood said they should be thrown into the Regent's Canal, and, with that, he and Hart were told to dispose of the weapons and then drive to 174 Vallance Road where the twins' Aunt May kept spare clothes for them. Hart drove, and on reaching the bridge over the canal at Queensbridge Road, he pulled over and got out, throwing the gun first, then the knife. Hopwood said he heard the gun fall into the water, but heard the sound of the knife hit the gravel towpath.

The knife would never be found, but the gun was ultimately dredged from the canal on 23 August 1968 by police diver PC Philip Johns.[60] It was examined by John McCafferty, the Senior Experimental Officer for the Metropolitan Police Forensic Science Laboratory (who had also examined evidence collected at the Blind Beggar after the Cornell shooting), and he quickly found out why the gun had failed:

> *It is a German Mauser .32 calibre self loading pistol. It is commonly called an automatic. There were 4 live rounds of appropriate ammunition in the magazine. None was in the chamber. Missing from the pistol were the recoil spring and its guide. It was otherwise complete. The lack of spring & guide would prevent the pistol from working normally.*[61]

Alas, unlike with George Dixon, the failure of this particular firearm did not guarantee that its intended victim would get a second chance at life.

---

59 Statement by Henry Hopwood, undated (1968); DPP 2/4583, ff. 53-60 (National Archives).
60 Statement by PC Philip Johns, 9 September 1968; DPP 2/4583, f. 95 (National Archives).
61 Statement by John McCafferty, undated (1968); DPP 2/4583, ff. 62-64 (National Archives).

On their return to the flat, Hopwood and Hart delivered the clothes to the twins, who promptly changed into the newly supplied trousers, shirts and suit jackets. Ronnie was given a tie. Hart was then told to remove his own clothing and change and when all the offending articles were collected, they were stuffed into the case in which the other clothes had been brought from Vallance Road. Whilst this was happening, Hopwood, who had no telephone, was told to go to the phone box outside the Odeon on Hackney Road, call Charlie Kray, and get him to come over.

Charlie later claimed to have remonstrated with the twins when they told him what had happened and, angry and exasperated, returned home where he gave wife Dolly "some cock and bull story about the twins having a row."[62] But Ronnie Bender gave a different account, again from his 1969 appeal statement. He claimed that after being dropped off by the Lambrianou brothers, he went to Charlie's place as intended. The door was answered by Dolly Kray who told Bender that Charlie had recently gone out without saying where or why; he was obviously at Harry Hopwood's at this time. Bender came right out with it: "They have killed Jack McVitie." Dolly appeared shocked and looked about to faint. Her first instinct was to call somebody, that somebody being Tommy Cowley, who, after being told what had happened, arrived within twenty minutes. Bender explained the situation and, without mentioning the Lambrianou brothers, told him where the body of McVitie had been left.

Charlie Kray arrived presently, seemingly less than his usual good-humoured self, and was distracted and tetchy enough to refuse Bender a lift home. Cowley did likewise and so Bender walked from Poplar to Millwall where he spent the night on his sister's sofa.

Back at Hopwood's flat, the twins and Hart were all cleaned up. Their paper money was taken away to the kitchen to be burnt and their jewellery was vigorously cleaned by Hart and Hopwood. Now there was the question of what to do with the incriminating case full of bloodstained clothing. Hopwood quickly realised it was going to be down to him to get rid of it and so, in the absence of any real ideas, suggested that the case should be handed over to his wife's cousin, Percy Merricks. He obviously felt that Merricks could be relied upon to do what was required and again ventured out to the telephone box

---

62 Charlie Kray & Robin McGibbon; *Me and My Brothers* (London:Grafton 1988).

in Hackney Road to phone him. Hopwood was correct and Merricks arrived in about five minutes with his van.

> *Harry turned round & said to me "Would you get rid of this case?"*
> *I saw an ordinary attaché case standing on the floor. I just turned round and said "Yes". I don't think anything was said by anyone as to how I was to get rid of it. I just picked up the case & went out & put it in the van.*
>
> *I did not go back into the flat. I went to my small holding.*[63]

The small holding was forty miles away in East Farleigh, Kent, a small village on the banks of the Medway. There, Merricks, who was never once tempted to see what was inside, took the case to a rubbish heap, poured several gallons of petrol over it and set it on fire.[64]

As day was breaking, the twins finally left Hopwood - who at the last minute had found a handkerchief to cover Reggie's hand wound - and Hart at the flat, casually saying, "Thanks very much," as they went.[65] The elimination of all potential evidence surrounding McVitie's murder was continuing apace. Back at Evering Road, Carole Skinner and George Plummer were also finally left alone and everything had been scrubbed from top to bottom. The sitting-room carpet was still awaiting disposal and at one point Skinner unfolded it so she could see about half of it: she noticed "a number of blood splashes as though blood had dripped on to it. These splashes were not in a line but confined to one small area of the carpet."[66] It was later removed by Ronnie Bender and burnt by a sympathetic scrap yard dealer in Poplar High Street.[67]

The only other consideration was the obviously important issue of Jack McVitie's body, lying in the back of the Ford Zodiac in that little cobbled street in Rotherhithe. Surely somebody would notice it before long. Speed was of the essence and, whilst it was still dark, moves had been made to address the thorny problem of disposal: it was time to

---

63 Statement by Percy Merricks, undated (1968); DPP 2/4583, ff. 59-60 (National Archives).
64 Leonard Read & James Morton; *Nipper Read: The Man Who Nicked the Krays* (London: MacDonald & Co 1991). The following year 'Nipper' Read would send a team to East Farleigh to sift the ashes in the rubbish heap for evidence, where they found some suit buttons and the clasps from the attaché case.
65 Statement by Henry Hopwood, undated (1968); DPP 2/4583, ff. 53-60 (National Archives).
66 Statement by Carole Skinner, 9 September 1968; MEPO 2/11404, ff. 1175-6 (National Archives).
67 Martin Fido; *The Krays: Unfinished Business* (London: Carlton Books 1999).

call in 'The Undertaker',[68] Freddie Foreman. Rather thoughtlessly, the car had been left in what was effectively Foreman's patch, whereby any discovery would direct the police in his direction. The issue of McVitie's confrontation with Foreman at the 211 club only months before would also have looked interesting to the authorities. Foreman, therefore, was none too pleased at the situation.

How Foreman heard about McVitie being left in Rotherhithe differs in the telling. Ronnie Hart claimed that Charlie Kray had called at Foreman's pub, the Prince of Wales, to give him the bad news, yet Foreman claimed it was Tommy Cowley. By now it was 3.00 a.m.:

Now I've got this little ginger bastard, Tommy Cowley, ringing my doorbell, getting me out of bed at fucking three o'clock in the morning to tell me about Jack The Hat. There was two cars brought over. One was Ronnie Bender's Mini, which they left behind. They needed the other car to go back in.

It was bloodstained, the Mini. The twins and Hart left the murder scene in it, and Reggie's hand was cut, so it was bleeding in the Mini. The reason they brought it to my pub was to have it washed and cleaned. Why can't they wash a fucking Mini out themselves? Why bring it and dump it outside my pub?

But I don't know who was driving the second car. I didn't see anybody other than Cowley.[69]

The driver of the second car was in all probability Charlie Kray, who was obviously with Cowley that morning. If Foreman realised who it was, he wasn't letting on.

I waited till early morning when it's still dark, just before breaking daylight. About six o'clock, I started to move. It's pissing down, and I thought, well, that's handy, it's raining.

Cowley told me it had been left outside a church. My old pal Alf [Gerrard] was tailing me up. It took me a while cos there's plenty of churches in the area. But I reckoned they'd want to dump it as quick as possible after they come through the tunnel, and I just drove around until I found it... Anyway, I looked in and Jack was just

---

68 A nickname that Tony Lambrianou said was used occasionally to refer to Foreman owing to his ability to dispose of bodies, but which Foreman himself was none too enamoured with. This was mentioned in their book, *Getting It Straight: Villains Talking* (London: Sidgwick and Jackson 2001).

69 Ibid.

laying there, all curled up, in a candlewick bedspread. You can see it's a body by the shape of it, and I thought, Oh, that's fucking nice.[70]

Fortunately for Foreman, the few people who were walking past had their heads down because of the rain. Using a screwdriver, he forced the window and let himself in. He had a large set of various car keys to hand and he tried each one in the ignition until finding the one that worked; as the car spluttered into life, it was apparent that the windscreen wipers were not working and a little later, as Foreman and Gerrard drove to Camberwell to some lock-up garages, Gerrard let Foreman know one of the back lights wasn't working either. This could certainly increase the risk of being pulled over. It so happened that they got to Camberwell without any problem and, later that day, McVitie's body was put in a van and his Zodiac was taken to a wrecker's yard, after which it disappeared off the face of the earth.

On the Monday - 30 October - Foreman drove McVitie's body to the south coast where, with the help of his fishing contacts, Jack 'The Hat' joined Frank Mitchell and 'Ginger' Marks in the depths of the English Channel beyond Newhaven.[71]

◆

The day before McVitie's burial at sea, Jack Dickson went to Pellicci's Café on Bethnal Green Road and Charlie Kray was pulling up outside at the same time; it was around 11.30 a.m. There was a brief exchange, during which Charlie said that "the twins did McVitie last night",[72] which Dickson merely took as meaning there had been a big fight. After downing a quick cup of tea, Dickson left for Dodger Silver's Club. At about 6.00 p.m., Albert Donoghue arrived and passed on a message that the twins wanted to see Dickson at Tommy 'The Bear' Welch's flat in Tottenham, where they were now lying low. On arrival, Dickson was instructed to go to 178 Vallance Road and pick up some clothing as they were intending to go away for a few days.

---

70 Ibid.
71 Until Foreman confessed in 1997 to disposing of the bodies of McVitie and others, numerous rumours about what happened to them abounded; fed to pigs, chopped up and incinerated at the Cheshire Street Bath House or a smelting works, or buried with other bodies. Tony Lambrianou was adamant that McVitie had been secretly buried in an unmarked grave in a Gravesend Cemetery.
72 Statement by John Dickson, 14 September 1968; MEPO 2/11404, ff. 1281-1287 (National Archives).

Ronnie said to me, "We done McVitie last night" and I said, "How bad is he?", thinking they had only hurt him. His words were to the effect, "they had done him properly" but even then it did not register with me they had killed him. Reggie was in a bit of a daze and I saw one of his hands was swollen and appeared to have a big gash in it. I thought it looked bad enough to need a stitch.[73]

Dickson went off to Charlie's flat and saw Violet there, passing on the message about getting the twins some fresh clothing.

The following day, Connie Whitehead was summoned to the Tottenham flat by Ronnie. Unlike Dickson, who had no idea what had gone on, Whitehead had been on the periphery of the McVitie incident and was certainly complicit in the operation to clean up the evidence. It was no secret that Ronnie Kray hated Whitehead, although nobody ever really knew why. In some of his fits of anger and paranoia, Ronnie had given various members of the Firm the unenviable task of killing Whitehead, which, luckily for him, they made sure never came to pass. At Welch's flat, Reggie began telling Whitehead about how he should react and what to say if the police came snooping round him, only to be interrupted by Ronnie who said, "Don't fuck about with him." Ronnie wanted Reggie to tell Whitehead what had happened but, before he could do so, he interrupted again, this time brandishing a flick-knife.

"Me and Reggie done McVitie last night and keep your fucking mouth shut or otherwise I'll stick this through your head," Ronnie growled.[74] Reggie then gave Whitehead the reason why McVitie was killed, citing the abortive shooting of Leslie Payne and the withholding of the pre-payment money, and that he "tried to make us look cunts, and he was getting too flash anyway."[75]

Rumours about McVitie's whereabouts were quick to manifest themselves: Carole Skinner, whose flat was soon totally redecorated by Albert Donoghue, had heard that McVitie had been blown up or stabbed, but it was unknown by whom or where.[76] Kathleen Collins was drinking in the Coach and Horses one evening when a friend

---

73 Statement by John Dickson, 14 September 1968; MEPO 2/11404, ff. 1281-1287 (National Archives).

74 Statement by Cornelius Whitehead, 1 October 1968; MEPO 2/11404, ff. 1398-1400 (National Archives).

75 Ibid.

76 Statement by Carole Skinner, 13 May 1968; MEPO 2/11404, ff. 1158-60 (National Archives).

said to her, "What a tragedy about Jack getting blown up in his car on London Bridge," suggesting that it had happened in a collision with a milk float (a truly preposterous scenario).[77] Jack Dickson had also heard the story about McVitie being blown up. Not only was the misinformation service beginning to function, but money began to change hands to pay for any inconveniences, favours done, or the promise of silence. On the Monday when McVitie was buried at sea, Skinner received £40 in £10 notes from Vicky James at the Regency and would go on to receive regular small payments for a few weeks to come.[78] Whilst at work at the Green Dragon Club, George Plummer received money for new furniture after a relative of Tommy Welch had cleared the Evering Road basement of any further possible blood-stained items.[79] A while later, at the Carpenter's Arms, Percy Merricks received an envelope from Harry Hopwood's daughter containing £20.[80] No doubt numerous others were paid off. Hopwood, to his lasting unease, received a few threats from Ronnie Kray to keep him quiet, for, as they say, familiarity breeds contempt.

Perhaps to the relief of people like Hopwood and Whitehead, the twins took themselves away from London and went to Suffolk for a while to stay with Geoff Allen. The rumour mill turned and turned, and the damage limitation procedures continued in the twins' absence, but the fact that there had been no public mention of anything suspicious happening in Stoke Newington on that October weekend, and no official reports about McVitie being missing, gave the Firm the chance to breathe a sigh of relief. Foreman had worked on the premise of 'no body, no case' and, for the moment at least, Jack 'The Hat' had just vanished without causing so much as a ripple of concern anywhere. In fact, Sylvia Barnard waited a fortnight, until 13 November 1967, before filing a missing person's report at West Ham Police Station.[81]

Before moving on from this infamous and revolting episode in the Kray story, it is worth looking at Reggie's motives for what he did that

77 Statement of Kathleen Collins, 14 May 1968; MEPO 2/11404, ff. 1459-1462 (National Archives).
78 Statement by Carole Skinner, 8 August 1968; MEPO 2/11404, ff. 1161-1174 (National Archives).
79 Statement by John Dickson, 24 September 1968; MEPO 2/11404, ff. 1288-1292 (National Archives).
80 Statement by Percy Merricks, undated (1968); DPP 2/4583, ff. 59-60 (National Archives).
81 A copy of the report, made by Sergeant Anthony Mepham, can be found at MEPO 2/11404, ff. 1432-3 (National Archives).

October night in 1967, a night which would go on to change his life, and the lives of several others, forever. Both Lambrianou brothers, particularly Tony, felt that Reggie probably did not intend to kill McVitie; Tony would repeatedly pronounce, in print and on television, that he firmly believed Reggie did not mean to commit murder that night. Much of this may have been Tony's attempt to assuage the guilt he felt for literally luring McVitie to his death – it cannot have been an easy thing to live with. However, such is the fragility of villains' recollections that in his personal memoir[82] Tony said that McVitie, owing to his violent and unpredictable nature, which had been building up fast over two years, had it coming to him in any case. Freddie Foreman agreed that Reggie did not intend to kill, citing the very public nature of the crime, in front of several witnesses, including non-Firm members like the Mills brothers, Trevor Stone and Terry Clulow, as reasons to exonerate Reggie of any premeditated intent.

What is certainly clear is that Reggie intended to harm McVitie, probably seriously, to teach him a long-overdue lesson. He had a gun and as far as everybody who saw it was concerned, he had every intention of using it. Reggie was getting pretty trigger-happy by this point and it is possible that, in an alternative scenario, McVitie would have been knocked about a bit and sent off to Dr. Blasker with the obligatory bullet wound in the leg. But by the time he had arrived at the Regency and spoke to Tony Barry, Reggie was well gone on alcohol, and very likely pills. His judgement was profoundly affected and his mental state was still chaotic so soon after the death of Frances.

But this is not meant to be an apologist's stance on Reggie Kray, the murderer. The man himself said a few telling things during his life, until he was literally drawing his dying breaths. Not long after the killing, Tony Lambrianou asked Reggie one night in the Carpenter's Arms why he had done it; he was looking for a reason, a justification. Reggie could only say, "He was just a nuisance."[83] From the 1968 committal hearings onwards, Reggie never openly admitted to the murder; that is until the publication of *Our Story* in 1988. In that book, he claimed that "...I didn't intend to kill him – just to give him a bloody good hiding..." and that the gun was taken as a precaution in case McVitie "started anything nasty."[84]

82 Tony Lambrianou with Carol Clerk; *Inside the Firm* (London: Smith Gryphon 1991).
83 Ibid.
84 Reggie & Ronnie Kray, with Fred Dinenage; *Our Story* (London: Sidgwick and Jackson 1988).

Three years later, in *Born Fighter*, Reggie was telling a different story. Using the shared meal in the Regency to sound McVitie out, to see how he responded to the noises of disapproval about his behaviour from the Kray camp, Reggie considered that McVitie's arrogance had caused him to fail the test. Reggie paid for McVitie's meal, "knowing it would be his last... During my conversation with McVitie at the restaurant, he continued to talk himself into an early grave... I then left the Regency that October night knowing that the next time I saw 'The Hat' I would kill him."[85]

Martin Fido's observation - that Reggie over-egged the distasteful characteristics of his foe to justify his later actions – was quite apparent in what he said in the pages of *Born Fighter*. Importantly, however, he did say that he most definitely intended to kill McVitie. Almost ten years later, lying on his death-bed with only days left before succumbing to terminal cancer, Reggie had one last chance to put the record straight in front of a television camera. In what was his last ever interview, Reggie Kray was asked about that night in 1967 and the man whose life he ended:

> *I wanted to get rid of him... He was very uncouth... he was loud and aggressive, which I find is a vexation to the spirit... Indeed, he was just something that was erm... the sort of thing I despised...*
>
> *I thought I'd been pushed into it too quick, because to me it was common sense to wait a bit longer. I don't say you could prolong a thing like that for ever... I see it was getting a bit close... so it's still debatable... I say I had a lot of frustration in me. And anger. Probably more anger than I had had on any other night in my life.*[86]

Did "pushed into it too quick" relate to Ronnie's now infamous taunts that he had killed George Cornell and that Reggie now needed to show his commitment and do his own murder? Nearly every member of the Firm who gave interviews or wrote memoirs refers to these taunts. Sometimes Ronnie would be merciless in his ribbing of his brother and often Reggie would lose his temper in frustration. All this must have counted for something.

Reggie showed no remorse for killing McVitie, even as he was about to meet his maker; in truth, he never had done, although he did make the death-bed concession of saying that he was sorry for the effect it

---

85 Reggie Kray; *Born Fighter* (London: Arrow Books 1991).
86 Interviewed in *The Krays – The Final Word* documentary (DVD; WMV 2001).

had on his victim's family. He had done what he had done and there was no point in trying to change it; for Reggie, such behaviour was "negative."

Like George Cornell, Jack McVitie died as a result of a long-term build-up of incidents and other exacerbating circumstances; but unlike Ronnie's cold, arrogant execution of Cornell in the Blind Beggar, Reggie killed McVitie in a chaotic assault fuelled by anger, frustration, hatred, alcohol, drugs and no little amount of goading. It was a mess. As for the still-unanswered question of whether Reggie intended McVitie to die that night: people can assume what they want and they can pick through the claims and counterclaims for all they're worth, but only one person, Reggie Kray – and just maybe his twin – would be in any real position to give anything approaching a definitive answer to that. And one imagines that even if he were alive today, he still wouldn't be able to bring himself to do it.

SIXTEEN

CULTURE OF VIOLENCE

The twins' brief stay with Geoff Allen in Suffolk was a chance for them to escape the aftermath of the murder of Jack McVitie, and perhaps recharge their batteries and contemplate what to do next. It is no secret that the Krays, despite being the hardened product of the gritty East End, had a distinct love of the countryside, Suffolk in particular, a feeling that had stayed with them from their brief year of evacuation during the war. Allen's current home was Gedding Hall, a "rambling pseudo-Elizabethan country house",[1] complete with large gates and a moat which in itself was home to black swans.[2] The Krays, particularly Ronnie, aspired to the kind of life Allen was leading, and the thought of decamping to the country as 'Lords of the Manor' living off the proceeds of their dealings in the big city was growing more enticing as negotiating the chaotic life of London villainy became more challenging. But it wasn't all relaxation; it was also an excellent venue to meet, for the first time, a man who was to play a big part in the Kray story for decades to come, the author John Pearson.

Pearson, a former Fleet Street journalist who had worked with Ian Fleming at the *Sunday Times* (and who wrote Fleming's biography

---

1 John Pearson; *The Cult of Violence* (London: Orion Books 2001).
2 Gedding Hall was established as a fortified manor house by the Chamberlayne family in the early 16th century, although it has been said that some of it goes back as far as 1480. Much of the manor house itself was incorporated into the original buildings in 1897. In 1968, Geoff Allen sold Gedding Hall to former Rolling Stones bassist Bill Wyman, who still lives there today.

after the James Bond creator's death)[3] had been living in Rome and was 'between jobs' when, in November 1967, he received a call from his American publisher Frank Taylor, who was excited about a meeting he had had a month or two before with "the twins who run the London underworld."[4] It appears that the Krays were extremely anxious to have a book written about themselves, not surprising considering their egotistical love of being in the limelight.

Pearson was given an all-expenses paid ticket to London which included a stay at the Ritz Hotel. On the morning of 9 November 1967, he was picked up from the Ritz by Tommy Cowley and Tommy 'The Bear' Welch in a silver-grey Mercedes and taken to Gedding Hall to meet the brothers. Short of hearing various rumours about one of the twins having dubious dealings with a member of the House of Lords a few years previously, Pearson was none too familiar with the Krays, so he was predictably impressed by Gedding Hall, which he assumed was something to do with the men he was due to meet.

Geoff Allen made the introductions in his grand, oak-panelled dining room; present were Charlie, the twins, Cowley, Tommy 'The Bear' and a number of other men whom Pearson never got to speak to. After being introduced to Charlie, Pearson was acquainted with the twins, first Ronnie, then Reggie:

> *Ron Kray would have fascinated Ian Fleming, with his strong yet clammy handshake, the way he spoke as if suffering from a hidden speech impediment, the big gold bracelet watch and the eyes that seemed to bulge with painfully suppressed aggression. Here was Dr. No and Goldfinger and Mr. Big in one extraordinary person.*
>
> *Although they were obviously identical twins – the same height, of around five foot ten, the same dark hair and eyes of some gypsy forebear, and much the same mannerisms, Reg Kray was quicker and thinner than his twin, with a certain shifty charm. When we sat down for lunch, it was Reg who did the talking.*[5]

Reggie explained, over a frugal meal of tinned ham and tongue, coleslaw and light ale, that he and his brothers were planning to retire from big time crime and that now they felt that it was time

---

3   *The Life of Ian Fleming* (New York: McGraw-Hill Book Company 1966). Pearson would also write *James Bond: The Authorised Biography* in 1973.

4   John Pearson; *The Cult of Violence* (London: Orion Books 2001). The meeting had been arranged via Taylor's Mafia connections.

5   Ibid.

for somebody to record their 'achievements' and to set the record straight. Pearson was naively taken in by the charisma of the Krays and their apparent success, unaware, of course, that Gedding Hall, the flash cars and the free flight and stay at the Ritz were put together as a package of deception to make Pearson feel suitably impressed. Nonetheless, they all felt that there was a decent book in the Kray story. And so there was. John Pearson had entered the Krays' world at a dangerous time. As they made conversation in the imposing dining hall, Pearson noticed Reggie's bandaged hand; when he asked how the injury happened, Reggie replied glibly, "Gardenin'".[6]

It was a successful meeting, although Pearson's next experience of the twins' world could not have been any more different. A few weeks later, he once again flew over from Rome and, having asked the twins to show him their East End origins, was put up in Flat 2, Blackwall Buildings, just off of Vallance Road:[7] Ronnie had apparently said, "I'll show him the fucking East End,"[8] probably his idea of a joke. It was the antithesis of Gedding Hall, a squalid one-bedroom flat with mildew, cockroaches, bare lightbulbs, boarded-up windows, a payphone and a second-hand television. The bed was propped up on one corner by a packing crate. It was used by the Firm for meetings and, strangely, given the conditions, drinking parties, and occasionally people would crash out there after a particularly long night; it was known to all as 'The Dungeon'. Pearson had to make do with the arrangement, but was interested in the contrast between this rotting Victorian slum and Gedding Hall; two bedraggled and totally unappealing prostitutes, 'Tall Tess' and 'Trixie', arrived shortly after he did, a comfort offering from Reggie, but all they got up to was small-talk and tea-drinking. A while after the ladies left, Reggie himself arrived and took the bewildered author to the Old Horns pub where he was to meet the 1967 version of the Firm, quite an experience in itself.

The noisy, smoke-filled pub had essentially been commandeered by the Krays for the London villainy to meet their biographer. Ronnie

6   Ibid.
7   Built in Thomas Street (later Fulbourne Street, then Lomas Street) Whitechapel c.1890 by the Great Eastern Railway Company to replace homes demolished during the widening of the London Blackwall Railway. It has been alleged that George Cornell once lived in the Buildings; however, the claims (from www.guysinger.com) do not seem to be backed up with hard evidence. Having been in a state of deterioration for many decades, they were demolished in 1969.
8   Tony Lambrianou with Carol Clerk; *Inside the Firm* (London: Smith Gryphon 1991).

had brought along two midgets who tugged at Pearson's trouser leg and threatened to kill him if he didn't write the truth. Conversations with associates like Teddy Berry (the landlord), Sammy Lederman and 'Nobby' Clarke veered in the same reverential direction, in favour of the twins. It was, of course, another set up, engineered by the Krays to show them in the best light possible in the less than glamorous surroundings of their 'manor'.

Bizarrely, the arrival of John Pearson, another innocent drawn into the Krays' uncertain world, came at a time when attention should have been the last thing the Firm wanted. Ronnie and Reggie had now murdered one man apiece, been instrumental in the execution of another, were still reaping the benefits of their links with the Mafia, were branching out into drug trafficking and conspiracy to murder (courtesy of Alan Cooper) and, worryingly, were becoming increasingly prone to random acts of extreme violence. Indeed, two associates, 'Mad' Teddy Smith and one of their occasional drivers, Billy Frost, had disappeared under suspicious circumstances, presumed dead at the behest of the Krays. In the case of Frost, he would later resurface, alive and well, to become an outspoken commentator and critic in the media (alongside his old friend Lenny Hamilton) on all things Kray, but Teddy Smith's disappearance is an enduring mystery to this day.

Sometime after the Frank Mitchell affair, Smith, who had been heavily involved and obviously knew more than was healthy for him, just disappeared off the face of the earth. Whenever anybody asked of his whereabouts, people would just say things like, "Teddy Smith is a goner," without venturing why.[9] The rumour has often been that he had been done away with at the behest of the twins, although the 'official' Kray line was that he had emigrated to Australia.[10] Frankie Fraser, on his website, claimed that Smith was indeed alive and well, and had "headed for the sunshine, and peace and quiet" after his arguments with Ronnie Kray had become too much for him.[11] Years later, as more former members of the Firm spoke out about those dangerous times, the suggestion that Reggie was responsible for killing Smith became a favoured opinion in the media, although few of the old faces (Lenny

9   Leonard Read, quoted in Lenny Hamilton & Craig Cabell; *Getting Away With Murder* (London: John Blake 2006).
10 Ibid.
11 'Reggie Kray's Parting Gift', posted 29 March 2001 at www.madfrankiefraser.co.uk/ frankiefraser.htm?viewpoints/views16.htm~mainFrame.

Hamilton notwithstanding[12]) said as much. Interviewed in 2001, Albert Donoghue even claimed to have been present the moment he vanished:

> *He showed up in the Regency, drunk as a skunk, shouting about Mitchell. We got him in the car, taken him round to the twins' house and he said, "Stop the car, I wanna take a leak." So he goes behind a house, or something, and that's it, never see him again.*[13]

Significantly, Reggie Kray was asked outright during his death-bed interview in August 2000 if there had been any more killings. His only reply was, "One... one."[14] Any chance of him openly confessing to another murder he had yet to be charged with would have been out of the question in his lifetime and again, just as when Reggie recounted his reasoning behind killing Jack McVitie, the possibility of him opening up and laying down the absolute truth would have been entirely dependent on what he wanted people to know at any given time. The real facts about the fate of Teddy Smith, if Reggie was indeed responsible for his disappearance, have been buried with him.

The willingness to inflict violent retribution during this period appeared to be a constant threat. In late 1967, Ronnie Hart and Ronnie Bender were sent by Ronnie Kray to 'do' a man who worked at Romford Market, as a favour to boxing friend Roy 'Pretty Boy' Shaw, who was in prison at the time.[15] Bender quickly distanced himself from the plot, so on the day, 'Scotch' Jack Dickson drove an armed Ronnie Hart to Romford to do the deed, but by then it had already been agreed that it "would be silly to shoot the geezer and get twenty years all for Ronnie Kray."[16] Hart actually had no intention of "doing the fellow" and when he returned from the abortive shooting, he told Dickson that he had thrown the gun away. Sensibly, Hart told Ronnie Kray that the job had been done, Ronnie believed him, and no more

12 Hamilton claimed that, apart from Smith, the Krays had been responsible for the deaths of several others, including Brian Scully, Billy Bannister, Tony Mafia and an unnamed 'rent boy'.
13 Interviewed in *The Krays – The Final Word* documentary (DVD; WMV 2001).
14 Ibid.
15 Shaw, also known as 'The Mean Machine', had known the Krays since the early 1960s, and was criminally active in the East End, as well as a notorious unlicensed boxer. He later became a millionaire through real estate investment and a minor media figure. He died in 2012.
16 Statement by John Dickson, 14 September 1968; MEPO 2/11404, ff. 1281-7 (National Archives).

was said.

The amount of orders being given out to do such things, by Ronnie in particular, had caused a significant shift in the loyalties of the Firm. Reggie and Ronnie were often referred to as 'Gert and Daisy',[17] behind their backs of course. There was no longer the promise of allegiance through respect or the guarantee of lucrative villainy, as fear was quickly becoming a significant motivator; the disappearances of Billy Frost and Teddy Smith, the occasional suggestions to kill off Connie Whitehead and the ease with which Frank Mitchell and Jack McVitie, very much part of the Krays' world, had been eliminated must have made the members of the Firm realise that nobody was free from the threat of serious harm or even death if they stepped out of line. Even steadfast henchmen like Albert Donoghue were beginning to feel the strain:

> Generally the mood on the Firm was dipping fast. The laughs were getting fewer and fewer. Ronnie was on a one-way trip, sinking deeper and deeper. He had become a slob. At the morning meets he'd sit there in a collarless shirt, with braces and baggy trousers, chain-smoking and infecting us all with his depression like a plague, barking manic orders just like Hitler must have done in his bunker during the final days.
>
> Around the murders the twins were getting even more paranoid. Reggie was drinking more and more. Instead of getting drunk once or twice a week, he was drunk practically every night. Ronnie would hole up with crates of brown ale and whether he was drunk or not, to him everybody was a spy, everybody was trying to fuck the twins up.[18]

Even when Billy Exley had a heart attack and was cooped up in the London Hospital undergoing treatment Reggie Kray was suspicious, certain in the belief that he was faking it just to get off the Firm. He went so far as to visit Exley and study his medical charts, even though he would have had no idea what the data represented. In this case, Reggie's paranoia served him well; although the ailing Exley had indeed had a heart attack, he was by now utterly disenchanted with

---

17 As maintained by Albert Donoghue. Gert and Daisy were a British female comedy act particularly remembered for their contribution to film and radio entertainment during the Second World War. They were sisters Elsie and Doris Waters, whose brother, Horace, was also an actor working under the stage name Jack Warner, most famous for his role in the popular TV police drama *Dixon of Dock Green*.

18 Albert Donoghue & Martin Short; *The Enforcer* (London: John Blake 2002).

the Krays. One night, not long after Exley's discharge from hospital, Jack Dickson went to his small house off Brick Lane to invite him to the pub at Ronnie's request. Exley looked ill, unsurprisingly, but he was resolute in his feelings about the Krays:

> *I've finished with them. I have had enough. I've been loyal to them for years and now I have been ill and they didn't even send a few quid round for my wife. I don't care what happens, they will never use me again.*
>
> *I think they are through. All they are getting around them now is a lot of idiots. You should try to get out before it's too late. Do you think they've forgotten about our involvement with Mitchell? Or that bird Lisa or Lennie? We all know too much. Either we will be reading about them in the papers or they will be reading about us.*[19]

In addition, it was becoming known, thanks to the Krays' police informants, that 'Nipper' Read was back on the case.

◆

Detective Superintendent Read had begun his reactivated investigation into the Krays in September. To his horror, when he reacquainted himself with the material that had been gathered over the years, not one new piece of evidence, intelligence or information had been added since Read's days on the Kray case back in 1965. Because the documentation regarding the Cornell murder and the Mitchell case was not officially linked to the Krays, such material was rightly absent; and yet, despite the information that Tommy Butler had gathered from Bobby Teale about the Krays since the spring of 1966 - which resulted in the arrest of the twins, the failed identification parades and their subsequent release – there was no record of any of it.

Read realised that he had to effectively start from scratch yet again. He also realised at an early stage that he would need to make sure that the Firm was out of action in some way before he could get key witnesses to talk – fear of the Krays was something that Read was only too aware of. But in his previous dealings with anybody associated with the Kray enterprise, Read had always maintained respectful relations with his targets and did not use bullying tactics to get what

---

19 John Dickson; *Murder Without Conviction* (London: Sidgwick and Jackson 1986).

he wanted. Knowing that it would not all be entirely straightforward, he drew up a list of thirty-two people he wanted to speak to, many of whom were former members of the Firm, or those who he knew may well be becoming disenchanted with the way things were now going.

There were plenty of rejections. However, one associate who seemed open to dialogue was Billy Exley: Read was aware of his health problems and felt that he was becoming distanced from the Krays sufficiently to open up. Their first meeting (Read approached everybody personally), at Exley's home in December 1967, did not produce any information straight away, but Read could tell by Exley's reaction that here was somebody who had had enough of the twins and who could well crack at a later date. Realising that he was putting himself in an awkward situation, Exley made his position clear. "Don't worry about me," he said. "If they come looking for me I've a shotgun behind the door and that's what they'll get. Don't worry, it's licensed."[20]

Read made more headway with Leslie Payne that same month:

> *He was far more intelligent than most of those I saw, the sort of guy who might want to do a deal, but I had to remember he was a most experienced, even brilliant, con-man. I knew he couldn't be bullshitted, but he might be tempted.*[21]

According to Leslie Payne, a supposed 'problem' with the number plates on his car was used as an excuse to pull him in, whereupon Read made his initial overtures.[22] Read said that the initial meeting was held at the Lyons Corner House in the Strand, where they got to know each other a little better as they chatted over their coffees. Read discovered that Payne no longer associated with the twins because of his disapproval of their increasingly violent ways and their stupidity when it came to business: he wanted the company of like-minded people in his schemes and the twins and their hangers-on could not be relied upon to fulfil that requirement. Payne knew 'Nipper' Read of old and realised that this was a police officer who could be reasonable (otherwise he would never have agreed to see him) and, after the initial cautious discussion, further appointments were arranged. Eventually, after numerous meetings, Payne agreed to

---

20 Leonard Read & James Morton; *Nipper Read: The Man Who Nicked the Krays* (London: MacDonald & Co 1991).

21 Ibid.

22 Leslie Payne; *The Brotherhood* (London: Michael Joseph 1973).

talk about what he knew of the Krays' affairs: Read had heard through the grapevine that the twins had wanted Payne liquidated and, but for McVitie's unreliability, may well have been successful, a fact that alarmed the normally unflappable 'Man with the Briefcase' enough to drop his guard and consent to making a statement.

Although Payne was aware that he would be implicated in many of the crimes he would be outlining, Read promised that he would do as much as he could to help Payne avoid prosecution, a technique that would be used throughout the enquiries and which would ultimately produce the results Read's team were after. The Director of Public Prosecutions agreed with Read that Payne could have immunity from prosecution regarding any charge except murder and violence. Payne's only crimes were related to fraud, and thus, with a deal struck, over numerous days he sat in a quiet room in a police section house at Marylebone Station and gave Read a 146-page statement, making him effectively the very first 'Supergrass'.[23]

Leslie Payne was a superb witness; his sharp intelligence and excellent memory furnished the Kray investigation with a tremendous amount of information about the long-firm frauds and the various companies created to execute them, the selling of stolen bearer bonds, examples of blackmail, drug-running and, of course, the numerous acts of violence. Facts, figures, names and addresses; all were set out to the delight of Read and his team. It wasn't long before Payne used his charm on Freddie Gore, his long-standing business partner, who quickly came on-side to give a statement of his own. It was a major breakthrough in the case against the Krays.

The sheer weight of information given by Payne and Gore required an enlargement of the investigation team, in order to corroborate all the details now being received. The complex jigsaw of the stolen bearer bonds was assigned to Inspector Frank Holt, and two women police officers, Sheila Acton and Pat Allen, were also brought in. Chief Inspector Harry Mooney, later to become such a valuable link in looking after key witnesses, joined the squad. As the information

23 The term 'Supergrass' was coined by journalists in the early 1970s to differentiate a regular informer from one who testified against big criminal organisations in high-profile trials, resulting in the conviction of many individuals. Derek 'Bertie' Smalls has always been considered the first well-known 'Supergrass' after he turned Queen's evidence - against literally everybody he had ever worked with - in 1972; he struck a deal with the Director of Public Prosecutions for his information and was never prosecuted for any of the crimes he did himself. His case has many of the attributes of Leslie Payne's situation almost five years previously.

rolled in, Read found out about the assault on Lenny Hamilton at Esmeralda's Barn (as Payne had witnessed it), and Hamilton too became a key witness, giving his first statement as early as February 1968.[24] With Hamilton, and others who were reluctant at first to give Read anything, a unique proviso was written into the deal, "that the statements wouldn't be used without their consent or until such time as we had substantial evidence to arrest the Krays."[25] In fact, many statements would go unsigned until those who gave them were ready to commit.

And there was more. Around the same time that Payne was granted immunity, Sylvia Barnard, Jack McVitie's partner, walked into New Scotland Yard, again to report him missing. Her previous approach, in November 1967, had seen little action, as she was unaware of any further information at the time that could help the police, but here was yet another avenue for Read to explore.

By early 1968, the Kray investigation was gaining ground quickly. 'Nipper' Read had learnt by his previous mistakes when it came to dealing with the Krays, and his revised investigative methodology, unconventional as it was turning out to be, was proving profitable for the shrewd Detective Superintendent and his now extremely busy team.

◆

By the start of 1968, Braithwaite House, an eighteen-storey modern tower block overlooking Bunhill Row, had become the new Kray family home.[26] The edifice of concrete and steel, utterly in keeping with the architectural style of 1960s urban development, cast its long shadow over Bunhill Fields burial ground, the final resting place of such luminaries as Daniel Defoe, William Blake, John Bunyan and Susanna Wesley. Today, such soulless architecture is considered in a poor light, but back then, many of the new occupants felt lucky to have homes free of damp and mice, and with proper bathrooms.

The Kray and Lee families had been relocated gradually to their new accommodation, all of which would have been palatial compared to Vallance Road, despite lacking the much-missed character and,

24 Statement by Lenny Hamilton, 28 February 1968; MEPO 2/11387, ff. 684-694 (National Archives).
25 Leonard Read & James Morton; *Nipper Read: The Man Who Nicked the Krays* (London: MacDonald & Co 1991).
26 Proposed in 1963 as part of the Banner Street housing project, it was completed in 1967.

perhaps more significantly, all those memories. Violet and Charlie Snr were first to go, moving into Flat 43 of Braithwaite House, on the ninth floor. "If you'd seen our tears you'd have thought she was emigrating instead of going a short bus ride to a flat in Bunhill Row," cousin Rita Smith later recalled.[27] Over time, the Vallance Road terrace that had seen so much happiness and sadness began to empty in readiness for demolition; Grandad and Nanny Lee, now in their 80s, had become stuck in their ways enough to be dragged protesting to a maisonette in Cheshire Street; Aunt May and Albert would later move to the brand new Charles Dickens House in Mansford Street, Bethnal Green, and cousin Rita ended up in nearby Blythendale House.[28]

Braithwaite House became the new centre of Kray operations, and the airy living room, with its huge picture windows commanding excellent views of the City of London, would immediately replace its cosy Vallance Road equivalent as a venue for regular Firm meetings. But the Krays had also acquired another property in Suffolk, demonstrating, at least, that their bid for a life in the country was becoming a reality. Perhaps with no little help from Geoff Allen, they had found a house in Bildeston, Suffolk, not far from Hadleigh, and had snapped it up for £12,000,[29] putting the property in their mother's name. Called The Brooks, it was a potential idyll, set in eight acres of land, with stables and a paddock and a small stream running alongside it. It needed a great deal of work, and some of it was almost derelict, but the twins were excited enough to get their hands dirty redecorating, assisted, of course, by a team of builders. Ronnie in particular seemed to delight in his new surroundings and was a different man to the one who scowled and threatened back in London. He had bought a donkey, named Figaro, which was kept in the paddock, and he let local children ride it round the grounds.[30] He spoke optimistically of living there full-time - accompanied by 'Duke' Osbourne, who was about to be released from prison - as a man of leisure, and of being driven to London occasionally for 'business.'[31] Violet Kray was in her element and, despite a lifetime growing up

---

27 Joe Lee, Rita Smith and Peter Gerrard; *Inside the Kray Family* (London: Carlton 2008).

28 Both Charles Dickens House and Blythendale House were opened in 1969, suggesting that the Vallance Road properties were still partially occupied up until that time.

29 Charlie Kray & Robin McGibbon; *Me and My Brothers* (London: Grafton 1988).

30 John Pearson; *The Cult of Violence* (London: Orion Books 2001).

31 Ibid.

in the grime of East London, she felt right at home at The Brooks, enjoying the company of her family, making big Sunday lunches for one and all and being very much the matriarch once again.

But once back in London, the Kray twins had no option but to revert to type. Suffolk seemed a million miles away from 'Nipper' Read, the nagging problems with the Firm, and the constant, cyclical routine of earning and spending. John Pearson, as an outside observer, was quick to notice that Reggie did not share his brother's confidence:

> As he was not living in Ron's schizophrenic dreamland he knew exactly what was happening. He had seen through Cooper from the start, he knew what Nipper and his men were up to, and he knew by now that there was no escape.
>
> Reg was no Colonel, no General Gordon, not even Al Capone or Meyer Lansky. He was a wretched, guilt-torn gangster, haunted by his dead wife's ghost and recurring nightmares of the killing of Jack McVitie...
>
> Whenever I saw him now there was always the same anxious face, the bloodshot eyes, the haunted expression.[32]

At this stage, Reggie was still drinking heavily and taking pills – usually five milligrams of Valium, three times daily - in an attempt to quell his anxiety.[33] Ronnie, still fuelled by his illness and his feelings of being the untouchable 'Colonel', expressed his feelings of power with renewed fervour; he had even ordered two pythons from Harrods, one of which was named 'Read' by Reggie[34] in honour of the persistent police officer who was now on his tail (the other was named 'Gerrard'). David Bailey came to Braithwaite House to take some appropriately menacing photographs; in one of them, the twins appear to be laughing as they manhandle the two snakes, but Ronnie's expression of mirth is decidedly sinister, in what can only be described as the face of a madman – and probably with good reason.

One morning at Braithwaite House, Ronnie said he wanted Ronnie Bender to kill Frankie Shea. Bender said he could not, as by now he was living with Shea's former partner 'Bubbles'; it was typical of the moral dilemmas the twins were fond of putting their associates into. On Bender's refusal, Ronnie flew into a rage, yelling, "All right then

---

32 John Pearson; *The Cult of Violence* (London: Orion Books 2001).
33 CRIM 1/4927, f. 1321 (National Archives).
34 *Sydney Morning Herald*, 18 February 1973.

fuck off, you're sacked – and if you tell her I'll do you."[35] Later, when Reggie chastised Ronnie for the terrifying threats, Ronnie replied, "Well, you don't keep dogs and bark yourself. They've either got to do as they're told or fuck off. They're either with us or against us."[36]

Ronnie's acts of violence, when they came, were typically unpredictable, and becoming increasingly frequent, and all for the slightest reasons. John Pearson got a huge shock when he was present at the Old Horns pub and Ronnie approached a man named Johnny Wakefield, known as 'Johnny Guitar', and slashed him down the face with a glass for no other reason than "for looking at him the wrong way."[37] On another occasion, during a social gathering in a West End club, boxer Johnny Cardew sent over some drinks to the Krays' table, "including the fat one", meaning Ronnie. Tony Lambrianou later remembered that Ronnie said to Cardew, "'I wanna see you in the toilet,' and left half his face on the floor."[38]

When he wasn't consolidating his position as the most feared villain in London, Ronnie Kray was also looking to extend the influence and power of the Kray operation. Alan Cooper was seen by Ronnie as a veritable 'Mr. Fix It', who could, and seemed more than willing to, make Ronnie's dreams of expansion come true. They spoke again of narcotics; Cooper knew the European drugs market, and felt that this was an easy way to make considerable amounts of money. There was also talk of large-scale gold smuggling, illegal trafficking of Asian immigrants from Belgium and, most significantly, increased links with the North American Syndicates. For a while, the Krays' associations with the Mafia-controlled West End club scene and the stolen bonds rackets suggested that more could be done between the big gangs of America and Britain. It was decided that a trip to the United States was calling, but Reggie, increasingly suspicious of Cooper, wanted none of it. Ronnie, on the other hand, was excited, and once he'd made his mind up about something, there was no going back.

The only problem was Ronnie's criminal record. He had been refused entry to the USA before, and since then the Krays had risen in notoriety, a sure way of being barred yet again. But Cooper was

35 Statement by Ronald Hart, 3 September 1968; DPP 2/4583 (National Archives).
36 Ibid.
37 Freddie Foreman & Tony Lambrianou; *Getting It Straight: Villains Talking* (London: Sidgwick and Jackson 2001).
38 Ibid.

confident that it could be arranged, so on 2 April 1968 Cooper and Ronnie, accompanied by old Kray stalwart Dickie Morgan, flew to Paris on a chartered flight; Morgan had not long before been released from a nine-month prison sentence for stealing a car[39] and was probably only too happy to get a free trip to the Big Apple with his old friend.

It was in the French capital that Cooper worked his magic. As he busied himself at the American Embassy, he found no impediment to getting Ronnie and Morgan their required visas to America. It was almost too good to be true, but everybody, particularly Ronnie, was happy that the American trip to meet the movers and shakers of the Mafia was going ahead as planned. On 3 April, they flew to New York, where they were met by Mafia go-between Joey Kaufman. Ronnie had met Kaufman on a number of occasions in London when the Jewish Sicilian had come over on business in relation to the Mafia-controlled West End clubs and the stolen bonds operation, and, on his home turf, Kaufman made Ronnie and the others very much at home. He booked them rooms at the Warwick Hotel on West 54th Street and immediately settled into his role as host, introducing Ronnie to various boxers (including Rocky Marciano), taking him to clubs, and when needed, supplying him with a young boy or two, all the while footing the bill.

However, when the time came for Ronnie to reacquaint himself with the illustrious figures of the New York underworld, they appeared to be strangely unavailable. Angelo Bruno and George Raft were out of town or unavailable, so Ronnie had to make do with little tours of Harlem, Brooklyn, and other New York locales where he would meet old-time criminals whom Kaufman knew. There was no stellar line-up of big time Mafiosi, yet Ronnie appeared to be enjoying the trip nonetheless. Cooper appeared to be less comfortable: he seemed anxious, kept disappearing to telephone 'important' people, and Dickie Morgan noticed he stuttered more than usual. Morgan also noticed that they were being followed by two men who looked for all the world like plain-clothes detectives.[40] Something wasn't right, but Ronnie was enjoying the experience so much that he didn't seem to notice.

On 7 April, a discussion was held regarding "a shortage of 'readies', or money", and it was suggested that this could be rectified by doing

39 CRIM 1/4927 (National Archives),
40 John Pearson; *The Profession of Violence* (London: Weidenfeld & Nicolson 1972).

a favour for one Bernie Silver, which would allow the Krays to have a large equity in a club in London as a reward.[41] Silver, alongside Maltese 'Big' Frank Mifsud, headed a crime gang in London known simply as 'The Syndicate', which was active in pornography, prostitution and racketeering.[42] During their heyday, between 1967 and 1972, The Syndicate had most of the Metropolitan Police's Obscene Publications Squad on their payroll,[43] and thus exerted considerable influence. At this point, discussion only touched on the opportunities, and the nature of the favour was not divulged. The matter would be followed up in London, for, on 8 April, Ronnie decided it was time to go home.

The trip to New York did not really open up any new leads or opportunities, but Ronnie had returned jubilant and ready to take things forward. He returned to an unusual situation. Only three members of the Firm had been aware of Ronnie's trip; old time friends such as Johnny Squibb and Tommy Welch were noticeable by their unusual absence and those that still hung around were now becoming concerned for the future.[44] Much of this was the very real fear that the police were about to pounce; that 'Nipper' Read and his team were making the required inroads, were finding out about the serious crimes of murder, and that it was only a matter of time before the shelf-life of the Firm would expire. Albert Donoghue later recalled that,

> The law wasn't the only danger. A far bigger danger was the twins themselves. At any moment they might turn against you directly, and try and finish you off. There was always the chance that, even by accident, you could do something that would spark them off. You could be done for saying the wrong word. You might talk to somebody who, they've heard, is co-operating with the police, so they might think you were in there with the traitor, cooking something up, preparing your own destiny.[45]

Secret code words were established between Firm members, to tip each other off if one had been ordered to 'do' the other, and anybody who had gone missing for a time was automatically deemed to have

41 Statement by Alan Bruce Cooper, 17 July 1968; CRIM 1/4927 (National Archives).
42 Donald Thomas; *Villains' Paradise: a History of Britain's Underworld* (New York: Pegasus Books 2008).
43 *The Independent*, 28 November 2010.
44 John Pearson; *The Profession of Violence* (London: Weidenfeld & Nicolson 1972).
45 Albert Donoghue & Martin Short; *The Enforcer* (London: John Blake 2002).

been killed by the twins for some unknown misdemeanour, such was the paranoia at that time. The situation was fast becoming oppressive and terrifying in equal measure.

◆

Part way through the Kray enquiry, with good progress being made, 'Nipper' Read was sent to Ireland to investigate the case of a murdered woman found at Sandycove Point in Dublin back in February 1966. Read's assignment there had much to do with the pretence of him being seen to be active as a jobbing Murder Squad Detective, thus removing any suspicion that he may have been devoting all of his time to something very big and very secret. To Read, the interruption was a colossal waste of his own time and energy which took him away from "an increasingly demanding investigation"[46] and, when he returned to the fold at Tintagel House, he was alarmed at what had transpired in his absence. The *Sunday Mirror* had run a story with the headline "Murder for Silence by the Big Time Racketeers", stating that Read was conducting an investigation into the deaths of Cornell, Mitchell and McVitie.[47] It could only be referring to the Krays.

Despite the co-operation of Leslie Payne and Freddie Gore, the diligent Detective Superintendent had been unaware of Ronnie's visit to New York. The team had acquired much important evidence about fraud, assault, blackmail and other misdemeanours. It was all good stuff, but Read needed something big with which to claim the twins: the confidential nature of the investigation was being compromised by unknown sources within Scotland Yard and the press, and time was fast running out. It would turn out that the plot to do Bernie Silver a 'favour', briefly discussed between Ronnie, Dickie Morgan and Alan Bruce Cooper on the American trip of which Read had been ignorant, would be the major breakthrough that the Kray investigation needed, and the catalyst for decisive action.

Just after returning from New York, another meeting about the plan was held at Braithwaite House with Ronnie, Reggie, Cooper, Dickie Morgan and Tommy Cowley in attendance. Ronnie announced that a certain person - whose name was not mentioned - "was trying to horn

46 Leonard Read & James Morton; *Nipper Read: The Man Who Nicked the Krays* (London: MacDonald & Co 1991).
47 *Sunday Mirror*, 18 February 1968.

in on some clubs owned by Bernie Silver",[48] and because the twins were in some kind of partnership with Silver, they felt compelled to help him out. The Krays must have already intimated to Silver that they were going to do something for him, because it was said that he had expressed the desire that nothing drastic should happen to the man: he was only to be taught a lesson. The twins, however, wanted the man killed, and wanted Eugene Elvey, despite his failure to execute Jimmy Evans with the booby-trapped briefcase over a year before, to be recalled to do the job, for a fee of £1,000. Further meetings took place at Braithwaite House and a pub called the Horn of Plenty,[49] and it was decided that stabbing and shooting were not appropriate, although the idea of using explosives in some way was considered.

In a meeting with Cooper at the Westland Hotel in Bayswater, around 15 April, Elvey agreed to the job and a number of methods of killing were discussed, including using a rifle with a telescopic sight, an underwater harpoon and a crossbow, the latter being Elvey's idea. Cooper seemed keen on the harpoon, but there were financial considerations and the idea was ditched in favour of the crossbow, with the alternative possibility of acquiring explosives for a remote-controlled car bomb.[50] Soon after, Cooper met Tommy Cowley outside the Dominion Theatre in Tottenham Court Road in order to go to Soho and see the man who was to be assassinated. After driving to Greek Street, Cowley caught sight of a heavy-set, tall, swarthy man, who was pointed out to Cooper as the target, and he was finally given a name: George. This was George Caruana, a Maltese club owner (said to resemble the actor Tony Curtis), who had once been a part of the gang said to be responsible for the shooting of early Kray hero Tommy Smithson in 1956.[51]

Elvey was made familiar with his target, as well as being supplied with the description and number plate of Caruana's red Mini. He then went to Whiteley's, the famous Bayswater department store, and bought a crossbow, arrow tips and barbs for a total of £51 2s 6d,[52] and he was given £100 the following day to go towards the cost of the

48 Statement by Alan Bruce Cooper, 17 July 1968; CRIM 1/4927 (National Archives).

49 It is unclear which pub this was; if in the East End it could have been the pub of that name in Underwood Street, not far from Vallance Road, or the one in Globe Road, Bethnal Green which still operates today.

50 Statement by Eugene Elvey, 19 July 1968; CRIM 1/4927, ff. 36-49 (National Archives).

51 James Morton; *East End Gangland* (London: Little, Brown and Company 2000).

52 Statement by Eugene Elvey, 19 July 1968; CRIM 1/4927, ff. 36-49 (National Archives).

crossbow and any other items he would need. Elvey later recalled:

> *I found that this cross-bow was really not suitable though it was*
> *obviously a very lethal device. It required setting up by an expert*
> *and there wasn't time to get an expert. I just played around with it*
> *at home and had very bad results. I did this at home in my garden*
> *and in the garage.*[53]

The weapon was most certainly dangerous; at a range of fifty yards, it was positively lethal. When fired over its maximum range of about one hundred and twenty yards, despite an erratic trajectory, it was still judged to be able to cause serious injury.[54] John McCafferty, Scotland Yard's Senior Experimental Officer, had this to say after he tested it:

> *It could be that the bolt could go right through somebody's body. It*
> *could penetrate through a body; certainly up to 50 yards, the head*
> *of the bolt would penetrate a considerable distance into the body,*
> *provided it didn't hit thick bone. It would cause very severe multiple*
> *injuries.*[55]

Elvey's lack of confidence with this bulky weapon soon rendered it unsuitable for use, and, at a meeting on 28 April, Elvey told Cooper of his concerns. But Cooper had already been considering the explosives option and had secured a supply of gelignite from a contact in Glasgow. All that was needed was for somebody to go there and fetch it back to London. On Monday, 29 April, Elvey bought a £20 air ticket to Glasgow and boarded a plane at Heathrow Airport.[56] He had no idea where he was to go on arrival, only that he had two telephone numbers he could contact when he got there. Landing at around 10.55 a.m., Elvey telephoned one of the numbers and spoke to a man named Charles Elliott, who gave him an address, 178 Maxwell Road,[57] from where he could collect a parcel of gelignite.[58]

The pick-up went without a hitch. The explosives consisted of six

---

53 Statement by Eugene Elvey, 19 July 1968; CRIM 1/4927, ff. 36-49 (National Archives).

54 Statement of John McCafferty, Senior Experimental Officer, 18 June 1968; MEPO 2/11387, ff. 1052-3 (National Archives).

55 Statement of John McCafferty, Senior Experimental Officer, undated (1968); CRIM 1/4927, ff. 30-32 (National Archives).

56 From its creation in 1929, today's Heathrow was called London Airport, changing to its current name in 1966. The statements regarding Elvey's trip use the name London Airport (Heathrow), as the change had been so recent.

57 Statement by Detective Inspector John Buchanan (Glasgow Police), undated (1968); CRIM 1/4927, f. 73 (National Archives).

58 Statement by Eugene Elvey, 19 July 1968; CRIM 1/4927, ff. 36-49 (National Archives).

sticks of ICI Polar Ammon gelignite, all wrapped in brown greaseproof paper,[59] which were placed in Elvey's hand luggage, a small blue suitcase. Elvey then took a cab back to the airport. It was then that he noticed what seemed to be a little 'buzz' around him, as if a number of people were becoming interested in where he was going. At around 11.45 a.m., after Elvey had been in Glasgow for less than an hour, he was arrested by Inspector John Dougall of the Glasgow Airport Police. The blue case was opened to reveal its deadly contents and Elvey was taken into custody.

According to Dougall, he had been told to look for Elvey at the airport only five-to-ten minutes before making the arrest, having received instructions from Detective Sergeant Waldman of Glasgow City Police, who had obviously received a tip-off. That particular, and significant, piece of intelligence had come from London, from Tintagel House.

As part of the Kray investigation, 'Nipper' Read had sought permission from the Home Secretary to use wire-tapping on the phone lines of a number of individuals,[60] one of whom was Alan Cooper. Indeed, following his arrest, Elvey was perplexed, as only his wife and Cooper knew that he was travelling to Glasgow; he couldn't believe for a moment that Cooper would be the source of the information, as he would be implicating himself in the murder conspiracy by talking to the authorities.

The day after the arrest, one of Read's team, Detective Sergeant Algernon Hemingway, travelled to Paisley to speak to Elvey and negotiate the possibility of him making a statement. That same morning Detective Sergeant Alan Wright went to Cranford Hall Car Park at Heathrow Airport and located Elvey's Riley motor car. On the rear seat he found three arrows and, in the boot, the crossbow, fully assembled with string and telescopic sight, as well as an arrow with a large barbed tip.[61]

On 1 May, Elvey agreed to make a statement and, two days later, 'Nipper' Read himself went to Paisley and spoke to Elvey. From information gleaned from these conversations, Elvey's house in

---

59 Statement of Inspector John Dougall (Glasgow Police), undated (1968); CRIM 1/4927, ff. 23-25 (National Archives).

60 Leonard Read & James Morton; *Nipper Read: The Man Who Nicked the Krays* (London: MacDonald & Co 1991).

61 Statement by Detective Sergeant Alan Wright, 14 July 1968; MEPO 2/11387, f. 1050 (National Archives).

Hornchurch, Essex, was searched, whereupon Detective Sergeant Hemingway found a veritable treasure trove of incriminating evidence: arrows, arrow fletchings and arrow tips; a spring-loaded bolt; a hypodermic syringe; a hypodermic needle; various tools; a hide document case with spring; and a bottle marked 'acid'.[62] The murder briefcase, which the Krays had hoped would eliminate Jimmy Evans in the foyer of the Old Bailey, was now in the possession of the police, along with six sticks of gelignite and one seriously dangerous crossbow, all of them evidence of a plot to commit murder. Read sent out an 'all points' to effect the arrest of Alan Bruce Cooper immediately.

When Cooper and Read finally faced each other in those first days of May 1968, the American denied any knowledge of a conspiracy to murder, and even of the existence of Eugene Paul Elvey. He was obviously anxious and stuttered more than usual, but when Read hit him with the threat of being charged with conspiracy to murder, Cooper came back with something that Read was not expecting: "If you contact John du Rose, he will tell you that I am his informant."

Cooper then went on to say that he had been working with du Rose in this capacity for two years.[63] Read couldn't believe what he was hearing and immediately asked his superior to pay a visit to Tintagel House:

He accepted that they had been in contact for some time, but he was, he said, not really running him as an informant as such, and had really received no information worth passing on. 'If there had been, I'd have let you know, Nipper.' At the time I was furious and du Rose knew it. I got a bit emotional and queried whether I was trusted, but John was conciliatory and played the whole thing down. Eventually I calmed down, but as far as Cooper was concerned, there was to be no messing about.[64]

Cooper's unlikely role as John du Rose's informant came in an indirect way via the involvement of Admiral John H. Hanly, a *chargé d'affaires* for the US Treasury attached to the American Embassy in Paris. This title was merely a front for his work in the US Secret Service, in which he had been closely linked with the Bureau of Narcotics; since the

62 Statement by Detective Sergeant Algernon Hemingway, 26 June 1968; MEPO 2/11387, ff. 973-987 (National Archives).

63 Leonard Read & James Morton; *Nipper Read: The Man Who Nicked the Krays* (London: MacDonald & Co 1991).

64 Ibid.

war, Hanly had been a major player in the fight against the Mafia. He had become aware of the twins in the early days of their involvement with the syndicates in the running of London gambling clubs; he had noted the media interest surrounding the Boothby affair; and he was particularly intrigued by the description of Ronnie Kray as "King of the London Underworld."[65] It was this negative image of the Krays that ensured that Ronnie was refused entry to the United States in 1964, and Hanly's persistent interest in the Krays' activities led to the cessation of the stolen bonds operation in April 1967.

It was this interest in all things Kray/Mafia related, and the fact that their influence was apparently spreading in Europe, that led Admiral Hanly to visit London, where he met Chief Commissioner of the Metropolitan Police Sir Joseph Simpson, and ultimately John du Rose. Hanly promised Simpson that he would help in any way with the thorny problem of the Kray twins and, in 1967, he got the breakthrough that would prove so vital the following year. Early that year, a man named David Nathan was arrested in Washington DC in possession of a shipment of LSD which had been sent by his son-in-law from Marseilles: Alan Cooper. Hanly realised that if he played right by Cooper, he would have the best link to the Krays' operations he could hope to get, and when Cooper was given the choice of a long prison sentence for narcotics offences or the chance of freedom as a Secret Service informer, he wisely chose the latter. And so, as part of the anti-Kray operation being engineered Stateside, Cooper was introduced to John du Rose. The two got on well and du Rose gave Cooper the responsibility of being a covert middle-man between Scotland Yard and the Firm; this meant creating bogus paperwork to impress - and mislead - the twins, as well as concocting imaginative schemes which would ultimately fail, yet still be based on enough content to incriminate. It explained the failure to con Congolese representatives out of £75,000, the sudden termination of the bearer bonds racket, the ease with which visas were acquired for Ronnie and Dickie Morgan in Paris, Elvey's botched attempt at killing a man at the Old Bailey, and his subsequent arrest for possession of explosives. Reggie and Charlie Kray were absolutely right when they first met Cooper and smelt a rat.

Although at this stage, in early May 1968, police protection and immunity from prosecution were not a given, Alan Bruce Cooper, now

---

65 John Pearson; *Notorious* (London: Century 2010).

faced with very serious charges, agreed to make a statement and, seeing as he was effectively backed by the men at the top, had little to lose by doing so. It contained information about the plans to murder Evans and Caruana, told how the murder briefcase was devised, and disclosed Elvey's involvement in all of it. Cooper also fleshed out information regarding the stolen bearer bonds and, of course, as he did so, he drove the nail even deeper into the Krays' coffin.

◆

Ronnie and Reggie did not need the police attention to make things difficult for everybody; they were quite capable of doing it themselves by this time. The fear within the Firm was at a critical point as the twins continued to exert their brutal influence on what was, in some ways, an empire on the road to ruin. In April 1968, as plans were well underway to kill George Caruana, the twins were involved in a serious piece of violence involving their old Tottenham adversaries, Billy and Ron Webb.

The Webb brothers had had little to do with the Krays since those days at the Tottenham Royal in the early 1950s. By now, they worked their own business and chose prudently not to tread on the Firm's toes; besides, they didn't need the Krays. One racket from which they earned well was the protection of a smuggler who brought pornography and handguns into Britain from Denmark in large quantities. The twins, always with their eye on others' successes, made it known that they would like to be a part of this lucrative operation. Billy Webb was reluctant:

> As could be expected, I would not allow this. Inevitably a quarrel started as Ronnie Kray assumed I could be persuaded into taking them in as partners. This could not be achieved and a war started. It began when we received an invitation to meet the twins and talk about the business.
>
> Many times we had got word that they were anxious to have a meeting with us. Ron and I discussed the possibility of a meeting with the Krays many times but Ron was against it and I, whilst I was not too keen, was a bit curious.[66]

Eventually, the Webbs reluctantly agreed to a meeting, to see what the Krays had to say. It was to be held on Kray territory, at the Old

---

66 Billy Webb; *Running With The Krays* (Edinburgh: Mainstream Publishing 1993).

Horns pub, on 18 April.

When the Webb brothers entered with two friends, they were very much outnumbered. The Old Horns was a long-standing Kray stronghold and the twins were surrounded by assorted members of the Firm: 'Scotch' Jack Dickson, Albert Donoghue, Tommy Cowley, Sammy Lederman and the three Lambrianou brothers, Chris, Tony and young Nicky, were just some of the recognisable faces present in the packed pub, some of whom had had fallings-out with the Webbs on a number of occasions. Billy Webb noticed that some of the older members of the Firm, like Tommy Welch, were absent, although he was unhappy to see 'Checker' Berry, the brother of landlord Teddy, in the bar, as there was little love lost between the two.

The conversation between the Webbs and the Krays started cordially enough, with talk about how well the Webbs were doing and a brief chat about the sentences passed on the Richardson brothers the previous year.[67] Suddenly, out of the blue, Ronnie went to hit Billy Webb, who retaliated, sparking a fight which included the use of stools and bottles. The Webbs' companions were told by Reggie, who was probably armed, not to get involved as he "would blow their heads off",[68] and though Reggie did not get involved himself, various people present joined in the assault, including Nicky Lambrianou. It was a furious attack, with broken glass ricocheting off heads; Tommy Cowley made a move to stab Billy Webb, but was beaten back with a bar stool. Both Webb brothers were soon taking a hammering, all the while moving painfully under the hail of fists and blunt objects to the door.

They were in a bad way as they dashed away from the pub, blood streaming down their faces as they made their way through the pouring rain to Hackney Hospital. There they were seen by the casualty officer, Dr. Mary Murphy, who examined their injuries:

> On examination I found that William Webb had a laceration of the right eyebrow and a laceration of the forehead just inside the hair line and lacerations to the top of the skull and a laceration of the left ring finger. He was X-rayed and a number of sutures were inserted into the lacerations.

---

67 Ibid.
68 Statement by John Dickson, 24 September 1968; MEPO 2/11404, ff. 1288-1292 (National Archives).

> *On examination of Ronald Webb I found he had lacerations on the*
> *top of his head, a peri-orbital haematoma [black eye] and a sub-*
> *conjunctival haematoma [blood in the eye] and fragments of glass*
> *in his hair. He was X-rayed and then refused to have any further*
> *treatment. His wounds definitely needed sutures.*
>
> *In my opinion the lacerations caused to these two patients were*
> *probably by a blunt instrument, and most unlikely with just a fist.*[69]

This unprovoked and mob-handed assault was typical of the kind of violence being dished out by the Krays at this time. Around the same time, a 'Scouse fellow' was shouting in the bar of the Old Horns and so Reggie 'belted him'; the same punishment was meted out at the Green Dragon Club by Reggie to a man who had been bad-mouthing one of his friends, 'Old Duchy Sam.'[70] The behaviour of the Kray twins, invariably fuelled by paranoia, pills and alcohol, appalled the last loyal members of the Firm. And with this, drastic measures were contemplated – the Krays had to be 'ironed out'.

Albert Donoghue would later recall how the possibility of killing the Krays, to end the spiralling chaos and madness, was something that had been talked about for a little while, although nobody seemed to want to take it any further than the talking stage:

> *I'm sure Ronnie was a psycho. He really did enjoy 'doing' people.*
> *And when we saw his murderous paranoia at its worst, this only*
> *drove the rest of us on the Firm to thinking we might have to kill*
> *them both before they tried to kill us.*[71]

For the most part, it had been a bit of banter, a way of relieving the tension, but the respect had gone, and the possibility was now there. Only a few trusted individuals – Donoghue, Connie Whitehead, Jack Dickson and Ronnie Hart – dared talk about the idea, such was the fear of word getting back to the twins. What always stymied the assassination plot was the fact that if the twins were gone, what little work the Firm still had, with its financial benefits, would also disappear. In many ways, these men were stuck between a rock and a hard place: being seen to pull out of the Firm was dangerous, but staying in it was similarly fraught with perils. The only way to

---

69 Statement by Dr. Mary Murphy, 17 June 1968; MEPO 2/11387, ff. 1104-5 (National Archives).

70 Albert Donoghue & Martin Short; *The Enforcer* (London: John Blake 2002).

71 Ibid.

maintain the status quo of earning a living, essentially off the Kray name, was to put oneself in jeopardy twenty-four hours a day, seven days a week.

But the idea of killing the twins had already been considered by others. Mickey Fawcett, that old-time associate who had first been drawn in by the Krays' dark gravity during the Double R days, had deliberately removed himself from their orbit as much as possible. After the murder of George Cornell, he had contemplated killing the twins, but instead had chosen to use the public show of murder as an excuse to part ways with his former friends. Now he was ready to kill Reggie; it had all been pre-arranged. Fawcett followed his target to Albert Bigg Point in Stratford,[72] a block of flats which was home to a girl whom Reggie was dropping off after a night out:

> *Cutting myself off from the Krays made me a marked man. Getting them first struck me then as only logical, but the truth was that I was under almost as much pressure as the twins. My own grasp on reality was slipping as I sat in a car in the shadows and believed I could shoot Reggie Kray and get away with it. I just felt that I didn't have a choice.*[73]

But where did the order to kill Reggie Kray come from? It wasn't until 2015 that the possible answer came courtesy of Freddie Foreman in one of his many media interviews. Filmed for a documentary,[74] Foreman admitted that he and other leading figures in the London underworld had hatched a plan to kill the Krays, in what has become known as the 'Kill Order'. As far as the plotters were concerned, the twins had become too dangerous, too reckless, and now, with their increasingly unpredictable and violent behaviour, they threatened to bring them all down. It was a matter of survival of the fittest:

> *What sparked the plot against the Krays was Foreman being 'summoned' by psychotic Ronnie to be ready to dispose of the body of Billy Gentry who was about to be lured into an ambush.*
>
> *"Billy Gentry was a good fellah," Foreman recalls. "I've done loads of 'bird' with Gentry, so I told Ron to forget about it and calm down. I thought he was raving mad."*
>
> *That was the turning point. Foreman held his notorious "council of*

---

72 In his book *Krayzy Days*, Fawcett mistakenly calls it John Bigg Point.
73 Mickey Fawcett; *Krayzy Days* (Brighton: Pen Press 2013).
74 *The Krays: Kill Order* (Metronome Distribution 2015).

war" at Simpson's in The Strand with some of London's top gang leaders.

"I reported that night back to my pals and said there's only one thing for it," Foreman admits. "I thought the twins should be 'ironed out'.

"The two of them should be shot because they were dangerous to everybody. That was my thought and several other people. If the twins hadn't been arrested, that's what would have happened. That was on the cards." [75]

Whether Mickey Fawcett was operating on the orders of Foreman and the others is not clear. What is clear is that Fawcett lost his nerve and the 'Kill Order' never got the chance to be implemented.

◆

With the charges being built up against the Krays and their contemporaries at Tintagel House by 'Nipper' Read and his overworked team, the time was swiftly approaching for direct action. Alan Cooper was proving a most voluble witness; as there was no way he could be released back into the Krays circle, Read was presented with a dilemma. As somebody who was in constant contact with the twins, his unavailability would look extremely suspicious in their eyes, and so Read had to devise a plan whereby Cooper could be allowed to interact with the Firm, yet still be under police scrutiny. The answer came with Cooper's stomach ulcer. Under the pretence of having complications with his recurring gastric complaint, he consented to take part in a bogus stay at a nursing home in Weymouth Street, Marylebone,[76] where he could accept visits by the Krays and others, all the while being wired up to record potential incriminating conversations. It was known that Joey Kaufman was on the way over from America, and the opportunity to garner information, by cunning means, from yet another key character was looked on as too good to miss. Cooper began his stay on 6 May 1968.

Ultimately, the twins never got see Cooper, as they were enjoying The Brooks (accompanied by John Pearson) at that time, but they sent Tommy Cowley over with some "nice eggs."[77] A number of telephone

75 *Docklands and East London Advertiser*, 10 September 2015.
76 Statement by Alan Bruce Cooper, 18 July 1968; CRIM 1/4927, ff. 9-22 (National Archives).
77 Leonard Read & James Morton; *Nipper Read: The Man Who Nicked the Krays* (London: MacDonald & Co 1991).

conversations between Ronnie and Cooper were recorded, mainly regarding whether the twins would be visiting and the reasons why they would not be, but all that could be heard was Cooper's side of the conversation, which proved as good as useless. It was all looking to be a bit of a waste of time until Joey Kaufman bounded into the room with an ebullient, "Hi there, how ya doin'?" and proceeded to have a conversation with Cooper about a new batch of bearer bonds that would soon be arriving. It was invaluable stuff.

It would have been imprudent to wait around any longer. Enough evidence had been gathered to arrest the Krays and many of their associates on an assortment of charges: assault, selling stolen bearer bonds, long-firm fraud, demanding money with menaces and conspiracy to murder. It was all meaty stuff and enough to convince 'Nipper' Read, on 7 March 1968, that the arrest of the Krays was imminent.

That night, Reggie and Ronnie spent time with friends and associates in the Old Horns until closing time. A little party was being held to welcome Joey Kaufman to Britain and, once the pub had closed, they decamped to the Astor Club where they wined and dined until the early hours of the morning. The twins went back, with their respective companions, to an empty Braithwaite House (their parents were still at The Brooks) and, "very tired and fairly pissed after a night of pubbing and clubbing",[78] fell quickly into a sleep that would last only a couple of hours. It was to be their last night of freedom.

78 Reggie & Ronnie Kray, with Fred Dinenage; *Our Story* (London: Sidgwick and Jackson 1988).

SEVENTEEN

END OF EMPIRE

5.55 a.m., Wednesday, 8 May 1968. As the dawn light cast its first rays over a chilly London, Detective Superintendent Read, Detective Inspector Cater and Detective Sergeants Hemingway and Donaldson, accompanied by a number of uniformed officers - some of them armed - made their way by elevator to the ninth floor of Braithwaite House. On arrival outside Flat 43 they stood and listened at the door for any movement within. At that moment, the lift door slid open and a milkman walked out; the look on his face must have been a picture to behold as two police officers quickly and silently bundled him back into the lift and sent him down to the ground floor, as much for his own safety as anything else.

At 6.00 a.m., Read knocked loudly on the door and rang the bell. Further loud knocking received no reply and so Read gave the order for the door to be forced. DS Hemingway jemmied the door and, as the door frame splintered and the door itself fell impotently to one side, the men charged in, making their way first to the living room. Sleeping on the sofa, John Lucy, a young man of twenty-two, was rudely awoken by the invasion and arrested. Read and Cater went upstairs to the bedrooms; they found Reggie Kray in bed with a young woman, June MacDonald, and Ronnie Kray in bed with Martin Morgan, who was sixteen-years-old.[1] All were arrested and Ronnie was handcuffed

---

1   Statement by Detective Sergeant Algernon Hemingway, 26 June 1968; MEPO 2/11387, ff. 972-987 (National Archives).

before being led downstairs.[2]

Read said to Ronnie, "You know who I am. You are under arrest. I am going to take you to West End Central Police Station," and then cautioned him. Ronnie appeared unflustered by the events confronting him, seeming more concerned with his routines. He replied calmly, "Yes, all right Mr. Read, but I've got to have my pills, you know that." As he was about to reach over and pick up a tin from the table, he was stopped by Cater. Ronnie was insistent; "But I've got to have them. You know what they are, they're Stemetal [sic]. I've got a letter from my psychiatrist what says I have to take two a day. I'll have to have that as well could you bring that along please Mr. Read. It's in that book there, my address book, would you bring it. I must have it please."[3]

Read assured the compliant Ronnie that all would be taken in hand and went to the bedroom where Reggie had been sleeping. He was naked, so was told to dress himself before being cautioned; he appeared less calm than his brother.

"What's this all about anyway?" he asked.

Read ignored the question, answering, "Why didn't you answer the door?" When Reggie claimed to have heard nothing, he was reminded that the door had been noisily smashed in. Reggie added, "Well, I never heard nothing. We was up late last night we had a bit of a party matter of fact."[4] This was not news to Read, who had had the Krays under surveillance for the preceding twenty-four hours. With the twins now under arrest, they were taken to West End Central Police Station where a number of cells had been made available for what was going to turn out to be quite a number of new arrivals.

Simultaneously, brother Charlie received a rude awakening at his flat in Poplar when three plain-clothes detectives knocked at the door. Donning his dressing gown, Charlie went downstairs and opened the door with the security chain on: before he could ask what the men wanted at such an ungodly hour, the door was pushed with force and the chain broken. Charlie was led into the lounge where he demanded to know what was going on. As he was informed that he was to be

---

2   In *Me and My Brothers*, Charlie Kray said that as Ronnie opened his eyes to be faced with guns aimed at him, he muttered with his characteristic sense of humour, "I'd be careful with those, one of them might go off."

3   Statement by Detective Superintendent Leonard Read, undated (1968); MEPO 2/11387, ff. 939-960 (National Archives)

4   Ibid.

arrested on a charge of conspiracy to defraud, wife Dolly and children Gary and Nancy came downstairs, bemused and concerned by what was happening. Charlie was told to dress, but not to bother shaving. Then, strangely, a pot of tea was made and all assembled in the kitchen, sipping their tea and making polite conversation.[5]

When Charlie arrived at West End Central Police Station, unrestrained (the handcuffs were too small to be used),[6] the activity was considerable. After being formally charged at 7.20 a.m. he was placed in a cell and over the next few hours, all he could hear were urgent voices, the rattling of keys and the clanging of cell doors as other members of the Kray Firm were brought in.

That morning, twenty men were arrested in an operation involving over one hundred and twenty police officers, described as "one of the biggest and most secret in the Yard's history."[7] It had all begun the previous day when 'Nipper 'Read', after discussing his intentions with John du Rose, informed the Detective Inspectors of the ten regional crime squads of London to have men ready at his disposal at short notice. A pre-arrest briefing was scheduled for 4.30 a.m. on 8 May, although for security's sake up until the meeting had started nobody present had been made aware of what was about to unfold. There was no way Read was prepared to risk even the slightest leak.

That day, one after the other, key players in the Krays' multifarious enterprises were brought in and charged with numerous offences. Some were not in London and officers had been dispatched to places as far afield as Bournemouth and Southend in order to reach their quarry.[8] Not everybody was rounded up on that first day, and arrests continued throughout the following day and beyond. Many of those who had worked with the stolen bearer bonds were taken in on 9 May, including Gordon Anderson, Freddie Bird and Robert Gould. Joey Kaufman was arrested at his room in the Mayfair Hotel; he protested his innocence until a parcel intended for him was intercepted at the hotel two days later; it contained $190,000 of stolen bonds, covered with Kaufman's fingerprints.[9] Significant individuals like Tommy Cowley, Connie Whitehead and Tommy 'The Bear' Welch were brought

5   Charlie Kray & Robin McGibbon; *Me and My Brothers* (London: Grafton 1988).

6   Ibid.

7   *Daily Mirror*, 9 May 1968.

8   *Daily Express*, 9 May 1968.

9   Leonard Read & James Morton; *Nipper Read: The Man Who Nicked the Krays* (London: MacDonald & Co 1991).

in quickly; others, like Albert Donoghue, 'Scotch' Jack Dickson and Ian Barrie, remained at liberty for some time before being rounded up.

By this time, with the twins behind bars and many of their perceived henchmen out of action too, there would be very little risk of intimidation to those witnesses, such as the ordinary citizens, who had refused to speak out against the twins through fear of retribution. Those members of the Firm who were enjoying their last few days of freedom whilst the others languished in jail posed little threat. Nonetheless, Read ensured a major deployment of officers to provide protection for potential witnesses whilst Chief Inspector Harry Mooney rounded up the remaining Kray associates.

In that regard, the first avenue Read wanted to follow was a tantalising lead that brought about the discovery of 'Blonde' Carole Skinner at Evering Road. An anonymous woman (possibly Kathleen Collins) had approached Read claiming that she had information about what may have happened to Jack McVitie at a party in Evering Road. Although she gave little away, two women police officers, posing as market researchers, called at the houses in Evering Road and came across Carole Skinner in her basement flat.[10] Before long, she was taken to see Read and Cater at West End Central Police Station, but despite the soft approach, assurances of safety and eventually threats, she refused to acknowledge that she knew anything, or even that she knew the Krays. It was a frustrating dead-end which would eventually come good, but for the moment, Read and his team had other work to do, and moved on apace. The production of the formal charge sheets was a major job and a relay of typists worked relentlessly for thirty-six hours to create the eleven page document.[11] Two of the arrested men had been allowed to go, and so charges were read to the remaining eighteen; this started at 12.45 a.m. on 10 May and was wrapped up by 2.00 a.m.[12] In the midst of intense press scrutiny, the committal hearings began the same day at Bow Street Magistrates' Court:

> The doors of the court at Bow-street, London, were locked during the 26-minute hearing. Inside, twelve uniformed policemen stood shoulder-to-shoulder around the dock. About twenty Scotland Yard

10 Leonard Read & James Morton; *Nipper Read: The Man Who Nicked the Krays* (London: MacDonald & Co 1991).

11 *Daily Express*, 10 May 1968.

12 Leonard Read & James Morton; *Nipper Read: The Man Who Nicked the Krays* (London: MacDonald & Co 1991).

detectives stood at the back of the court.[13]

During those brief twenty-six minutes the three Kray brothers, and those with them, were read the initial charges:

Reggie, Ronnie and Tommy Cowley: two charges of conspiracy to commit murder.

Reggie, Ronnie and Charlie: Demanding money with menaces and intent to steal.

Reggie, Ronnie, Charlie, Charles Mitchell, Robert Gould, Gordon Anderson, Marshall Goldblatt, Joseph Kaufman, Arnold Davis, Mark Kennedy: various charges of fraud relating to stolen Canadian bearer bonds and debentures.

Reggie, Ronnie, Charlie, Charles 'Nobby' Clarke, Billy Exley, Tommy Welch, Fredderick Bird, Alfred Willey, David Forland, Samuel Lederman: conspiracy to defraud relating to long-firm frauds.

Tommy Welch: Grievous bodily harm.

These charges, significant as they were, were essentially used as an excuse to keep the twins and their associates out of the way whilst Read and his team built up a really major case against them. The Krays had shown time and time again that they could wriggle out of situations like this, and for Scotland Yard, any sentences they would receive from any convictions resulting from these charges would not be long enough. Read was playing a long game, but he was to benefit from the publicity surrounding the committal hearings and the enthusiasm of a number of journalists who were happy to use their own enquiries to help out. The pressure was now on for those who had something to say to come out and say it.

As Read had hoped, a terrified Billy Exley came forward and spoke of the escape, harbouring and death of Frank Mitchell. Lennie Dunn, the long suffering tenant of the East Ham flat where Mitchell saw his final days, made a nervous approach. As a result, Lisa, the hostess who provided the 'Mad Axeman' with companionship and sexual gratification during his last days, was traced in what Read would later call "possibly the most brilliant piece of detective work in the case."[14] Detective Inspector Frank Cater took Exley to West London,

---

13 *Daily Mirror*, 11 May 1968.

14 Leonard Read & James Morton; *Nipper Read: The Man Who Nicked the Krays* (London: MacDonald & Co 1991).

where he identified the house to which he had taken Lisa to pick up fresh clothes back in December 1966. Lisa had long gone, but the woman occupier, Valerie Fiske, was helpful, supplying Cater with a photograph of Lisa and the name of her doctor. Having traced the doctor, the address of Lisa's family in Leeds was obtained and, from her mother, a new address in Battersea; however, it was believed that Lisa and her new boyfriend had gone abroad. Although the couple were indeed found to have left the flat in Battersea, the other occupiers were confident that the couple were still in London. In fact, they had the details of a vehicle repair garage where Lisa and her boyfriend had taken their camper van after it had broken down; the owner of the garage remembered hiring them a courtesy car which was soon traced, found parked outside a hotel in Earl's Court. The search was over – Lisa was found asleep in the hotel and told she was going to be taken to Scotland Yard.

It was an incredible piece of work by Cater, but it nearly came to nothing when, as she was being driven over Westminster Bridge on her way to Tintagel House, Lisa realised she was going in the opposite direction to the Scotland Yard headquarters and fearing a trap panicked, flinging open the car door and leaping out. Cater managed to pull her back in before she could run to the edge of the bridge and throw herself into the Thames. Such was the fear of the Krays.

Once she had calmed down, Lisa was a superb witness, blessed with a formidable memory. Her account tallied with Exley and Dunn's stories, and implicated Albert Donoghue and Jack Dickson, who were traced and taken to Tintagel House. Further enquiries in Dartmoor and London soon meant that Read and his team were building up enough evidence to press charges for the escape, harbouring and possible death of Frank Mitchell. Those charged would be all three Kray brothers, Donoghue, Dickson, Wally Garelick, Connie Whitehead, Tommy Cowley and 'Big' Pat Connolly.[15]

As more work continued with the other charges, extra people were brought in: with regard to conspiracies to defraud concerning the stolen bonds and long-firm frauds, John Chappell, David Levy, Michael Kenrick, Robert Buckley and Wally Garelick were charged.[16] Ronnie

---

15 Court Register: Special Sittings of Bow Street Magistrates, 26 June 1968; PS/BOW/B/04/002/D (London Metropolitan Archives).
16 Ibid.; 31 May 1968.

was charged with the assault on Lenny Hamilton[17] and Dickie Morgan was added to the list of those charged with conspiracy to murder. But it would be the women, who, like Lisa, were drawn into the chaos surrounding the twins, who would go on to make the biggest splash.

Frances Sanders, the Blind Beggar barmaid, had been under considerable police protection since the shooting of George Cornell. During that stressful time, she had struck up a respectful friendship with Chief Inspector Harry Mooney and WDC Pat Allen, and had been gradually considering her options. The possibility of coming clean and exposing Ronnie Kray as a murderer had not been an easy thing to live with. She had already lied to a Coroner's Court in 1966 after the murder, claiming that she did not know the man who had shot Cornell. Sadly, her fear of Ronnie Kray, and her anxiety about her own safety and that of her children, would still not allow her to make a statement saying that Ronnie was the killer. What she possessed was vital evidence, and the police were careful about how they handled this frightened woman. Ultimately, the gentle approach of Read and his team paid off, and on 10 June 1968, Sanders gave a statement to the police at West End Central Police Station; Mooney took the situation very seriously indeed: "Don't tell anyone what you are doing. If people ask, don't tell them, just say you know nothing about anything,"[18] he said. As a result, Ronnie was charged with Cornell's murder on 25 June.[19] The following day, Ian Barrie was arrested in the East End, broke and directionless without the Firm. On 3 July, Sanders was brought in to identify him, which she did without hesitation, and Barrie was formally charged with the murder of Cornell the same day.[20] The Kray enquiry was now taking on a whole different character, and was looking better and better for 'Nipper' Read and his intrepid detectives; they were now being told that Jack McVitie was dead, not missing, and another murder enquiry presented itself.

Inroads had been made with Carole Skinner, who, after repeated denials about knowing anything of the McVitie murder, broke down in front of Read and told all she knew. This implicated Ronnie

17 Court Register: Special Sittings of Bow Street Magistrates, 10 July 1968; PS/BOW/B/04/002/D (London Metropolitan Archives).
18 Mrs X with James Morton; *Calling Time on the Krays: The Barmaid's Tale* (London: Little, Brown and Company 1996).
19 *Daily Mirror*, 26 June 1968.
20 Court Register: Special Sittings of Bow Street Magistrates, 3 July 1968; PS/BOW/B/04/002/D (London Metropolitan Archives).

Bender, Ronnie Hart, Connie Whitehead, Albert Donoghue and the Lambrianou brothers. Skinner's confirmation that her flat had been redecorated led to an examination by a forensic team, where minute blood spots were found under the newly-applied wallpaper. Ronnie Bender's Mini, which had apparently been cleaned up, was examined and blood spots were found on the backs of the front seats.[21]

When Harry Hopwood was interrogated, he was reluctant to speak at first, and then suddenly broke down in front of 'Nipper' Read, telling him about the night the twins came to his place covered in blood. He spoke of disposing of the gun and the knife with Ronnie Hart, leading to a police diver retrieving the now grime-encrusted weapon from the bottom of the Regent's Canal on 23 August. An attempt was also made to locate the murder weapon, the carving knife, from the river bed; three knives were actually found, but none were any use as evidence.[22]

By late August 1968, Ronnie Hart was the only person involved in the McVitie murder who was still at large. He knew full well that Read was looking for him, and eventually, at 4.30 a.m. on 31 August, he called Tintagel House and said he was ready talk. And talk he did, turning Queen's Evidence and effectively producing the longest account of the McVitie affair the police would get, albeit with certain alterations to the truth designed to save his own skin. In this way he would avoid prosecution; however, thanks to his evidence and the combined testimony of Carole Skinner, Harry Hopwood, Percy Merricks, Albert Donoghue (who had also turned), the police forensics men, and other side players like Trevor Stone, Terry Clulow and the Mills brothers, Read had enough evidence to make a go of it. On 19 September, Reggie, Ronnie, Bender and the Lambrianou brothers were charged with the murder of Jack McVitie. Charlie Kray was charged with being an accessory to the fact. Tony Barry was also charged, as were Donoghue and Whitehead, and Freddie Foreman was charged with disposing of McVitie's body on 10 October.[23]

◆

21 Report by Brian Culliford, Principle Scientific Officer, 18 October 1968; DPP 2/4583, ff. 102-104 (National Archives).

22 Statement by PC Philip Johns, 9 September 1968; DPP 2/4583, f. 93 (National Archives).

23 Court Register: Special Sittings of Bow Street Magistrates, 10 October 1968; PS/BOW/B/04/002/D (London Metropolitan Archives).

The foregoing account of the Krays' arrest and the subsequent committal hearings, as well as the machinations going on behind the scenes during those highly publicised five months is, by necessity, simplistic due to the sheer weight of information available, but it is hoped that it gives some idea of how the case against the Krays snowballed during that important period in 1968. The sheer number of people, both within and outside the Krays' trusted circle who were willing to turn to the police and give crucial evidence on serious crimes going back years is astonishing. It seems that, with few exceptions, old friends, strangers, people who had earned a good life as members of the Firm, and others, just felt that they were doing something that was now justifiable, despite their reservations and fear. Hart, Donoghue, Dickson, Barry, Hopwood, Exley, Hamilton and Dunn are just some of the names who turned against the Firm and the twins that governed it. Frances Sanders, Carole Skinner and Lisa, three women who by their bravery made heart-wrenching decisions that would affect the rest of their lives, were crucial to the success of Read's investigation, for they confirmed that the twins were not just East End villains who ducked and dived and flexed a little muscle where necessary, but murderers, killers with little remorse for their actions.

It was for this reason that, when the cases were considered for trial at the Central Criminal Court, all charges would be set aside, save for those of murder. The serious crime of taking somebody's life, and the repercussions for the perpetrators if found guilty, was considered more than enough for Scotland Yard to finally bring the Krays down for good. Fraud, no matter how extensive, a little GBH here and there, or conspiracy to do away with somebody: all were smothered into insignificance by the deaths of three London villains. It could be said that the murders of Cornell and Mitchell were a warning sign that all was not well within the Kray organisation, that it had lost its sense of purpose in the face of a rising, and some would say misguided, desire for power. But from the moment Reggie Kray plunged that knife into Jack McVitie's body in the first hours of 29 October 1967, the Krays were as good as over. The money-go-round, the schmoozing with the rich and famous, the charity galas and the photocalls with celebrities and heroes, would all count for nothing. The Firm knew it early on, and the situation could continue only for a finite amount of time. As a potent force in the underworld, the Kray Empire expired in October

1968 as the trial dates were set. 'Nipper' Read and his squad had worked a miracle in the face of tremendous odds: uncompromising and unconventional, they gathered unsurpassable evidence, re-assured the frightened, gained the trust of the enemy within and got the result that Scotland Yard hoped they would. The Krays did not stand a chance, no matter how hard they tried.

The Krays were finished, but the great trial of 1969, the 'Trial of the Century', would serve to reinforce their status as anti-heroes; and the fractured 1970s and the years beyond would feel their legacy.

AFTERWORD

'LEGEND'

It cannot be denied that Ronald and Reginald Kray have become legends, or at least legendary, if indeed there is a distinction. This is not intended to promote the Krays as upstanding or admirable: Ghengis Khan, Jack the Ripper and even Adolf Hitler have become legendary, and one could hardly admire them for what they became famous for. One definition of legend is "a very old story or set of stories from ancient times, or the stories, not always true, that people tell about a famous event or person"[1] and thus, in this context, the Krays are legends in the sense that not only were they well-known and spoken of in their lifetime and beyond, but also because there are innumerable (now very old) stories associated with them which often change depending on the storyteller. Rumours and conjecture also help to reinforce their almost mythical status in the history of British crime, and there is a definite blurring of what is truth and what is not.

Regardless of their high status – or disdain - in the public's opinion, what is undeniable is that their story is an incredible one. During the writing of this book, two feature films about them – one a big-budget affair starring popular actor Tom Hardy as the twins, the other a more modest independent production – were released, adding to 1990's successful biopic *The Krays*.[2] Each film took on a different aspect of the twins' story; the first, starring brothers Martin and Gary Kemp

---

1   *Cambridge Dictionary Online* definition.
2   *The Krays* (Fugitive/Parkfield Entertainment 1990); Dir. Peter Medak; Martin Kemp, Gary Kemp, Billie Whitelaw.

as the brothers, was an overview of their life and career, paying close attention to the relationships with each other and their family. *The Rise of the Krays*[3] looked more at the key incidents, often violent, which shaped their criminal empire. *Legend*[4] famously came from the perspective of Frances Shea, her relationship with Reggie and the almost tragic-comic aspects of the Krays' life, all bound together by excellent performances, most notably Hardy's dual role as the twins themselves. The fact that three motion pictures have been produced about the Krays demonstrates that there is a story to tell, and a story that engages many.

They have also been the subject of numerous documentaries, independently produced DVDs and most significantly, books, written by biographers, former associates (both loyal and disloyal), family members and even the twins themselves. To date, John Pearson must hold the mantle of producing the definitive works on the Krays - three books in all - but it is his first, 1972's seminal *The Profession of Violence*, that has done much to shape the vision of the twins in the minds of the book-buying public. It was the basis of the two movies *The Krays* and *Legend*, and in 2015 was reprinted for the umpteenth time, on this occasion with Tom Hardy adorning the cover.

Interestingly, being such infamous and noteworthy characters the twins have received their fair share of pastiche over the years. Just over a year after their imprisonment in 1969, Monty Python's Flying Circus ran their now famous 'Piranha Brothers' sketch.[5] The recalled violence was comical, obviously, perhaps with one eye on the Richardsons' methods (screwing a victim's pelvis to a cake-stand is particularly memorable) and, with the other eye on Ronnie's mental illness, the character of 'Spiny Norman', a giant hedgehog, would make an appearance when Dinsdale, the mentally unstable brother, grew increasingly agitated. In 1988, comedians Gareth Hale and Norman Pace introduced TV viewers to regular characters the Two Rons, a straight mickey-take if ever there was one. Bristling with menace, they were invariably filmed with one Ron looking over the shoulder of the other, *à la* David Bailey's iconic photo, threatening the viewer

3 *The Rise of the Krays* (Saracen Films 2015); Dir. Zachary Adler; Simon Cotton, Kevin Leslie, Nicola Stapleton.
4 *Legend* (Studio Canal 2015); Dir. Brian Halgeland; Tom Hardy, Emily Browning, Christopher Eccleston.
5 *Monty Python's Flying Circus*, Series 2 Episode 1; first transmitted on BBC2, 15 September 1970.

before ruining the sinister effect with lines like, "Do we Ron?" "We do Ron Ron, we do Ron Ron." And, in 1989, the lofty Roy Marsden and the diminutive Christopher Ryan made a one-off appearance as Peckham's much-feared Driscoll Brothers in BBC Television's ever-popular comedy *Only Fools and Horses*.[6]

What the twins themselves thought of such comedy at their expense is unknown. What is clear is that such spoofs were ideal for comedy writers and, perhaps more significantly, when the characters appeared, everybody knew who they were based on. It is the unique characteristics of the Kray twins that set them apart from many other criminals: being twins was, of course, a major part of it all. Their desire for publicity and their courtship of celebrities, recorded in innumerable photographs, allows the ordinary public to see them in a number of ways, most of them glamorous, and none of which involve violence. That privilege was reserved for those who knew them or crossed them. Being so detached from the reality of their crimes is what has allowed so many to give the Krays some kind of 'benefit of the doubt'.

When I first started working on this book, I decided that I would not offer my own opinion about them. After all, I had never met the twins or anybody associated with them, save their biographer, Fred Dinenage, and that occasion had nothing to do with the Krays in any case. In April 2015, a launch party was held at the Blind Beggar for Maureen Flanagan's book *One of the Family: 40 Years With the Krays* and I was a little disappointed that I could not attend for personal reasons. However, after subsequently seeing photos of the event on a social networking site, I was glad I did not go; it was obvious from the images of many of the attendees that I would not have been comfortable. No disrespect to Chris Lambrianou, Dave Courtney, Freddie Foreman or any of the other celebrity 'villains' who were there, but this was not my world. My parents, coincidentally both from the East End, were not part of that world either. If any of those associated with the Krays are reading this, I would hope that they would understand.

However, as my research developed, it became very difficult not to form an opinion about these infamous twins – after all, everybody else has one. On the one hand, you have what I would call 'Kray Fans',

6 'Little Problems'; first broadcast on BBC1, 12 February 1989.

those who aspire to the view that the twins were good at heart, that they only hurt other villains, that they gave generously to charity, and that the streets of the East End were safe when they were around; it is the enduring cliché. These are the people who also applaud the twins for being smart, professional and gentlemanly in appearance, suggesting that modern 'wannabe' villains, wearing their trousers slung below their buttocks and baggy hoodie tops, in the style of American 'gangstas', could learn a thing or two about style and presentation. Facebook has a number of Kray-related sites, featuring photos and discussions and, sometimes, interesting archive material from members' personal collections. They also have news of upcoming social events, invariably themed around boxing or charity, but the imagery is usually based on an element of thuggery. A serious reading of many of the comments on these sites shows a distinct support for the Krays, and words like 'respect' are thrown about liberally. And anybody who denigrates the twins is in for a tough time.

For there are certainly those who confidently decry them as mindless thugs, evil and cold-blooded murderers, who let nothing and nobody prevent them from getting what they wanted. To them, there is no 'respect' – that commonly-used word in the underworld – there is only fear. I was astonished to see, in the numerous statements made to the police (particularly in 1968 after the Krays had been arrested for the last time), how many said words to the effect that, 'It is more than my life's worth,' 'I am frightened for myself and my family,' and 'Don't tell anybody I am doing this.' These are terrible things to have to say, and the fear emanating from those stark, typewritten pages is tangible.

These are very black-and-white opinions. After what I have read and researched, I cannot sit comfortably in any one camp. Essentially, the Kray twins were everything to everybody; the fact that people can call Ronnie Kray a great friend, despite his numerous problems, demonstrates to some at least that there was a side to him that did not inspire fear. He was generous, could be incredibly humorous, apparently loved animals and certainly longed for a life in the idyllic countryside. Reggie could be selfish and brutal, but he could be an excellent host, charming when necessary, and although he found great difficulty demonstrating it, he felt great love. Both twins would go on to write poetry and paint; they were strangely sentimental for the old East End and truly idolised their mother. They certainly had a moral compass, but of a kind that many of us would not recognise; the letters on the dial were in unfamiliar places and the needle itself was somewhat bent.

The sentences they received at the Old Bailey in 1969 were tough, and served as a warning to others who may wish to take on the Kray mantle as overlords of the Underworld. It was their legendary status and the publicity they craved, even whilst in prison, that made it such a difficult decision to grant Reggie parole; Ronnie, as a patient at Broadmoor, would never have the chance to receive that honour.

But what I have decided is that, despite what the 'Fans' say, there is nothing wrong in disliking the Krays. Had I been a local at the Grave Maurice or the Old Horns back in the 1960s, I would probably have made myself scarce at the arrival of the twins; I spoke to one elderly East End resident once who said that when the Krays came into a pub, the entire atmosphere would change and not necessarily for the better. They never hurt me or anybody I know personally; they never lent me money when I was struggling, or slashed my face in a pub toilet; they never took over my business or protected me from troublemakers. But this is what they did to many others, and in the process built up a reputation second to none.

Ultimately, they were the architects of their own downfall, alienating their supporters and recklessly ignoring the signs of imminent action by the authorities. In their arrogance, and some would say desperation to maintain their standing in the London Underworld, they imploded. They were not immortal: they were humans, and drastically-flawed humans at that. They had the ability to be very successful criminals, and for a brief period they were. Had they gone about things differently, they could well have retired to the country or the south of Spain, as so many have. They would be a small chapter in British criminal history, as opposed to the iconic, David Bailey-immortalised gangsters who are now a big part of London's iconography. Their convictions did not permit them to continue their criminal enterprise with diminishing returns and a dwindling reputation, as has-beens gracing the club circuit or attending movie premieres like some of their contemporaries and imitators, but it sealed their fate dramatically. It is noteworthy that they are among the few public figures recognisable from one iconic image, Bailey's one; that is how many remember the Kray twins, or choose to remember them. Despite the occasional photos taken in prison or the footage of them attending funerals, their enduring image is in black and white, for they will forever be stuck in 1965, preserved in amber if you like, when they were at their peak.

It is a hackneyed phrase – 'crime doesn't pay.' In the case of the Krays, it may well have done for a while, but when one thinks that Ronnie and Charlie died in prison, with Reggie freed merely because he was about to die anyway, the end was hardly glamorous and blessed with riches.

As many have said before me, it was all such a bloody waste.

APPENDIX ONE

SELECT BIBLIOGRAPHY

There has been a tremendous amount of literature on the Krays since the first book by Brian McConnell in 1969 and innumerable other writings contain references to them. The footnotes in this book mention all the books which were consulted, however the select list below is a distillation of those which the author feels are of particular interest or importance.

Brian McConnell;
The Rise and Fall of the Brothers Kray
(London: David Bruce and Watson Ltd 1969).

John Pearson;
The Profession of Violence
(London: Weidenfeld & Nicolson 1972).

Leslie Payne;
The Brotherhood
(London: Michael Joseph 1973).

John Dickson;
Murder Without Conviction
(London: Sidgwick and Jackson 1986).

Charlie Kray & Robin McGibbon;
Me and My Brothers
(London: Grafton 1988).

Reg & Ron Kray, with Fred Dinenage;
Our Story
(London: Sidgwick and Jackson 1988).

Reggie Kray;
Born Fighter
(London: Arrow Books 1991).

Tony Lambrianou with Carol Clerk;
Inside the Firm
(London: Smith Gryphon 1991).

Leonard Read & James Morton;
Nipper Read: The Man Who Nicked the Krays
(London: MacDonald & Co 1991).

Colin Fry & Charlie Kray;
Doing the Business (London: John Blake 1993).

Ron Kray, with Fred Dinenage;
My Story
(London: Sidgwick and Jackson 1993).

Billy Webb;
Running with the Krays
(Edinburgh: Mainstream Publishing 1993).

Chris Lambrianou and Robin McGibbon;
Escape From the Kray Madness
(London: Sidgwick and Jackson 1995).

Mrs X with James Morton;
Calling Time on the Krays: The Barmaid's Tale
(London: Little, Brown and Company 1996).

Martin Fido;
The Krays: Unfinished Business
(London: Carlton Books 1999).

Laurie O'Leary;
Ronnie Kray – A Man Amongst Men
(London: Headline 2001).

John Pearson;
The Cult of Violence
(London: Orion Books 2001).

Craig Cabell;
The Kray Brothers: The Image Shattered
(London: Robson 2002).

Albert Donoghue & Martin Short;
The Enforcer
(London: John Blake 2002).

Lenny Hamilton & Craig Cabell;
Getting Away With Murder
(London: John Blake 2006).

Joe Lee, Rita Smith and Peter Gerrard;
Inside the Kray Family
(London: Carlton 2008).

Reg Kray;
Reggie Kray's East End Stories
(London: Sphere 2010).

John Pearson;
Notorious
(London: Century 2010).

Bobby Teale with Clare Campbell:
Bringing Down the Krays
(London: Ebury Publishing 2012).

Mickey Fawcett;
Krayzy Days
(Brighton: Pen Press 2013).

Jacky Hyams;
Frances: The Tragic Bride
(London: John Blake 2014).

Maureen Flanagan with Jacky Hyams;
One of the Family: 40 Years With the Krays
(London: Century 2015).

APPENDIX TWO

THE KRAYS FAMILY TREE

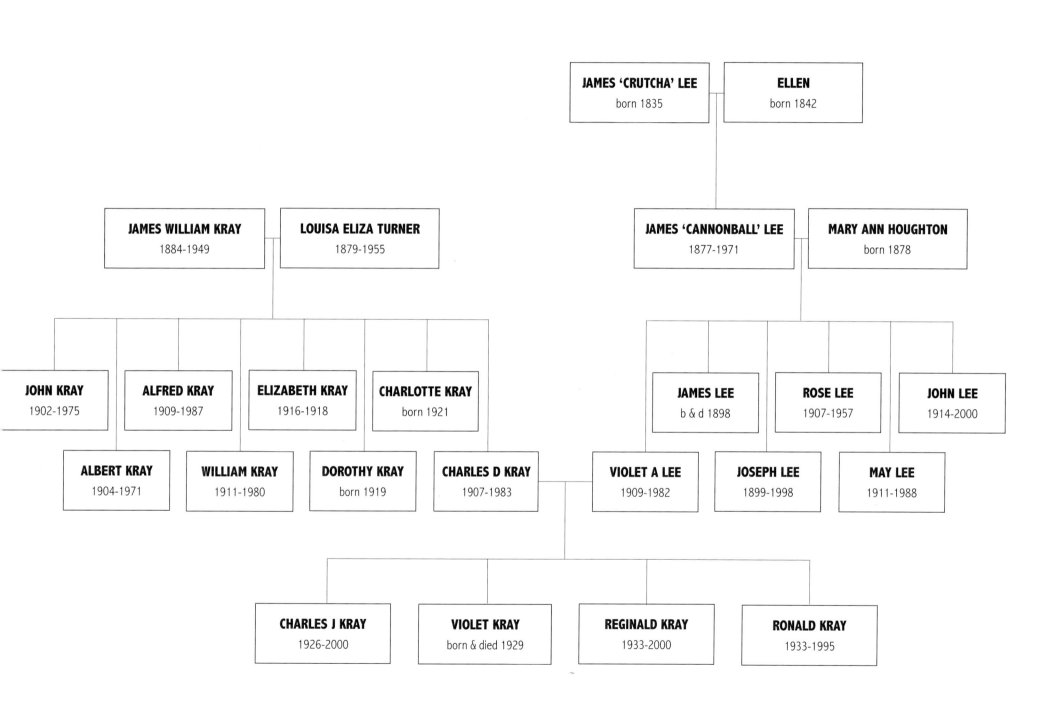

APPENDIX THREE

MAPS OF THE KRAYS' EAST END

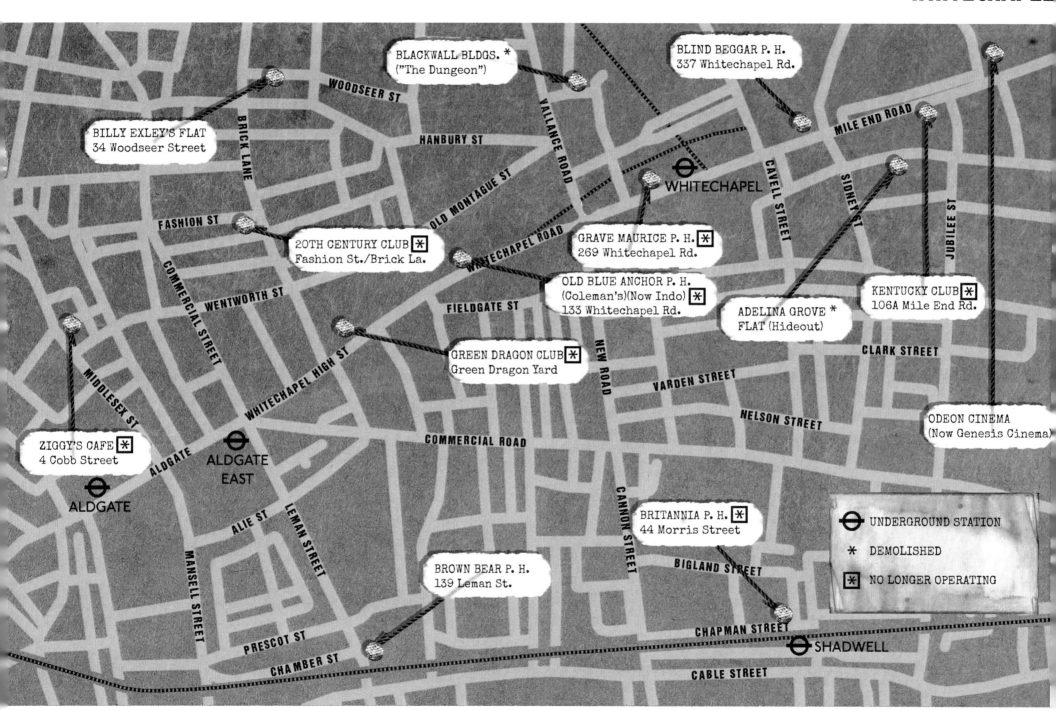

BLACKWALL BLDGS. *
("The Dungeon")

BLIND BEGGAR P. H.
337 Whitechapel Rd.

WOODSEER ST

HANBURY ST

BILLY EXLEY'S FLAT
34 Woodseer Street

BRICK LANE

OLD MONTAGUE ST

VALLANCE ROAD

MILE END ROAD

CAVELL STREET

WHITECHAPEL

SIDNEY ST

JUBILEE ST

FASHION ST

20TH CENTURY CLUB ⊠
Fashion St./Brick La.

WHITECHAPEL ROAD

GRAVE MAURICE P. H. ⊠
269 Whitechapel Rd.

COMMERCIAL STREET

WENTWORTH ST

OLD BLUE ANCHOR P. H.
(Coleman's)(Now Indo) ⊠
133 Whitechapel Rd.

FIELDGATE ST

ADELINA GROVE *
FLAT (Hideout)

KENTUCKY CLUB ⊠
106A Mile End Rd.

CLARK STREET

WHITECHAPEL HIGH ST

GREEN DRAGON CLUB ⊠
Green Dragon Yard

NEW ROAD

VARDEN STREET

NELSON STREET

ODEON CINEMA
(Now Genesis Cinema)

MIDDLESEX ST

COMMERCIAL ROAD

ZIGGY'S CAFE ⊠
4 Cobb Street

ALDGATE

ALDGATE
EAST

ALDGATE

ALIE ST

LEMAN STREET

CANNON STREET

BRITANNIA P. H. ⊠
44 Morris Street

⊖ UNDERGROUND STATION

* DEMOLISHED

⊠ NO LONGER OPERATING

MANSELL STREET

BIGLAND STREET

BROWN BEAR P. H.
139 Leman St.

PRESCOT ST

CHAMBER ST

CHAPMAN STREET

SHADWELL

CABLE STREET

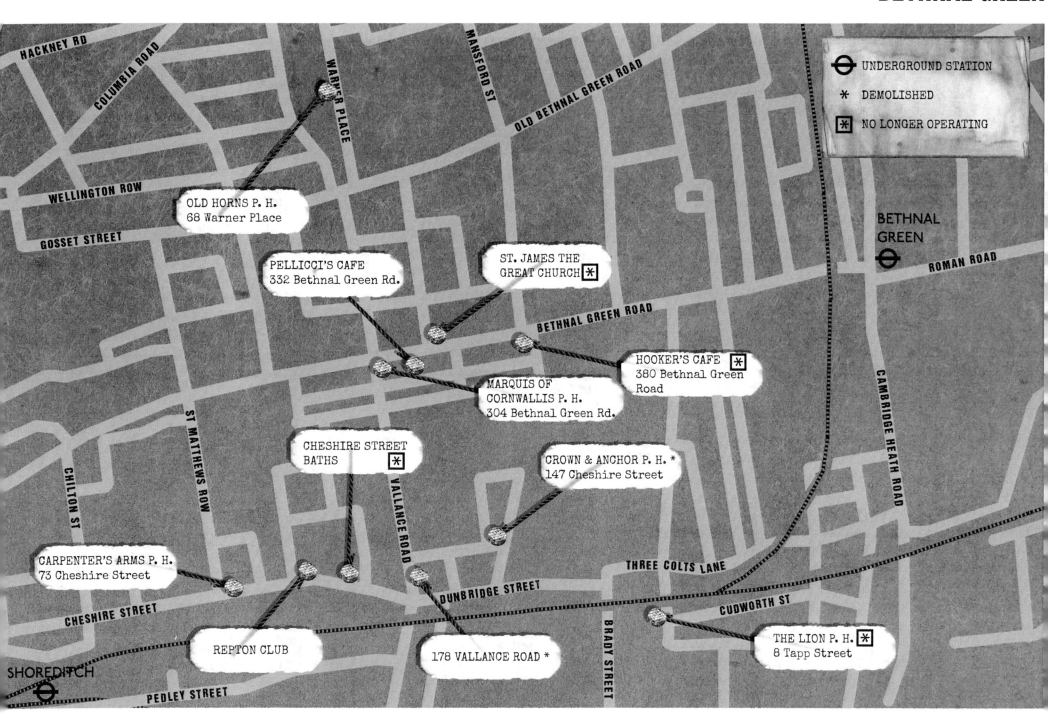

BETHNAL GREEN

UNDERGROUND STATION

* DEMOLISHED

NO LONGER OPERATING

HACKNEY RD

COLUMBIA ROAD

WELLINGTON ROW

GOSSET STREET

WARNER PLACE

MANSFORD ST

OLD BETHNAL GREEN ROAD

BETHNAL GREEN

ROMAN ROAD

OLD HORNS P. H.
68 Warner Place

PELLICCI'S CAFE
332 Bethnal Green Rd.

ST. JAMES THE
GREAT CHURCH

BETHNAL GREEN ROAD

HOOKER'S CAFE
380 Bethnal Green
Road

MARQUIS OF
CORNWALLIS P. H.
304 Bethnal Green Rd.

CAMBRIDGE HEATH ROAD

ST MATHEWS ROW

CHESHIRE STREET
BATHS

CROWN & ANCHOR P. H. *
147 Cheshire Street

CHILTON ST

VALLANCE ROAD

CARPENTER'S ARMS P. H.
73 Cheshire Street

THREE COLTS LANE

DUNBRIDGE STREET

CUDWORTH ST

CHESHIRE STREET

BRADY STREET

THE LION P. H.
8 Tapp Street

SHOREDITCH

REPTON CLUB

178 VALLANCE ROAD *

PEDLEY STREET

ACKNOWLEDGEMENTS

First and foremost I would like to thank Adam Wood at Mango Books, whose generosity, vision, and open-mindedness made this book a reality after many false starts; Mark Ripper, for his thorough editorial work on the manuscript; David Green for his extremely helpful suggestions and indexing; Andrew Firth for his wonderful maps; Laura Prieto at Laura P Imagery; Sharon Adams at the BBC; Laurie Allen; David Barrington; Paul Begg; Neil Bell; Paul Bickley at New Scotland Yard's Crime Museum; Richard Cobb; Denis Ellam; Kate Lambert and Candy Vincent Smith at Studiocanal; Keith Skinner; Robert Smith; Andrew Tigue and Angus Watts at Thinkjam; Staff at the National Archives, Kew; London Metropolitan Archives; the Museum of London; Stefan Dickers at the Bishopsgate Institute; Malcolm Hamilton-Barr and the staff at Tower Hamlets Archives.

This book is dedicated to my family (East Enders one and all) and to Laura who, for the first time in one of my book dedications, I can proudly say is my wife.

INDEX

20th Century Club, Brick Lane, 131, 161, 220
21 Rooms (West End club), 69
66 Club, Islington, 202–3
99 Public House, Moorgate, 41, 68
211 Club, Balham, 301, 322

Aarvold, Carl, Judge, 173, 174
Abberline, Chief Inspector Frederick, 154
Aberfan Disaster Fund, 283–4
Abrahams, Harry, 63, 67, 81, 110, 125
Abrahams, Joe, 79
Ackerman, Bill, 106, 170, 171, 215
Acton, Detective Constable Sheila, 337
Adams (barber's shop), Leyton, 242
Adams Casino Enterprises, 124, 125
Adelina Grove: safe house, 89, 105
Agate, Dick, 74
Albert Hall, 51
Alford, Eddie, 62
Allen, Geoff: meets the twins, 69–70; Hadleigh retreat, 88; and Townshend bribery case, 246, 263; at twins' thirty-fourth birthday party, 303–4; at Evering Road party, 309; Gedding Hall, 325, 329–31; finds Suffolk property for twins, 339
Allen, Detective Constable Pat, 337, 362
Allen, Terry, 189

Allpress, Danny, 124
Amass, William, 219, 224, 232
Ambrose, Billy, 106–7, 218
American Mafia, 133–4, 183–5, 299, 341–3, 349
Anderson, Detective Constable, 226
Anderson, Gordon, 194, 358, 360
Andrews, Jimmy, 219
Anglo-Pakistani Club, Campbell Road, 81–3
Armstrong-Jones, Anthony, 123
Artichoke (pub), Wapping, 74
Astor Club, Mayfair, 111, 203, 204, 205, 206, 355
Athens: Reggie and Frances honeymoon in, 191
Atlantic Machines, 204, 205, 209
Aucott, Patrick, 47–8
'aways' (displaced ex-cons), 63, 101, 121, 203, 263
Axon, Detective Superintendent James, 228–9, 232, 234, 241

Bacon, Francis, 171
Bailey, David, 186–7, 189, 283, 340
Baker's Arms (pub), Hackney, 244–6, 263
Barker, Detective Constable Peter, 244
Barking Road (206A), East Ham, 265–7, 270, 272, 274–6, 277, 284

Barnard, Sylvia, 249–50, 301, 303, 325, 338
Barratt, Michael, 157
Barrie, Ian ('Scotch Ian'): background, 160; meets Krays and joins Firm, 161, 163; at Glenrae Club, 171; and Ronnie's kill list, 208; silent about time with Krays, 213; and Cornell shooting, 220–2, 223, 225, 233; returns to Lion pub, 229; gets out of East End, 229–30; in Chingford with Ronnie, 241; police identification parade, 242; and Townshend bribery case, 244, 263; reconnaissance mission at Stoke Newington club, 253; arrested, 359; charged with Cornell murder, 362
Barrie's Dance Hall, Hackney, 47, 48
Barry, Anthony, 125n, 247–8, 307–8, 310, 363
Barry, John, 125n, 208, 247–8, 301
Bart, Lionel, 171
Bartlett, PC Robert, 225–6
Baynton, PC Donald, 49–50
BBC News: interview with Kray twins, 177–8, 183
bearer bonds racket, 184–5, 194, 255, 299, 349
Beatles (band), 192, 283
Bellamy, Billy, 58
Bender, Ronnie: background and joins Firm, 202; introduces Chris Lambrianou to twins, 288; affair with 'Bubbles', 303; on night of McVitie murder, 307–9, 310; involvement in McVitie murder, 312, 314–17, 320; leaves body in Rotherhithe, 317–18; removes bloodstained carpet, 321; mission to shoot Romford man, 333; refuses to kill Frankie Shea, 340–1; charged with McVitie murder, 363
Bending, Joan, 106
Berry, Edward, 110, 121, 332
Berry, Henry 'Checker', 62, 110, 351
Bethnal Green, 15–16, 32
Bethnal Green Mob (gang), 63
Bethnal Green Police Station, 50

Billingsgate Market, 44
Binfield, Ena, 138
Bird, Freddie, 170, 358, 360
Black, Bernard, 141, 143
black market, 35
Black Swan (pub), Bow Road, 162
Blackwall Buildings (Flat 2), off Vallance Road, 331
Blasker, Dr Morris, 61–2, 96, 171, 200, 253, 254, 296
Blind Beggar (pub), Whitechapel: as tourist attraction, 212; regular drinking spot for Cornell, 216, 218; premises and staff, 217–18; evening of the murder, 219–20, 222; shooting of Cornell, 223–6; emergency services at scene, 225–6; crime scene forensics, 227, 231, 232; Olive Myers arrives, 227–8; Maureen Flanagan's book launch party, 369
Blonde Carole see Skinner, Carole Anne
Blueboy, Moishe, 45–6, 69–70
Blythe, Billie, 68
bombing raids (and blitz), 30–1, 32, 38–9
Booth, Charles, 11
Booth, James, 122
Boothby, Robert ('Bob'), Baron: background and political life, 134–6; relationship with Leslie Holt, 136; illicit parties at Cedra Court, 138–9; Eaton Square meetings, 140–1; revelations in Sunday Mirror, 141–4; sexual proclivities, 145; named in Stern, 146–7; considers libel action, 147–8; Parliamentary cover-up, 148–9, 152; denial letter to The Times, 149–51; damages and apology, 151–2; pays off Holt, 152–3; campaigns on behalf of Krays in Lords, 171–3; sends wedding telegram to Reggie, 189
Botton, Henry, 209
Bow Police Station, 102
Bow Street Magistrates' Court, 359–60
boxing, 13, 16, 27–8, 37–8, 43–4, 51–2, 57

Braithwaite House, 338–9, 340, 344–5, 355–7
Brick Lane, 13, 41, 160–1
Briddon, PC Bernard, 91
briefcase assassination plot, 256–8, 348
Brisco, Derek, 91, 259–60, 261–2, 264
Britannia (pub), Chapman Street, 74–5
Broadmoor, 91, 104, 371
Brodie, Assistant Commissioner Peter, 298
Brooks, The, Bildeston, Suffolk, 339–40, 354
Brown, Tommy *see* Welch, Tommy
Brown Bear (pub), Leman Street, 214, 304
Brown Derby (club), Soho, 203
Bruno, Angelo, 133, 170, 183, 342
Bryant, John, 125
Bryant, Ted, 56
Bryant, Tom, 101
'Bubbles' (Lily; Frankie Shea's common-law wife), 285, 292, 303, 308, 340
Buckley, Robert, 133, 361
Budd, William, 22
Burch, Walter, 47
Butler, Pat, 45, 49, 62, 64, 110
Butler, Detective Superintendent Tommy, 238, 241, 242, 248, 335; report on Kray activities, 107–8
Byrne, Peter, 174, 175–6

C11 (Criminal Intelligence) branch, Metropolitan Police, 140, 141
Cabell, Craig: *The Kray Brothers: The Image Shattered*, 213
Cable, Vince, 193
Caine, Michael, 58n, 186, 187
Callaghan, Jerry, 276, 280
Cambridge Rooms (club), Kingston Bypass, 120, 167
Cambridge University Union, 193
Camp Hill Prison, Isle of Wight, 77–8, 83
Camps, Francis, 257n, 258
Canadian bearer bonds racket, 184–5, 194, 255, 299, 349
car bomb plot, 345, 346–7

Cardew, Johnny, 341
Carpenter's Arms (pub), Cheshire Street, 289–90, 303–4, 306
Carsten Securities Ltd, 114
Caruana, George, 344–5
Castro, Fidel, 133
Cater, Detective Inspector Frank, 356–7, 359, 360–1
Cavendish, Diana, 136
Cedra Court, Stoke Newington: twins rent apartments, 137; illicit parties, 138–9; under police surveillance, 140; courtyard photograph of twins, 151; unpaid bills, 159, 170; police search, 170–1; Reggie and Frances move into, 198; twins avoid, 241
celebrities, 81, 100, 122–3, 171, 187, 189, 192
Cellini, Dino, 133–4
Ceville, Don, 194
Chappell, John, 361
Chequers (pub), Walthamstow, 230
Chester, Lewis, 185
Chingford Mount Cemetery, 293
City Road Police Station, 156, 169
Clapton, Eric, 115
Clarke, Charlie 'Nobby': in the Firm, 112, 171; and Ronnie's kill list, 208; gets out of East End, 229; disposes of guns, 230; Ronnie stays with, 241; and Townshend bribery case, 244; shot by Reggie, 250, 252–3; and Frank Mitchell, 265, 274; meets John Pearson, 332; charges against, 360
Clarke, Brigadier Terence, 141
Clein, Dr Lewis, 200–1, 290
Clinton Road, Mile End, 53, 54
Clulow, Terry, 304, 309, 311, 313, 363
Coach and Horses (pub), Mile End Road, 64–5
Coach and Horses (pub), Stoke Newington, 306, 324
Coates, Sheila, 47–8
Cohen, David, 79
Colchester Military Detention Barracks, 55

Collingburn, Leonard, 91

Collins, Mrs (friend of Olive Myers), 227

Collins, Jackie, 100

Collins, Kathleen ('Kitty'), 305–6, 309, 315, 324–5, 359

Colony Club, Mayfair, 184, 203

Commercial Street Police Station, 154, 242

Congo rescue scam, 195–6

Connolly, 'Big' Pat: at the Double R Club, 80, 110; criminal record, 80n; cameo in *Sparrows Can't Sing,* 122; protection racket at Adams Casino Enterprises, 124; at the Regency Club, 125; at Reggie's wedding, 189; visits Frank Mitchell in Dartmoor, 240, 262, 268; questioned by police, 268; at Pellicci's Cafe, 287; rents room on Evering Road, 305; at Evering Road on night of McVitie murder, 309, 310; charges against, 361

Conservative Party: 1964 general election, 142; and Boothby affair, 145–6, 149

Constantino, Matty, 106

Cook, George and Betsy, 19

Cook, Peter, 130–1

Cooney, Selwyn, 106–7

Cooper, Alan Bruce: background and criminal life, 194–5; and Congo rescue scam, 195–6; drug-smuggling scheme, 201; and stolen Canadian securities, 201–2; and contract to kill Jimmy Evans, 255–8; New York trip with Ronnie, 341–3; and plot to murder George Caruana, 344–6; wire-tapped by 'Nipper' Read, 347; arrested, 348; as Secret Service informer and *agent provocateur,* 348–9; makes statement, 349–50; hospitalised as trap for Krays, 354–5

Cooper, Henry (boxer), 81

Cooper, Henry (Marie McVitie's partner), 117

Cooper, Sergeant Walter, 75–6

Coote, Colin, 142–3

Cope, Harry 'Jew Boy', 171, 244, 263, 287, 303

Cornell, George: background and criminal career, 65–7; at Stragglers club, 73; henchman for Richardson brothers, 104, 203, 297; and Lenny Hamilton, 128; 'fat poof' put-down, 206–8, 213–14; and Ronnie's kill list, 208–9; feud with Ronnie, 213–17; regular customer at Blind Beggar, 216, 218; in wrong place at wrong time, 217; movements on day of murder, 219–20; shot by Ronnie, 222–6; taken to hospital, 226–7, 228; dies, 228; post-mortem, 232; body identified and death registered, 232; press coverage, 231, 235; murder investigation, 228–9, 231, 232–5, 242–3, 286–7, 335, 362; Ronnie and Ian Barrie charged, 362

Cornell, James, 65, 232

Cornell, Joseph (friend of Mary Ann Garrett), 65–6

Cornell, Joseph (George's brother), 216, 232

Cornell, Olive see Myers, Olive

Corri, Adrienne, 192

Courtney, Dave, 369

Cowley, Tommy: joins the Firm, 112; and contract to kill Jimmy Evans, 255–6; procures female companion for Frank Mitchell, 268, 269–70; and plans to kill Frank Mitchell, 274; at Pellicci's Cafe, 287; connection with McVitie murder, 320, 322; at Gedding Hall, 330; and plot to murder George Caruana, 344–5; assault on Webb brothers, 351; visits Alan Cooper in nursing home, 354; arrested, 358; charges against, 360, 361

Cox, Frederick, 137, 139

Crowder, Peter, QC, 173, 174

Crown and Anchor (pub), Cheshire Street, 120, 161, 163, 255–6

Cuba: gambling outlawed, 133

Cudlipp, Hugh (*later* Baron Cudlipp), 141–2, 149

Daily Express, 151, 192, 235

Daily Mirror, 141, 231, 267, 271

Dale, John: in Blind Beggar pub, 219–20, 222; witnesses shooting of Cornell, 223; identified by fingerprints, 232; gives statement to police, 233; unofficially identifies Ronnie Kray, 233–4

Daniels. Billy, 171

Darling, Dennis, 267–8

Dartmoor Prison: Mitchell at, 240–1; Honour Party system, 259–60, 262, 271–2; Mitchell's escape from, 263–5

David Bailey's Box of Pinups (book), 187

Davidson, PC Francis, 225–6

Davis, Arnold, 360

Davis, Johnny, 81, 110, 170, 171

Davis Feather Mills, Whitechapel, 44

De Faye, Stefan, 114–15

deserters (from Second World War), 50n

Devlin, George, 175, 192, 244, 246

Dew, Walter, 154

Diamond, Ronnie, 58

Dickson, John ('Scotch Jack'): background, 160; joins the Firm, 161, 163; at Glenrae Club, 171; and Congo rescue scam, 195–6; and Ronnie's kill list, 208; getaway driver at Cornell shooting, 220–2, 225; returns to Lion pub, 229; gets out of East End, 229–30; tails McVitie, 250; and Reggie's attack on 'Nobby' Clarke, 252; and shooting at Stoke Newington club, 253–4; minder for Frank Mitchell, 266, 272, 274, 277; warns McVitie, 302; at twins' thirty-fourth birthday party, 303; learns of McVitie murder, 323–4; mission to shoot Romford man, 333–4; visits Billy Exley, 335; talk of killing the Krays, 352; witnesses assault on Webb brothers, 351; arrested, 359; charges against, 361

Dillinger, John, 24

Dimes, Albert, 104, 128, 133

diphtheria, 25–6

Dixon, George, 248–9

Dodson, Sir Gerald, 76–7

Donaldson, Detective Sergeant, 356

Donoghue, Albert: on fights between the twins, 73; background and criminal career, 128, 190n; speaks out on Hamilton assault, 128–9; shot at by Reggie, 161–3; joins the Firm, 163; on relations between Reggie and Frances Shea, 190, 200; on Ronnie's obsession with Richardson gang, 206; and Ronnie's kill list, 208–9; and Cornell shooting, 220–1, 225n, 230; gets out of East End, 229–30; protection racket at Regency Club, 247–8; springing of Frank Mitchell, 240–1, 262, 263–6, 272; introduces Lisa to Mitchell, 269–70; and Mitchell's murder, 273–9, 280, 282; spends night with Lisa, 278, 305; at Frances Shea's funeral, 294; at twins' thirty-fourth birthday party, 303; redecorates Evering Road flat, 324; on disappearance of Teddy Smith, 333; oppressive atmosphere within the Firm, 334, 343; witnesses assault on Webb brothers, 351; talk of killing the Krays, 352; arrested, 359; charges against, 361, 363; turns Queen's Evidence, 363

Donovan, Billy, 64–5, 80, 128, 163, 171

Dore, George, 260

Dors, Diana, 189

Dorset Street (*later* Duval Street), Spitalfields, 106

Double R Club, 79–81, 89, 100–1, 102, 108, 110

Dougall, Inspector John, 347

Down, Clifford (cab driver), 261n

Drake, Charlie, 123

Drayson, George Burnaby, 141

Driberg, Tom, 138–9, 141, 143, 148, 171, 189

drug smuggling, 201, 301

Drury, Raymond: in Blind Beggar pub, 222; witnesses shooting of Cornell,

223–4; questioned by police, 232;
gives statement, 233
du Rose, Chief Superintendent John,
297, 299, 348–9, 358
Dunbridge Street, Bethnal Green *see*
London Street
Dunloe Place, off Hackney Road, 28
Dunn, Lennie, 265–6, 272, 274, 275–6,
277, 282, 284–5, 360
Durand, Victor, 76
Duval Street (*formerly* Dorset Street),
Spitalfields, 106

East End: black market trading, 35;
bombing raids, 30–1, 32, 38–9;
first Royal Premiere (1963), 123;
gang warfare, 76–7, 235; gangster
tours, 212; organised crime, 144–5;
slum clearance and redevelopment,
285–6; street gangs, 63, 65, 73, 103;
underworld hang-outs, 35–6, 58, 60;
women's lives, 111
East Farleigh, Kent, 321
East House, Hadleigh, 31
Eaton Square, Mayfair, 140–1;
photographs, 143–4, 146–7, 151
Effingham, Mowbray Henry, 6th Earl of,
115
El Morocco (*formerly* the Hideaway
Club), 191–2, 305
electrocution torture incident, 124–5
Elephant's Nest (pub), near Tavistock,
260, 261
Elvey, Eugene Paul, 256–8, 345–8,
349–50
Empire Cinema, Stepney, 122–3
Enugu project, Nigeria, 134, 139–40,
158–9, 166, 194
Epsom races, 68
Esmeralda's Barn: Krays acquire,
114–15; running of, 118–19, 131–2;
Hamilton assaulted at, 126–7; Tom
Driberg at, 138; debts and closes
down, 158, 159
Establishment Club, Soho, 130–1
Evans, Jimmy, 235n, 255–8, 348

Evans, William, 42
Evering Road (No. 97), Stoke
Newington: Donoghue and Lisa
spend night at, 278; regular party
venue, 305; McVitie murdered at,
309–11, 312–17, 318; flat cleaned and
redecorated, 321, 324, 325; police
visit, 359; searched for evidence, 363
Exeter Prison, 118
Exley, Billy: Kray associate, 81;
witnesses assault on Lenny Hamilton,
126; barman at Glenrae Club, 164,
168, 171; visits Frank Mitchell in
Dartmoor, 240; hires escape vehicle,
263; minder duties, 266, 270–1, 272,
274; accused of Mitchell's murder,
280; disenchanted with Krays, 282,
334–5; mission to shoot Payne,
300; hospitalised following heart
attack, 334; talks to Nipper Read,
336; charges against, 360; statement
concerning Frank Mitchell, 360–1

Fallon, PC Jeremiah, 99–100 & n
Farren & Barrow (traders), Billingsgate,
44
Farson, Dan, 122
Fawcett, Mickey: Kray associate, 80,
170; on the Double R Club, 101; on
relations between Reggie and Frances
Shea, 182, 200; on Ronnie's dislike of
Frances, 198; on Ronnie's selfishness,
199; on 'fat poof' story, 207; and
'Magic Bullet' incident, 248–9;
contemplates killing Reggie, 353, 354;
Krayzy Days, 71n
Fido, Martin: *The Krays: Unfinished
Business,* 213, 311–12, 327
Fielder's Tinsmiths, Bethnal Green, 44
Filler, Albert (May Lee's husband), 28,
33, 339
Firm, the: beginnings, 62–3; recruiting
and expanding, 80–1, 112, 159–61,
202–3, 236, 247–8, 287–9; local roots,
120–1; mobilised against Richardson
gang, 208; fear and paranoia within,

289, 334, 343–4, 350; shift of loyalties, 334–5; and talk of killing the twins, 352–3; rounded up by police, 358–9

Fisher, PC Roy, 55, 57

Fiske, Valerie, 269, 271, 282, 361

Flanagan, Maureen, 6, 180, 181, 188, 190, 294–5; book launch party, 369

Flannery, Michael: in Blind Beggar pub, 222; witnesses shooting of Cornell, 223–4; questioned by police, 232; gives statement, 232–3

Foreman, Freddie: criminal life, 104–5; relations with Charlie and the twins, 104–5, 171; on McVitie, 118; on Esmeralda's Barn, 132; foots bill for failed Enugu project, 159; at twins' acquittal party, 192; at London gangs summit, 206; accidentally kills Tommy Marks, 235n, 255; and contract to kill Jimmy Evans, 255; and murder of Frank Mitchell, 273–4, 276–7, 279; disposes of Mitchell's body, 280; Prince of Wales pub, 289n; confrontation with McVitie, 301; disposes of McVitie's body, 322–3; nicknamed 'The Undertaker', 322n; view on McVitie killing, 326; hatches plot to kill the twins, 353–4; charged with disposing of McVitie's body, 280, 363; as celebrity 'villain', 369

Foreman, George, 235n, 255

Forland, David, 81, 126, 360

Foster, Father John, 188

France, Gilbert, 165, 167

Francis, Johnny, 165–7, 169–70

Fraser, 'Mad' Frankie: background and criminal career, 37, 104; minder for Billy Hill, 68; in Exeter Prison with Jack McVitie, 118; owns club in Soho, 165; enforcer for Richardson brothers, 203; and Atlantic Machines, 204; axe attack on Eric Mason, 205–6; and Cornell's 'fat poof' put-down, 207; targeted by Ronnie, 208; and Mr Smith's gunfight, 209–10; charged with murder of Dickie Hart, 211; and 'Torture Trial', 297; on whereabouts of Teddy Smith, 332

Frazer, Ronald, 123, 171

Frederick (gunshot victim), 296

Freud, Lucian, 119, 171

Frith, Maude see Lee, Maude

Frost, Billy, 66, 332, 334

Fry, Colin, 114

gambling, 115

Gaming Act (1960), 115

gang warfare, 2, 52, 63–4, 76–7; Pen Club shooting, 106–7; London gangs summit, 206, 208; Mr Smith's gunfight, 209–11; press coverage, 231, 235 see also Nash brothers; Richardson brothers

gangster tours of East End, 212

Gardner, William, 209

Garelick, 'Fat' Wally, 240, 252, 262, 268, 361

Garland, Judy, 171, 187, 189

Garrett, Mary Ann (George Cornell's mother), 65–6

Gedding Hall, Suffolk, 329–31

general election 1964, 141–2, 148

Gentry, Billy, 353

Gerrard, Alfie, 276–7, 280, 322–3

Gerrard, Chief Superintendent Frederick, 154, 156, 168–9, 170, 190

Gerreli, PC Kenneth, 225–6

Gert and Daisy (comedy act), 334n

Gill, Ronnie, 34

Ginette's gay disco, 115–16, 119

'Ginger' (barman at Anglo-Pakistani club), 82

Glasgow airport: Elvey arrested at, 346–7

Glenrae Hotel and Club, 163–5, 168, 170, 171, 190–1

Goldblatt, Marshall, 360

Goodman, Arnold (later Baron Goodman), 148–9, 151, 152

Gore, Frederick, 112, 114–15, 131, 134, 139, 158–9, 337

Gorsuch Street, Bethnal Green, 12, 19
Gould, Robert, 166n, 358, 360
Grave Maurice (pub), Whitechapel Road,
    89n, 120, 156–7, 161, 166–7, 208,
    221n, 257, 300
Great African Safari (GAS) scheme, 134,
    139–40, 158–9, 166, 194
Greek Civil War (1946–49), 191n
Green Dragon Club, 105–6, 215, 248,
    326, 352
Greenways (private hospital),
    Hampstead, 200–1, 290

Hackett, Richard, 74n
Hackney Hospital, 290, 351–2
Hadleigh, Suffolk, 31–2, 88
Haines, Corporal Ted, 56
Hale and Pace (comedians), 368–9
Hall, Detective Sergeant, 168
Hamilton, Lenny: first encounter with
    twins, 54–5; on George Cornell, 66;
    becomes Kray associate, 81; on Jack
    McVitie, 118; branding incident,
    125–8; on Ronnie Bender, 202; on
    feud between Ronnie and Cornell,
    214; and 'Magic Bullet' incident,
    248–9; claims Krays responsible for
    other deaths, 333n; gives statement
    to police, 338; Ronnie charged with
    assault on, 362
Hammersmith nude murders (1964–
    65) see Jack the Stripper murders
Hanly, Admiral John H., 348–9
Haque, Anwar, 81, 83
Hardy, Tom, 368
Hare, Robert, 121, 122
Harper, Greta, 94n
Harris, Detective Superintendent
    Edward, 268
Hart, Richard ('Dickie'), 209–11,
    215–16, 217
Hart, Ronnie: joins the Firm, 247–8;
    protection racket at Regency Club,
    247–8; and Reggie's attack on 'Nobby'
    Clarke, 252; at twins' thirty-fourth
    birthday party, 303–4; on night of

McVitie murder, 307–11; collects
    knife from Regency, 310; involvement
    in McVitie murder, 312–14; at Harry
    Hopwood's flat, 318–21; disposes
    of weapons, 319; mission to shoot
    Romford man, 333–4; talk of killing
    the twins, 352; turns Queen's
    Evidence, 363
Harvey, Roy, 47–9
Harwood, Winnie, 305
Hatfield, Michael, 289–90
Hayes and English (Hoxton funeral
    directors), 293
Hayward brothers, Billy and Harry,
    209–10, 211, 216
Hemingway, Detective Sergeant
    Algernon, 347–8, 356
Hennessey, Peter, 209–10
Hertzberg, Lily (and husband), 119
Heseltine, Michael, 271–2
Hetherington, Father Richard Neville,
    42, 45, 49, 187–8, 293, 294
Hideaway Club, 165, 166–8; reopens as
    El Morocco, 191–2, 305
Highbury Vale Police Station, 164, 169
Hill, Billy, 46, 61, 68–9, 103, 104, 239
Hill, David (Dartmoor farmer), 262
Hinds, Alfred ('Houdini' Hinds), 193
Hobbs, Charlie, 230
Holt, Inspector Frank, 337
Holt, Leslie Stanley: affair with Lord
    Boothby, 136; background and
    criminal career, 136–7; Eaton Square
    meeting, 140–1; link to MI5 informer,
    145; paid-off and threatened, 152–3;
    death, 153
Homerton Isolation Hospital, Hackney,
    26
homosexuality, 58–9, 59n, 116, 147; of
    Reggie, 93, 200; of Ronnie, 59, 71–2,
    92–3, 116, 138–9, 238
Honour Party scheme (Dartmoor
    prison), 259–60, 262, 271–2
Hooker's Cafe, Bethnal Green, 50n
Hopwood, George, 56
Hopwood, Harry: best man at Charlie

and Violet's wedding, 19; 'on the knocker', 41; abets twins' escape attempt from Canterbury jail, 56; at Glenrae Club, 171; flat used for Mitchell meeting, 273–4; and Carpenter's Arms, 289; twins stay with after McVitie murder, 318–21; disposes of weapons and bloodstained clothing, 319, 320–1; threats from Ronnie, 325; interrogated by police, 363

Hotel Organisations Ltd, 115
Houghton, Mary Ann see Lee, Mary Ann
Howe Barracks guardroom, Canterbury, 55–6
Hoxton, 9, 10–12, 27–8
Hughes Mansions, Vallance Road, 38
Humperdinck, Engelbert, 283
Hunter, Detective Sergeant James, 227
Hutton, Johnny, 70–1, 79
Hyams, Jacky, 292

International Publishing Company (IPC), 142, 151–2
intimidation see 'Wall of Fear/Silence
Ireson, Sandra, 94n
Isaacs, Henry, 219–20, 232

Jack the Ripper, 35, 106n, 154, 219n
Jack the Stripper murders, 202, 299
Jacobs and Sons (solicitors), 166
James, Vicky (later Hart), 304, 309, 310, 315, 317, 325
Jeffrey, Ronald, 209
Jenkins, Roy, 240, 271
Johns, PC Philip, 319, 363n
Jones, Billy, 73–5, 76
Jones, Howard, 227
Jones, Roberta (Reggie's second wife), 93
Jordan, Jackie, 51
jury tampering, 175

Kankus, Solly ('Solly the Turk'), 46
Kaufman, Joey, 342, 354–5, 358, 360
Keating, John, 218
Kells, Dr, 153

Kennedy, Ludovic, 135, 136
Kennedy, Mark, 360
Kenrick, Michael, 361
Kentucky Club, 121–4, 159
'Kill Order' (plan to kill the Krays), 353–4
King, Cecil, 142, 152
King, Henry, 225, 226, 232
King, Lionel 'Curly', 72, 86, 97
Kramer, Isaac, 219, 220
Kray, Alfred (uncle), 12, 161
Kray, Billy (uncle), 12, 161
Kray, Charlie (brother): birth, 19; childhood, 19–20, 21, 22–3, 27–8; and birth of twins, 9–10, 25; boxing, 27, 37–8, 43; in Hadleigh, 31, 32; job as messenger boy, 37; discharged from Navy, 41; on twins' adolescence, 44–5; reaction to police assault on Ronnie, 50; marriage to Dolly Moore, 51; pro boxing career, 51; frustrated at twins, 57; starts up travel business, 71; on Ronnie's sexuality, 71–2; and Double R Club, 80, 110; questioned over damage at Anglo-Pakistani Club, 82; and Ronnie's escape from Long Grove, 86, 87; on Ronnie's medication, 97; affair with Barbara Windsor, 100n, 122; relations with Freddie Foreman, 104–5; criminal record, 105; and Esmeralda's Barn, 114; and Lenny Hamilton, 128; and Great African Safari scheme, 140, 158–9; at Glenrae Club on night of twins' arrest, 168; at acquittal celebrations, 176; and stolen Canadian securities, 184–5, 194, 255; and Bailey photo shoot, 186; refused entry to Canada, 194; reservations about Alan Cooper, 195, 196; visits Frank Mitchell in Dartmoor, 240; and 'Magic Bullet' incident, 249; enraged at Clarke shooting, 253; and contract to kill Jimmy Evans, 255–6; and Frank Mitchell, 273–4; opens nightclub in Leicester, 288; and the Carpenter's Arms, 289; at Frances's inquest,

292; at twins' thirty-fourth birthday party, 303; connection with McVitie murder, 318, 320, 322, 323; meets John Pearson, 330; arrested, 357–8; in court at Bow Street, 359–60; charges against, 360, 361, 363

Kray, Charlie (father): birth, 12; work, 13, 18, 20; courts and marries Violet, 18–19; drinking and domestic violence, 20–1, 22, 41; moves to Stean Street, 22; on Violet's care of Ronnie, 26; encourages son Charlie's interest in boxing, 27; house moves, 28; prints business cards for Vallance Road, 29; at Hadleigh, 32; as deserter, 36–7, 50; abets twins' escape attempt from Canterbury jail, 56; on Ronnie's homosexuality, 71n; pleads leniency for twins, 76; visits Ronnie in Long Grove, 86; argument with Olive Myers, 235; at twins' thirty-fourth birthday party, 303; moves to Braithwaite House, 339

Kray, Dolly (*née* Moore; brother Charlie's wife), 51, 304, 320, 358

Kray, James (great-grandfather), 12

Kray, James ('Mad' Jimmy; grandfather), 12–13, 16, 19 & n, 27, 41

Kray, James (uncle), 12

Kray, Louisa Eliza (*née* Turner; grandmother), 12, 19n

KRAY, REGGIE: biographical sources, 3–6, 308, 311–12; appearance (*see* photographs and physical appearance); family background, 12–14, 16–22; birth, 9–10, 23; babyhood, 24–5; hospitalised with diphtheria, 25–6; personality development, 26–7; childhood and upbringing, 29–37, 41–3; at school, 29–30, 41–2; evacuated to Hadleigh, 31–2; interest in boxing, 37–8, 43–4; early trouble with railway police, 39–40; joint fighting force with Ronnie, 43, 64–5; first jobs, 44; as tearaway and street thug, 44–5; first gun, 46; acquitted of GBH (Harvey case), 47–9; assault on police officer, 49–51; becomes professional boxer, 51–2; *détente* with Webb brothers, 52; National Service, 52–3, 55–7; on run from army, 54–5; imprisoned for assault, 55; dishonourable discharge, 57; end of boxing career, 57; mixes with villains, 58, 60–1; early criminal activities, 59, 61; on Billy Hill, 61; and the Regal, 62–3, 83–4, 101–2; Coach and Horses fight, 64–5; charged with attempted murder (African case), 67–8; association with Jack Spot and Billy Hill, 68–9; and Ronnie's shooting of docker, 70–1; aggressive instincts, 72; memory for grudges, 72, 129; fights between twins, 73; door-work, 73–4, 80; acquitted of GBH (Martin case), 74–6; opens Double R Club, 79–81; gambling club ventures, 81–3; intimidation and 'Wall of Fear', 82–3; and Ronnie's escape from Long Grove, 86–8; hands Ronnie over to authorities, 90; sexuality, 92–4, 200, 295; engages Frankie Shea as driver, 94, 95; falls for Frances Shea, 96; demands money with menaces, 98–100; imprisoned then released on bail, 100; remonstrates with Ronnie over running of Double R Club, 101; harbours Ronald Marwood, 102; assaults Sonny the Yank, 105–6; at Pen Club trial, 107; writes to Scotland Yard denying criminal interests, 107; police raids, 110; courts Frances, 111; beats up Bobby Ramsey, 113; partnership with Leslie Payne, 114–15; and Esmeralda's Barn, 114–15, 131–2; returned to Wandsworth, 116; meets Frank Mitchell, 116; first meeting with Jack McVitie, 118; release from prison, 119; success and wealth, 119, 120, 123, 130; acquitted of burglary, 119–20; marriage intentions, 120; philanthropy and charity work, 121–3, 283–4; cameo in *Sparrows Can't Sing*,

122; torture incident, 124–5; foothold in West End, 130–1; dealings with the American Mafia, 133–4, 183–5, 299, 349; at Cedra Court, 137, 151; Nigerian investment scheme, 139, 158–9; precarious finances, 159, 163; shoots Albert Donoghue, 161–3; and the Glenrae Club, 163–5, 171, 190–1; dealings with McCowan, 165–8; arrested on menace charges, 168–9; bail refused, 169, 171; trial, 173–6; admits to jury tampering, 175; acquittal celebrations, 176–7, 192; television interview, 177–8, 183; celebrity status, 171, 185–7, 193, 282–4, 367–9, 371–2; relationship with Frances, 180–3; and stolen Canadian securities, 185, 194, 255, 299; and Bailey photo shoot, 185–7; wedding and reception, 187–90; honeymoon in Athens, 191; invited to debate at Cambridge University Union, 193; reservations about Alan Cooper, 195, 196, 341; married life, 197–200; couple move into Cedra Court, 198; feelings for Frankie Shea, 200; sexual relations with wife, 200, 295; and drug-smuggling, 201, 301; relations with the Richardson gang, 105, 204–5; and Eric Mason assault, 205–6; at London gangs summit, 206, 208; Ronnie's kill list, 208–9; hitman story, 214; alarmed at Ronnie's threat to 'do' Cornell, 221; gets out of East End, 229–31; at Moresby Road flat, 237; in Morocco, 239; detained by police, 242–3; on Ronnie Hart, 247; McVitie double-crosses, 250; marriage over, 251–2; heavy drinking, 252; shoots 'Nobby' Clarke, 252–3; shoots club owner in Stoke Newington, 253–4; lies low, 254; and Frances's suicide attempt, 255; personal and financial pressures, 255; and contract to kill Jimmy Evans, 255–8; visits Frank Mitchell, 266; plans to

murder Mitchell, 273–4; debriefs Lisa, 278; reaction to Mitchell's death, 279; and the music business, 283; and the Carpenter's Arms, 289–90; seeks reconciliation with Frances, 290–1; premonition, 291; reaction to Frances's death, 291–2; at inquest, 292; Frances's funeral, 293–4; doomed marriage, 294–6; twin bond, 295; increasingly unpredictable and violent behaviour, 296; shoots Frederick, 296; plans murder of Leslie Payne, 300; McVitie disrespects and threatens, 301–2; McVitie's 'last' meal with, 301, 327; thirty-fourth birthday party, 303–5, 306; quarrels with Ronnie, 307; lead-up to McVitie murder, 307–11; murders McVitie, 312–14; at Harry Hopwood's flat, 318–21; lies low in Tottenham, 323–4; motives for killing McVitie, 325–8; with Geoff Allen in Suffolk, 325, 329–31; meetings with John Pearson, 330–2; and disappearance of Teddy Smith, 332–3; continued heavy drinking, 334, 340; buys The Brooks in Suffolk, 339–40; and plot to murder George Caruana, 344–5; and stateside anti-Kray operation, 348–9; assault on Webb brothers, 350–2; other unprovoked attacks, 352; as assassination target, 352–4; last night of freedom, 355; arrested, 356–7; in court at Bow Street, 359–60; charged with murder, 361, 363; collapse of the Kray empire, 364–5; legacy and legendary status, 365, 367; film and TV representations, 367–9; author's opinion of, 369–72

KRAY, RONNIE: biographical sources, 3–6, 212–13, 308, 311–12; appearance (*see* photographs and physical appearance); family background, 12–14, 16–22; birth, 9–10, 23; babyhood, 24–5; hospitalised with diphtheria, 25–6;

personality development, 26–7; childhood and upbringing, 29–37, 41–3; at school, 29–30, 41–2; evacuated to Hadleigh, 31–2; accidentally shoots boy in eye, 32; interest in boxing, 37–8, 43–4; joint fighting force with Reggie, 43, 64–5; first jobs, 44; as tearaway and street thug, 44–5; gangster aspirations, 46; first gun, 46; acquitted of GBH (Harvey case), 47–9; first conviction, 49; assault on police officer, 49–51; beaten up by police, 50; becomes professional boxer, 51–2; détente with Webb brothers, 52; National Service, 52–3, 55–7; on run from army, 54–5; imprisoned for assault, 55; dishonourable discharge, 57; sense of humour, 57, 101, 123, 249, 357n; end of boxing career, 57; mixes with villains, 58, 60–1; sexuality, 59, 71–2, 92–3, 116, 138–9, 238, 283; early criminal activities, 59, 61; and the Regal, 62–3, 83–4, 101–2; obsession with weapons, 63, 72, 75–6, 169; scares off Maltese gang, 63–4; Coach and Horses fight, 64–5; charged with attempted murder (African case), 67–8; association with Jack Spot and Billy Hill, 68–9; shoots docker at car-dealers, 70–1; nicknamed 'The Colonel', 72; sadism and uncontrollable violence, 72–3, 127; fights between twins, 73; door-work, 73–4; assault on Terry Martin, 74–6; in Wandsworth Prison, 77, 90; transferred to Camp Hill Prison, 77–8; mental health, 78, 84–6, 88–90; moved to Winchester Prison psychiatric unit, 83–5; certified insane, 85; at Long Grove Hospital, 85–6; escapes, 86–8; in hiding, 88–90; sees Harley Street psychiatrist, 89; back in Long Grove, 90; attitude toward women, 93, 111, 181, 198; continuing mental health problems after release, 96–7, 216–17;

hospitalised following seizure, 97; alibi for Finchley Road extortion, 100; business mismanagement, 100–1, 118–19, 158; at Pen Club trial, 107; writes to Scotland Yard denying criminal interests, 107; police raids, 110; bound over and fined, 110; disapproves of Reggie's life with Frances, 111–12, 181, 188, 198, 295; beats up Bobby Ramsey, 113; partnership with Leslie Payne, 114–15; and Esmeralda's Barn, 114–16, 118–19, 131–2; success and wealth, 119, 120, 123, 130; acquitted of loitering with intent, 119–20; philanthropy and charity work, 121–3; knife incident at the Kentucky, 123–4; torture incident, 124–5; assaults Lenny Hamilton, 125–8; foothold in West End, 130–1; and David Litvinoff, 133; dealings with the American Mafia, 133–4, 183–5, 299, 341–3, 349; at Cedra Court, 137, 138–9, 151, 198; relationship with Leslie Holt, 137; grand tour of Enugu, Nigeria, 139–40; meetings at Eaton Square, 140–1; supposed homosexual affair with Lord Boothby, 141; 'Peer and a Gangster' scandal, 141–52; gangster swagger, 157; precarious finances, 159, 163; and failed Nigerian investment scheme, 158–9; intervenes in shooting of Albert Donoghue, 162; and the Glenrae Club, 163–5, 171, 190–1; dealings with McCowan, 165–8; arrested on menace charges, 168–9; bail refused, 169, 171; trial, 173–6; acquittal celebrations, 176–7, 192; television interview, 177–8; celebrity status, 171, 185–7, 282–4, 367–9, 371–2; refused entry to US, 183–4, 349; and stolen Canadian securities, 185, 194, 255, 299; and Bailey photo shoot, 185–7; best man at Reggie's wedding, 189–90; and Congo rescue scam, 195–6; drug-smuggling, 201,

301; relations with Richardson gang, 105, 204–5, 206; and Eric Mason assault, 205–6; at London gangs summit, 206, 208; and Cornell's 'fat poof' put-down, 206–8, 213–14; mobilises troops against Richardsons, 208–9; kill list, 208–9, 217, 237; feud with Cornell, 213–17; hitman story, 214; medication and alcohol, 217; dislikes the Blind Beggar pub, 218; shoots Cornell, 220–6, 233; returns to Lion pub, 229; gets out of East End, 229–31; at Moresby Road flat, 237–9; possible paedophile interests, 238; in Morocco, 239; regains confidence, 239–40; plans Frank Mitchell escape, 241, 262–3; detained by police, 242–3; identity parade shambles, 242; entraps DS Townshend, 243–6; and 'Magic Bullet' incident, 248–9; McVitie double-crosses, 250; and contract to kill Jimmy Evans, 255–8; generosity of, 263, 284; refuses to give evidence in Townshend case, 263, 266, 284; nearly a year in hiding, 266, 284, 297; and Frank Mitchell, 279–80; deteriorating mental health, 284, 296; and the Carpenter's Arms, 289–90; twin bond, 295; plans murder of Leslie Payne, 299–300; McVitie disrespects and threatens, 301–2; thirty-fourth birthday party, 303–5, 306; quarrels with Reggie, 307; lead-up to McVitie murder, 309–11; murders McVitie, 312–14; at Harry Hopwood's flat, 318–21; lies low in Tottenham, 323–4; threatens Connie Whitehead at knifepoint, 324; with Geoff Allen in Suffolk, 325, 329–31; taunts Reggie to kill, 327; meetings with John Pearson, 330–2; orders shooting of Romford man, 333–4; sinks into paranoia and depression, 334; buys The Brooks in Suffolk, 339–40; pet pythons, 340; orders killing of Frankie Shea, 340–1; attacks Johnny Wakefield,

341; attacks Johnny Cardew, 341; looks to expand business, 341; trip to New York with Cooper and Morgan, 341–3; pornography and prostitution opportunities, 343; and plot to murder George Caruana, 344–5; and stateside anti-Kray operation, 348–9; assault on Webb brothers, 350–2; as assassination target, 352–4; last night of freedom, 355; arrested, 356–7; in court at Bow Street, 359–60; charged with murder, 361, 362, 363; collapse of the Kray empire, 364–5; legacy and legendary status, 365, 367; film and TV representations, 367–9; author's opinion of, 369–72

Kray, Violet (*née* Lee; mother): birth, 14; childhood and upbringing, 17–18; courtship and marriage, 18–19; birth of son Charlie, 19; beaten by husband, 20, 22; birth and death of daughter Violet, 21–2; moves to Stean Street, 22; birth of twins, 9–10, 23; raises family, 25, 27, 30; nurses twins through diphtheria, 26; adored by her children, 20; and move to Vallance Road, 28; with twins at Hadleigh, 31; attends juvenile court hearing, 39; doting influence on twins, 49, 294; twins visit while on run, 54; on last days of sister Rose, 84; visits Ronnie in Long Grove, 86; celebrates twins' acquittal, 176–7; on Reggie's wedding day, 188; argument with Olive Myers, 235; visits Moresby Road flat, 239; fifty-sixth birthday, 243; on Frances Shea as a wife, 294; at twins' thirty-fourth birthday party, 303; moves to Braithwaite House, 339; at The Brooks, 339–40

Kray, Violet (sister who died at birth), 21–2

Kray fandom, 369–70

'Krayology': origin of term, 7

Krays, The (film), 64n, 133n, 367–8

Labour Party: general election 1964, 141–2, 148; and Boothby affair, 148–9

Laburnum Street School, 27

Lal, Dr Jaivant, 226

Lambrianou, Chris: criminal background and reputation, 94–5; on the Regency Club, 247; dealings with the Krays, 288–9; at twins' thirty-fourth birthday party, 304; with McVitie at Regency Club, 306–7; arrives at Evering Road, 310–11; involvement in McVitie murder, 312–13, 315–17; leaves body in Rotherhithe, 317–18; returns to Evering Road, 318; on death of McVitie, 318; witnesses assault on Webb brothers, 351; charged with McVitie murder, 363; as celebrity 'villain', 369

Lambrianou, Jimmy, 95

Lambrianou, Nicky, 287, 351

Lambrianou, Tony: criminal life, 95; on McVitie, 118; on feud between Ronnie and Cornell, 207, 214; side player in Firm, 287; pacifies Reggie, 296; at twins' thirty-fourth birthday party, 304; at Regency Club, 306; tasked with luring McVitie, 307–8; arrives at Evering Road, 310–11; involvement in McVitie murder, 312, 313, 314–17; leaves body in Rotherhithe, 317–18; reflections on McVitie case, 326; on Ronnie's attack on Johnny Cardew, 341; witnesses assault on Webb brothers, 351; charged with McVitie murder, 363; integrity as witness, 308

Land, Bernard, 261n

Lane, Googie, 52

Langlands, Diana, 244

Lansky, Meyer, 133–4, 183, 195n

Lavender, Edward see Woods, Edward

Lawton, Mr Justice, 297

Lazar, Lew, 51

Lea Bridge Road, Leyton, 242

Lederman, Sammy: Kray associate, 69, 80, 112, 351; at Glenrae Club, 164, 171; at Pellicci's Cafe, 287; at twins'

thirty-fourth birthday party, 303; meets John Pearson, 332; charges against, 360

Lee, Cissy (née Whittington, wife of Joe Lee Snr), 9–10, 22

Lee, James ('Crutcha') (great-grandfather), 13–14, 85

Lee, James ('Jimmy') (grandfather): background and character, 14, 16–17; nicknamed 'Southpaw Cannonball', 14; objects to daughter's match, 18–19; delighted at birth of twins, 24; entertainer during blitz, 32; mixes with local villains, 35; celebrates twins' acquittal in McCowan case, 176, 177; at Reggie's wedding, 189; moves to Cheshire Street, 339

Lee, Joe (cousin), 9, 20, 22–3, 34, 86, 89

Lee, Joe (uncle), 14, 17, 18, 19, 21, 22, 28, 41, 49

Lee, John (uncle), 14, 28, 33, 39

Lee, Mary Ann (née Houghton; grandmother), 14, 17, 35, 49, 339

Lee, Maude (née Frith; John's wife), 28, 33, 39

Lee, May (aunt), 14, 17, 28, 31, 33, 177, 339

Lee, Rose (aunt): birth, 14; character and temperament, 17, 33–4, 36–7; marriage and birth of son, 21; and Vallance Road, 28, 33; accepting of twins' misdemeanours, 33, 49; influence on Ronnie, 33; attends juvenile court hearing, 39; illness and death, 84

Lee, Violet see Kray, Violet

Legend (film), 368

Leman Street Police Station, 75–6

Levy, David, 361

Lewis, Lynn, 133

Lewis, Stephen, 122

Lewis, Ted 'Kid', 27, 171, 189

Lewisham Hospital, 210

Limehouse Mob (gang), 63

Lion, The (pub), Tapp Street, 120–1, 217, 220–1, 229, 288–9

Lisa (Lisa Prescott/Patricia Watson), 268–71, 272, 275–6, 277, 282, 305, 360–1, 364
Liston, Sonny, 171
Little Dragon club, Whitechapel, 131
Littlewood, Joan, 122, 189
Litvinoff, David, 132–3, 138, 145, 157–8
Litvinoff, Emanuel, 132n
London Hospital, 75, 106, 107, 334
London Street (later Dunbridge Street), Bethnal Green, 14–15, 18, 21, 28
long-firm fraud, 113–14
Long Grove Hospital, Epsom, 13–14, 85–8, 90
Longman, Johnny, 227–8
Lucas, Norman, 141–2
Luciano, Lucky, 195
Lucy, John, 356
Luger, PC Frederick, 231
Lyell, Mr Justice, 176
Lynch, Michael, 231
Lyons, Detective Inspector, 242

MacDonald, June, 356
Macmillan, Lady Dorothy, 135–6
Macmillan, Harold (later 1st Earl of Stockton), 135–6, 142
Mafia, American, 133–4, 183–5, 299, 341–3, 349
'Magic Bullet' incident, 248–9
Maguire, Billy, 161
Maida Vale Hospital, 226, 228
Maltese gangs, 63–4, 103, 299, 343
Manito, Bobby, 51
Mansford House, Bethnal Green, 339
Marble Arch, flat in, 191, 197–8
Marciano, Rocky, 342
Margaret, Princess, 123
Mark, Robert, 272
Marks, Tommy 'Ginger', 235, 255, 323
Marney, Marie see McVitie, Marie
Marshall, Eric, 245–6, 263
Martin, Charlie, 74
Martin, Samuel, 60, 62, 83
Martin, Stephen, 81–3
Martin, Terry, 74–5, 76

Marwood, Ronald, 102
Maskell, Richard, 91
Mason, Eric, 203, 205–6, 288
Masters, Doreen, 106
Matthew, John, 175
Mayer, Thomas and Bertha, 28
McCafferty, John, 231, 319, 346
McCowan, Hew: background and character, 165; turns down Enugu investment, 165–6; dealings with Krays over Hideaway Club, 166–8; goes to police, 168; as prosecution witness, 170; discredited at trial, 174, 175–6
McCrystal, Cal, 185
McElligott, Neil, 169
McKew, Bobby, 194
McVitie, Jack 'The Hat': background and criminal career, 116–17; reputation, 117–18; first meets Reggie in Wandsworth, 118; life with Sylvia Barnard, 249–50; double-crosses the Krays, 250; attacks club owner in Stoke Newington, 253–4; funks contract killing of Leslie Payne, 300; shotgun incident at Regency Club, 301; confrontation with Freddie Foreman, 301; disrespects and threatens Krays, 301–2; 'last' meal with Reggie, 301, 327; movements on day of murder, 303, 306–7; lured to Evering Road, 310–11; murdered, 311, 312–17; body left in Rotherhithe, 317–18, 321–3; burial at sea, 323; rumours regarding disappearance, 324–5; missing person's report, 325, 338; Reggie's motives for killing, 325–8; police investigation, 359, 362–3; perpetrators charged, 363
McVitie, Marie (née Marney; Jack's wife), 116–17, 118
McVitie, Mary Elizabeth (Jack's daughter), 117
McVitie, Tony Jackson (Jack's son), 117
Merricks, Percy, 320–1, 325, 363
MI5 (Security Service), 145

Mifsud, 'Big' Frank, 343
Mile End Hospital, 70–1, 226–7
Millen, Commander Ernie, 298
Miller, Alfie, 39
Mills brothers, Alan and Ray, 304, 306,
    310–11, 312, 363; Alan's account of
    McVitie murder, 313
Mirror Group Newspapers, 141–2, 143,
    144–5
Mitchell, Charlie, 124, 194, 360
Mitchell, Frank ('The Mad Axeman'):
    background and criminal career, 90–2;
    idolises Ronnie, 92; gets nickname,
    101; first meets Reggie, 116;
    correspondence with Krays, 171, 240;
    in Dartmoor, 240–1; Ronnie plans
    escape of, 241, 262–3; on outdoor
    working party, 259–62; escape
    from Dartmoor, 263–6; in East Ham
    hideout, 266–8, 270–4; writes to the
    press, 267–8, 271; and Lisa, 270, 272,
    275; nationwide hunt for, 273; plan to
    murder Mitchell, 273–4; murdered,
    274–9; body disposed at sea, 280;
    tragic life, 280–1; police investigation,
    268, 360–1; perpetrators charged,
    280, 361
Mitchell, Sylvia Ann, 117
Mizel, George, 106
Mizen, Fred, 164
Montreal, 185, 194
Monty Python's Flying Circus, 368
Moody, Jimmy, 209
Mooney, Chief Inspector Harry, 337, 359,
    362
Moore, Doris see Kray, Dolly
Moore, Roger, 123
Moresby Road, Clapton, 'siege' of, 231,
    237–9
Morgan, Dickie: family and criminal
    background, 53–4; on run with twins,
    54; at Canterbury jail, 56; at the Regal,
    60, 62; in Wandsworth, 77; employed
    by Rachman, 114; at the 66 Club
    with Ronnie, 203; protection racket
    at Regency Club, 247–8; trip to New

York with Ronnie, 342–3; and plot
    to murder George Caruana, 344–5;
    charged with conspiracy to murder,
    362
Morgan, John 'Chunky', 53, 62
Morgan, Martin, 356
Morocco, 239
Morton, James: The Krays: Crime Archive,
    213
Mottram, Brian, 204, 208
Moughton, Dickie, 81, 110
Mr Smith's (club), Catford: gunfight at,
    209–10, 215–16, 231, 235
Mrs X (Blind Beggar barmaid) see
    Sanders, Frances
'murder briefcase', 256–8, 348
Murphy, Dr Mary, 351–2
Myers, George see Cornell, George
Myers, Olive (née Hudd; George Cornell's
    wife), 67, 219, 227–8, 232, 235, 239

Nairn, Sergeant John, 226, 227
Nash brothers (Islington villains), 58,
    103, 105, 106–7, 111n, 171, 203, 206;
    tip-off concerning Lord Boothby and
    Ronnie, 141
Nathan, David, 349
National Service, 52
Newcombe, Dr Raymond, 228
Newell, Detective Sergeant Perry,
    99–100 & n
News of the World, 267–8
Nicholls, Dr Lewis, 76
Nigeria: proposed project in, 134,
    139–40, 158–9, 166, 194
'nipping' protection rackets, 130, 164–5,
    247–8
Norris, Stephen, 47
North Eastern Fever Hospital,
    Tottenham, 26
North London Magistrates' Court, 47–8

Okpara, Dr Michael, 139
Old Bailey: Roy Harvey assault trial, 49;
    Terry Martin assault trial, 76–7; Pen
    Club trial, 107; McCowan trial, 173–6;

and trick briefcase murder plot, 256, 257–8; Townshend bribery case, 296–7; 'Torture Trial', 297
Old Blue Anchor (pub), Whitechapel Road, 306
Old Horns (pub), off Hackney Road, 121, 331–2, 341, 350–1, 352, 355
Old Nichol (London slum), 15
Old Street Magistrates' Court, 49, 169, 191, 263, 266
O'Leary, Laurie, 32, 33, 45, 46, 49, 50n, 65n, 77
Oliffe, Ronnie, 276n
One Armed Bandit murder (1967), 47n
Only Fools and Horses (TV programme), 369
Organ, Thomas, 47–8
Orkin, Harvey, 193
Ormsby Street, Hoxton, 95–6, 182, 198, 200–1, 254, 285
Osbourne, Detective Sergeant, 227
Osbourne, Colin 'Duke', 62, 112, 157, 161, 170, 236, 339
Osbourne, Georgie, 80, 86–7, 98–100

Parker, Rodney, 220
Patmore, Bill, 74
Patterson, Floyd, 309
Paul, Andy, 126
Payne, Leslie: background, 112; meets the Krays, 113; and Esmeralda's Barn, 114–15; witnesses assault on Lenny Hamilton, 126; business frauds, 130; and Nigerian project, 134, 139–40, 158–9, 165–6; leasee of Cedra Court, 137, 159, 167; and stolen Canadian securities, 184–5, 194; drifts away from Krays, 201–2; on Eric Mason's injuries, 205; Kray hitmen story, 214; on Ronnie's murderousness, 214; twins conspire to kill, 237–8, 299–300; and 'Magic Bullet' incident, 248–9; McVitie fails to assassinate, 300; Read approaches, 336–7; granted immunity from prosecution, 337; gives statement, 337

Payne, Reginald, 142
Pearson, John: commissioned to write the Kray story, 329–30; meets the twins, 330–2; on Reggie's haunted look, 340; witnesses attack on Johnny Wakefield, 341; auctions Kray memorabilia, 141n, 284n; view on the Krays' charity-giving, 284; his books on the Krays, 368; *The Cult of Violence*, 187–8; *Notorious*, 113, 114, 148–9, 214–15; *The Profession of Violence*, 368
Peggs, Edward and Eva, 92
Pellicci's Cafe, Bethnal Green, 50n, 287, 323
Pen Club shooting and trial, 106–7
'pension' protection rackets, 130
Pentonville Prison, 129
Peter Tavy Inn, near Tavistock, 260–1
Peters, Lennie, 171, 189
Petticoat Lane Market, 45
photographs and physical appearance (of the Krays): as babies, 24; likeness as twins, 53, 70–1, 86–7; Ronnie's weight gain, 97; Eaton Square pictures, 140–1, 143–4, 146–7, 151; cameo in *Sparrows Can't Sing*, 122–3; strolling through Cedra Court, 151; gangster swagger, 157; at Vallance Road after acquittal, 176–7; on television, 177–8; David Bailey photo shoot, 185–7; wedding and honeymoon pictures, 189, 191; and Edmund Purdom photograph, 192; witness descriptions in Blind Beggar, 233; 'cup of tea' pictures at Vallance Road, 242; formal attire, 283; John Pearson's description, 330; Ronnie as chain-smoking slob, 334; menacing photos with snakes, 340; Reggie's haunted look, 340
Pigalle club, Piccadilly, 131, 203, 204, 287
Pine, Wilf, 214, 217
Platts-Mills, John, QC, 7
Plumley, Tommy 'Red Face', 71

Plummer, George, 305, 309, 315–16, 321, 325

Podro, Murray, 98–9

Pogue, Detective Sergeant Joe, 241

Pokla, Jack, 69

Polowski, Lisa see Lisa

Poplar Accident Station, 225

Poplar Mob (gang), 63

pornography, 343

Power, Reg, 124

Prescott, Lisa see Lisa

Prince of Wales (pub), Lant Street, 279, 289n, 322

Private Eye (magazine), 130–1, 148n

Profumo affair, 142n, 145, 146

protection rackets, 62, 70, 106, 124–5, 130–1, 144–5, 147, 164–5, 166–8, 247–8, 253–4

Purdom, Edmund, 192

Purfleet army punishment institution, 55

Pyle, Joey, 106–7

Quarry, Jerry, 309

Quill, Frances, 220

Quill, Jimmy, 105, 218

Quill, Patrick ('Patsy'), 105, 216, 218, 224–5, 231, 232

Quinn, William, 219, 222

Rachman, Peter, 114

Raft, George, 184, 299, 342

Rampton Hospital, 91

Ramsey, Bobby: Kray associate, 60–1; and twins' assault on African, 67; attacks Terry Martin, 73–5; tried and convicted, 76; beaten up by Krays, 113; and Albert Donoghue shooting, 161–2; doorman at Glenrae Club, 164, 171

Rawlings, Henry, 209, 210

Raynor, Trevor, 288

Read, John, 106–7

Read, Superintendent Leonard ('Nipper'): background and career, 154–6; assigned Kray case, 156; first sight of Ronnie, 156–7; initial enquries, 157–8; on McCowan's sexuality, 165; twins arrested on menace charges, 168–9; and Johnny Francis, 169–70; arrests Teddy Smith, 170; reaction to Krays' acquittal, 178; and Phoebe Woods, 190–1; at Krays' acquittal party, 192; and photograph of Edmund Purdom, 192; promoted Chief Inspector, 193; on Lennie Dunn, 265; promoted Detective Superintendent, 298; re-assigned Kray case, 298–9, 335–6; approaches Billy Exley, 336; takes statement from Leslie Payne, 336–7; expands team, 337; offers safeguards to witnesses, 338; Reggie's pet python named for, 340; side-tracked by Dublin murder investigation, 344; Kray enquiry leaked to press, 344; and Caruana murder conspiracy, 347; interviews Elvey, 347; learns Cooper is du Rose's informant, 348; ploy to trap Krays, 354–5; arrests twins, 356–7; Kray gang rounded up, 358–9; McVitie enquiry, 359, 362–3; Frank Mitchell enquiry, 360–1; Cornell enquiry, 362; successful work, 365; on the term 'Krayology', 7

Rees, Gwynneth, 202

Regal Billiard Hall, 60, 62–3, 83–4, 101–2, 110

Regan, Micky, 301

Regency Club, Stoke Newington: altercation at, 125; protected by Krays, 247–8; 'Magic Bullet' incident, 248–9; McVitie shotgun incident, 301; Reggie and McVitie dine at, 301, 327; evening of McVitie murder, 306–10

Regent's Canal, 11

Reid, Chief Inspector Edmund, 154

Repton Boxing Club, 43, 61, 121

Reynolds, Ernest John 'Jackie', 83, 110

Reynolds, Timmy, 287

Richards, David, 218

Richards, William ('Ivor'), 217, 218, 219,

220, 224, 232
Richardson, Kenneth, 173
Richardson brothers, Eddie and Charlie: criminal empire, 103–4, 203–4; relations with the Krays, 105, 204–5; mining interests, 134, 204; and attack on Eric Mason, 205–6; at London gangs summit, 206, 208; Kray troops mobilised against, 208–9; Mr Smith's shootings, 209–11; gang members arrested, 210–11, 297; 'Torture Trial', 297; absence from London crime scene, 299
Rise of the Krays, The (film), 368
Robert Browning Institute (boxing club), 38, 43
Roberts, Edgar, 260–1
Robertson (witness to Cornell shooting), 242
Rood, Joseph, 99
Rosa, Ray, 118
Rosen, Hymie ('Little Hymie'), 45–6
Rotherhithe: St Marychurch Street, 317–18, 321–3
Royal Fusiliers, 52–3, 55–8
Roza, Lita, 171, 189

St Andrew's Hospital, Bromley-by-Bow, 162–3
St Clement's Hospital, Bow, 97
St James the Great Church, Bethnal Green, 42, 187, 189–90
St Leonard's Hospital, Hoxton, 255, 285
St Mary's Church, Rotherhithe, 317–18
St Pancras Coroner's Court, 292
Sampson, Alistair, 193
Sampson, Jacob, 246
Sampson and Company (solicitors), 242
Sanders, Frances: barmaid at Blind Beggar, 218, 220, 222; witnesses shooting, 223–5; questioned by police, 232; first statement, 232; unofficially identifies Ronnie Kray, 234; fails to show at identity parade, 242; makes second statement and identifies Barrie, 362; bravery, 364

Scawfell Street School, Bethnal Green, 41–2
Schack, Bernard ('Sonny the Yank'), 46, 106
Second World War: evacuation of civilians, 30; bombing raids (and blitz), 30–1, 32, 38–9; black market, 35; amnesty to army deserters, 50n
Security Service (MI5), 145
Seigenberg, Denis, 47
Sewell, George, 100
Shaw, Roy 'Pretty Boy', 333
Shay, Daniel, 98–100
Shea, Elsie (Frances's mother), 95, 111, 182–3, 189, 292n, 293
Shea, Frances (Reggie's wife): Reggie falls for, 96; courted by Reggie, 111; contact with Reggie in prison, 116; marriage intentions, 120; celebrates Reggie's acquittal, 176–7; shy and undomesticated, 180, 294; early relationship with Reggie, 180–3; wedding and reception, 187–90; ill-fated honeymoon, 191; married life, 197–200; sexual relations, 200, 295; returns to live with parents, 200, 239; depression, 200–1; changes name and seeks annulment, 251; letters to Reggie, 251–2; suicide attempts, 254–5, 285; moves into brother's flat, 285; possible reconciliation, 290; death, 291; inquest, 292; suicide note, 292–3; funeral, 293–4; doomed marriage, 294–6; depicted in *Legend*, 368
Shea, Frank (Frances's father), 95, 110, 111, 254, 285
Shea, Frankie (Frances's brother): becomes Reggie's driver, 94, 95; criminal activities, 94; Reggie in love with, 200; lets Frances stay at flat, 285; finds Frances dead, 291; funeral arrangements, 293; twins want dead, 296, 340–1
Shepton Mallet military prison, 56–7
Shinwell, Ernest, 134

Shinwell, Manny, 134n
Shots, The (band), 283 & n
Silver, Bernie, 343, 344–5
Silverstone, Dr Julius, 290
Simmonds, Dave, 81, 171
Simms, Charlie, 43
Simpson, Dr Keith, 232
Simpson, Sir Joseph, 142, 144, 349
Skinner, Carole Anne ('Blonde
    Carole'): parties at Evering Road,
    278, 305; background, 305; on
    night of McVitie murder, 309–10,
    315–17; bloodstained carpet, 321;
    hears rumours about McVitie's
    disappearance, 324; inconvenience
    payment, 325; denies all knowledge
    of Krays, 359; tells all to police, 362–3;
    bravery, 364
Skinner, Colin, 305
Slarke, Thomas ('Pop'), 220, 224, 225 &
    n, 232
Sliney, Bill, 51
Smalls, Derek 'Bertie', 337n
Smith, Edward ('Mad' Teddy):
    relationship with Ronnie, 80;
    background and character, 80, 137–8;
    at Double R Club, 110; relationship
    with Tom Driberg, 138; Eaton Square
    meeting, 140–1; causes trouble at
    Hideaway Club, 167, 170; arrested
    on menace charges, 170; trial and
    acquittal, 173–6; and Townshend
    bribery case, 244, 263; and springing
    of Frank Mitchell, 262, 263–5; helps
    Mitchell write to press, 267–8, 271;
    at Pellicci's Cafe, 287; disappearance,
    332–3
Smith, Rita (twins' cousin): on Charlie
    Kray Snr's domestic violence, 20;
    childhood, 28, 31; at Tottenham Royal,
    52; visits twins in military prison, 57;
    dates Bobby Ramsey, 61; adored by
    Reggie, 93; Reggie seeks advice from,
    96; on redevelopment of Vallance
    Road, 285–6; moves to Blythendale
    House, 339

Smithson, Tommy, 58, 345
Sonny the Yank (Bernard Schack), 46,
    106
Sparrows Can't Sing (film), 122–3
Spinetti, Victor, 192
Spinks, Terry, 171, 189
Spot, Jack, 45–6, 60, 68, 104
Squibb, Johnny, 343
Starlite club, Mayfair, 131, 203, 301
Stayton, Billy, 204, 209
Stealey, Eric, 155
Stean Street, Hoxton, 9–10, 22, 28
Steeple Bay, Essex: Krays holiday at, 119
Stephens, George, 223
Stern (magazine), 146–7
Stewart, Alfie, 38
Stone, Trevor, 304, 309, 311, 313, 363
Stork, The (West End club), 204, 207
Stow Club, Walthamstow, 230
Stragglers (West End club), 73
Style, Clare, 31
Style, Dr Arthur, 31
Suffolk, 31–2, 88, 325, 329, 339–40
Summers, PC Raymond, 102
"Sun Ain't Gonna Shine Anymore, The"
    (song), 222–3
Sunday Mirror, 141–5, 151, 152, 344
Sunday Pictorial, 267
Sunday Times, 185–6, 187, 329
Supergrass: as term, 337n
Swain, Inspector, 268
Swinging Sixties, 282–3
Swiss Travel Goods (shop), Finchley
    Road, 98–9
'Syndicate, The' (London crime gang),
    343

Tappin, George, 30
Tarlton, Roland, 230–1
Tarron, Leonard, 225, 226
Tavistock, West Devon, 261
Taylor, Frank, 330
Teale, Alfie, 80–1, 202–3, 220–1, 236–7,
    240, 286–7
Teale, Bobby: joins the Firm, 203, 236–7;
    on feud between Ronnie and Cornell,

214, 230; summoned by Reggie, 220–1; failed marriage, 236; becomes police informant, 238–9, 241–2; imprisoned for own safety, 286–7

Teale, Christine, 237

Teale, David: joins the Firm, 203, 236; summoned by Ronnie, 220–1; gets out of the East End, 229; flat beseiged, 231, 237–9; imprisoned for own safety, 286–7

Teale, Paul, 238

Tebbell, Detective Inspector Edward, 233–4, 242

Ten Bells (pub), Spitalfields, 219

Thompson, Carol, 303, 307, 309, 310, 315

Times, The, 149–51, 267, 271

Tintagel House, 299

Tippett, Jimmy, 210

'Top Bunk, The' (play), 137n

'Torture Trial' (1967), 297

Tottenham Royal Ballroom, 52, 53

Tower of London army barracks, 52–3, 55

Townshend, Detective Sergeant Leonard: bribery case, 243–6, 263, 266, 284, 296–7

Toynbee Hall Juvenile Court, Whitechapel, 39

Tullen, Joe, 164

Turner, Louisa Eliza *see* Kray, Louisa Eliza

Turner, Roy, 260

Turtle, Dr Stanley, 47

V1s (flying bombs), 38

V2s (rockets), 38

Vallance Road: living conditions, 28–9; Kray and Lee families move into, 28, 33; bombing raids, 30–1, 32, 38–9; twins' acquittal celebrations, 176–7; Reggie's wedding day, 188–9; brick through window, 235, 239; 'cup of tea' photographs, 242; slum clearance and redevelopment, 285–6; families move out, 338–9

Varnes, Anita, 223

Vaughan, Sidney, 166, 167–8, 174, 175–6

Vienna Rooms (club), Edgware Road, 54, 60–1

Wakefield, Johnny, 341

Waldman, Detective Sergeant, 347

'Wall of Fear/Silence', 82–3, 157–8, 170, 179, 239, 253, 254, 278

Waller, Mr Justice, 297

Wally's Cafe, Hackney, 58

Wandsworth Prison, 77–8, 90, 92, 116, 120, 203

Ward, Bonner, 125

Ward, Henry 'Buller', 125–6

Wardle, Henry, 219, 220

Warhol, Andy, 187

Warner, Jack, 334n

Waterman, Squire 'Split', 256–8

Watney Street Gang, 63, 65, 73, 103, 215

Watson, Patricia *see* Lisa

Watts, Queenie, 123

Webb, Billy: early relations with the Krays, 52, 54, 58–9; first aware of Ronnie's homosexuality, 59; and George Cornell, 66, 208, 219; attacked by the Krays, 350–2

Webb, Ron, 52, 219, 350–2

Welch, Tommy 'The Bear', 62–3, 80, 170, 264, 330, 343, 358, 360

Wellington army barracks, 52–3, 55

Wellington Way Club, 81, 110, 111

West End Central Police Station, 357–8, 359, 362

West Ham Police Station, 325

Westminster Public Mortuary, 232

Whelan (convict companion of Frank Mitchell), 260–1, 264

Whitehead, Connie: background, 202; suspect for Jack the Stripper murders, 202; and Ronnie's kill list, 208; Ronnie berates, 221; minds Frank Mitchell, 266; as driver, 278–9; and Chris Lambrianou, 288; at twins' thirty-fourth birthday pary, 303–4;

on night of McVitie murder, 309, 310; involvement in McVitie murder, 312–13, 317; Ronnie threatens at knifepoint, 324; talk of killing the twins, 352; arrested, 358; charges against, 361, 363

Whittington, Edward and Caroline, 22, 23

Wilkinson, PC Kenneth, 48

Willey, Alfred 'Limehouse', 80, 122, 126, 171, 230, 240, 360

Williams, Dr David, 75

Williams, George, 163n

Wilson, Harold, 148

Wiltshire, Billy (cousin), 21, 26, 33, 34

Wiltshire, Rose see Lee, Rose

Wiltshire, William (husband of Rose Lee), 21, 28, 33

Wimbourne Court, Shoreditch, 285, 290

Winchester Prison: psychiatric unit, 83–5

Windsor, Barbara, 100 & n, 122, 171

Winston's nightclub, Mayfair, 268, 269

Wisbech, Cambridgeshire, 44

Wood, Albert: in Blind Beggar pub, 219–20, 222; witnesses shooting of Cornell, 223–4; phones Olive Myers, 227; identified by fingerprints, 232; gives statement to police, 233; identification parade, 242

Wood, Edwin, 218

Wood Close School, Hoxton, 29–30

Woods, Edward (Edward Lavender), 163–4

Woods, James, 83

Woods, Phoebe, 163–5, 190–1

Wormwood Scrubs, 55

Wray, S. (solicitors' clerk), 242

Wright, Detective Sergeant Alan, 347

Wrightson, Paul, QC, 173

Wylie, William, 219–20, 232

Wyndham, Francis, 185–6, 187

Ziggy's Cafe, 45, 60